HUTTERITE SOCIETY

JOHN A. HOSTETLER

HUTTERITE SOCIETY

THE JOHNS HOPKINS UNIVERSITY PRESS
Baltimore and London

This book has been brought to publication with
the generous assistance of the Andrew W. Mellon
Foundation.

Manufactured in the United States of America

The Johns Hopkins University Press, Baltimore, Maryland 21218
The Johns Hopkins University Press Ltd., London
The Johns Hopkins University Press Ltd., London

Originally published, 1974
Second printing, 1975

Library of Congress Catalog Card Number 74-6827
ISBN 0-8018-1584-3

Library of Congress Cataloging in Publication data
will be found on the last printed page of this book.

Frontispiece: Hutterite child (photograph by Kryn Taconis)

Dedicated to
Robert Friedmann (1891–1970),
Grete Mecenseffy, and Elizabeth Horsch Bender
for their patient scholarship and timeless contribution

Contents

APPENDIXES

MAPS

CHARTS

TABLES

Preface

This volume offers a holistic, ethnographic account of Hutterite culture beginning with the historical background. A knowledge of the history of the Hutterites and of how they incorporate the past into the present is central to understanding Hutterite society. I have attempted to place Hutterite history in perspective for the modern reader and to some extent for the Hutterites themselves. Such a perspective has been difficult to obtain in the past because much of the pertinent historical literature is eclectic, fragmentary, and covered with a nostalgic overlay, and the primary sources are in the German language. The heart of this book, which deals with the social and cultural organization of Hutterite society, is the outcome of fifteen years of personal contact with the Hutterites.

My initial contact with the colonies began in 1959 in Edmonton, soon after I had accepted a teaching position at the University of Alberta. Five Hutterite elders who had been summoned to the provincial capitol for legislative hearings came to visit me. At issue was a law that restricted them from buying additional land. The following day, I instructed my class in minority groups to observe the legislative debates from the balcony of the provincial assembly. Seated below us were twenty-six bearded apostles in an arena of lawyers and lawmakers arguing opposing viewpoints. Having been raised Old Order Amish, I understood something of the Anabaptist tradition and the ethnic conflict that was inevitable. In a short time, the elders accepted me as one of their kind of people.

Many of the colonies were within driving distance of our home in Edmonton. As a visitor, often accompanied by members of my family, I was the recipient of Hutterite hospitality on their holidays and on my weekends during the three years I lived in Alberta. The success with which the Hutterites trained their children for living communally impressed me as extraordinary. Realizing that here was an opportunity for acquiring basic knowledge about communal living, I set about designing a study of communal education.

After receiving a grant from the U.S. Office of Education for the study of socialization in Hutterite culture, I selected a panel of consultants and a staff of trained field workers who lived for extended periods in colonies. Three colonies were selected for intensive observation on the basis of their geographic location, area, size, age, affiliation, and willingness to cooperate. We chose "normal" rather than atypical colonies and visited many more than the original three.

The objective was to observe the basic unit of Hutterite culture, which is a relatively small number of persons. The combined population of the three colonies was 280 persons. These colonies, fictitiously named Dariushof, Lehrerhof, and Schmiedehof, were located in Manitoba, Montana, and Alberta. The purpose of the research was to acquire a knowledge of the methods of socialization in a highly communal-oriented society, to learn how persons were equipped to live in such a society, and to discover why persons defect from the society. To answer the questions we were asking, we needed a knowledge of the Hutterite environment and of the basic culture.

The research project was operative from June 1, 1962, to September 30, 1965, and the findings are contained in a monograph: *Education and Marginality in the Communal Society of the Hutterites*, Cooperative Research Project no. 1683, U.S. Office of Education, 1965. The cultural analysis was published in part in "Case Studies in Cultural Anthropology," a series of instructional books edited by George and Louise Spindler, under the joint authorship of John A. Hostetler and Gertrude E. Huntington, with the title *The Hutterites in North America* (Holt, Rinehart and Winston, 1967).

The research for the European period consisted of integrating recorded history with visits to places of Hutterite origin in Eastern Europe. This was made possible by a yearlong study leave from Temple University during 1970-71 and was supported by grants from the National Science Foundation, the National Endowment for the Humanities, and the American Philosophical Society. My family was living in Vienna, and from this location I was able to absorb the landscape and to visit the archives, museums, libraries, villages, and archaeological sites essential to the study.

This volume incorporates the basic findings of the socialization study, together with additional observations and field work to the year 1974. With the passing of time, some of our conclusions have matured. By making at least annual field trips to the colonies—often two or three trips a year—I have maintained continuous contact with them. In rare instances the Hutterite people have reciprocated by visiting my family in Philadelphia and the Amish people in Pennsylvania.

Consultants who gave valuable assistance were Bert Kaplan (psychology), Laura Thompson (anthropology), Calvin Redekop (sociology of religion), and Joseph Britton (human development). On the informal level I have profited from interchanges with, and insights from, the late Robert Friedmann and from Karl Peter, Dale Harris, and Dennis Kleinsasser. I wish to thank Irene Bishop for her initial journey to the colonies and for cheerfully braving subzero weather and snow banks between Manitoba and Alberta. I owe much to the generous help of Gertrude Enders Huntington, principal field worker on the education project, and to those who assisted her: her mother, Abbie C. Enders, of Swarthmore, Pennsylvania, a teacher for many years; her husband, Professor David C. Huntington; and her children, Abigail, Daniel, and Caleb, who also lived in a colony. Daniel and Arie Hochstetler, who taught school in a colony for several years, also assisted me, as did Gary Waltner, of Germany.

I am grateful to Dr. Adolf Mais, of the Museum für Volkskunde in Vienna, for valuable historical counsel; to Dr. Karl Steininger, Wirkl. Hofrat, Direktor der Druckschriften Versammlung, Österreichische Nationalbibliothek, for library accommodations; to Herman Landsfeld of Strážnice, Czechoslovakia, who took me along with his village translator, Johann Skácel, to many Hutterite sites, excavations, cellars, castles, and museums in both Moravia and Slovakia; and to Horst Klusch, Sibiu, Romania, who introduced me to the former Hutterite landscape and to the libraries and ceramics in that country.

Beulah S. Hostetler deserves much credit for her assistance in the organization of the historical material and for editorial work. In the more technical translations from German to English, it has been my good fortune to have the services of Elizabeth Bender, wife of the late Harold S. Bender and daughter of John Horsch, author of *The Hutterian Brethren* (1931). And I am grateful to Maria H. Krisztinkovich, who gave valuable advice on Hungarian culture, history, and place names.

My thanks go to Jan Gleysteen, Kryn Taconis, and Philip Garvin for photographs and to Professor David J. Cuff of Temple University, who drew the maps.

A small society that comes under the scrutiny of scientific investigation exposes itself to the risks of disclosure—of its weaknesses and its strengths. I found the Hutterite people fully knowledgeable of this fact, yet admirably open and fearless of anything science might uncover about them. I acknowledge not only the courtesy and help of many Hutterite men and women who were my informants but also my gratitude to them for acquainting me with communities of people who live a satisfying, stable, and rewarding life.

HUTTERITE SOCIETY

Introduction

The people of this book live in collective agricultural colonies, each of which is called a *Bruderhof*, meaning a dwelling place of the brothers. Each colony considers itself symbolic of Noah's Ark, a God-given provision for living in a world that is otherwise hopelessly lost. The colonists derive from the sixteenth-century Anabaptist tradition but identify with neither Catholic nor Protestant theology.

Of hundreds of recorded attempts to establish communal societies in North America,[1] the Hutterites are the only group that has managed not only to survive but to expand and prosper. Yet the members work without the incentive of private gain, and privileged positions are few. There are no extremely poor or wealthy persons among them, and individuals never worry about food, shelter, clothing, or dependency in old age. Identity problems and alienation are virtually nonexistent. In their history, which spans more than four centuries, there has never been a single homicide. There are no high walls around the colony and no police force. Communal Christian sharing of goods and property permeates all aspects of their existence, while competiton between

1. Harold Barclay, "The Renewal of the Quest for Utopia," *Canadian Confrontations,* Proceedings of the Eleventh Annual Meeting of the Western Association of Sociology and Anthropology, Banff, Alberta, December 28–30, 1969, pp. 60–65.

individuals for a livelihood is considered to be carnal, an evil tendency inherent in a fallen society.

From 400 emigrants to South Dakota in 1874, the Hutterite population in North America has grown to more than 22,000, distributed across the northwestern United States and the Canadian prairies. These people in plain clothes are no longer a strange sight to shoppers in the major cities of this region. To encounter them on their home ground, whether along the ravines of the James River in South Dakota or along the banks of the Saskatchewan in the prairie provinces of Canada, is another matter. The Hutterites prefer geographic isolation and a supply of natural water. Once inside one of their colonies, you are confronted with a strong presence. Dozens of children and a few men gather around. Each male is dressed in black pants with suspenders, a colorful shirt, and a black hat. In a few minutes women begin to appear from behind various buildings. They are dressed in long skirts and practical shoes, and they wear black polka dotted bandanas on their heads. Suddenly you feel as though you have entered another country or been dropped back in time. Everyone stands there sternly, looking at you intensely. It is not just the beards and clothes; the people have a distinctive way about them.

Suddenly you feel like an outsider, the product of an easygoing, loose culture, whereas here are a disciplined, hardy people with very strong ideas about how to live. You can feel it in the way they stand around you. But their curiosity is genuine; they will lose no time in evaluating you. The tourist who is improperly dressed will be sent away, but a salesman, a government official, a real estate broker, or an innocent visitor will likely be given a nod of hospitality.

part one

HISTORICAL
DEVELOPMENT

chapter one

The Birth of
Hutterite Society

Anabaptism

The Hutterian Brethren were an outgrowth of sixteenth-century Anabaptism. Anabaptist, meaning "rebaptizer," was a derogatory name given to a wide range of left wing groups during the Reformation; the repudiation of infant baptism had for centuries been a heresy condemned by civil and ecclesiastical law and was punishable by death.

That the movement should acquire the name "Anabaptist" is of more than passing interest, for baptism was only one of several major points at issue, although it was without question the most conspicuous. By seeking to found a "new" and voluntary church free from the state, the movement incurred the displeasure of both Catholic and Protestant leaders. As is often the case in heated controversy, nonconformists who were for any reason in opposition to the established order were labeled indiscriminately; thus the epithet Anabaptist was at various times applied to revolutionaries, rebelling peasants, anarchists, millenarians, fanatical prophets, and dreamers, irrespective of their attitude toward baptism.

Among the diverse ideologies of the so-called Anabaptists two types stand out: (1) the Old Testament–oriented revolutionaries, who have until very recent times been considered by some leading historiographers as the originators of the entire Anabaptist movement, and (2) the New Testament-oriented pacifists. The former originated in Zwickau in Saxony about 1520 and came to an end in the disastrous Peasant War of 1525. Although opposed to infant baptism (they did not, however, practice adult baptism), they were distinguished from the pacifist Anabaptists by their emphasis on the Old Testament call to war against the "Canaanites" and by their elaborate chiliastic speculations. Another group of revolutionaries (who did practice adult baptism) attempted to establish by the force of arms a communist "kingdom of God" in the city of Münster (1533-35); this group also came to a catastrophic end. Thomas Müntzer and his militant revolutionaries have also often been classed as Anabaptists, but two leading scholars in the twentieth century, Ernst Troeltsch and Harold Bender, have dissociated him and his followers from the Anabaptist movement.[1] None of these groups has survived.

The New Testament-oriented pacifist Anabaptists, forerunners of the Hutterites, originated in lay Bible-study groups in Zürich, Switzerland (1523-25). Here a group of Ulrich Zwingli's associates, including Conrad Grebel, Felix Manz, George Blaurock, and later Balthasar Hubmaier, impatient with Zwingli's reforms and his interpretation of the nature of the church, took the initial step of practicing believers' baptism in 1525.[2] Following their expulsion from Zürich, the movement spread all over central Europe. In the Netherlands and Northern Europe, the Anabaptists found an eloquent leader in Menno Simons. Blaurock carried the new teaching to South Tyrol and the Hapsburg empire, where it found ready acceptance among the common people and led to the founding of the Hutterites.

Interpretations of Anabaptism have varied widely, and in this respect it is helpful to distinguish between the "inner view" and the "view from the outside." Marxist writers have interpreted Anabaptism as an early stage of modern class warfare. Socialists have seen the movement as the religious counterpart of class struggle or as a renewed attempt at Christian communism. Some have regarded the movement as a forerunner of the French Revolution. From the viewpoint of the great reformers Martin Luther, Ulrich Zwingli, and John Calvin, Anabaptism was a revolt against duly constituted political and religious authority,

1. Ernst Troeltsch, *The Social Teachings of the Christian Churches*, trans. Olive Wyon (New York: Macmillan Co., 1931), p. 754; Harold S. Bender, "The Zwickau Prophets, Thomas Müntzer, and the Anabaptists," *Mennonite Quarterly Review* 27 (January 1953): 3-16. (Hereafter *Mennonite Quarterly Review* will be cited as *M.Q.R.*)
2. Harold S. Bender, *Conrad Grebel, c. 1498-1515. The Founder of the Swiss Brethren Sometimes Called Anabaptists* (Goshen, Ind.: Mennonite Historical Society, 1950).

and its adherents were society's worst enemies. Since official histories were written by opponents of the movement who had been trained in universities and state churches, this view from the outside has been perpetuated for centuries.

Sociologically, an understanding of the Anabaptists has been greatly advanced by Ernst Troeltsch.[3] In the tradition of Max Weber, Troeltsch distinguishes between "church" and "sect" sociological types, identifying Anabaptism as a Protestant sect type structurally different from the institutional church as well as from mysticism and spiritualism. He characterizes the Anabaptists as a "gathered church," a brotherhood of the regenerate, a congregation of volunteers committed to a disciplined life centering in the teachings of Jesus, especially the Sermon on the Mount—a group separate from the state and aloof from the world. The church type is defined as an institution dispensing baptism, salvation, and education to all members of society.

The sectarianism of the Reformation has been characterized as "Left-Wing Protestantism" by Roland Bainton and as the "Radical Reformation" by George Williams.[4] "Left" and "Radical" refer to sectarians' interpretation of the sacraments, to their church organization, and to their independence from civil government. Franklin Littell saw in Anabaptism a form of Christian primitivism, a struggle to restore the true nature of the early church along New Testament lines.[5] To the Anabaptists the medieval church was "fallen" and apostate—a view still adamantly expressed by their descendants and shared by many Protestants.

After a stormy period of rejecting the established religious practices and customs, including images, an elaborate hierarchy, and the Mass, the Anabaptists introduced a fundamentally different understanding of the church and the Christian life.[6] Central to their beliefs were the reconstruction of the church according to the New Testament pattern and entirely separate from the state; adult baptism following repentance and confession of faith; the "priesthood of all believers,"

3. Troeltsch, *The Social Teachings of the Christian Churches*, pp. 691–728.

4. Roland Bainton, *The Reformation of the Sixteenth Century* (Boston: Beacon Press, 1952); George H. Williams, *The Radical Reformation* (Philadelphia: Westminster Press, 1962). "Left" would also include pacifism, but Anabaptists were not uniformly pacifist, as recent studies by Karl-Heinz Kirchhoff ("Was There a Peaceful Anabaptist Congregation in Münster in 1534?" *M.Q.R.* 44 [October 1970]: 357–70), James M. Stayer ("Anabaptists and the Sword," *M.Q.R.* 44 [October 1970]: 371–75), and Walter Klassen ("The Nature of the Anabaptist Protest," *M.Q.R.* 45 [October 1971]: 291–311) point out.

5. Franklin H. Littell, *The Anabaptist View of the Church* (Boston: Beacon Press, 1958); Littell, *The Origins of Sectarian Protestantism* (New York: Macmillan Co., 1964).

6. John Dillenberger and Claude Welch, *Protestant Christianity* (New York: Charles Scribner's Sons, 1954), p. 63.

referring not only to man's relation to God but also to the equality of all men in Christian community; a disciplined way of life incorporating only persons who are Christian by free decision and excluding those who became apostate; and the practice of nonconformity to the world. They refused to participate in war or to swear oaths of any kind, since these acts violated the new life in Christ and the injunctions of the New Testament. Anabaptists admitted that the state was a necessary institution for mankind, but they themselves felt unable to assume any responsibilities for functions of the state involving coercion.

As Anabaptists, they attempted to found a "pure" church,

not necessarily a church composed of men and women who were sinless, but rather sin-conscious; adult men and women, not children; men and women who knew right from wrong, and who of their own volition as a result of deep-seated religious conviction had formed themselves into a voluntary band of worshippers after the example of apostolic times. This small company holding these views was in the habit of meeting in the homes of various members of the group, spending their time largely in Bible study, in which Zwingli had at first occasionally joined for a time. The more they studied the New Testament the more they were convinced that their conception of the true church was the right one.[7]

Present-day Anabaptist groups can be traced to three distinct streams: the Hutterites derive from South Germany and Austria, the Mennonites from the Netherlands and North Germany, and the Swiss Brethren, now also known as Mennonites, from Switzerland and South Germany. The latter two groups are distinct historically and in practice from the Hutterites. (See map 1.)

Many of the Dutch Mennonites emigrated to Prussia during periods of persecution, then to the Ukraine, and later to the plains areas of the United States and Canada and to Mexico and South America. There is still a large denomination of Mennonites, or *Doopsgezinnde*, in the Netherlands. Also of Dutch origin are the Old Colony Mennonites in Canada, Mexico, and Latin America.[8] As the most agrarian and conservative of the Mennonites of Dutch descent, they have repeatedly sought new frontiers in order to escape assimilation. They speak a Low German dialect called *Plattdeutsch*.

The Swiss Brethren migrated under persecution to South Germany, to Alsace, and to Pennsylvania and nearby states. In Switzerland, where a few congregations still remain, they call themselves *Alt-*

---

7. C. Henry Smith, *The Story of the Mennonites* (Newton, Kans.: Mennonite Publication Office, 1950), p. 4.

8. Calvin W. Redekop, *The Old Colony Mennonites: Dilemmas of Ethnic Minority Life* (Baltimore: Johns Hopkins Press, 1969).

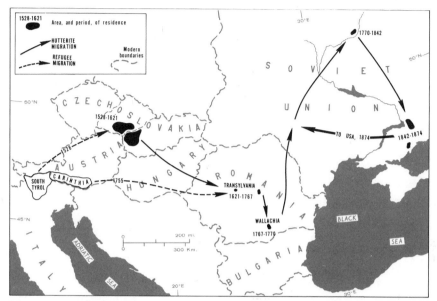

Map 1. Hutterite Migrations and Areas of Residence, 1528–1874

Evangelische Taufgesinnten, but they are generally known as Mennonites because of the similarity of their beliefs to those of the early Netherlands group. A major division of the Swiss Mennonites at the close of the seventeenth century gave rise to the Amish, named after Jakob Ammann, whose most representative adherents, the Old Order Amish, live in North America; they embody the conservative elements of the Swiss movement.[9] The Amish speak Pennsylvania German, a dialect similar to that of the Rhineland-Palatinate area from which they emigrated.

Since their origin the Hutterites have been distinguished from Mennonite groups by their pattern of communal living. The speech of the Hutterites, a German dialect resembling that spoken in the province of Carinthia in Austria and influenced by the Slavic languages, reflects a cultural and geographic background different from the Dutch and Swiss groups.

South German and Austrian Anabaptists

The Hutterite identity was formed in the Hapsburg domain at a time when rulers were hard pressed to exterminate heresy. Charles V of the

9. John A. Hostetler, *Amish Society*, rev. ed. (Baltimore: Johns Hopkins Press, 1968).

house of Hapsburg, Holy Roman emperor and king of Spain, having inherited vast territories, turned the administration of the Austrian lands over to his brother Ferdinand (Ferdinand I of Austria, who reigned from 1521 until 1564). The collaboration that followed between the two Hapsburg lines, the Spanish and the Austrian, was close. Charles was burdened with war against the French, and Ferdinand, who ruled the Austrian lands from Alsace to Hungary, had two great worries. First, there was the overhanging threat of the Turks; some thirty thousand Turkish troops had reached the gates of Vienna in 1529. Second, there was the threat of Protestantism from within in a variety of forms. Having been reared in Spain as a devout Catholic, Ferdinand viewed with dismay the immense strides made by Lutheranism and other nonconformist religions within the Hapsburg lands. Charles had convened the Diet of Worms in 1521, which resulted in the outlawry of Martin Luther's reforms and the restriction of his activities. Ferdinand invited Ignatius Loyola, founder of the Society of Jesus, to send some Jesuit teachers to Vienna. In 1529 an imperial law (Diet of Speyer) asked the death penalty for any person who did not desist from Anabaptism. It was in this political context that the teachings of Anabaptism in Switzerland and South Germany began to spread eastward to Tyrol and Austria.

A South German Anabaptist whose teachings had a major influence on Austrian Anabaptists was Hans Denck.[10] Trained in German universities, he was well grounded in Latin, Greek, and Hebrew and at home in the humanistic circles of his day in Augsburg, Strasbourg, and Basel. He was appointed rector of a school in Nürnberg in 1524 at the age of twenty-three but was deposed for unorthodox remarks he allegedly made about baptism and communion. He was disappointed in the Lutheran reform movement, particularly in the doctrine of justification by faith, for it tended to give the believer a high standing with God regardless of the character of his life. Denck was earnest, sensitive, and spiritually discerning and one of the few of that rough era who could enter into a debate without being abusive or brutal in language and conduct. He taught the discipleship of Jesus, emphasizing that no one may truly know Christ except one who follows Him in life. Although he died of the plague in Basel at the early age of twenty-seven, his writings had a profound impact on all Anabaptists. In his basic position he moved from Catholicism to Humanism to Lutheranism to Anabaptism and,

---

10. *The Mennonite Encyclopedia*, s.v. "Denk, Hans." (Hereafter *The Mennonite Encyclopedia* will be cited as *M.E.*) See also Walter Fellman, *Hans Denck, Religiöse Schriften* (Gütersloh: Gerd Mohn, 1956).

finally, to "evangelical Spiritualism."[11] Denck and his sympathizers stressed the freedom of the will and the belief that "there is no other way to blessedness than to lose one's self-will." The deemphasis of self was one of the elements leading to a communal interpretation of Christianity.

One of Denck's followers, Hans Hut, was rebaptized in 1526 and became a zealous missionary in South Germany and Austria.[12] Three of his converts were Leonard Schiemer, a Franciscan friar; Hans Schlaffer, a priest; and Ambrose Spittelmaier, a university-trained layman. Schlaffer wrote nine tracts (eight of them in prison shortly before he was beheaded), which survive in Hutterite codices.[13] The theological writings of these three converts influenced the whole development of Austrian Anabaptism. They stress the imminence of Christ's second coming, personal suffering as a necessary condition for following Christ, and the sharing of goods—an element destined to be fully developed in the Christian communism of the Austrian refugees in Moravia.

The converts to Anabaptism came from all classes.[14] In Tyrol in particular it was the laborers in the famous mines in Rattenberg, Kitzbühel, and Schwaz who constituted the major portion of the membership of the Anabaptist churches.[15] The mines had drawn many foreigners into the valleys, and the parishes had become overcrowded and understaffed. Social patterns were disrupted, and the area was ripe for Anabaptist missioners. While many who joined the Anabaptists were poor, there were also some among them with property. Many were artisans and tradesmen—printers, booksellers, schoolteachers, publishers, weavers, ropemakers, shoemakers, and furriers have been specifically mentioned among Anabaptist converts. Some of the nobility joined the group. Peasants came in greater numbers from Lower Austria than from Upper Austria, as can be attested by the records of their confiscated property in the Tyrol archives. Throughout Austria the government ruthlessly suppressed all heretics wherever they could be found. As Holy Roman emperor, Charles V was responsible for protecting the Roman Church, and he decreed that Anabaptists were to be "exterminated by fire and sword." The town of Zürich introduced the death penalty for Anabaptists on March 1, 1526, and by the end of the

11. Williams, *The Radical Reformation*, p. 149.
12. Wilhelm Neuser, *Hans Hut: Leben und Werken bis zum Nikolsburger Religionsgespräch* (Berlin, 1913).
13. *M.E.*, s.v. "Schlaffer, Hans."
14. Paul Peachey, *Die sociale Herkunft der Schweizer Täufer* (Karlsruhe: Heinrich Schneider, 1954).
15. Paul Dedic, "The Social Background of the Austrian Anabaptists," *M.Q.R.* 13 (January 1939).

same year extended the law to include persons who attended Anabaptist meetings.[16] By 1530, one thousand Anabaptists are believed to have been executed.

Moravia, the Land of Promise

Since Moravia and Bohemia had experienced a national religious reformation in the fifteenth century, by 1526 these lands had already been through a century of pre-Protestant uprisings. Those rebelling were the followers of John Huss in Bohemia, the Czech Brethren, the Utraquists, the Picards, the Minor Unity, and others.[17] A divergence of beliefs in Moravia had, over a period of time, led to a considerable degree of religious toleration there.

As the tolerance in Moravia became more widely known, a continuous stream of Anabaptist refugees from Tyrol, Switzerland, Austria, Hesse, Bavaria, and Württemberg moved into this land that was to become the country of Hutterite origin, although the Hutterites themselves were not native to it. Moravia was "the Promised Land," and for half a century the Hutterite colonies grew with the enormous influx of persecuted Anabaptists. During the first one hundred years, not a single Hutterite leader was a native Moravian. The thronging of the Anabaptists into southern Moravia evoked strong edicts on the part of King Ferdinand.[18] He could not eradicate the Anabaptists because of the protection given them by the sympathetic nobles, especially the Liechtensteins, who were not only sympathetic but one of whom, Leonhard von Liechtenstein, had himself baptized into this new faith.

One of the first to take an active role in bringing Anabaptism to Moravia was Balthasar Hubmaier.[19] A native of Bavaria, Hubmaier studied at the University of Freiburg and was ordained a priest. He held the positions of corrector of the University of Ingolstadt and chaplain at the cathedral in Regensburg. As his views became known, he was deposed from these positions and given a parish at Waldshut. After attending the disputations of 1523 in Zürich, he returned to Waldshut and there instituted reforms discussed at the meetings; he introduced

16. *M.E.*, s.v. "Mandates." For lists of executions, see Claus-Peter Clasen, *Anabaptism: A Social History* (Ithaca: Cornell University Press, 1972).

17. Peter Brock, *The Political and Social Doctrines of the Unity of the Czech Brethren in the Fifteenth and Early Sixteenth Centuries* (The Hague: Mouton and Co., 1957). See also Henry A. DeWind, "A Sixteenth-Century Description of Religious Sects in Austerlitz, Moravia," *M.Q.R.* 29 (January 1955): 44-53.

18. Grete Mecenseffy, *Geschichte des Protestantismus in Österreiech* (Gratz-Köln, 1956).

19. Thorsten Bergsten, *Balthasar Hubmaier: Seine Stellung zu Reformation und Täufertum, 1521-1528* (Kassel: J. G. Oncken Verlag, 1961).

the German service, abolished fasting regulations, and married. He was baptized in 1525 along with sixty others by the Swiss Anabaptist Reublin. In the days that followed, he baptized over three hundred persons, using a milk bucket and water from the faucet in the town square. For a short time Waldshut was predominantly Anabaptist, but in December 1525, the imperial forces recaptured the town and Hubmaier fled to Zürich, where he was held in confinement until April, when he offered a semirecantation of his views.

Hubmaier came to Nikolsburg in Moravia in May 1526 on the personal invitation of Leonhard von Liechtenstein. He at once set out to transform the Lutheran congregation located there into an Anabaptist congregation and to merge it with the Anabaptist refugees. He converted both the pastor, Oswald Glait, and Leonhard von Liechtenstein to Anabaptism.[20] Here Hubmaier found the peace and quiet necessary to put some of his beliefs into writing. Like Denck, he emphasized the importance of man's will. He said the cause of the "original fall" was man's will rather than man's flesh. He postulated a trichotomous man: spirit, soul, and body, each of the three aspects of man having a separate will. The spirit-will did not participate in the fall; the soul-will assented to the temptation of the flesh; the body, completely corrupted by the fall, carried the soul about as a helpless accomplice to its deeds. He taught that salvation consists in restoring to the soul the capacity to distinguish good from evil, for only then can it throw its weight with the spirit against the body. This is accomplished by the saving word, that is, the gospel of Christ, which restores the believer within the disciplined community of grace, the gathered church, to the condition of paradise before the fall. The believer can only be admitted to the church by baptism, and he can be excluded by the ban. Within his system of interpretation, Hubmaier permitted some room for others to have the truth and for government officials to be Christian.

Fragmentation and Purification

Refugees from numerous localities made up the Anabaptist community around Nikolsburg. (See figure 1.) The Anabaptist groups soon found themselves at variance with each other on the questions of pacifism, the payments of war taxes to Ferdinand, and the use of the sword. The group supporting complete pacifism, led by Jakob Wiedemann and Phillip Jäger, lived outside the town wall in the neighboring village of Bergen. They were dubbed *Stäbler*, or men of the staff, for they would not bear the sword. Within the walled town, Hubmaier, Spittelmaier,

20. Williams, *The Radical Reformation*, pp. 205, 219.

Figure 1. Scenes of Liechtenstein Castle, Nikolsburg, Czechoslovakia, where Anabaptists were given refuge. (Photograph, 1970)

Liechtenstein, and Glait represented a group of moderates which the Wiedemann group called *Schwertler*, or those who permitted the use of the sword.

Early in 1527 Hans Hut, a reformer, writer, and pamphleteer, came to Nikolsburg. His was an intensely apocalyptic message, for he exhorted his hearers "to sell house and goods" in view of Christ's return to establish his kingdom on earth at the approaching Pentecost of 1528. The Wiedemann group supported Hut and arranged a disputation between the leaders of the two groups. They charged that Hubmaier baptized on the simplest request without adequate examination and that he and the group associated with the lords of Liechtenstein discriminated against the refugees who practiced true Christian sharing of material goods. The basic disagreements, however, were over the use of the sword and the propriety of paying taxes for military purposes in order to defend Christianity.

Hut's fervent advocacy of nonresistance sounded seditious to the Liechtensteins, especially in view of the protection they were giving the Anabaptists and the pressure that came from King Ferdinand for the payment of taxes and for military support against the Turks. Leonhard von Liechtenstein, alarmed at what he heard, forcibly detained Hut in the castle. News of his imprisonment caused an uproar among the extremist elements.

Hubmaier arranged a meeting and spoke to the Wiedemann group, defending as legitimate the right of government to levy war taxes to protect its citizens. He reminded them that even Christ did not attempt to predict the exact time of his second advent. This did not satisfy them. Hubmaier responded to the charges against him by writing a book on the legitimate use of force. His writings drew wide attention, and when the Hapsburg authorities learned of his activity they had him imprisoned in the ancient castle of Kreuzenstein in Lower Austria. Charged with heresy and sedition for his part in the conditions that led to the Peasants' War, Hubmaier was sentenced to death at the stake and was executed in Vienna on March 10, 1528. A few days later his wife, who had staunchly encouraged him, was cast into the Danube with a stone tied around her neck.

As a theologian and reformer, Hubmaier's influence has extended not only to the Hutterites; today he is revered by the Baptist denominations in North America as one of their founders. His writings are in almost complete agreement with the Schleitheim Articles of the Swiss Anabaptists, and it is likely that Peter Riedemann incorporated much of Hubmaier's thought into his *Rechenschaft* ("Account of Religion"), which today is the Confession of Faith of the Hutterites.[21]

The many disputes during the founding period resulted in fragmentation within the Anabaptist movement—a phenomenon that invariably occurs in religious social movements. Sociologically, this serves the important function of "refinement"—separating the peripheral adherents from the most loyal believers, reducing the size of the group, and simplifying the focus of the ideology.

Community of Goods

With the penetration of the Turks into the Hapsburg lands, the imperial government put great pressure on the Moravian nobles for tax revenues and men. In response to the continued refusal of Leonhard von Liechtenstein to expose the Anabaptists on his estate, an imperial emissary threatened him with force. Liechtenstein replied that if imperial troops should cross the border they would be met with cannon balls. At this point the Wiedemann Stäbler group, whose pacifism went as far as refusing protection by arms, offered in good conscience to leave the estate and find a nobleman who would grant toleration without armed

21. Franz Heimann, "The Hutterite Doctrine of Church and Common Life: A Study of Riedemann's Confession of 1540," *M.Q.R.* 26 (January 1952): 142–60.

protection. Wiedemann reasoned: "Since you threaten to protect us by the use of force we cannot stay." Many who were not Stäbler, sensing that there might be armed conflict, fled to nearby hiding places; but they soon returned.[22] One account says that the Liechtensteins at one point asked the Wiedemann group to leave. At any rate the Hutterite chronicle describes the historic occasion in the spring of 1528 when *Gütergemeinschaft*, or "community of goods," was launched by Jakob Wiedemann and his followers:

Therefore they sought to sell their possessions. Some sold, but others simply abandoned them and they departed with one another from thence. Whatever remained of theirs the Lords of Liechtenstein sent after them. And so from Nikolsburg, Bergen and thereabouts there gathered about two hundred persons without [counting] the children before the town [Nikolsburg]. Certain persons came out . . . and wept from great compassion with them, but others argued. . . . Then they got themselves up, and went out and pitched camp . . . in a desolate village [Bogenitz] and abode there one day and one night, taking counsel together in the Lord concerning their present necessity, and appointed [*geordnet*] ministers for their temporal necessities [*dienner in der Zeitlichen Notdurfft*]. . . . At that time these men spread out a cloak before the people, and every man laid his substance upon it, with a willing heart and without constraint, for the sustenance of those in necessity, according to the teaching of the prophets and apostles. Isaiah 23:18; Acts 2, 4, and 5.[23]

Leonhard von Liechtenstein apparently followed the group and protested that they need not leave. When they refused to return, he rode with them for a time, providing them with drink and freeing them from the usual tolls. The group sent four men north to Austerlitz to see whether Ulrich von Kaunitz and his brothers, who already had a Unitas colony on their estates, would allow them to live there. The lords agreed to their conditions concerning war and taxes—they were to be exempted from all services, interest, and taxes for a period of six years—and welcomed them. For three weeks, with their sick and their children, they had been under the open sky. The local inhabitants helped them to get settled.

22. Josef Beck, *Die Geschichts-Bücher der Wiedertäufer* (Vienna, 1883), p. 58.
23. A. J. F. Zieglschmid, *Die älteste Chronik der Hutterischen Brüder* (Philadelphia: Carl Schurz Memorial Foundation, 1943), p. 86 (hereafter cited as Zieglschmid, *Die älteste Chronik*). The English translation of this quotation is by Elizabeth Bender. Reference to Hutterite chronicles is made at various places in the text. For a full discussion of the versions of the chronicles, see appendix 1, "Hutterite Historiography." References are made in the text to three published chronicles: (1) Rudolf Wolkan, *Geschichts-Buch der Hutterischen Brüder* (Vienna: Carl Fromme; Macleod, Alta.: Standoff Colony, 1923) (hereafter cited as Wolkan, *Geschichts-Buch*); (2) Zieglschmid, *Die älteste Chronik*—the letter-perfect, or philologic, edition for use by German language scholars; (3) Zieglschmid, *Das Klein-Geschichtsbuch der Hutterischen Brüder* (Philadelphia: Carl Schurz Memorial Foundation, 1947) (hereafter cited as Zieglschmid, *Das Klein-Geschichtsbuch*).

In the course of the year the group at Austerlitz received many refugees into their community, some of whom apparently brought with them a written constitution for communal living—probably one of the tracts that had been worked out by Leonard Schiemer while in prison at Rattenberg in Tyrol.[24] One version of the Rattenberg regulations, ca. 1527, is included in the Hutterite chronicle with the indication that it became the constitution of the Austerlitz community in 1529.[25]

Wiedemann's group was not the only Anabaptist colony to establish itself in Moravia. At nearby Rossitz, a small colony had been founded by Gabriel Ascherham's Anabaptist followers in 1527. It was greatly expanded in 1529 when all of his followers were forced to leave Silesia. Another community, under the leadership of Philip Plener, called themselves the Philippites. They were established on lands at Auspitz, south of Austerlitz.

Jakob Hutter Emerges as Leader

Jakob Hutter, who was the chief pastor of the Tyrolese Anabaptists, made his first appearance at Austerlitz in 1529.[26] He was not a highly educated man, but he possessed unique leadership ability. He was born and raised in the hamlet of Moos (see figure 2) and, according to tradition, learned the skill of hat-making. Whether he acquired his name from his occupation, as some sources infer, is doubtful. Later he lived at Spittal in Carinthia, where he succeeded George Blaurock, who had been executed by burning near Klausen, as pastor in the Puster Valley.

Hutter began looking for a place of refuge for his stricken followers, for the persecution in Tyrol was extremely severe. His reputation as an effective Anabaptist leader reached King Ferdinand; it was reported that he "baptized others for money," but in reality each applicant had to make a contribution to a common treasury. Hutter heard of the opportunities for peaceful colonization in Moravia, and he and Simon Schützinger visited Austerlitz to assess the situation there. Hutter was so favorably impressed that he joined Wiedemann's congregation in the name of his own flock. He then returned to Tyrol to organize small bands of refugees for the flight to Moravia.

Because migration to Moravia was very dangerous, it was carried on in small groups called *Völker*. These small groups traveled the river routes on the Inn and the Danube and then proceeded on foot from Wachau (near Krems) through the forests to Moravia. Many had to leave

---

24. Williams, *The Radical Reformation*, p. 168.
25. Ibid., p. 232; and Zieglschmid, *Die älteste Chronik*, p. 84.
26. Hans Fischer, *Jakob Huter: Leben, Froemmigkeit, Briefe* (Newton, Kans.: Mennonite Publication Office, 1956).

Figure 2. Moos (Moso) Alto Adige, South Tyrol, Italy, birthplace of Jakob Hutter. (Photograph by Jan Gleysteen, 1970)

everything behind, even small children, whom they left with relatives or friends; little ones could hardly have survived the flight and would certainly have betrayed the secret flight route. The property of the fugitives was confiscated and frequently applied in whole or in part to the rearing of the children.[27]

The incoming refugees at Austerlitz were so numerous that it was impossible to adequately house and feed them, for the community there had been in existence for only a year and lacked the physical and spiritual resources to absorb them.

Wiedemann was initially the undisputed leader of the Austerlitz community. Hutter arranged that, in addition to Wiedemann, George Zaunring be especially responsible for the Tyrolese refugees in Moravia. In the winter of 1530 the Austerlitz community grew so large that when the weather became too cold for them to meet for religious services

27. Dedic, "The Social Background of the Austrian Anabaptists," pp. 6, 10. The extent and causes of the emigration are given serious attention by Clasen, *Anabaptism*, pp. 234–43.

out-of-doors, they had to meet in three different shelters, each with its own leader. These groups soon developed into factions.[28] In addition to Wiedemann and Zaunring, William Reublin, a former priest at St. Albans in Basel, also exerted a leadership role. Reublin had been an associate of Conrad Grebel, one of the initial leaders of the Swiss Brethren. It was Reublin who had baptized Hubmaier. Now, at Austerlitz in the winter of 1530, Reublin became a vigorous spokesman for a faction vexed by Wiedemann's authoritarian administration.

Reublin drew up ten charges against Wiedemann, which appear in a long letter to Pilgrim Marpeck.[29] He charged Wiedemann with a lack of humane consideration, since more than twenty infants had died for want of milk even though their parents, upon entering the group, had turned over all their funds, sometimes as much as fifty guilders. Girls were obliged to accept as husbands whomever the elders decreed. Maladministration was claimed: the elders and their wives were better fed and clothed than the common members. Reublin criticized the elders for failing to turn over to their patrons taxes for the war against the Turks, as they had promised. Wiedemann, according to Reublin, held that water baptism was absolutely essential to salvation and that infants who died unbaptized were condemned to hell—a teaching quite contrary to the very concept of Anabaptism.

During one of Wiedemann's absences, Reublin and Zaunring presented their complaints to the group and introduced rules to check Wiedemann's authority; the group supported them. When Wiedemann returned he spoke to the congregation and then took another vote without giving Reublin and Zaunring a chance to defend themselves. This time the majority supported Wiedemann, and Reublin and Zaunring were placed under the ban. Reublin and Zaunring considered this treatment unfair, and in the dead of winter, with 350 followers, they moved to Auspitz, leaving some 250 members with Wiedemann.

Both sides, unhappy at this outcome, appealed to Jakob Hutter to come from Tyrol to arbitrate. Hutter found the group at Austerlitz under Wiedemann to be most at fault. He then returned to Tyrol, considering the difficulties solved. But soon there was more trouble at Auspitz. It was discovered that Reublin had secretly retained several guilders for his own private emergency use. He was accused of being an Ananias and was removed from office. Zaunring then became sole leader of the group, but he too was soon in trouble. His wife was taken in adultery, and he refused to bring her before the group for disciplining;

28. Williams, *The Radical Reformation*, p. 419.
29. Ibid., p. 420.

for this he was excommunicated. Schützinger and Hutter again came from Tyrol to set things in order, and Schützinger was appointed leader.

The two communities at Auspitz, one led by Philip Plener and the other by Schützinger, formed an affiliation. With the help of Hutter, a nearby third community, the Gabrielites at Rossitz, was drawn in. Gabriel Ascherham was their leader, and he was made overseer of the three groups.

On August 11, 1533, Hutter came to Moravia to make his residence there. He felt specifically called of God to give leadership to the fragmented groups. But when he told the colonists that the failings and difficulties that they had experienced were due to their insufficient detachment from worldly considerations, family ties, and jealousies, all three groups rejected his immediate leadership.

Hutter's opportune moment came when two new converts were discovered to have secretly retained part of their possessions. Hutter then made a very bold assertion. He suggested that perhaps Schützinger's wife was a Sapphira, with secret possessions stowed away. The accusation was upsetting to the congregation, but they finally consented to have Schützinger's bedroom searched, provided Hutter's bed and chest were also examined. To the amazement of his followers, Schützinger himself was found to have hidden a number of things, including four Bernese silver pounds. He was deposed, as were Ascherham and Plener for having supported him. Although each man still had sympathizers, the major leadership position was now left to Hutter, who was elected chief elder, or *Vorsteher*.[30]

Hutter now effected a thoroughgoing communal organization. He instructed his followers that they were indeed God's elect, who, as despised sojourners in the world, could expect only hardship and suffering. He taught insistently that the complete break with the past—leaving homeland and kindred to share with fellow pilgrims what little possessions there were—was a necessary form of resignation (*Gelassenheit*). "With Hutter it was not the inner peace of a sectarian convent that was the goal of communal production and sharing but the discipline of spiritual warriors persevering against all obstacles until their vindication at the second advent of Christ."[31]

Hutter's leadership in Moravia was to last for only a short time— from August 1533 until late spring 1535—but during this time he demonstrated decisive leadership and channeled the skills of his people into

---

30. For Jakob Hutter's interpretation, see Robert Friedmann, "Jakob Hutter's Epistle Concerning the Schism in Moravia in 1533," *M.Q.R.* 38 (October 1964): 329–43.
    31. Williams, *The Radical Reformation*, p. 423.

building an economically durable and socially cohesive Bruderhof organization. The capacity to missionize proceeded more rapidly than ever.

Persecution and Dispersion

As early as 1528, King Ferdinand had demanded that the Moravian nobility expel the Anabaptists. The nobles refused to carry out the mandate. But in 1535, alarmed by the Münster disaster, Ferdinand appeared in person in Moravia and repeated his demand, threatening to use force if the nobles failed to comply. Thereupon the Philippites, Gabrielites, and all other Anabaptists who had sought refuge in Moravia were expelled from their villages. The Hutterite group spent the Easter of 1535 in the fields and forests. For months the harassment and persecution were severe. Agents and informants collected bounty for every Anabaptist they produced. Hutter and his followers, with bundles on their backs, wandered in small groups and pairs. "They were thus driven into the field like a herd of sheep," says the chronicle.[32] They reached the village of Tracht, and there "lay down on the wide heath under the open sky with many wretched widows and children, sick and infants."[33] In a passionate letter to the governor, Hutter wrote: "Now we are camping on the heath, without disadvantage to any man. We do not want to harm any human being, not even our worst enemy. . . . If all the world were like us there would be no war and no injustice. We can go nowhere; may God in heaven show us where we shall go."[34]

During the persecution the brotherhood urged Jakob Hutter to leave for his own safety, for he better than anyone knew the hiding places in Tyrol. He fled Moravia, leaving the overseeing of the group to his assistant, Hans Amon, who had also worked closely with him in Tyrol. With "grief and pain" the group saw Hutter leave. They scattered, some settling on smaller estates of lords who did not feel bound by the royal decree, and a few returned to their former homes in Tyrol.

Typical of the experience of the Anabaptists is an incident that occurred at Steinabrunn in Lower Austria, not far from Nikolsburg. In December 1538 a group of 136 persons representing several Anabaptist branches were meeting to discuss uniting with the Hutterites when they were surprised by the police and taken under guard to the Falkenstein Castle. (See figure 3.) After eight days imprisonment in Falkenstein, they were visited by several priests and an executioner sent by the king, demanding information about their faith and the location of their

---

32. Wolkan, *Geschichts-Buch*, p. 109.
33. Ibid., p. 110.
34. Ibid., p. 111.

Figure 3. Falkenstein, Austria, site of castle where Hutterites were imprisoned. (Photograph by Jan Gleysteen, 1970)

money and trying in vain to convert them to the state religion. Later they returned, threatening that if the prisoners refused to give up their Anabaptist beliefs they would be delivered to Trieste and sold as galley slaves to serve in the war against the Turks on the Mediterranean. Ninety of the men were chained in pairs and taken to Trieste, while the sick and the women were released. By making a rope of their chains, the men were able to escape over the wall of their prison in Trieste. Twelve of them were seized in Carinthia on their return and taken back to Trieste; nothing more was ever heard of them. The happenings at Steinabrunn are of special significance to modern Hutterites, for their hymns recapitulate this sad event.[35]

The several other communal groups in the area fared even worse. The Austerlitz group was almost totally wiped out in the persecution of

35. Adolf Mais, "Der Überfall von Steinabrunn im Jahr 1539," *Jahrbuch für Landeskunde von Niederösterreich* (Vienna), 1964, series 36, pp. 295–310. See *Die Lieder der Hutterischen Brüder* (Scottdale, Pa.: Die Hutterischen Brüder, 1914), p. 89.

1535. Wiedemann and many others met death in Vienna. The Hutterite chronicle records the names of over two thousand men and women who died at the hands of the executioners.[36] The Philippites left Moravia, passing through Austria en route to South Germany, but were caught and imprisoned in the castle at Passau. Here they composed many songs, forty-seven of which survive in the *Ausbund*, the hymnal of the Old Order Amish. Some of the Philippites stayed in Upper Austria, and a few years later Peter Riedemann visited them and managed to unite them with the Hutterite Brethren. The Gabrielites moved back to Silesia. They gradually became disillusioned with their leader, and between 1542 and 1545 most of them returned to Moravia and merged with the Hutterite group.

Most of Hutter's followers did not leave the area during the persecutions of 1535 but went into hiding in the surrounding fields or forests or were kept secretly by lesser nobles. While in hiding Hutter wrote letters to the scattered Brethren in Moravia. His apostolic style shows the extent to which he considered himself especially called to serve "the elect of God." Hutter's "Remonstrance" to the government of Moravia, in which he movingly reassured the lords of the peaceful intentions of the Brethren and pleaded for a small place on "the God-created earth" where his followers might live, was of no avail.

King Ferdinand demanded that both Hutter and Amon be imprisoned.[37] A price of 40 guilders had been placed on Hutter's head by the king, and on the night of November 29, 1535, he and his wife were captured in the home of Hans Steiner at St. Andrews in Austria. The small group was imprisoned and Hutter was promptly taken back to Innsbruck for trial. Even under torture on the rack and after severe whippings, he refused to reveal the names of his associates or the manner in which he conducted his mission. Hutter was sure that he was dealing with an emissary of Satan, and so were his questioners. Ferdinand, determined to make a public spectacle to warn anyone who might be inclined to follow Hutter, demanded a public execution by fire. The officials arranged for special torture. They held Hutter bound and gagged in freezing water, then took him to an overheated room. In public they poured brandy over his lacerated flesh and set it aflame. His public burning occurred in Innsbruck on February 25, 1536. His wife, who managed to escape the prison at Gufidaun, was executed about two years later.

36. Zieglschmid, *Das Klein-Geschichtsbuch*, pp. 53–55. See also Beck, *Die Geschichts-Bücher der Wiedertäufer*, pp. 277–80.
37. Grete Mecenseffy, *Österreich*, pt. 1, Quellen zur Geschichte der Täufer, vol. 11 (Gütersloh: Gerd Mohn, 1964), p. 273.

Jakob Hutter was the acknowledged leader of the Moravian Hutterites for scarcely three years. Into an area where there were at least fourteen different Anabaptist groups, he brought decisive leadership which gave permanent form to a segment of these groups. He impressed upon them the necessity for communal living, for working fearlessly in the face of external threats and internal problems of jealousy and division. The selection of leaders by lot was not as important to Hutter as a leader's own sense of inner awakening; he himself felt compelled to give the utmost in leadership. He could not escape the call of God, and as he stated in one of his letters, "[The Almighty] has appointed me to be a watchman, shepherd and guardian of His Holy people, of His elect."[38] His message was, "Resign yourselves to tribulation and trial." It is from Jakob Hutter that the surviving group received its name.[39]

Leadership after Hutter

Hans Amon was elected to succeed Hutter. His first task was to minister to the scattered flock hiding in the fields and forests. On Easter 1536, one year after they were driven from their homes, the Brethren celebrated the Lord's Supper in the forest. There they decided to break into groups of six or eight and to quietly find employment with the nobles; in this they succeeded. In a few years the communities began to reestablish themselves and eventually to prosper. One of their able organizers was Jakob Mändl, formerly an administrator for Lord Liechtenstein at Nikolsburg.

Amon was the leader of the brotherhood until his death in 1542. During his administration, missionaries were systematically sent out in an effort to cover all of Europe. The Hutterites thought of themselves as members of the true church and regarded their location in Moravia as the special place in the wilderness that was saved for the righteous. They considered it their task to turn it into a paradise in preparation for Christ's second coming.[40] About four-fifths of the missionaries who were

38. Fischer, *Jakob Huter*, letter 4.
39. Following the account of the execution of Hutter, the chronicle (Zieglschmid, *Die älteste Chronik*, p. 158) states: "Von diesem Jakob Hueter hat die gemain den Hueterischen Namen ererbt das man sie die Hueterischen Brüder genennt hat." At the outset, the Brethren called themselves "The Brothers, known as Hutterians." Today both "Hutterian Brethren" and "Hutterite" are common usages. When conversing with outsiders, members themselves use "Hutterite." Like "Mennonite," it carries no derogatory overtones. Naming has varied in past centuries and in various regions. In the Italian language the Brethren were called *Nouvi Christiani*, or "New Christians"; in Transylvania, "Black Germans," because they wore black cloth and spoke German; in Slovakia, *Habaner* (from *Haushaben*)—besides other frequently uncomplimentary epithets. Huter in American English is rendered Hutter.
40. Williams, *The Radical Reformation*, pp. 673 ff.

sent out were martyred, but their converts, many from the German states, came to Moravia.

Peter Riedemann, a Silesian cobbler, was one of the most influential early Hutterites, emerging as a leader in the early 1530s. In 1529, before he had become a Hutterite, Riedemann was imprisoned for his Anabaptist faith. He escaped from prison and went to Moravia, where he joined the Hutterite brotherhood and married. In 1533 he was sent as a missionary to Franconia and in 1535 to Hesse. He also went to Austria, Tyrol, Swabia, and Württemberg and induced many to come to Moravia.[41]

Riedemann was captured in Hesse and imprisoned by Landgrave Philipp.[42] While imprisoned, first in a dungeon and later in more comfortable quarters, he wrote his great *Rechenschaft* (about 1540), which has been accepted by the Hutterites as a definitive statement of their faith and which serves this function even to this day.[43] Riedemann also wrote many hymns, forty-five of which appear in the Hutterite hymnal.

Before Amon died in 1542 he named Leonard Lanzenstiel as his successor. Lanzenstiel urgently requested that Riedemann, who was still in prison in Hesse, share the leadership with him. This urgent plea induced Riedemann to escape. He returned to Moravia and served as coleader until his death in 1556. Lanzenstiel remained leader until his death in 1565. Together Lanzenstiel and Riedemann guided the Brethren through the difficult years between 1545 and 1551.

King Ferdinand personally visited Moravia for the second time in 1546. This visit again put the Hutterite Brethren in great danger. By 1548 the nearby settlement in Upper Hungary (Slovakia) was also threatened. The chronicle speaks of the Brethren fleeing to mountains and caves and forming small groups; some were probably disguised as wandering monks.[44] Though many deserted the colonies during this period, the majority remained steadfast. Around 1551-52 the

41. Robert Friedmann, "Peter Riedemann, Early Anabaptist Leader," *M.Q.R.* 44 (January 1970): 5-44. *Riedemann* is variously spelled (*Rideman, Rydeman, Ryedeman*). In this book, I shall use *Riedemann* in keeping with the usage of Riedemann's modern biographer (Friedmann).

42. Philipp consistently refused to execute Anabaptists for their faith; see Franklin H. Littell, *Landgraf Philipp und die Toleranz* (Bad Neuheim, 1957).

43. Peter Rideman, *Rechenschaft unserer Religion, Lehr und Glaubens, von den Brüdern, so man die Hutterischen nennt, ausgangen 1565* (n.p., 1565), translated into English by Kathleen Hasenberg as *Account of Our Religion, Doctrine and Faith, Given by Peter Rideman of the Brothers Whom Men Call Hutterians* (London: Hodder and Stoughton; Rifton, N.Y.: Plough Publishing House, 1950; reprinted by Plough Publishing House in 1970) (hereafter cited as Rideman, *Account of Our Religion*).

44. Zieglschmid, *Das Klein-Geschichtsbuch*, p. 68. The elders, according to this account, disbursed the members *kuttenweis* (as wandering monks), and they lived in secrecy among the population.

political tension eased. The Moravian noblemen reasserted their right to administer their own domains, and in 1553 the Hutterites managed to form three new colonies. During the next several decades there was a remarkable increase in the number of colonies formed.

Summary of the Founding Period

The Austrian Anabaptists represent a consistent development of the Zwinglian reform movement. Like other Anabaptists, the Hutterites accepted the teaching of the Bible as authoritative, particularly the ethic of love and discipleship of the New Testament. Their attitude toward the Bible was one of obedience rather than the philosophical speculation or intellectualism of other nonconformists.

Hutterite society was formed in Moravia by the influx of religious refugees from the Austrian Tyrol and from other German-speaking regions who had responded to the message of itinerant Swiss and German preachers and were subsequently forced by authorities to leave their homes. This message was a return to the discipleship of the Apostolic church, on the one hand, and future fulfillment in the Kingdom of God (salvation), on the other.

While the practice of rebaptism, and particularly baptism of adults only, was heresy to the authorities, it was not the most distinguishing feature of the Hutterite interpretation of Christianity. Like other Anabaptists, the Hutterites were formally apolitical, and they were pacifists, the Schwertler having died out by 1530. They differed from the Swiss and Dutch Mennonites in their practice of community of goods. To be Christian was to give all material resources to the community of believers and to live in a state of submission to the will of God within the believing community.

In addition to the issue of adult baptism, the Moravian Hutterites faced three more internal crises before the movement acquired a stable character. There was (1) the dispute over pacifism (at Nikolsburg in 1527), which fragmented the group into Schwertler and Stäbler. This was followed by (2) the dissension over community of goods (from 1529–33), which separated the Philippites and the Gabrielites and others from the proto-Hutterite group. Finally there was (3) the wrangle over leadership within the group that practiced pacifism and community of goods, with Jakob Hutter emerging as the charismatic leader.

Following the execution of Hutter, there was no further fragmentation, for as a social movement integration had been achieved. The group had moved from a diverse to an integrated ideology, from unintegrated to integrated social structure, and from a heterogeneous to a homogeneous membership. After its identity was formed and integrated, the movement expanded rapidly by absorbing incoming persecuted refugees. Bruderhofs were formed in many parts of Moravia after the same basic ideology, social pattern, and function. Once the Hutterite movement achieved integration, many individuals joined who had earlier been deterred from entering the movement.

Although the community of goods was instituted by the pacifist faction under Jakob Wiedemann at Nikolsburg, it was Hutter who later brought decisive leadership to the several groups. He offered hope to the persecuted Brethren in Tyrol, helping them to escape the executioner and organizing their escape routes to Moravia. Hutter spoke of himself as "a servant and apostle of Jesus Christ" and described his followers as "saints, chosen and elect, fighters and witnesses of God" ready "to suffer poverty, need, tribulation, pain, torture, suffering and even death itself, that we might show fellowship, love, and faithfulness."[45]

Hutter envisioned no utopia on earth. He emphasized absolute obedience to God, stressing the denial of self and of private property in the community of believers. His epistles to the Moravian groups brought them consolation in their struggle but also the warning; "resign yourselves to tribulation and trial."[46]

The sufferings and tragedies of the Moravian Hutterites form a significant part of the present-day Hutterite world view. The hardships came not only from church and state and from Jesuit priests but from roving bands of plunderers and from successive wars between Catholic and Protestant states. Viewed from without, the Hutterites were obdurate and bigoted, and in the Jesuit Christoph Fischer's words, "worse than Turks or Jews."[47] But viewed from within, "The fire of God burned within them. They would rather have died the bitterest death, yea ten deaths, than to forsake the truth which they had espoused. They would take nothing in exchange for their faith in Christ, no lordship, no principality, no kingdom, yea not all the wealth and pleasures of the world; for they had a firm ground and assurance of their faith."[48]

45. Robert Friedmann, trans., "Jakob Hutter's Last Epistle to the Church in Moravia, 1535," *M.Q.R.* 34 (January 1960): 41.

46. Ibid., p. 42.

47. Christoph Andreas Fischer, *Vier und fünfftzig Erhebeliche Ursachen Warumb die Widertäufer nicht sein im Land zu leyden* (Ingolstadt, 1607), p. 119.

48. John Horsch, *The Hutterian Brethren, 1528–1931: A Story of Martyrdom and Loyalty* (Goshen, Ind.: Mennonite Historical Society, 1931), p. 42.

chapter two

The Golden Period in Moravia

The chronicles speak of a "good" period (1554–65) and a "golden" period (1565–92) when the Hutterite communities experienced growth and unhindered development.[1] During this time the Moravian nobles were strong; jealous of their local autonomy, they ignored the mandates from the government in Vienna to expel or prosecute the Hutterites. Between 1529 and 1621, one hundred two Bruderhofs developed in Moravia with an estimated population of twenty to thirty thousand inhabitants.[2] This phenomenal growth was aided by the itinerant Hutterite missionaries in Austria and South Germany. (See map 2.)

The genius of Hutterite culture during the golden period manifested itself particularly in economic organization, ceramic making, the

---

1. Josef Beck, *Die Geschichts-Bücher der Wiedertäufer* (Vienna, 1883), pp. xi–xli; Zieglschmid, *Das Klein-Geschichtsbuch*, p. 83.

2. Estimates vary from twenty to seventy thousand. The claim of sixteenth-century authors that as many as one thousand persons lived in a single community appear exaggerated. Estimates occur in Walter Kuhn, *Geschichte der Deutschen Östsiedlung in der Neuzeit* (Cologne: Böhlau, 1957), suppl. map no. 18; František Hrubý, *Die Wiedertäufer in Mähren* (Leipzig: Verlag M. Heinsius Nachfolger, 1935), p. 62; Rideman, *Account of Our Religion*, appendix 1, pp. 274–75; *M.E.*, s.v. "Hutterian Brethren"; and Claus-Peter Clasen, *Anabaptism: A Social History* (Ithaca: Cornell University Press, 1972), p. 244. Hereafter the term *Bruderhof(s)* will be used instead of community and without italics. *Colony* will be used in speaking of the North American Hutterites.

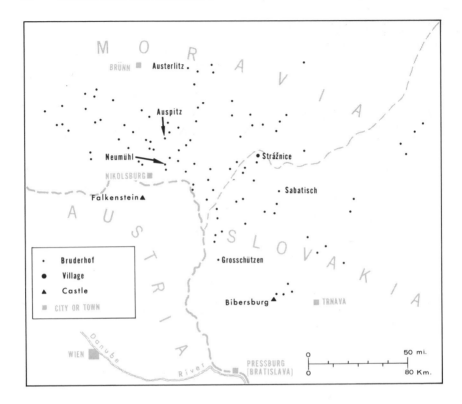

Map 2. Czechoslovakia, Showing Former Hutterite Bruderhofs, 1528–1686

development of education, missionary activity, medicinal cures and practices, and handicrafts. In this chapter we shall discuss the Bruderhof activities essential to Hutterite identity.

The Social Structure of the Bruderhof

In the Catholic monastic groups, monks and friars shared in a common life and in common goals, but they were individualists given to devotional exercises and to working at their own salvation. The Hutterites were different. They were a religious community of wedded couples with their offspring, practicing common ownership of possessions. Under the theology of *Gelassenheit*—a term indicating peaceful submission to God and to the believing group together with the forsaking of private property—they practiced the communism of love, in production as well as consumption, looking to the future for the ultimate vindication of their faith.

It was Hutter who, regarding himself as an apostle appointed of God, firmly established the practice of communal living as a means of salvation. Under Hutter and Hans Amon the group had capable leadership during the first and second generations. Peter Riedemann, called by some "the second founder of the brotherhood," was concerned with the practical organization, "How to Build the House of God."[3] One of the most capable leaders, Peter Walpot, who served as Vorsteher from 1565 to 1578, left an imprint on all of Hutterite history by his contribution to the organization of schools and other distinctive Hutterite institutions. He was followed by Hans Kräl (1578-83) and Claus Braidl (1583-1611); they, like Walpot, were residents at Neumühl, a place recognized for its Hutterite leadership.[4]

The source of Hutter's concept of the Bruderhof is not known, for he makes no reference whatever to a model for such an institution. But it is known that the practice of communal living was nothing new in Hutter's time; there were other pacifistic communal groups in Bohemia and Moravia, and several Hutterite writers allude to still other communitarian groups. A Hutterite document of 1577 mentions the Therapeutae,[5] whose description by Philo of Alexandria was incorporated in the well-known *Ecclesiastical History* of Eusebius. The Hutterites probably found a precedent for communal living in the writings of Hubmaier against Zwingli, and they cited a pseudo-Clementine epistle, a spurious letter allegedly written by Clement, Bishop of Jerusalem, to James the brother of Jesus.[6]

The early Hutterites based their support of communal living primarily on the Scriptures. They cited with great skill many passages

---

3. Rideman, *Account of Our Religion*, pp. 154-65.

4. Throughout this book, German place names (as in the chronicles) will be used; for their modern counterparts, see appendix 3. For an extensive treatment of Walpot, see Leonard Gross, "The Golden Years of the Hutterites: Life, Mission, and Theology of the Communistic Moravian Anabaptists during the Walpot Era, 1565-1578" (Ph.D. dissertation, University of Basel, 1968).

5. Peter Walpot, *Von der wahren Gelassenheit und der christlichen Gemeinschaft der Güter* (n.p., 1577). See English translation by Kathleen Hasenberg in Robert Friedmann, "A Notable Hutterite Document: Concerning True Surrender and Christian Community of Goods," *M.Q.R.* 31(January 1957): 22-62.

6. George H. Williams, *The Radical Reformation* (Philadelphia: Westminster Press, 1962), p. 431.

and allusions in the Old and New Testaments in support of this view. Their claim was to represent the faithful church, the community of God's elect. Parents and teachers taught their children that from the beginning God had commanded the communitarian way of life in which all of man's activities should be sacred.

Decisive leadership emerged from the start, for there were talented persons among the Brethren. A few of the early leaders were learned men; they knew Latin or had some knowledge of Hebrew, Greek, or French. The former priests among them were men who had been educated. But the large majority of Hutterite leaders, like Jakob Hutter, were craftsmen. They knew how to read and write and were acquainted with the Scriptures. Catholic writers downgraded their qualifications, asking how a straw-cutter, a vinedresser, a blacksmith, a weaver, or a carpenter could rule over thousands of people? In their view these ignorant people were qualified to make shoes, select a solid pitchfork, and take a wife, but to preach and conduct the sacraments was something else. Nonetheless, it was these adamant believers, largely craftsmen, who set about to establish a new form of society based on communal sharing of property.

At least five different offices were recognized by the early Hutterites: (1) apostles, "who are sent out by God to go through the country and establish through the word and baptism the obedience of faith in His name"; these apostles, also called *Sendboten*, or "missioners," were ordained for this function; (2) pastors (preachers), or shepherds, who have the same duties as apostles "except that they remain in one place"; (3) helpers, "who serve along with the shepherds, exhorting and calling people to remain true"; (4) stewards, who minister to the temporal needs, and (5) elders, who, like the trustees, consider "the good of the church together with the preacher, helping the latter to bear the burden."[7]

Distinctions between religious and secular offices were minimal. The church (*Gemein*) was the ruling body, and in every Bruderhof there was a preacher-pastor and usually an assistant. These spiritual leaders were called *Diener am Wort*, or "ministers of the word." Those appointed to temporal duties were called *Diener der Notdurft*, or "stewards."

The Spiritual Leaders. Candidates for the position of preacher were nominated by the group; one of the nominees was chosen by lot, following the practice of the early Church in choosing Matthias (Acts 1). After much searching and praying, "those who have been recognized through God's counsel to be suitable, are presented to all." However,

7. Rideman, *Account of Our Religion*, p. 82.

no one could be confirmed (by the laying on of hands) unless he be "proven and have the testimony of a good life." The chronicles register the names, dates, and often the places of all elections and confirmations to office of both preachers and stewards.[8]

The duties of a Hutterite preacher were similar to those described in the Anabaptist Schleitheim Confession of 1527: "His office shall be to read, to admonish and to teach, to warn, to discipline, to ban in the church, to lead out in prayer for the advancement of all the brethren and sisters, to lift up the bread when it is broken, and in all things to see to the care of the body of Christ that it may be built up and developed."[9] Each Bruderhof had at least one fully ordained spiritual leader (head pastor) and often others who were sent out as missioners.

From the Bruderhofs one preacher was chosen to serve as *Vorsteher* (or *Aelteste*) ("bishop," "moderator," or "chief elder") for the entire brotherhood. His charge was the overall welfare of the brotherhood. He corresponded with the missioners who were traveling abroad and sent epistles of comfort to those who were suffering in prisons. He presided at the assembly of the ordained leaders when there were ordinations and special problems. He issued regulations embodying the disciplines of the brotherhood. The oldest chronicle begins by listing all the Vorsteher from Hutter (d.1536) to Johannes Rücker (d.1687). There are thirteen names in all, including that of Peter Riedemann, who was considered a coleader. The Waldner chronicle, following the same procedure, lists twenty-two Vorsteher from the time of Hutter to 1762 and five more to 1857. All members were to esteem their leaders as "worthy of double honor" (1 Tim. 5:17). Although *Vorsteher* is often translated as "bishop," it would be inaccurate to regard the Vorsteher as a pope or a bishop; his function is more nearly that of a moderator. Among present-day Hutterites the person who occupies this position is called "elder." Should he be restricted on account of health or age, he may recommend a successor.

The Stewards. Diener der Notdurft did not designate a single position but comprised at least four different role allocations—the *Haushalter*, or "general manager" of the Bruderhof; the *Einkäufer*, or "buyer"; the *Furgestellte*, or "foremen" of the various trades and shops; and the *Meier*, or "overseer" of the farming activity. Other positions mentioned in the literature are those of *Weinzierl*, an assistant to the *Haushalter*, who served in his absence; *Kellner*, or "manager of the vineyards";

8. The number of leaders has been tabulated by Clasen (*Anabaptism*, p. 247).
9. John C. Wenger, intro. and trans., "The Schleitheim Confession of Faith," *M.Q.R.* 19 (October 1945): 250.

and *Kastner,* or "caretaker of the storage bins." Persons were nominated and voted into office, but permanent appointments were made
only after a period of probation. The principles of organization today
are very similar to those of the sixteenth century, but since Hutterites
are now large-scale farmers rather than craftsmen, some of the functions allotted to these positions have changed, as will be noted later in
the discussion of modern economic life.

The Haushalter was the manager of material needs—the housekeeper and general steward of the Bruderhof. He was the first to awake
in the morning and the last to retire. He supervised the distribution of
material goods, clothing, and bedding, and he supervised the work. He
kept account of all business transactions and collected the income from
the persons in charge of the various enterprises. The welfare of the aged,
the sick, and to a certain extent the children was his responsibility.
Major purchases were made only with the approval of an elected body of
elders that included the preacher. The Haushalter worked closely with
the preacher at all times.

The Einkäufer maintained a liaison with the "world." On the one
hand, he was to be careful in all purchases and never to squander the
savings of the Bruderhof; on the other hand, he was to be honest and,
according to the Discipline of 1599, was not to "fall into the tricks of the
traders, butchers, or Jews." When in doubt he was to ask the counsel of
the elders. Funds entrusted to him were not to be left with the women
but were to be deposited with the elders or the general steward.

The Furgestellten, or foremen of the shops and the various trades
(smiths, weavers, tanners, shoemakers, potters), managed their particular business by buying what they needed, selling their product on the
market, and turning the proceeds over to the general steward.

The Meier and the Kellner each held an important position of
trust: they were responsible for the farm, orchard, vineyards, barns,
and cellars, and also for the maintenance of buildings, tools, and roads.
The services of these men and their assistants were invaluable to the
manorial lords. They worked conscientiously and reliably. All of these
offices were held in honor, for the chronicle records the names not only
of those who were elected as preachers but also those who were chosen
to serve as stewards. In 1548, for example, four preachers and fourteen
stewards were chosen. Two years later, seventeen preachers and thirty-
one stewards were chosen.[10]

The early Hutterite writers describe the Bruderhof as "a big
clockwork where one wheel drives the other, promotes, helps and makes
the whole clock function" and as "a big beehive where all the busy bees

10. Beck, *Die Geschichts-Bücher der Wiedertäufer,* pp. 193–95. Between 1539
and 1618, the number of Servants of the Word elected was 150; see Clasen, *Anabaptism,*
p. 246.

work together to a common end, the one doing this and the other that, not for their own needs but for the good of all."[11] The basic motivation for the organization was not profit, as many contemporaries seemed to think, but the call to discipleship in keeping with a disciplined life of Christian obedience. The result, however, was a rational establishment of great efficiency. There was hard work, frugality, little waste, and no motive for private gain. This approach to large-scale enterprise, developed by the Hutterites in the sixteenth century, was practically unknown before the Industrial Revolution. The Hutterites of today continue to demonstrate this rational efficiency in their farm enterprises in North America.

The Bruderhof was an elaborate establishment and its houses were acknowledged by contemporaries to be "the most beautiful." There were forty or more dwellings in a single Bruderhof. A cluster of long buildings was usually arranged around a village common or square, as can still be observed at Grosschützen and St. Johann. The ground floors of the larger buildings were used for workshops, for carpentry, for spinning, weaving, and sewing, for the laundry and for communal functions—the dining hall, kitchen, school, and meeting place for worship were all there. The roofs were steep and the attics consisted of two stories with rooms (*Stuben*, or *Oertel*) where the married couples lived with their small children. The thatch on the roofs was mixed with clay to make it fireproof as well as durable. (See figure 4.) The wood partitions in the attics were also coated with a white claylike substance, thus making the rooms lighter as well as providing insulation and fireproofing.[12] Many of the original thatched-roof buildings in Grosschützen were still standing in 1937. The author found only one such roof in 1971, as all others had been replaced with tile. A 1589 woodcut shows thatched roofing and rows of windows for each of the attic floors.[13] A man, woman, and child are shown in typical Hutterite dress. (See figure 5.)

11. Wolkan, *Geschichts-Buch*, pp. 434–35.

12. Straw roof construction is described in Adam Landgraf, *Beschreibung des Habaner Strohdaches . . .* (Pressburg: Printed by Franz August in Patzko, 1772).

The two traveling Hutterites, David Hofer and Michael Waldner, who observed the dwellings at Grosschützen (Velké Leváry) in 1937 observed that the houses "are about 67 feet long and look very nice and tidy with their thatched roofs. . . . The *Stuben* in the living quarters are 14 by 16 feet and the *Oertlein* are somewhat smaller, 10 by 12 feet, having room just for one big bed and two chairs. The roofs are beautifully preserved and perfectly tight, made of straw with clay intermixed in several layers. They are said to be absolutely fireproof. The floors downstairs are exactly the same as we used to have them until recently in our American Hofs, namely of stamped clay or loam with yellow sand strewn on top" (Robert Friedmann, ed. and trans., "Hutterites Revisit European Homesteads: Excerpts from the Travel Diary of David Hofer," *M.Q.R.* 33 (October 1959): 310–11).

13. Christoph Erhard, *Gründliche und kurz verfasste Historia. Von Muensterischen Widertauffern* (Munich, 1589), title page.

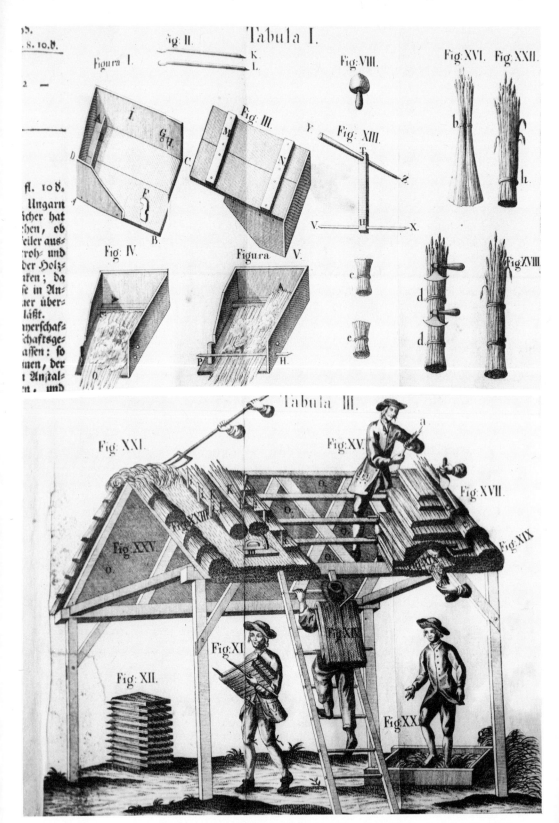

Figure 4. Illustration of Hutterite straw roof construction. (Reprinted from Landgraff, 1772)

Figure 5. Sixteenth-century woodcut showing Hutterite dwelling and dress. (Photograph from title page of Erhard, 1589)

While the brethren thought of their Bruderhof as a "bee hive" or a "large clockwork," Catholic foes had other conceptions. Christoph Fischer symbolized the Bruderhof as a *Taubenkobel* ("pigeon shed") and illustrated his contention on the title page of his book on the Hutterites.[14] (See figure 6.) He describes the Bruderhof as accommodating five to six hundred persons living in each of seventy places in southern Moravia. Although intended as a satire, the woodcut is in some respects revealing. The dress is probably authentic and typical of this period for the Hutterites. It is similar to but appears less rigid than that in the Erhard illustration.

To Fischer, the pigeon hut represented the Bruderhofs and their enterprises, "their offal, manure, mud, and filth—that is, their false, stinking, filthy and abominable doctrines. . . ."[15] The activities pictured are supervised by an elder, with Hutter himself peering from the top.

14. Christoph Andreas Fischer, *Der Hutterischen Widertauffer Taubenkobel* (Ingolstadt, 1607), title page.
15. The quotation is the subtitle of Fischer's book (see fn. 14), translated by Elizabeth Bender: "In welchem all ihr Wust, Mist, Kott und unflat, das ist ihre falsche stinckende unflaetige und abscheuliche Lehren verfasset; auch dess grossen Taubers dess Jakob Hutters Leben."

Figure 6. Conception of the Bruderhof as a pigeon hut. (Photograph from title page of Fischer, 1608)

The elevated position of the pigeon house symbolizes isolation and inaccessibility. Various activities are illustrated on the beams extending outward from the hut. On the top left side is the alchemist, or *Hexen-Meister*, holding his instruments. Below him is a tailor with scissors and cloth. The owl symbolizes the potter; the bats symbolize the astronomer and the alchemist, who ply their secret arts by night. At the top right is a laborer with a shovel. Beneath him is a shoemaker displaying stockings and shoes. Other wares depicted are tools of various sorts, a drawing knife, a carding comb, brushes, and pottery. Above the woodcut is the caption *Die Zauberer solst tu nicht lassen leben* ("Thou shalt not permit sorcerers to live").

Early Economic Organization

Driving through the rolling countryside of Moravia today, one gets the impression that those places where the Bruderhofs were once located are productive agricultural areas. For anyone who knows the large-scale and almost exclusively agricultural enterprises of the colonies in North America, it is startling to realize that agriculture was but one of a dozen or more economic activities engaged in by the Moravian Hutterites. They had no access to land or living space except with the permission of ruling princes and barons, so that their potential economic development was limited to the kind of reciprocity they could obtain. The Hutterites possessed skills which the ruling princes could not find in their native populations. They gave the Hutterites permission to live on the land in exchange for their services. The first generation of Hutterites, refugees from Tyrol and other religiously oppressed countries, had left most of their possessions behind, but the skills they brought with them were a great asset.

The manorial lords formalized their relationships with the Hutterites in a charter, or *Hausbrief*. The earliest known charter (Neumühl, in Moravia, 1558) stipulates in detail the space, resources, and privileges of the Brethren;[16] these charters specified precisely, for example, which lands were to be used for pasture for the various kinds of animals (even geese), which waters could be used for fishing, and from which swamps reeds could be gathered for making thatched roofs and baskets. The Bruderhof established in 1546 in Sabatisch, Slovakia, just across the border from Moravia, had a charter, renewed in 1713, with the lords of Berencs (today Branc) that specified the various kinds of taxes that were to be paid and the privileges that were to be accorded each party.[17] The charter for Grosschützen dates from 1558. This charter illustrates the many reciprocal relationships and the range of activities the Brethren engaged in:

Hans Bernhart, lord of Lembach at Grosschützen, offered the Brethren the following opportunities:

> For wages they shall serve in my cattle yards and dairy and the mill at *Nagy-Levard*.
>
> I have granted them a plot on the open meadow for buildings necessary to a *Hof*.
>
> The house is to have all the necessary perquisites—rooms for living and sleeping, also sheds, stables, workshops as they may require for their needs, crafts, and other work. For this house and its land I promise them for ten years release from the great tithe and the small tithe, and from the payment of interest and feudal service. With this house I give them a field adjoining the house or *Hof*. . . . Likewise I give them a meadow that adjoins the *Hof*. . . . I agree to give them still more lands and meadows that I will designate. I have also given them land for vegetable gardens and orchards, as much as they may need, and a plot, as much as they may need, for a vineyard, which shall also be free of feudal obligations and other payments for ten years.

16. Adolf Mais, "Das Hausbuch von Neumühl, 1558–1610, das älteste Grundbuch der huterischen Brüder," *Jahrbuch der Gesellschaft für die Geschichte des Protestantismus in Österreich* (Vienna, 1964), pp. 66–68.

17. Beck, *Die Geschichts-Bücher der Wiedertäufer*, p. 364.

I specify that they and their families may now and for all time enjoy this house and its land and whatever more they clear, to possess and occupy it with many or few persons, craftsmen and others, entirely in accord with their wishes and practices as they see fit for their welfare.

I agree to let the Brethren keep in any year now and in the future seven hundred milk-giving sheep and their lambs. They may also keep as many cattle—oxen, cows and calves—as they can use. Also hogs as many as they want and one hundred goats with their kids.

They may keep a stallion on the meadow with thirty or forty horses and their colts which they may keep until they are usable and then dispose of them as they wish. All of these cattle and livestock they may herd with mine if they wish; but if they prefer to herd theirs separately, they may do so wherever they can find pasture, but without damaging any cultivated meadows and with the exception of the estate forest.

I promise them all the wood and charcoal they need for fuel, also the wood for buildings and crafts—wheelwrights, cabinet-makers or other craftsmen. Also the wood for making tiles, all free of any charges.

I give them from my ponds and swamps all the reeds they need for roofing at any time. They also have the right to buy what they need in grain, wine, salt, iron, etc., whenever they can, whether in Austria, Moravia, or Hungary.

In exchange Bernhart asked for the following:

For these freedoms and for the aforesaid buildings and land they shall be obliged at the end of the ten free years, to pay me, my heirs or my successors as interest, service and labor as follows: First, for the house, fields, gardens and meadows, with all freedom and justice, annually 32 Talers—16 on St. George's day and 16 on St. Wencesles', each Taler to be figured as 100 Hungarian Pfennig. For the cultivated fields, one-tenth of the grain as is customary.

The fields in which they break ground shall be free of all payments of the tithe for ten years, after which they shall pay a tithe, as is customary.

Also on the vineyards they shall pay after ten years the usual tithe.

Concerning kids and lambs, after ten years they shall give me the customary tenth annually. Because this tithe goes to the Pressburg Chamber and I must redeem it every year if I want the income, this tithe is taken from my subjects and the aforesaid Brethren, they shall not be obliged to pay me another tenth. Beyond this they shall have no further obligations to pay taxes or tithes or labor. I, my heirs and my successors and all of our officials, such as captains, judges or other shall not demand of them more than specified herein or express it from them by deceit or pretense or secret design.

Bernhart guaranteed religious freedom and assured the Brethren the same protection afforded to all his other subjects:

We shall consider ourselves as their protectors and keep them and their people and possessions like our other [immigrant] subjects at home and outside, protecting, guarding and supporting them in all justice, as is our duty whenever they need it, to the extent of our ability in order that they may be protected from arbitrariness, injustice or harm, as God gives grace and permits, be it from our subjects or those of other lords.

They shall also be excused from all things that are against their faith and conscience and shall not be harassed; whether in the matter of tips [gifts] to the shepherds, money for military service, war taxes or money for any warlike purpose, by whatever name, that is against their religion, whether for barracks or imperial taxes. I or my heirs or the owners of this estate will be responsible for and pay such things so that no one will have the right to demand such payments from them.

[Since] I do not want to look upon them with disfavor or anger through talebearing and unverified accusations, I will let them at all times answer for themselves, and in general grant them honorable and favorable opportunities.[18]

The Hutterites were careful not to make themselves liable for war taxes or peasant servitude, and in this document they attempted to protect themselves against the arbitrariness and deceit used by previous manorial lords. The charter also stipulated that should the Brethren need to move for any reason, they might sell their buildings after first offering them to the lord, keep the money, and take their possessions with them without interference. This, too, was an important provision for a group that was consistently forced to migrate. The charter provides for the basic conditions needed for the Bruderhof. The Brethren could work for wages on the estate of the lord, they could engage in the manufacture and sale of crafts, and they could produce livestock and crops.

In Moravia relationships in the manorial system between the lords and their workers were still characterized by feudalism. The lords, some wealthy, others of lesser power, owned the land which was tilled by the peasants. Some of the peasants were partially free and others were serfs who had very limited freedom. But whether partially free or not, all tenants were under the jurisdiction of the manor. It was common practice for the lords to require of all their tenants certain services in the fields (*Frohndienst*, or "corvée") with "cart and horse." The Branc estate, which at this time contained Sabatisch, belonged to thirteen different lords. Instead of serving each of these lords with "cart and horse," the Hutterites agreed in the charter of 1613 to pay a certain sum of money, and they were thus exempted from any claim to corvée. As renters, their relationship to the lords was different from that of the peasants. The charters to which they became parties were decisive, clearly

18. A. J. F. Zieglschmid, "An Unpublished Hausbrief of Grimmelshausen's Hungarian Anabaptists," *Germanic Review* 15(April 1940): 91–97 (translated for the author by Elizabeth Bender).

indicating which obligations were due and which were not. Little room was left for misunderstanding. The charter at Sabatisch stipulated that the Brethren would not appeal to any court, manorial or otherwise, in case of conflicts; their principles prevented it, and the lords were obviously willing to agree to a stipulation that was to their advantage.

The social and occupational background of the people who joined the early Hutterite movement represented a wide range of skills. Although there were poor and propertyless people among them, they were not "course, ignorant, inexperienced and foolish poor people . . . a mob collected from the common rabble," as asserted by contemporary Catholics.[19] Among them were former priests and monks, a few noblemen, and freemen, peasants, laborers, and artisans.

The productive activities during this period included the following: agriculture, bookbinding, brewing, carpentry, carriage- and wagon-making, cutlery, lantern-making, leatherworking, harness and saddle-making, masonry, milling, nursing, pharmacy, ropemaking, shoemaking, tanning, pottery-making and glazing, tailoring, watchmaking, dying, weaving, warping, and caring for vineyards. There were barber-surgeons (and bath houses), coppersmiths, tinsmiths, locksmiths, roof thatchers, scythe makers, and wheelwrights.

A Hutterite clock was sold to an Austrian Archduke for 170 talers. Another was sold to Franz Cardinal von Dietrichstein of Nikolsburg, a longtime foe of the Hutterites. Hutterite carriages were in great demand by the nobility. Also mentioned in the documents is a newly fashioned type of iron bedstead. The creativity of these communities, combined with their technological skills, was a real asset to the manorial lords.

The productive activities were centered in the Bruderhof, where the community's products were made and sold. These Hofs had all the buildings and facilities for carrying on with marked efficiency all of the trades mentioned above. The earnings of members who worked outside the Bruderhof were pooled in a common treasury. Such work not only brought in needed cash but earned for the Brethren the reputation of being good workers, thus eliciting the favor of the manorial lords whose protection they needed. The Brethren were managers of farms, dairies, vineyards, wineries, mills, and sawmills. For noblemen they built various buildings, breweries, mills, wagons, and carriages. Their reputation as skilled craftsmen and reliable workers gained them the utmost confidence of the lords, so that in all of Moravia and Slovakia there was scarcely an estate that did not have at least one Hutterite workman.

19. Paul Dedic, "The Social Background of the Austrian Anabaptists," *M.Q.R.* 13(January 1939): 8.

Even after the Bruderhofs were destroyed and their members forced out of Moravia, a few of the Brethren still worked on these manorial estates as overseers and as physicians.

Most of the crafts were governed by a set of regulations (*Ordnungen*), which were read to the incoming artisans and to the young, who then pledged to follow the rules faithfully. There exist today over thirty different Ordnungen; the oldest, dated 1561, is for the shoemakers.[20] There were separate rules for millers, carpenters, dyers, barber-surgeons, stewards, buyers, potters and ceramicists, coppersmiths, watchmakers, and other assignments of a less economic character, such as child-rearing and education. That these regulations existed in the golden period is evidence that they did not originate only during periods of fossilization or decline. The rules for economic activity required the approval of the religious leaders.

Each trade had an overseer who knew the skills of his trade, organized the work, settled disputes, paid the bills, sold the products, and brought the proceeds to the brotherhood treasury. The overseer was responsible for efficiency and "quality control." In the making of cutlery, for example, the rules say: "Blades that are seen to be defective shall not be sold, and imperfect work shall be sold for less than perfect work. . . . Good wares only are to be given, so that the good and honorable name of the brotherhood be not lost or maligned and that people be not cheated." "Cutlers shall insist on good workmanship, so that the people will get something decent for their money, as the price of knives is high. Hungarian and Silesian iron shall not be offered for sale in the place of Styrian iron, for defamation would follow, and it would not be right."[21]

A few crafts were forbidden, and merchandising as an occupation was not allowed: ". . . We permit no one to buy anything for the purpose of selling it, as merchants are accustomed to do. But one who sells to provide for the needs of the household or to obtain material for his trade, and sells the article he has made we regard not as doing wrong, but as doing right. But we consider it wrong if one buys an article and then sells the same article and takes his gain, thereby making the article more expensive to the poor and taking the bread from their mouths, and thus

---

20. For a list of Ordnungen, see *M.E.*, s.v. "Gemeindeordnungen." See also a subsequent list by Robert Friedmann, with the assistance of Adolf Mais, *Die Schriften der Huterischen Täufergemeinschaften* (Vienna: Hermann Böhlaus, 1965), pp. 171–72; for a ceramic Ordnungen, see also Maria H. Krisztinkovich, "Wiedertäufer und Arianer in Karpatenraum," *Ungarn-Jahrbuch* (Mainz, 1971).

21. Béla Krisztinkovich, "Unbekannte Messerschmied-Kunstwerke der Ungarischen Habanen," *Iparmüvészeta muzeum évkönyvei* (Budapest, 1964), pp. 59–82.

the poor man must become nothing more than the servant of the rich man." The making of weapons was forbidden, and knife making was restricted "to the daily use of men, such as breadknives, axes, hoes, etc. . . . We make no swords, spears, guns, or similar weapons for arms." Tailoring was permitted conditionally: "Christians shall not apply their industry on outward ornamentation to please the world. Whatever tends to create pride, haughtiness, and vanity . . . we permit no one to make, in order that our conscience be preserved spotless before God." Likewise in the making of pottery, especially bowls and tankards, "superfluous painting" was not allowed, and so such items were to be left unpainted. Innkeeping as an occupation was prohibited, for serving wine and beer "goes with all that is unchaste, ungodly and decadent." Although Hutterites in the past and even today drink alcoholic beverages, "standing drinks" were expressly forbidden and viewed as a source of evil.[22]

The Ceramic Industry

Swiss and Dutch Anabaptists acquired renown as agriculturists. That the Moravian Hutterites acquired the potter's trade has puzzled historians. Their remarkable skill is authenticated in the beautiful white enamel-like tableware, vessels, and varied containers we know as Anabaptist pottery.[23] This pottery is today displayed in private collections, in palaces, and in national and regional museums in Central Europe. Museums in Budapest, Brno, Prague, Bratislava, and Vienna have fine collections. Special exhibitions are held from time to time.

Haban ("Hutterite") pottery was called faience, after Faenza in Italy, or majolica, after the island of Majorca near Spain.[24] In both countries ceramic production flourished in the fifteenth century. Pottery was made in Moravia long before the Hutterites came to the area, but it was the Hutterites who introduced a ware of superior craftsmanship and design. Special studies of Hutterite ceramics have been made by several European scholars.[25] Heřman Landsfeld, a ceramist living in the village of Strážnice, Czechoslovakia, has devoted a lifetime to excavating Hut-

22. Quotations from Rideman, Account of Our Religion, pp. 127, 128.

23. In Austria it is called Täufergeschirr; in Hungary, Habán edénhek; in Czechoslovakia, Habánská Fajans.

24. Haban rather than Hutterite is the name commonly used in Europe today.

25. A bibliography of these specialized studies appears in Béla Krisztinkovich, Haban Pottery (Budapest: Corvina Press, 1962), p. 42. Krisztinkovich has published studies in Hungarian, German, Italian, and Dutch. See also Adolf Mais, "Literarisches und Graphisches auf Habaner Keramiken," Österreichisches Zeitschrift für Volkskunde (Vienna), n.s. 15(1961): 149-94.

terite pottery.[26] His collection consists of thousands of sherds and the kiln-waste from twenty-four different sites. For the past few years the castle in his town has exhibited a selection of his findings. From a study of the "trademarks" or initials and the dates on the pottery, Landsfeld concludes that it originates from the period 1576–1690. In 1970 he published a catalog of his major discoveries.[27] His display consists of seventeenth-century bowls, plates, pitchers, jugs, apothecary jars, bottles, basins, inkwells, candlesticks, toy dishes for children, saucepans, sieves, chamber pots, some hitherto unknown forms of lids, deep bowls with decorative ears, and sherds excavated from the kiln sites. These excavations clearly reveal the breadth of the Hutterite ceramists' technical skill. (See figure 7.)

Ceramic blocks were manufactured for floors and building materials. The Bruderhof shops produced hollow tiles, conical water pipes, and various kinds of paving tile, some of which were beautifully decorated. Among the finest discoveries are seven glazed-tile stoves.[28] They produced once-fired tiles without a shiny glaze as well as glazed tiles (20.5 x 20.5 cm.), usually green or marbled tiles with a dark violet

26. Heřman Landsfeld, "Thirty Years of Excavation," trans. (from the Czech) Michael Mrlik and ed. Robert Friedmann, *Mennonite Life* 14(October, 1964): 167–73; Landsfeld, "The Discovery of Hutterite Books," *Mennonite Life* 12(July 1962): 140–44. Also relevant are the two illustrated articles of Robert Friedmann, "Hutterite Pottery or Haban Fayences," *Mennonite Life* 8(October 1958): 147 ff., and "More About Habaner Pottery," *Mennonite Life* 9(July 1959): 129–39.

27. Heřman Landsfeld, *Habánské památky* (Strážnice: Ústav Lidohévo Umění, 1970).

28. Several of these stoves have been restored and placed in museums. According to Heřman Landsfeld, three of the green glazed ceramic stoves in the well-preserved Bibersburg Castle at Častá (Slovakia) were built by Hutterites.

Figure 7. Hutterite ceramic trademarks: design of a tree on the bottom of a painted faience cup, Sabatisch, ca. 1640; design of a bird on the bottom of a faience bowl, Sabatisch, ca. 1670; design of a stag on a pottery dish, Kostel, ca. 1670; design of a tree with blossoms on a faience jug, Sabatisch, ca. 1650. (Reprinted from Landsfeld, 1970)

underglaze. The most expensive were the majolica tiles decorated with relief work and colored enamel. Also manufactured were upper and lower friezes to harmonize with the general decoration. Clay matrices have also been excavated, the earliest dating from 1589.

In all of the sites where ceramics were discovered remains made of iron were also found: nails, keys, locks, hammers, horseshoes, sickles, and knives. Materials made of bone include awls, handles for knives, combs, and needle cases. Also uncovered were artifacts of stone: whetstones, faces of sundials, and mortars for grinding colors. Copper and brass were found on the corners and clasps of large bound books, and on rings, thimbles, buckles, buttons, small chains, and large clock hands. In many of the Bruderhof rubbish heaps there were hundreds of glass fragments from various products—window panes, beakers, and bottles.

Forty-five "trademarks" and 402 different signatures have been identified by name and place, according to Landsfeld.[29] The initials or symbols are scratched either on the bottoms or painted under the handles. In view of the potters' regulation of 1612,[30] which forbade the inscription of names on ceramics, what does this mean? Most scholars believe that no Hutterite potter would have dared initial his creation. But according to Landsfeld, the prohibition concerned the name of the owner of the vessel and not its creator or the workshop in which it was made. Much of the excavated material, however, dates from 1621, after the Hutterites were expelled from Moravia. Hutterite renegades who remained in Moravia likely continued to make ceramic wares long after the Bruderhofs were destroyed.

There are four basic colors in the faience pieces—blue, green, yellow, and manganese-violet. To achieve these four "high temperature" colors, the craftsman needed oxides of cobalt, copper, antimony, manganese, and especially tin and lead oxides for the basic white glaze and the shiny surface. These ores were probably obtained from the mountain region of present-day eastern Slovakia.[31] It seems clear that the Hutterite potters were familiar with the writings of the alchemist Valentius,[32] for among other representations many of the vessels have chemical and alchemical signs. The methods of glazing were secret, and the preparation for the firing of the pottery was usually done at night.

---

29. The earliest signature found was dated 1576; see Landsfeld, *Habánské památky*, pp. 49–50, 71.

30. Zieglschmid, *Das Klein-Geschichtsbuch*, pp. 543–44.

31. Krisztinkovich, *Haban Pottery*, pp. 9, 20.

32. Basilius Valentinus wrote *Currus teriumphalis antimonii*, which was pursued by Paracelsus; *Jöcher's Allgemeines Gelehrten Lexikon*, 4:406.

The Hutterite wares differed from other pottery in design, in motif, and probably in manufacture. Shapes were limited in keeping with the Bruderhof rules (see figure 8).[33] Jugs and cups, for example, were not to be shaped like books or shoes. Neither the human figure nor animal forms could serve as ornamentation during the early period. Tableware made for their own use was to remain unglazed and unadorned. The white color was the most expensive and the most difficult of all to obtain because of the scarcity of tin oxide. The white resembled that found in wares from the Far East and hence was coveted by every lord.

Some pieces bear an inscription or a design surrounded by a wreath of leaves. Plants and leaves were common motifs. Many motifs can also be found in the Hutterite manuscripts.[34] There was undoubtedly

33. Zieglschmid, *Das Klein-Geschichtsbuch*, pp. 543–44.
34. A conclusion of Adolf Mais, "Literarisches und graphisches auf Habaner Keramiken," p. 188.

Figure 8. Regulations governing the making and marketing of ceramics, issued by Prince Bethlen to the Hutterites in Transylvania, 1627. (Photograph by Jan Gleysteen, Krisztinkovich Collection)

a conflict of interest between the demands of the customers, who wanted all kinds of designs and decorations (Catholic, military, or very fancy themes), and the austere standards of the Brethren, who nonetheless needed the money. Moderation and simplicity of style were characteristic of the early Hutterite period. After the forced evacuation from Moravia in 1621 and especially after the decline of the Slovakian communities, when craftsmen continued their workshops after leaving the faith, the design patterns became more elaborate. With assimilation and change in language from German to Hungarian or Slovakian, there was a change in the inscriptions on the ceramics.[35] Those Hutterites who turned Catholic and their descendants who remained in Europe (now known as Habaner) continued their pottery making long after the Hutterites had migrated to Russia and North America. (See figure 9.)

35. Ibid., p. 170.

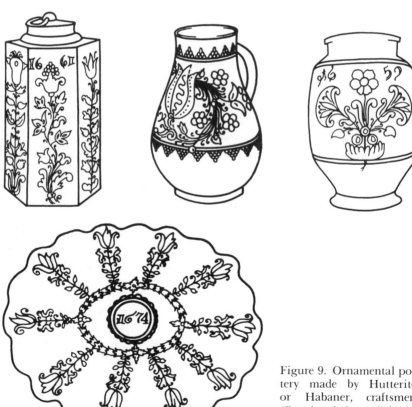

Figure 9. Ornamental pottery made by Hutterite, or Habaner, craftsmen. (Reprinted from Krisztinkovich, 1962)

The verses inscribed on the ceramics during the times of religious toleration are very different from those of later periods. Many of the inscriptions have a biblical theme. The Hutterite use of scriptural verses does not indicate a slavish conformity to the text: the ceramist omitted a word here and added one there as he pleased.

The earliest known pitcher, made in 1593, has this paraphrase from the Proverbs of Solomon: "He who lives piously and innocently/ Has happiness and salvation/ But he who tries to get rich quickly/ Will not be innocent."[36] A legend not found in the Bible appears on a spherical jug from the first half of the seventeenth century: "There is on earth no/ Better quality than to be master of one's tongue/ To know much and not/ To answer all questions./ Therefore speak little, make it true, buy little, pay cash/ And let each one be/ Who he is, and then you will remain/ Who you are."[37] A common saying among North American Hutterites appears on a Hutterite plate in the National Gallery in Prague: "In Gottes segen/ ist alles gelegen."

The post-Hutterite era of pottery making, when communal organization was broken up and craftsmen founded their own workshops, gave rise to a variety of decorative motifs and many more individualistic themes. On a jug from the year 1661 we read: "I love what is fine/ Even if it is not mine/ And cannot benefit me/ I still have pleasure in it."[38] This verse appears on a jug made in 1723, long after the communities were Catholicized: "To love God makes blessed/ To drink wine makes happy/ Therefore, I love God and drink wine./ Thus I can be happy."[39]

The skills developed by the Hutterite potters were passed on to succeeding generations in Moravia and Slovakia and are reflected in family names to this day. A well-known ceramic factory in Modra, Czechoslovakia, continues to make ceramics in modified Hutterite styles. Craftsmen with the names Odler and Tschetter made pottery well into the twentieth century. A private collection in the possession of Maria Odler in Dechtice was assembled by her father who died in 1951. (See figure 10.) He was commemorated in a monument made by ceramist Heřman Landsfeld.

In addition to performing a utilitarian function, the ceramics also filled an esthetic need, as is evidenced by the pride taken in their possession. The products of Hutterite craft, particularly tableware, won the admiration of the nobility, especially the lords of the Hutterite

36. Mais, "Literarisches und Graphisches auf Habaner Keramiken," p. 161. The inscriptions in this chapter were translated by Elizabeth Bender.

37. Ibid., p. 163.

38. Ibid., p. 165.

39. Ibid., p. 167.

Figure 10. Maria Odler, Dechtice, Slovakia, showing Haban pottery made by her father. (Photograph, 1970)

estates. The filigree plates, for example, were attractive and of superior workmanship. Many of these ceramic pieces were made to specification and sold at a reduced price to the lords, who kept them for their own use or gave them as gifts to other noblemen. The Hutterites also took their products to local markets and to the annual village fair (*Jahr markt*), where they brought in needed income. The quality of their ceramics, cutlery, earthenware, and bedsteads was widely recognized. Catholic leaders complained that their members patronized the Hutterite colonies far too much, especially at times when they should be attending Catholic worship services. "Do I not see on every Sunday and holiday, especially in the morning, the people come to you in droves and purchase their necessities of you? And this is the case not only here . . . but throughout the land." So wrote the priest Christoph Fischer.[40]

The skill of pottery making was an asset to the Hutterites when they were expelled from Moravia in 1621, following the defeat of the Protestant cause. Largely because of this skill, Gabriel Bethlen,

---

40. As quoted by Johann Loserth, *M.E.*, s.v. "Crafts of the Hutterian Brethren."

elected king of Hungary, invited a group of Hutterites to settle in his country of residence, Transylvania (at that time a province of eastern Hungary, now in Romania). The prince had apparently seen the attractive faience table service when he visited western Hungary. He ordered the registration of all skilled workers and transported a number of Hutterites to Transylvania (see chapter 3). They were obliged to deliver their ceramics to the prince at half-price and were free to sell their surplus to anyone except the Turkish merchants and the nearby Saxons. The pottery in this area appears to reflect Italo-Turkish influence—blue ground colors and a motif of fish scales. After a delegation had visited Holland in 1665, where they learned new decorative styles and brought back specimens of Delft ware, the blue and white ornamentation appeared on Haban pottery. (See figure 11.)[41]

How the Hutterites obtained a knowledge of pottery making remains a subject of speculation. That an ascetic, "puritanical" group like the Hutterites should cultivate a sophisticated artistic style and tech-

41. Two emissaries, one a potter named Benjamin Poley, were sent to the Palatinate and Holland to seek financial help following the Turkish invasion of 1663. See Zieglschmid, *Das Klein-Geschichtsbuch*, p. 188; Krisztinkovich, *Haban Pottery*, pp. 28–30.

Figure 11. *Left*, small Haban tankard, painted in white with fish scales on a deep blue ground. Loop handle to which a pewter top is attached. ¼". Early 17th century; *center*, small Haban tankard, painted in white with monogram and an alchemist sign within a wreath. Loop handle to which a pewter top is attached. Dated 1665; *right*, Haban bowl, painted on the outside with characteristic floral pattern in four high-temperature colors on white ground. Diam. 8". In the well a coat of arms is inscribed GEORG HERMAN: EFVA HÖRMANIN 1690. (Photographs by J. E. Horvath. Private Collection, Vancouver, British Columbia)

nique is not easily explainable. It is doubtful that the technique originated with the Hutterites. Béla Krisztinkovich, a Hungarian authority
on ceramics, believes that a knowledge of ceramics was brought to
Moravia and Hungary by the Anti-Trinitarians, or "New Christians,"
of Faenza, Italy, who fled the Inquisition.[42] A few of these refugees
from northern Italy joined the Hutterites from about 1555 to 1560. It is
believed that many came from majolica workshops and that in their
new country they produced faience for the nobility and thus introduced
the new techniques to the Hutterites. Several Italian converts to the
Hutterites returned to Italy as missionaries and were arrested and put
to death.[43] An Italian master-craftsman, Nicolo Stefano, was one of the
signatories to the contract which permitted the Hutterites to locate at
Grosschützen in 1588.[44] Since the designs during the early period of
Hutterite ceramic making were not artistic creations indigenous to
Hutterite culture but were copied or made to specification, there is good
reason to believe that both the technique and the patterns were borrowed from outside Hutterite culture.

The archaeological excavations by Heřman Landsfeld and the
beautiful specimens preserved in the castles throughout the centuries
are evidence that ceramics was not a peripheral or marginal activity of
the Hutterites. The size of the Bruderhofs, probably ranging from one
to four hundred persons, meant that production had to take many forms.
Furthermore, ceramics existed in all places where the Hutterites lived:
Moravia, Hungary (now Slovakia), and Transylvania. The craft was also
developed in the Ukraine, and the rules for potters were reissued there
in 1785.[45] At the Bon Homme colony in South Dakota, Michael Waldner,
who descended from a family of potters, was called "Hafner Michael."
In the New World, however, the Hutterites gave their attention entirely
to large-scale agriculture and livestock raising.

One of the houses in Grosschützen still carries a decorative design made by a Hutterite potter. On the gable end of the house, about
half way to the top, is a ceramic ornamental insert bearing the initials

42. Krisztinkovich, *Haban Pottery*, p. 7. One traveler notes that "there were many
Italians" in Moravia in 1568; Henry A. DeWind, "A Sixteenth-Century Description of
Religious Sects in Austerlitz, Moravia," *M.Q.R.* 29(January 1955): 45.

43. Documents in the Archives of the Inquisition at Venice leave no doubt about
Italians who became converts to the Hutterites; see Williams, *The Radical Reformation*,
p. 572. See also Henry A. DeWind, "Italian Hutterite Martyrs," *M.Q.R.* 28(July 1954):
163–85, and DeWind's article in *M.E.*, s.v. "Italy," which discusses three survivors of the
Inquisition who sought asylum with the Hutterites but were eventually executed.

44. Krisztinkovich, *Haban Pottery*, p. 8.

45. See Maria Krisztinkovich, "Die verschollene Keramik des Bartmennoniten in
Russland," *Keramos* (Cologne) 51(January 1971): 3–17.

J.H., H.H., I.M. and the date 1781. J.H. stands for Joseph Horndl, a recognized *Krüglmacher*, or potter.[46]

A well-known potter in Hungary by the name of Imre Odler (also Adler) continued his trade after he was forced to renounce his faith. He was later knighted for his artistic work. Following their conversion to Catholicism, some of these craftsmen acquired substantial private fortunes. Odler, who lived in Dejthe (today Dechtice), traveled widely, according to some reports as far as China, and is believed to have introduced Chinese ceramic techniques into Hungary.[47]

Education and Training

Schools were developed during the first generation of the Hutterite movement. Of all the Anabaptist groups, none were as systematic as the Hutterites in the maintenance of schools. The character of Hutterite education is known through the preserved documents of this period.[48] Even before there were permanent settlements, there was evidence of genuine interest in training the young, especially by such personalities as Hieronymus Käls (executed in Vienna in 1536), who "among his brethren . . . had the reputation of being an excellent, learned schoolmaster, who wrote many good teachings and prayers for the children."[49] The highest goal of education was to teach "the fear of God" and the right ways of living. Disregarded was higher education or worldly scholarship, which to them was "groping in Egyptian darkness." After all it was the highly learned priests and clergy who were the "unenlightened" because, the Brethren reasoned, it was they who were exterminating the simple believers by fire and sword.

On every Bruderhof there was a "little school" and a "big school." As soon as they were weaned, children were placed in the little school where they were supervised by a "school mother." From the age of six to twelve they attended the big school, supervised and taught by a man. The school was not merely a place for instruction but also a care center, where children learned the proper manners important to communal living. Although parents had some responsibility for teaching their children, it was the schoolmasters who were charged with the major responsibility for training the young. Walpot's "Address to the School-

---

46. Maria and Béla Krisztinkovich, "Ein Habanerkrug ["A Haban jug"], *Keramos* (Cologne) 36(January 1967): 28–34.

47. Béla Krisztinkovich, "Nobilis amphorarius magister" ["The knighted master-potter"], *Müvészettörténeti értesitö* (Budapest) vol. 7, no. 2/3 (1958), pp: 131–41.

48. The six major primary sources are listed in Friedmann, *Die Schriften der Huterischen Täufergemeinschaften*, pp. 172–73.

49. *M.E.*, s.v. "Käls, Hieronymus."

masters" and his "School Discipline" of 1586 convey the principles and the methods by which children were to be brought up.[50] Good discipline was stressed, and teachers were to set a proper example. There are instructions for dealing with difficult children. Discipline was to be administered with mildness and love by teachers who have "the fear of God." Children "must learn to love the Lord, to be diligent in prayer," and they were to be guarded against becoming self-willed. Teachers were to give attention to such matters as cleanliness, hygiene, table manners, proper clothing, and sleeping habits, and there were special instructions for the isolation and care of the sick.

In a land where the great majority of people never attended a school, there was literacy in the Bruderhof. High standards of penmanship, stylized writing, and the skillful attention given to memory work and a knowledge of the Bible all helped to fortify the young for the difficult times to come. It was not until 1775, two hundred years after the first Hutterite settlements, that school attendance for children between the ages of six and twelve was made compulsory in the Hapsburg empire under Maria Theresa with the development of the *Normalschule* and the *Trivialschule*.[51] Hutterite little schools were in operation 270 years before modern kindergartens were founded by Friedrich Froebel in Germany in 1837.[52] The development of education for the very young was an important aspect of maintaining identity from the very inception of the Hutterite movement. The subject is given fuller treatment in later chapters.

Medical Practices

The large Hutterite communities in Moravia developed their own therapeutic arts and medical personnel. Their best physicians were in great demand by non-Hutterites. A knowledge of their medical practices is reflected in the management of their boarding schools, in their medicinal bathing houses and the regulations governing them, and in the activities of the practitioners.

The school discipline of 1568 mentions several hygienic practices. There are instructions for cleanliness, how linens are to be handled, and how children are to be dressed, washed, and exercised. Children coming to school for the first time should, according to the School Discipline

---

50. Harold S. Bender, ed. and trans., "A Hutterite School Discipline of 1578 [1568] and Peter Scherer's Address of 1568 to the Schoolmasters," *M.Q.R.* 5 (October 1931): 231–44. The full text of this document appears in appendix 4.

51. Edward Crankshaw, *Maria Theresa* (New York: Longmans, Green and Co., 1969), p. 308.

52. E. R. Murray, *Fröbel as a Pioneer in Modern Psychology* (n.p., 1914).

of 1568, be "carefully examined, and if any one is found to have a contagious disease . . . the same should be instantly separated from the rest in sleeping and drinking, and in particular in washing." Those with diseased heads and "bad mouths" were given special care, including separate combs and wash basins as well as separate utensils. Sick children were given special diets. Mothers were to wash their hands before examining the mouth of the child. These schools, supervised by the Bruderhof officials, were essentially boarding schools for children from nursery age to about age fourteen.

Medicinal bathing was widespread in the sixteenth century, and the practice is still common in European countries. In Hungary today there are over five hundred registered bathhouses. The Hutterite bathhouses and bathing therapy were administered by professionals—the barber surgeons (Bader).[53] The Bruderhofs maintained mineral baths both for their own use and as a source of income. The barber-surgeon was one who practiced, along with cutting hair, the operations of bloodletting (phlebotomy) and cupping. The sharp distinctions between physician and barber drawn by the medical profession was not made by the Hutterites. Codes were issued by the brotherhood to regulate the behavior of barbers.[54] The tendency of these practitioners to be independent presented something of a problem to the Bruderhof. The payments received for their services was a source of temptation—hence the need for strict regulations. There was to be no arrogance or overbearing spirit among the barbers, who, because of their work, enjoyed privileges others did not have, such as horseback riding and traveling outside the Bruderhof. Also emphasized were cleanliness and a knowledge of pharmacy and medicine, including bloodletting. When traveling from one place to another, the barber-surgeons used a wagon to transport their wares—extracts, pills, electuaries, ointments, and pharmaceuticals. The jars for these items were made by the potters.[55]

The Hutterite literature of this period mentions a number of outstanding physicians and also speaks of a head physician.[56] Georg Zobel of Nikolsburg was called to the Imperial Court in Prague to cure Rudolph II. He stayed six months and the emperor was cured. Balthasar Goller at Nikolsburg was the personal physician of Franz Cardinal

53. John L. Sommer, "Hutterite Medicine and Physicians in Moravia in the Sixteenth Century and After," *M.Q.R.* 27(April 1953): 111–27; Robert Friedmann, "Hutterite Physicians and Barber-Surgeons," *M.Q.R.* 27(April 1953): 128–36.

54. Beck, *Die Geschichts-Bücher der Wiedertäufer*, p. 440.

55. Béla Krisztinkovich, "Anabaptista orvosok, gyógyszerészek a higiénia szolgálatában" [Anabaptist physicians and druggists in the service of hygiene], *Communicationes ex bibliotheca historiae medicae Hungarica* (Budapest), no. 20 (1961), pp. 88–117.

56. Friedmann, "Hutterite Physicians and Barber-Surgeons," pp. 128 ff.

Dietrichstein, who later arranged the expulsion of the Hutterites from Moravia. Goller also served as the personal physician of the imperial ambassador, Count Herberstein, on his trip to Constantinople. Another Hutterite physician, Conrad Blossey, formerly of Zurich, returned to that city to render assistance in fighting an epidemic which had taken a toll of eight thousand persons. Sebastian Dietrich was a Hutterite physician who was also a Vorsteher (1611–19). The Protestant nobleman Karl von Žerotin said he was "cured of a serious and dangerous illness" by a Hutterite physician and declared "there are excellent masters among them."[57]

The large patronage from non-Hutterites is confirmed by Fischer, who remonstrated with his fellow Catholics for patronizing the colonies: "Every Saturday their baths are packed full of Christians [i.e., Catholics]. And not only the common people but also noble persons come running to them if they need any drug, as if Anabaptists were the only ones who possessed this art in the entire region."[58]

Fischer also lashed out at the ruling class for taking Anabaptist women for their midwives, wet nurses, and child nurses: "The children will get from them nothing but poison and contempt for the Christian faith. Already the children of the nobles have Anabaptist stomachs, for they have sucked these things from their nurses and have grown up under their influence."[59]

Most of the medical practitioners among Hutterites probably received their training before joining the movement. Little is known of their subsequent training, except that a knowledge of the healing arts was learned from the more experienced physicians in the community. The most famous physician of the sixteenth century, Paracelsus, lived in Moravia at Kromau, Mahrisch-Kromau (today Moravsky Krumlov) from 1537 to 1538 on an estate where Hutterites also lived. It is more than likely that he came into contact with the Hutterites, although no documents have been found indicating direct exchanges between Paracelsus and the Hutterite physicians.[60] Several old medical books, however, have been preserved by contemporary Hutterites, which embody medical beliefs and practices of the sixteenth century.[61]

---

57. Hrubý, *Die Wiedertäufer in Mähren*, p. 105.
58. Fischer, *Der Hutterischen Widertauffer Taubenkobel*, p. 12.
59. Ibid., p. 101. See also Béla Krisztinkovich, "Anabaptist physicians and druggists in the service of hygiene."
60. Friedmann, "Hutterite Physicians and Barber-Surgeons," p. 136.
61. These manuscripts are listed in Friedmann, *Die Schriften der Huterischen Täufergemeinschaften*, pp. 178–79. See also Ado Stella, "Intorno al medico padovano Nicolò Buccella, anabattista del 1500," *Atti` e Hemorie dell' Accademia Patavina di Scienze, Lettere ed Arti* 74(1961/62): 347. Paracelsus also traveled in Hungary. A branch

Missionary Travels and Literary Activity

The motivating force permeating economic and material aspects of communal living was an urgency, a missionary vision of a time "in which the Lord would establish His people and His Law throughout the earth."[62] At the time when they were forming economic, educational, and social codes of living, the Hutterites were the most aggressive missionaries of the sixteenth century. Among the rank and file there was a strong sense of being "called" to spread the Gospel, to summon people to repent, change their lives in a spiritual rebirth, and follow Christ as true disciples. The Hutterite communities "sent Brethren every year to lands near and far according to the commandments of Christ and the practice of the Apostles, to teach and to preach and to gather for the Lord God's people."[63]

Both the revolutionaries of the Peasant Revolt and at Münster and the pacifist Anabaptists possessed a missionary passion, looking forward to a new era, a restoration of justice. With the former, evangelism gave way to prophecy, to the "New Zion," and to the "slaying of the ungodly." The pacifist Anabaptists and others, such as the *Schwenckfelders*, adopted the method of free proclamation of the faith, visitation, and letter-writing, calling men to a disciplined community life, "gathered and governed by the Holy Spirit."[64]

Missioners were sent to many parts of Europe: Bavaria, Württemberg, Hesse, Thuringia, the Rhineland, Silesia, Prussia, Switzerland, Poland, Italy, Denmark, and Sweden. The missioners often had handwritten tracts (epistles) in their possession. These men held small meetings at night in remote places, often in forests, stone quarries, barns, or mills. Other places were unsafe. The selection and departure of these missioners was a very solemn occasion, for they could expect never to return alive. Most became martyrs, being burned, beheaded, drowned, or imprisoned for life. Each preacher was assigned his field of travels by the Bruderhof. Words of encouragement, wisdom, and guidance were given to him, and hymns were later composed to commemorate his departure. The itinerant missioner was supported by prayers and by letters of exhortation, and in the event of imprisonment, additional brethren were sent to maintain contact with him, carrying letters to and from the prisoner and giving an account of his circum-

---

of his family settled in Eperjes (today Prešov in Slovakia) and was extant until the eighteenth century. See *Révai Lexikon* (Budapest) 15(1922): 178.

62. Franklin H. Littell, *Origins of Sectarian Protestantism* (New York: Macmillan Co., 1964), p. 109.

63. Andreas Ehrenpreis, *Ein Sendbrief, 1652* (Scottdale, Pa., 1920), p. 122.

64. Littell, *Origins of Sectarian Protestantism*, p. 128.

stances to the Bruderhof. The prisoners wrote epistles and hymns, making frequent use of acrostics to express their "unshaken trust in God."[65]

The missionary activity had several important consequences. From all over the German-speaking lands converts came to join the Moravian communities. Martyrdom became a normative aspect of a "true and suffering" church, as in apostolic times. The public execution of these brave men was an event shared by large crowds. Their bravery, confident faith, and serenity touched many of the onlookers, so that as a consequence some of them also turned Anabaptist.

The number of handwritten codices arising out of this period and still coming to light today is seemingly endless. The first chronicle was begun during the early period in Moravia, as were all the writings considered basic by the colonies today. Testimonials (epistles) were written with a great passion, and during this period historical episodes and happenings were commemorated in hymns. Many Hutterites had their writings destroyed by the authorities or had little opportunity to write, for they died young. By recording their living experience—in their chronicles, tracts, epistles, and hymns—the Hutterites were among the most prolific of all Anabaptist writers in the Reformation period. The early tradition of literacy and schooling combined with high motivation for communal living gave rise to an impregnable identity and historical consciousness.

The early Hutterites never thought of themselves as a sect. The established churches contested the right of the Brethren to send out missionaries on the ground that they had not been ordained or authorized. To the accusation that the Anabaptist preachers came into Bavaria "to dissuade the people," Claus Felbinger replied: "We go not only into this land, but into all lands, as far as our language extends. For wherever God opens a door unto us, shows us zealous hearts who diligently seek after Him, have a dislike of the ungodly life of the world and desire to do right, and to all such places we aim to go. . . ."[66] When the authorities questioned missioner Hans Schmit concerning his training and qualifications he said: "I study with pick and flail."[67] In the Hutterite view, Schmit's craft equipped him better to "gather the sheep of the Lord" and "to fish for men" than participation in the wranglings of the philosophers.

65. Robert Friedmann, *Hutterite Studies* (Goshen, Ind.: Mennonite Historical Society, 1961), p. 73.

66. John Horsch, *The Hutterian Brethren, 1528–1931: A Story of Martyrdom and Loyalty* (Goshen, Ind.: Mennonite Historical Society, 1931), p. 29.

67. Littell, *Origins of Sectarian Protestantism*, p. 113.

It was during the thirty-eight years of the golden period that missionary passion was most ardent and the Hutterite Bruderhofs maintained their strongest internal discipline. Modern Hutterites regard this time as sacred, and they see in the great chronicle the account of God's intervention in the world to reestablish community of goods.

chapter three

The Decline and Fate of the Eastern European Communities

The Disaster in Moravia

Toward the close of the seventeenth century the prosperous Bruderhofs of Moravia and adjoining areas faced two insuperable forces that ultimately caused their total expulsion from Moravia—war and the Counter-Reformation. In 1593 war broke out between Turkey and the Hapsburg empire.[1] Soldiers, both Protestant and Turkish, were quartered in the colonies, often staying indefinitely and exhausting the surpluses of food. There were raids by Turkish and Hungarian soldiers who killed or took colonists into captivity. Emperor Rudolph II pressed all his lords for taxes and war contributions. When the Brethren declined, the lords confiscated their possessions, taking cattle or sheep annually as a means of

1. The Hapsburgs were members of a powerful ruling family with holdings far exceeding the boundaries of Austria as we know it today. Members of the family held thrones in central Europe from 1273 until 1918. Far from being a natural unit, the Hapsburg monarchy was "a geographic nonsense, explicable only by dynastic graspings and the accidents of centuries of history" (A. J. P. Taylor, *The Hapsburg Monarchy* [Baltimore: Penguin Books, 1948], p. 284), an alliance maintained by politically advantageous marriages between royal families. The lands controlled by the Hapsburgs were a collection of states, not a single state. As landlords on a grand scale, they changed ideas, territories, methods, alliances, and statesmen whenever it was advantageous to their dynasty.

extracting war taxes. Heavy taxes were withheld from the wages of those who worked away from the colonies. Noblemen on occasion permitted Hutterites to settle in their territory only to expel them later. Pressure from the government in Vienna was so great that the governor of Moravia, Fredrick von Žerotin, who was kindly disposed to the Hutterites, was unable to stop the persecution.[2]

The second force associated with the mounting disaster was the rise of the Counter-Reformation—the concerted effort of the Roman Catholic Church to regain lands and adherents lost to Protestantism. Nikolsburg became a place of intolerance when the Dietrichstein family acquired the estate in 1575. Franz Cardinal von Dietrichstein was made head of the Catholic Church in Moravia in 1599. Supporting him was a vigilant government in Vienna and two priests, Christoph Erhard and Christoph Fischer, who dedicated themselves to eradicating Hutterite "heresy." Erhard was specifically assigned to Nikolsburg to take charge of the Catholicization of the Hutterites. Fischer wrote several books, one of which was entitled "Fifty-Four Important Reasons Why the Hutterites Should Not Be Tolerated in the Land."[3] These polemics supported the grievances of the peasants, who for the most part were less well-off than the Hutterites. Fischer observed that the Hutterites kept their books so secluded that "scarcely one in a thousand gets to read them." By posing as a convert, he gained entrance to the Hutterite communities long enough to make a list of the Hutterite books and manuscripts.[4] Fischer used every means at his disposal to extinguish Hutterite heresy.

2. Like the Liechtensteins, the Žerotin nobles admitted Hutterites to their estates and protected them from imperial oppression. The Žerotins were adherents of the teachings of John Hus and members of the Bohemian Brethren. At least eighteen Bruderhofs were located on the estates of the different branches of the Žerotin family in 1589, eight of which were on the estates of Fredrick, who was governor of Moravia. The Hutterites acknowledged a thorough acquaintance with him and state that he protected them as a father does his children (Josef Beck, *Die Geschichts–Bücher der Wiedertäufer* [Vienna, 1883], p. 328). The Catholic polemicist Christoph Andreas Fischer noted (in *Vier und funfftzig Erhebliche Ursachen Warumb die Widertauffer nicht sein im Land zu leyden* [Ingolstadt, 1607], p. 39) that the Hutterites spoke of Fredrick von Žerotin in very intimate terms, calling him "unser Fritz." See also Zieglschmid, *Die älteste Chronik*, p. 575. One of the Bruderhofs was located at Gross-Selowitz (Židlochovice, Czechoslovakia), apparently also the residence of Fredrick von Žerotin. As recently as 1956, the burial place of the Žerotins was discovered there by a local historian, Josef Jeřábek. His findings appear in a booklet, *Žerotínové, a Židlochovice*, which he published in 1966 at Židlochovice.

3. Fischer, *Vier und funfftzig Erhebliche Ursachen.* . . . Fischer also wrote *Von der Widertauffer Verfluchten Ursprung* . . . (Bruck an der Teya, 1603).

4. For the list, see Adolf Mais, "Literarisches und Graphisches auf Habaner Keramiken," *Österreichische Zeitschrift für Volkskunde*, vol. 15, no. 64 (1961), p. 156, and Robert Friedmann, with the assistance of Adolf Mais, *Die Schriften der Huterischen Täufergemeinschaften* (Vienna: Hermann Böhlaus, 1965), pp. 92–94.

The war between Turkey and the Hapsburg empire raged for thirteen years (1593–1606), involving the area of Moravia where the Hutterites were located. In its last two years, two Protestant princes, Stephen Bocskay, Prince of Transylvania, and Bethlen Gabor of Hungary, joined the Turkish forces in a revolt against the empire, hoping in this way to defend their religious freedom. Sixteen Bruderhofs, including eleven schools, were burned, 87 persons killed, and 238 Hutterites taken captive and sent as slaves mostly to Turkey.[5] The search by Salomon Böger, a Hutterite miller, for the captives is a story of incredible courage. Böger spent thirty-two months in Turkey trying to find his wife and child and other captured Hutterites. From the twenty-four letters he sent to his home community, we learn that his travels took him throughout Hungary and Turkey as far as Constantinople and that he recovered six women and two men but found no trace of his wife and child. He died mysteriously in Turkey.[6]

Being pacifists, the Hutterites did not resist but literally took refuge underground. They hid in subterranean passages and underground rooms that had been excavated by hand. Although many of the tunnels, which can still be seen in Moravia, are undoubtedly older than the Hutterite movement, the Hutterites are believed to have made some of them. In addition to large cellarlike rooms, there are also concealed holes and hidden exits from these underground cellars. The chronicle states that during severe times the Brethren lived in "holes in the earth."[7] (See figure 12.) A Benedictine monk who spent twenty-five years investigating, sketching, and measuring all the more important arched tunnels thought they were of prehistoric origin.[8] Archaeologists today believe they date from the Middle Ages and that they were developed as hiding places during times of distress.

In 1618, before the brotherhood had time to rebuild its resources following the war between Turkey and Austria, the disastrous Thirty Years' War broke out. It was instigated by the rebellion of the Bohemian people, who were largely Protestant, against their Catholic ruler, Emperor Ferdinand II, and there followed a vicious religious struggle between the Protestant and Catholic states. The Moravian government,

---

5. Wolkan, *Geschichts-Buch*, pp. 482 ff. The sufferings of this period are recounted in a hymn of 158 verses still sung by the Hutterites ("Die Botschkei [Bocskay] Lieder," in *Die Lieder der Hutterischen Brüder* [Scottdale, Pa.: Die Hutterischen Brüder, 1914; and Cayley, Alberta, 1962], pp. 804–12.)

6. See Robert Friedmann, "Adventures of an Anabaptist in Turkey, 1607–1610," *M.Q.R.* 17(April 1943): 73–86.

7. Beck, *Die Geschichts-Bücher der Wiedertäufer*, pp. 184, 191. In Czechoslovakia these underground passages were called *lochy*. The very large underground cellars were used as storage bins as well as hiding places.

8. P. Lambert Karner, *Die künstlichen Höhlen aus alter Zeit* (Vienna, 1903).

Figure 12. Subterranean passages in Moravia, likely hiding places of the Hutterites in the sixteenth century. (Reprinted from Karner, 1903)

predominantly Protestant, made an alliance with Bohemia and expelled the Jesuits. Their victory was brief. In the following year a punitive army of Ferdinand's invaded Moravia and within two months completely destroyed twelve of the forty remaining Hutterite households and plundered and devastated seventeen others. During one night, in the year 1620, a Polish army killed fifty-six people outright in the Bruderhof at Pribitz and wounded sixty others, many of whom died as a result of their wounds. The chronicle records these terrors:

It is impossible to write or tell of all the great and inhuman cruelties which came upon us and others in this ungodly, accursed and devilish war at the hands of the . . . imperial forces. . . . Women with child and mothers in childbed as well as virgins were shamelessly attacked. The men were burned with glowing iron and red-hot pans; their feet were held in the fire until the toes were burned off; wounds were cut into which powder was poured and then set afire; fingers and ears were cut off, eyes forced out by inhuman tortures on the wheel; men were hung up by the neck like thieves; all sorts of such brutality and unheard of godlessness were committed, half of which is not to be written for shame.[9]

In the wake of war came devastating plagues. In 1621 alone the brotherhood lost one-third of its members by death.[10] Several of the Moravian colonies fled when they heard of the approach of the great imperial army in the late autumn of 1620. Most of the escapees went into Hungary (today Slovakia) and temporarily found refuge in the colony at Sabatisch. (See figure 13.) For a time the small Bruderhof at Sabatisch harbored three thousand refugees. In January 1621 many of the Brethren from Wessel and Neudorff in Moravia proceeded over the Carpathian mountains, taking refuge with private families around Gostolän (Kostelna), Schächtitz (Cechtice), Wadovitz (Wadovce), and other localities where the nobles were friendly to them. The Protestant rulers in Moravia were now scarcely better protected than the Hutterites. Many left the country, but twenty-seven lords were captured and publicly executed in Prague.

After the victory of the imperial army in 1620, Cardinal Dietrichstein, a sworn enemy of the Hutterites, was appointed governor of Moravia. He imprisoned Rudolph Hirzel, overseer of the entire brotherhood, and by deception persuaded him to reveal the various hiding places of Hutterite funds that had been saved for emergency use. The authorities said they "wished only to aid in their safekeeping so they would not fall into the hands of rebels." But the money was seized immediately. The brotherhood unanimously excommunicated Hirzel and, although he "acknowledged his guilt," he lost his position as overseer.[11]

In the summer of 1622 Dietrichstein received authority from Ferdinand to expel all Hutterites from Moravia. The Hutterites were forced to leave their dwellings. Officials locked and sealed all houses, granaries, and buildings. The homeless Hutterites were then told they could not remain, nor would they find any safety in any of the emperor's lands, unless they consented to be instructed by the Catholic priests. If they would do that, they could return to their property and enjoy prosperity and safety. Two hundred and thirty persons, overcome by suffering and weariness, accepted this offer. All others, including many of the sick and aged, were refused permission to remain for the winter. On

9. Wolkan, *Geschichts-Buch*, p. 565. A translation appears in John Horsch, *The Hutterian Brethren, 1528-1931: A Story of Martyrdom and Loyalty* (Goshen, Ind.: Mennonite Historical Society, 1931), p. 55.
10. Wolkan, *Geschichts-Buch*, p. 565.
11. Ibid., p. 576.

Figure 13. *Top*, scene from Sabatisch (Sobotušte, Czechoslovakia), site of a Bruderhof founded in 1546, showing a bell tower and a mill near the dwelling of Elder Andreas Ehrenpreis (Photograph, 1970); *bottom*, Hutterite dwelling, Sabatisch. (Photograph by Jan Gleysteen, 1970)

September 28, 1622, the cardinal issued a mandate that all men and women who called themselves Hutterites must leave Moravia within four weeks on penalty of death and never set foot in the land again. The Brethren were expelled from a total of twenty-four separate households. Famine conditions prevailed, for winter was setting in, and they had to leave with empty hands. Over twenty-four thousand bushels of wheat and rye were left behind, and also large holdings of corn, wine, cattle, linen, woolens, equipment, and furniture. The Hutterites fled to Slovakia (then a part of Hungary) where they were welcomed by Hungarian lords in defiance of the emperor in Vienna.

The influx of refugees from Moravia into the Bruderhofs at Sabatisch and Grosschützen caused a shortage of food, clothing, and bedding. There were severe hardships, and the chronicle says that although the Brethren had left Moravia "like the children of Israel from Egypt" when the suffering, tribulation, deprivation, hunger, cold, and nakedness came upon them, "many looked back to Egypt where they had bread to the full."[12] Thus, some returned to their houses and lands in Moravia. Between 1622 and 1626 there were a number of attempts by Moravian lords to reestablish the Hutterites on their estates, but these efforts were crushed by Cardinal Dietrichstein. The Brethren simply could not stay in Moravia unless they succumbed to Catholicism.

Life in Northern Hungary

Hungary provided an uneasy refuge.[13] As the Thirty Years' War progressed, large numbers of troops moved into the area: in 1626 Emperor Ferdinand quartered fifty thousand soldiers in the region; Gabor Bethlen of Transylvania had a great army of Hungarians, Turks, and Germans stationed there. All of them camped in the area for months, and though they were not constantly in battle, they devastated crops and land. By 1631 the number of Hutterite members in Hungary had been reduced to fewer than one thousand.[14]

Although Hutterite life in Hungary was undergoing a period of general decline, it produced at least one very important leader in Andreas Ehrenpreis. He was ordained at Sabatisch at the age of twenty-

12. Ibid., p. 571.
13. Today Slovakia is one of the three provinces of Czechoslovakia, the other two being Bohemia and Moravia. To be consistent with the chronicles, we will use the term Hungary (for present day Slovakia), in keeping with the historical-political situation. There were also Bruderhofs in what is present-day Hungary, in the counties of Sopron, Vas, and Zala. See Imre Katona, "Sárvár und die Familie Nádasdy im XVI. Jahrhundert," *Savaria* (Szombathely) 1(1963): 239-55.
14. Horsch, *The Hutterian Brethren*, p. 65.

two and spent the remainder of his life there. In 1639, at the age of fifty, he was elected Vorsteher for all of the colonies and served until his death in 1662. Under his leadership the brotherhood engaged in its last European missionary activity, strengthened internal discipline, and produced a rich manuscript literature, especially sermons (called *Lehren*).[15] Today there are several hundred such sermons extant and about as many *Vorreden* (shorter sermons). These sermons have been copied over and over and are read in all Hutterite church services. The Ehrenpreis community discipline of 1651 is read annually before the assembled members in many present-day Bruderhofs.[16]

Numerous factors contributed to the decline of Hutterite life during this period. Billeting of troops was a constant drain on already scanty supplies; not only the Hutterites but all the people of the area were suffering want and, at times, even famine conditions. During the famine of 1638 and 1639, they mixed clay with flour to make bread.[17] The Hutterite storehouses inevitably invited envy and animosity; there were even some who joined the Brotherhood because these storehouses promised sustenance. After years of pillage by the armies, the surrounding population began raiding the colonies for supplies, and finally the nobles, too, joined in the pillage.

Disheartened by their vulnerability, the Hungarian Hutterites dissolved their community of goods in 1685 and appealed to the government henceforth to consider them as individual householders. They did, however, retain some communal practices. Their general religious life and worship services were distinctively Hutterite even though they had forfeited the practice of community of goods. The chronicles provide a sad account of the breakdown.

After the war political and religious pressures increased, for the Hapsburg monarchs who were staunch Catholics gained greater influence in Hungary. Cardinal Kollonitsch personally visited Grosschützen in 1688. Following his visit religious persecution increased. Decrees demanded that no infants be allowed to die without baptism. For a time the mandates were ignored, but when this was no longer possible the Hutterites began to allow the priests to baptize their children (at Grosschützen in 1688; at Sabatisch in 1733). When the children became adult members of the brotherhood, the Hutterites rebaptized them. Little is known of life in these colonies after they were assimilated into the Catholic church.

---

15. For a discussion of the texts and chronology of the sermons, see Friedmann, *Die Schriften der Huterischen Täufergemeinschaften*, pp. 156–70; and also Robert Friedmann, "Hutterite Worship and Preaching," *M.Q.R.* 40(January 1966): 5–26.

16. Zieglschmid, *Das Klein-Geschichtsbuch*, pp. 519–32.

17. Wolkan, *Geschichts-Buch*, p. 621.

Stronger measures to exterminate Hutterite beliefs were taken by the Hapsburgs under Maria Theresa, who reigned from 1740 to 1780. She allowed the Jesuits free rein to convert everyone to Roman Catholicism. The chronicle describes some of the incidents in detail:

In the year 1759 when Maria Theresa was Empress, the clergy, especially the Jesuits and their ilk, petitioned the Empress for permission to attack the brotherhood, which they still accused of being an Anabaptist sect, and to compel it to accept the Catholic faith. . . .
There was a great gathering of officials for counsel which included the Jesuits who had the work in charge, the clergy of Sobotisch, Levare and Trentschin, and the magistrates. These all took counsel how they might effectively accomplish their purpose. They decided it was best to attack all the congregations at all four places on the same day without warning and seize the books of the brotherhood. This they decided to do on the 25th of November.[18]

One of the sympathetic magistrates told the colonists of the plan. The most precious books were hidden, but when the officials came and searched the houses they still carried off many books. There were book raids in 1757, 1758, and again in 1770. Many of the books confiscated in these raids are now in the state archives of Bratislava, Esztergom, Budapest, and elsewhere. More books have more recently been found hidden in the plaster walls of former Bruderhof buildings, in 1890 and again in 1961.[19]

The persecution was persistent. Children were taken from their parents. The meeting houses of the Brethren were sealed and Catholic services were established at the Bruderhofs; everyone was forced to attend, and when the order was defied, mercenaries were hired to stand guard and lash those who refused. The mercenaries were maintained by the Bruderhof, and in addition, the Brethren were required to pay each mercenary 1 guilder per day. The ministers were arrested first. So many of the male members were taken prisoner that the rest went into hiding in the forests. Only women and children were left in the colonies. The shops were idle, and the economy of the Bruderhofs was totally disrupted. Eventually most of the men in hiding were captured and im-

---

18. English translation of Zieglschmid, *Das Klein-Geschichtsbuch*, p. 231, is from Horsch, *The Hutterian Brethren*, p. 79.

19. Friedmann, *Die Schriften der Huterischen Täufergemeinschaften*, pp. 35-45; Robert Friedmann, "Newly Discovered Hutterite Manuscripts," *M.Q.R.* 42(January 1968): 73-74; Maria H. Krisztinkovich, "Anabaptist Book Confiscations in Hungary during the Eighteenth Century," *M.Q.R.* 39(April 1965): 125-46; and idem, "Hutterite Codices Rediscovered in Hungary," *M.Q.R.* 44(January 1970): 114-21; Béla Krisztinkovich, "Glimpses into the Early History of Anabaptists in Hungary," *M.Q.R.* 43(April 1969): 127-41; and Leonard Gross, "Newly Discovered Codices of the Hutterites," *M.Q.R.* 42(January 1968): 149-55.

prisoned. Their resistance was worn down by beatings and torture until one after another they consented to be indoctrinated by the Catholic clergy.

Everyone at Sabatisch, according to the Jesuits, had been converted to Catholicism by May 27, 1763. Descendants of the Hutterites continue to live in Sabatisch in the twentieth century. Known as Habaner, they live in the original dwellings and retain vestiges of the Hutterite tradition, but their religion is Catholicism.

The question may be raised whether Maria Theresa initiated the action against the Hutterites or whether the Jesuits persuaded the empress to convert the Hutterites to the Catholic faith. It is well known that the Jesuit order (founded in 1534) had by this time become "the most feared and hated organization in both Protestant and Catholic lands, a Black International."[20] Its original purpose was to assist the papacy in the fight against all foes of Catholicism and to work toward absolute obedience to the pope. Unlike older Catholic orders, the Jesuits did not necessarily live in monastic houses but could be active at any place where their work was needed. They exerted a powerful influence all over Europe in checking Protestantism. They became the father confessors of many rulers and their families—Maria Theresa was educated by a Jesuit and had a Jesuit confessor. There arose widespread misgivings over their principle that one need not trust or believe those who are not of the Catholic religion. Even the archbishop of Vienna informed the Pope that there was no longer any discipline among the Jesuits, that they neglected the Scriptures and "cared neither for morals nor for honesty."[21]

Maria Theresa was adamant about heresy, and during her reign there was to be no toleration of Protestants. A biographer notes that "Maria Theresa's faith was absolute, and this was a great part of her strength."[22] To entertain religious toleration was to her the same as to entertain the ruin of the state. She therefore condoned the raiding of bookshops, the arbitrary burning of undesirable volumes (Jesuits burned more than sixty thousand books in Bohemia), traditional forms of torture, and the resettlement of Protestants to remote areas of the Hapsburg lands.[23] In all these things she sided with the Jesuits. She

20. Saul K. Padover, *The Revolutionary Emperor: Joseph II of Austria*, rev. ed. (London: Eyre and Spottiswoode, 1967), p. 39.
21. Ibid., p. 21.
22. Edward Crankshaw, *Maria Theresa* (New York: Longmans, Green and Co., 1969), p. 21.
23. H. Klima, "Das Verhalten der Wiener Regierung unter Maria Theresa gegen die siebenbürgischen Wiedertäufer and Herrnhuter," *Sudöstforschungen* (Brno, Munich, and Vienna, 1942).

defended them not only to her closest advisers and to her son but also against the Pope, who in 1773 ordered that the Society of Jesus be dissolved and its property confiscated. Today the population in Austria is 95 percent Catholic, and the credit goes to Maria Theresa. Of all the Hapsburg burial vaults in the Capuchin church in Vienna, hers is the most ornate. Poets have memorialized her as "the noblest mother of the fatherland" and Austria has exalted her by erecting statues and naming the most prominent roads and public buildings in her honor.

It was Maria Theresa's son, Joseph II, coregent from 1765 to 1780, and emperor from 1780 to 1790, who opposed not only his mother's absolutism but also the inhumanity of the Jesuits and who on two occasions received delegations from the Hutterites. In 1777 Joseph II pleaded with his mother:

To drive away the living, good farmers and excellent subjects, in order to save the souls of the dead—What arrogance of power! . . . So long as men serve the state, obey the laws of nature and society, and do not dishonor your Supreme Being—what right has a temporal ruler to interfere in other matters? . . . This is my conviction, and Your Majesty knows it.[24]

As coregent Joseph had succeeded in abolishing the most grotesque forms of torture in 1776, and he issued the famed Edict of Toleration in 1781—but by this time the Hutterites had already settled in the Ukraine.

An altogether different view of the Hungarian Hutterites from that taken by the Jesuits is recorded by the novelist Grimmelshausen (1668), a contemporary who described the "Hungarian Anabaptists."[25] He eulogized them for their disciplined, simple life, for their care of infants and the aged, for their schools, and for their excellent health practices; he found "no anger, jealousy, pride, vanity, gambling, and no remorse," but "a lovely harmony that seemed to surpass even the monastic life."

24. Crankshaw, *Maria Theresa*, p. 301.

25. Hans Jakob Christoph von Grimmelshausen (1620-76) in *Der abenteuerliche Simplizissimus* (n.p., 1668), in book 5, chapter 19, has the main character in his novel tell specifically what he saw among the Brethren. The account is barely three pages long. An English translation appears in Horsch, *The Hutterian Brethren*, pp. 66-68. On the basis of biographical data, scholars doubt that Grimmelshausen ever visited Hungary. Some think he may have visited the Bruderhof which existed in Mannheim, Germany, from 1655 to 1684. See A. J. F. Zieglschmid, "Die ungarischen Wiedertäufer bei Grimmelshausen," *Zeitschrift für Kirchengeschichte* (Stuttgart) 59 (1940): 352-87. Studies by J. Szövérffy, "Die Hutterischen Brüder und die Vergangenheit," *Zeitschrift für deutsche Philogie* 82(1963): 338-62, and Elizabeth Bender, "Grimmelshausen and the Hutterites," *Mennonite Life* 18(October 1963): 187-89, testify to the truth of Grimmelshausen's statements.

Anyone who could convert these Anabaptists, said Grimmelshausen, so that they in turn might teach the Catholic Church their art of living, would be a second Saint Francis.

Life in Transylvania

While the Hutterites were being expelled from Moravia in 1621, Gabor Bethlen, prince of Transylvania, sent an "invitation" to the Brethren to settle in his country. (See map 3.) He needed carpenters, masons,

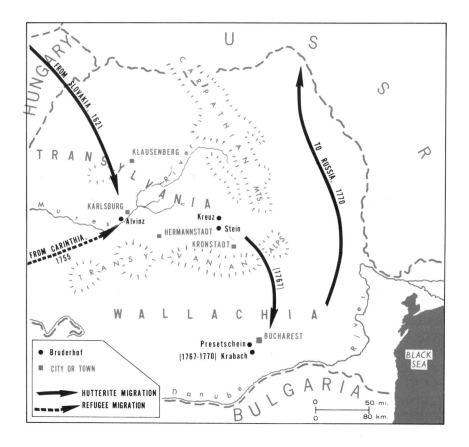

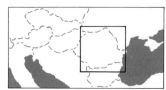

Map 3. Bruderhofs in Romania, 1621–1770

potters, craftsmen, and agricultural workers to develop his estates. His wife, Susanne Carolina, seems to have taken an interest in recruiting Hutterite craftsmen.[26] A delegation from Gabor came to the Hutterites at Neumühl, Schaechtitz, and Waidowitz "with a large number of horsemen and many wagons," bringing an eight-point letter of proposition. The message of the letter seemed like a command, but it promised everything necessary to start a colony, including freedom of religion, the development of trades, and protection. The Brethren were reluctant, thinking it a trap. The messengers then forcibly seized 85 souls, old and young, and eight days later took another 101 persons. This initial group of 186, with 70 guards and 18 wagons, started for Alwinz on April 2, 1621, a distance of over 500 miles.[27] To the Hutterite leaders in Hungary, the location seemed much too far away and in a land too much under the influence of Turkey. On arrival the group was given temporary quarters—a horse barn. Several hundred more Hutterites arrived during the next two years.[28]

The Brethren were treated kindly in Alwinz. In 1622 Prince Bethlen gave them a charter and in 1626 an even more comprehensive letter of protection. During the Thirty Years' War, while the settlements along the Hungarian border suffered privations, this group prospered.

26. This fact has been established in recent years in a study of Hungarian language documents by Maria H. Krisztinkovich, "Some Further Notes on the Hutterites in Transylvania," *M.Q.R.* 37(July 1963): 207-8. "Susanna Caralie" is also mentioned in the "Klaglied" of the Hutterites (*Die Lieder der Hutterischen Brüder* [1962], p. 834, vs. 61). For modern counterparts of the German place names mentioned in the hymn, see appendix 3.

The delegation of course went to the leaders of the Hutterite Gemeinde at Neumühl. Not only was Bethlen interested in craftsmen, but he wanted to obtain the consent of the Hutterites to the evacuation of these places in Hungary before they were destroyed. Bethlen knew very well what would happen to the country when his army retreated; therefore he saved the useful craftsmen and their families for himself. The places were actually plundered and burned later.

27. Alwinz is located ten miles southwest of Alba Iulia along the Mures River. In German the spellings appear as *Alwinz, Alwintz,* or *Winz*; in Hungarian as *Alvincz,* and in Romanian as *Vinţul de Jos.*

28. The initial journey was made without supplies, so that the group encountered great suffering. The long journey is memorialized in a hymn, "Klaglied," (*Die Lieder der Hutterischen Brüder,* pp. 827-35) of 67 verses. According to Zieglschmid, (*Das Klein-Geschichtsbuch,* p. 140), 690 persons migrated to Transylvania, of whom 400 died of the plague and other diseases. Another source, written by Jacob Werner, a participant and a school teacher, enumerates six subsequent migrations and concludes that, in all, 1,089 Hutterites came to Transylvania; see Robert Friedmann, "A Newly Discovered Source on the Transmigration of the Hutterites to Transylvania, 1621-1623," *M.Q.R.* 35(October 1961): 309-14. The last stop on the journey between Hungary and Transylvania was Tövis, on the present Hungarian-Romanian border. From there, one group was sent to Radnot and another to Bodola. By 1623 all 1,089 persons had settled at Alvinz. They were followed by more Hutterites in the years to come. The next migration, very similar to this one, came in 1645, when the prince of Transylvania, George Rakocy I, settled Hutterites in Sárospatak.

The Alwinz community sent aid to their Brethren in Hungary when there was opportunity. Descriptions of life in Romania by the schoolteacher Jacob Werner and by Horst Klusch, a modern scholar in Sibiu, indicate that the Bruderhof there had all the industries and crafts of the Hungarian communities.[29]

The good fortune and prosperity of the Alwinz settlement changed when war was waged between the Hapsburgs and Turkey from 1658 to 1661. The Hutterites at Alwinz took refuge in the high ridges about five miles from the Bruderhof. Here, as earlier in Moravia, they built hideouts, but this time in rocks instead of rich black soil. Some of the members of the Bruderhof lived in these hideouts for two years. The Bruderhof itself was plundered and burned by the raiders, a disaster from which the group never recovered. The group that survived the war was small.[30] Some joined other German-speaking religious affiliations. Ties with the Hungarian communities were weak, as was the leadership. Communal living was abandoned by the settlement about 1690.

Today nothing remains of the Bruderhof buildings in the Alwinz location. What was not destroyed by war and plunder in the seventeenth century was completely washed away in the eighteenth century when the flooding Maros River changed its course to flow through the site of the Bruderhof. Nearby still stand the deserted Alwinz castle (see figure 14) and a large thirteenth-century cathedral which was built by German immigrants from Saxony long before the arrival of the Hutterites. The cathedral had already been abandoned by the sixteenth century, and according to local informants, the Hutterites met there for their worship services. Many potsherds, unmistakably Hutterite, were found between the cathedral and the river by Horst Klusch and the author in 1971. Romania's enthusiastic pottery collectors will undoubtedly attempt a systematic search. Archaeological work on the nearby mountains where the Hutterites lived in hideouts has revealed several Habaner wares.[31] Modest exhibits of Hutterite pottery can be seen in museums in Hermannstadt (Sibiu) and Klausenburg (Cluj). Also nearby, in Karlsburg (Alba Iulia) in the Betthyány Library, are eighteen well-preserved codices, all of which were taken from the Alwinz Bruderhof by the Jesuits in 1767.[32]

29. Friedmann, "A Newly Discovered Source . . . ," pp. 309–14; Klima, "Das Verhalten der Wiener Regierung unter Maria Theresa. . . ."

30. Of twenty-four families in 1767, only four descended from the 1621 migrants.

31. Horst Klusch, "Die Habaner in Siebenbürgen," *Forschungen zur Volks- und Landeskunde*, vol. 11, no. 2 (1968), pp. 21–40, vol. 14, no. 2 (1971), pp. 101–7, illustrated. Archaeological discoveries, including Hutterite pottery, are reported in Gh. Anghel și Ion Berciu, *Cetăti Medievale Din Sud-Vestul Transilvaniei* (Bucharest: Meridiane, 1968).

32. Friedmann, *Die Schriften der Huterischen Täufergemeinschaften*, pp. 13–18.

Figure 14. Ruins of the Alwinz Castle (Vinţul de Jos, Romania) standing near the former Bruderhof. (Photograph, 1970)

The Carinthians Revitalize the Movement

Back in Carinthia (today a province of Austria), a revitalization movement within Lutheranism during the eighteenth century was becoming a source of alarm to the Catholic state. Books were being smuggled into the country, farmers were staying away from the state churches to read the Bible and hold meetings at night, "even when it rained or in spite of snow and wind." Authorities were ordered to "cleanse the archduchy of Carinthia of the heretics,"[33] and Maria Theresa commanded that they be deported and resettled in a far corner of her empire. They were loaded into wagons and promised that the proceeds of the sale of their property would be forwarded to them. The journey began at Klagenfurt and proceeded through Styria into Austria. In Ybbs on the Danube the group had to wait two months for others to join them. The total number was 270 before the journey was resumed, through Vienna, Pressburg, and Budapest to Pétervárad and Temesvár. The group traveled by land to within a half-day's journey of the Hutterite settlement in Alwinz, arriving there in October 1755.[34]

33. Johann Loserth, "The Decline and Revival of the Hutterites," *M.Q.R.* 4(April 1930): 94.
34. The transmigration of the Carinthian group was part of a larger resettlement effort of Maria Theresa between 1734 and 1756. There were at least fourteen such

In Transylvania a Lutheran magistrate received the Carinthians and informed them that they were free to practice their religion but that the queen required an oath of allegiance. A small group with Matthias Hofer as spokesman protested that the oath was contrary to the Gospel for which they had left their homes. The noncompliance of this small group and their repudiation of some of the Lutheran teachings cost them the right to free land. They were forced to be laborers, living and working in scattered nearby towns. Two of these men, Andreas Wurz and George Waldner, were assigned to the village of Alwinz, where they came into contact with former members of the Hutterite Bruderhof. They read the old Hutterite literature and entered into lively discussions with the Hutterites, who had abandoned communal living over sixty years previously. The Carinthians listened and were soon convinced that community of goods was required of Christians. They stopped attending the Lutheran services and began to meet in homes for study, prayer, and worship. By accepting the Hutterite faith, the Carinthian newcomers became the revitalizing group that reestablished communal living and carried the movement to Wallachia, Russia, and North America.[35] A careful reading of the sources gives one the distinct impression that the old Hutterites had an uneasy conscience about having given up communal living and were therefore naturally eager to explain their past life and beliefs to the newcomers. Joseph Kuhr seems to have played a major role in these exchanges.[36]

Hans Kleinsasser, also a Carinthian, was assigned to work in Kreutz, about seventy miles northeast of Alwinz. In 1761 several additional families moved there. Here, in the following year, a Bruderhof was established by the Carinthian exiles and patterned after the discipline of the old Hutterian brotherhood. Hans Kleinsasser was rebaptized in April 1762 and ordained by Elder Mertl Roth at Alwinz. Joseph Müller was made steward of temporal needs and George Waldner was

---

forced migrations to Transylvania involving several thousand Lutherans from many other parts of Austria. See Grete Mecenseffy, *Geschichte des Protestantismus in Österreich* (Gratz-Köln, 1956), pp. 198–206.

35. Of the fifteen most common Hutterite family names today, five are of Carinthian origin: Glanzer, Hofer, Kleinsasser, Waldner, and Wurz. All of these families originated in the area of Spittal on the Drau in the villages of Amlach, Stockenboi, and St. Peter. The Waldner and Kleinsasser genealogies have been traced to the transmigrants. Elias Gasser, a genealogist of Klagenfurt Austria, has traced the Kleinsassers back to 1528. An inn, or *Gasthaus*, called Kleinsasserhof, is operated by descendants six generations removed from a common Huttertie ancestor. Family names among the Carinthian Hutterites which have not survived include Amlacher, Egartner, Bichler, Gerl, Müller, Nägeler, Platner, and Resch.

36. *M.E.*, s.v. "Kuhr, Joseph."

elected schoolmaster. A common kitchen was established for the group under the direction of Dorothea Naegler. Additional members joined the group, making a total of forty-six. The town began to be uncomfortable with the growth of the group.[37] On orders from the regional government at Hermannstadt, the members were arrested and imprisoned and later distributed to isolated towns and estates. But they soon learned of each other's whereabouts and managed to restore fellowship. Gradually they reestablished themselves at Kreutz, only to suffer harsher treatment.

After concluding peace with Prussia, Maria Theresa concentrated on cleansing her land of heretics. The Jesuit missionary Delpini, who had directed the total suppression of the Brethren along the Hungarian-Moravian border, received permission to annihilate Anabaptism in Transylvania, too. He began his work at Alwinz. Out of fear, many of the Brethren, including their Vorsteher Mertl Roth, accepted Catholicism in 1762. When the rest refused to become Catholic, Joseph Kuhr, a courageous and strong personality, and "the leader" of the group (apparently Johannes Stahl), were imprisoned. Six weeks later, after they had been released, the Jesuit Delphini appeared at Alwinz and began to visit the Brethren daily. First, he demanded that they surrender their books. He preached to the group, and no one challenged his teachings except Joseph Kuhr. When Delphini was about to leave the meeting, Kuhr cried out that he would not attend any more of his sermons. Kuhr then challenged the congregation to walk out of the meeting with him. But not one person, not even his own son, followed him. The authorities thereupon imprisoned him again and after three years took him and Johannes Stahl to the Polish border and ordered them never to return.

Mercenaries who were kept on the property of the Brethren compelled everyone to attend Catholic services. For a time, in the face of the severe treatment they were receiving, all of the members at Alwinz appeared to succumb to Catholicism. But in the end, nineteen refused to give in. A number of times these scattered faithful ones fled to the group at Kreutz, but each time they were brought back to Alwinz by the authorities. Aware that the brotherhood at Kreutz was collaborating with the Alwinz group, Delpini carried his persecutions to Kreutz. The authorities scattered the Brethren throughout the villages in the hope that they would then be more easily converted. When this failed, the authorities made arrangements to place the Hutterite children in orphanages and drive the parents from the land. All the necessary preparations

---

37. Loserth, "The Decline and Revival of the Hutterites," p. 97.

were made, and the chronicle states that even the beds for the children were in readiness. But "God brought these intentions to naught."[38]

Joseph Kuhr and Johannes Stahl secretly returned from exile. They had spent the first part of their banishment in Poland, then, circling east of the Alps, had found their way through Moldavia and Wallachia to the south, crossing the mountains not far from Alwinz. Here they found available land where the soil was fertile and different religions were tolerated. Though it was highly dangerous, they returned to Alwinz to report their discovery to the Brethren.

Wallachia, Southern Romania

Applications for passports were denied to the Brethren, and the mountain passages to the east were guarded. But the determined members organized a quick departure. They secretly hired guides and smuggled keys to some of the prisoners. Three times they set the date for the escape, and each time the guides felt they could not go through with the plan, for they faced death if caught. Finally, the Brethren at Kreutz simply packed up and left, in broad daylight at ten o'clock in the morning on October 3, 1767. The villagers stood and watched. Sixty-seven persons, including sixteen from the old Hutterite group at Alwinz, made the departure.

The group traveled for seven days before they reached the high passes over the Carpathians. On October 13 they were ready for the most treacherous lap of their journey—they were about to attempt crossing the border, which was high in the mountains. The wagons had to be left behind. They started at sunset, following untrodden ways through the bush and wilderness with the aid of a guide. Zieglschmid's chronicle reads: "Each one can best imagine for himself what a difficult and tedious journey that was, with bag and baggage and little ones on their backs, to climb the high mountains with young and old and weak ones, and that at night" (*Das Klein-Geschichtsbuch*, p. 299). The chronicle continues: "Having crossed the border we were safe. . . . We travelled slower a distance on yonder side of the mountain until daybreak. Then we halted by the side of a brook and had a season of united prayer and thanksgiving and praised the Lord that he had led us out . . . without one of us being lost or harmed in any way."[39]

38. Zieglschmid, *Das Klein-Geschichtsbuch*, pp. 240 ff. The local authorities in Transylvania would not consent to such cruel measures, whereupon Delpini went to Vienna, where he obtained full permission from the Empress Maria Theresa to wipe out the Anabaptists. Portions of this dramatic account are available to English readers in Emil J. Waltner, *Banished for Faith* (Freeman, S. Dak.: Pine Hill Press, 1968).

39. English translation of Zieglschmid, *Das Klein-Geschichtsbuch*, pp. 303–4, is from Horsch, *The Hutterian Brethren*, p. 104.

Finally, the group considered it safe to encamp. Two men were sent back to Alwinz, a distance of about 170 miles, to tell those remaining in the prison where the main group could be found. Two others were sent to Bucharest to search for a location there.

The refugees were offered land by several landholders. They chose to settle 7 kilometers from Bucharest, at Tschoregirle, or in German, Kräbach (variously rendered as Choregirle and Ciorogirla, today a suburb of Bucharest). It was the sixteenth of November, and they had no dwellings; so they hastily built themselves houses of sod such as the native populace used. "It was indeed somewhat strange for us to live in earth, but we had peace and quiet and above all complete freedom of conscience," writes Waldner.[40] In the winter they began spinning and weaving. When their kind neighbor Wölfl died, they were able to purchase his house, garden, a portion of land, cattle, beehives, and household goods. The purchase was made on January 27, 1768.

The Brethren faced the problems of a poor climate and a lack of drinking water. They sought another location, while living in their earthen huts for two more winters. The following spring they moved a short distance to Presetschein (Presetchain), where they settled on the estate of a nobleman. But their general location in Wallachia was on ground being disputed in the Russo-Turkish war, and they found themselves continually caught between advancing and retreating armies, subject to the accompanying ravages. In addition there were roving bands which, under the pretense of driving out the Turks, robbed many of the nobles as well as the Hutterites of their goods and money. The bands used the whip, fire, and the sword to obtain their ends.[41]

The Hutterites again found it necessary to migrate, but before detailing their migration to Russia, we will summarize the external and internal threats they faced and the plight of those Hutterites who gave up their identity.

Identity Destruction and Assimilation

Historical Summary. The Hutterite brotherhood in Moravia, consisting of over one hundred known Bruderhofs and an estimated twenty to

---

40. Zieglschmid, *Das Klein-Geschichtsbuch*, p. 305.

41. The chronicler Johannes Waldner, then a boy of sixteen, relates his own experience of one of these raids: "One of the robbers led me out of the room into the yard, they threw me to the ground, held me by my head and feet and one of them struck me with a stick not less than fifteen or twenty times. Then they let me stand up. The German said to me, 'My child, tell me where your money is or who is hiding it, then we will not strike you anymore.' But God be praised that he protected me fatherlike, that I did not sin against brotherly love, for I answered, 'I have no money, I know of no money, not one penny' " (Zieglschmid, *Das Klein-Geschichtsbuch*, p. 314).

thirty thousand persons, was crushed. In a monolithic state where all religions but one were anathema, the Hutterites were put to death if they did not become Catholic or leave the territory. So long as the manorial lords or local princes operated autonomously with regard to the centralized government in Vienna, the industrious Hutterites were able to exchange their skills and goods for land and resources. When the central government was more powerful than the princes, soldiers and even citizens were given free rein to murder, loot, and rob all "heretics." By 1622 all the Bruderhofs in Moravia had been destroyed or evacuated.

Those who were not martyred or who refused to succumb to forced conversion fled to northern Hungary (today Slovakia). A small group had been taken to Transylvania. In both places the colonies fell victim to the many plunderers and armed troops who camped for unspecified periods in the same regions. Under these conditions it was difficult to maintain the practice of community of goods, and moral courage declined. Hutterites who remained in Hungary and Transylvania reluctantly became Catholic; by 1686 there were no Hutterite Bruderhofs in Hungary and by 1695 none in Transylvania.[42] The Transylvanian group was revitalized when transmigrants from Carinthia (in Austria) settled near them and accepted the Hutterite teachings. A small group of sixty-seven persons escaped to Wallachia and three years later to Russia.

What fate awaited those who succumbed to forced conversions and stayed in the Hapsburg lands? How were these individuals and groups assimilated into the national life of these countries? Are there any traces left of their culture? From their origin in Moravia until the remnant arrived in Russia, 242 years had elapsed. Summarized here are some of the main adaptations to external coercion made by the Hutterites and the resulting patterns of their assimilation in central Europe. Adaptations to external threats are illustrated and discussed under the headings *Martyrdom, Migration, Recantation, Assimilation,* and *The Habaner.*

Martyrdom. One adjustment to brute force is to die a willing death. The Hutterites did not resist or retaliate. Though there were defectors, many were steadfast in their biblical, pacifistic beliefs. They were willing to die and even rejoiced in the prospect. Under these circumstances a psychology and a theology of martyrdom developed. Confronted with the necessity of choosing, the believer gave his life for his faith. The Wolkan chronicle lists 2,173 Hutterite martyrs who "gave their lives for the sake of their faith" under the most torturous conditions.[43] All forms of

42. Communal life was abandoned in Sabatisch in 1685 and in Transylvania about 1695 (ibid., p. 223).
43. Wolkan, *Geschichts-Buch*, pp. 182–87. In a special study, Claus-Peter Clasen ("Execution of Anabaptists," *M.Q.R.* 47[April 1973]: 118) lists 706 executions for the

torture prevalent in a cruel era were employed: the rack, red-hot irons, burning, roasting on beams; groups were locked in houses that were then set on fire, bodies were quartered or chopped into pieces, and victims were starved in dark, vermin-infested dungeons.

Women were submerged in water and at the last moment taken out and asked if they would recant. Children considered too young to be slain were bound and beaten with rods. Gifts and riches were promised to any who changed their minds. Others, according to the Wolkan chronicle (*Geschichts-Buch*, p. 185), were offered freedom if they would simply utter a little profanity ("nur ein kleins Fluechl"), for such an act would be considered proof that they were not Anabaptists.

Monks, priests, and doctors of theology argued "with great cunning and cleverness, with many sweet and smooth words" (ibid.) day and night with the most able of the Hutterite leaders. In Tyrol where the prisons were full and where some authorities were reluctant to execute Anabaptists in public, some were killed secretly at night.

The legal basis for the execution of the Hutterites was the violation of civil law, heresy, and rebellion.[44] Protestant governments usually executed Anabaptists by decapitation, whereas Catholic governments burned the guilty ones at the stake in keeping with the medieval punishment for heretics. Special investigators were commissioned to pursue these secret believers. Paid informants, posing as converts, were very effective in reporting the Hutterites to the authorites. The death penalty was almost certain for Hutterite leaders from 1527 through 1537. As criticism of the death penalty began to be expressed in Protestant countries, lighter punishments were imposed.

Anabaptism could have been tolerated only if, like Lutheranism and Catholicism, it had been adopted by the prince of a city or territory as the official religion. For the Hutterites this was impossible, since they were opposed to the very idea of a territorial church. Hutterites were neither anarchistic nor opposed to governments. They maintained that secular rulers were necessary and "ordained of God" for maintaining order among the godless. Because they themselves claimed to be ruled by the community of love (rejecting the principle of coercion), they abstained from taking any part in the administration of territorial government.

The reaction of the prospective martyrs was resignation and joy. Many sang in their prisons or as they were being led to execution, "as though they were going to meet the bridegrooms at a wedding"

Hapsburg territories. For more on the psychology of adaptation to persecution, see Ethelbert Stauffer, "The Anabaptist Theology of Martyrdom," *M.Q.R.* 19(July 1945): 179-214.

44. Claus-Peter Clasen, *Anabaptism: A Social History* (Ithaca: Cornell University Press, 1972), p. 374.

(Wolkan, *Geschichts-Buch*, p. 186). Others came to the place of execution with smiles on their lips, praising God that they were worthy to die the death of a Christian hero.

Migration. Periods of hiding often preceded migration, which proved to be the only means of group survival. By dispersing into small groups, the Brethren went from place to place at night, hiding among rocks and cliffs, in forests, caves, and underground passages. Many of these holes and pits were probably made by skilled Hutterites. Not only were there complicated passages, with special arches, manholes, and secret hideouts, but there were large chambers used for the storage of food and supplies and for habitation. The early accounts state that during six years of persecution, the Hutterites lived in "holes of the earth."[45] Mention is made of "ungodly persons who made a fire before the hole and tried to suffocate them and smoke them out."[46] Most escapees took refuge in Hungary, whose northern lands contained fifteen Bruderhofs. In Transylvania the Brethren took to the mountains where dwellings were constructed on high stony ridges.

Recantation. The chronicle speaks of the number of God-fearing being greatly reduced because many could not bear the suffering, tribulation, hunger, cold, and nakedness. Jesuit purges came as late as the eighteenth century, even after Hutterite infants had, under compulsion, been baptized. In Hungary many men were imprisoned; in one instance, men were taken to the torture chamber, where each was tied to the floor and beaten until he promised to turn Catholic. The first man endured twenty-five strokes but did not yield; he was returned to prison with the assurance that he would be beaten again the next day. The second victim yielded after seven strokes, promising to turn Catholic. When they were about to beat the third, he preferred to turn Catholic without being beaten.

Other Bruderhofs, including the main Bruderhof at Sabatisch, fared similarly. Hans Schmid was beaten so badly he had to be carried away in a linen cloth, "since the flesh fell away from his feet and legs."[47] Some were crippled for life. Many were frightened, "since they saw that no one was able to endure it. So with the rest, not many strokes were necessary, and one after the other denied the truth, and turned Catholic." Leaders were also imprisoned in scattered towns and monasteries. When the imprisoned leaders returned to their villages "the members

45. Beck, *Die Geschichts-Bücher der Wiedertäufer*, pp. 184, 191.
46. Ibid., p. 186; Wolkan, *Geschichts-Buch*, p. 249.
47. English translation of Zieglschmid, *Das Klein-Geschichtsbuch*, p. 238, is from Horsch, *The Hutterian Brethren*, p. 88.

of the church had all fallen away. . . . So all the brethren in Hungary fell away from the faith, and not one remained faithful except Brother Heinrich Müller at Levar"; but he was soon put out of the way. In a disputation with the priests, Müller refused to agree that the sacrament was the literal body and blood of Christ; he quoted the words of Christ (Matthew 15:17), "What goes into the mouth enters the stomach, . . ." and said, "See to what a wonderful end your Christ comes." The priests charged him with blasphemy. That night he was killed and in the early morning thrown into the Danube.[48]

Misery, inconvenience, and harassment accompanied the weakening of the communities. Wives and children were left at home while the men wandered about in the forests. Workshops were deserted and the economic system deteriorated. Jesuits, accompanied by several soldiers, a corporal and four privates, were quartered in the houses. On Sundays they forced everyone to attend the Catholic services. In the winter the men hiding in the forest were easily discovered, if not by soldiers, then by hunters.

As the resilience of the Alwinz group declined, Elder George Geissy turned to Unitarianism. Another elder, Mertl Roth, was persuaded to recant, reasoning: "We do not observe our faith right, and community of goods has disappeared. Even if we resist a long time, we must finally become Catholic. God may still turn the tide; a way may come, and then we may live for our faith under another government."[49]

Poverty played an important role in the demoralization of the inner life. It was so severe that the Hungarian Hutterites sent a delegation to the Mennonites in Amsterdam in 1665 asking for financial help. The Mennonites contributed generously then and later, but even this help could not prevent the decline of the Hutterite movement.[50]

Assimilation. During the first half-century of the Hutterite movement, living in the Bruderhof was considered a privilege. There were deep feelings of gratitude for deliverance from oppressive Tyrol, and there was genuine charismatic sharing in the community of love. However, in the seventeenth century in Hungary, despite Grimmelshausen's favorable description (1668), communal living was less than harmonious beneath the surface. At the same time the chronicle speaks of persecution, it also speaks of an inner decline and of the struggle with self-regard.

48. The quotations in this paragraph are from Horsch, *The Hutterian Brethren*, pp. 88–89.
49. *M.E.*, s.v. "Kuhr, Joseph."
50. *M.E.*, s.v. "Slovakia."

There were varied complaints and problems. Men performed their day's duties, then hired themselves to outsiders, or they worked for their personal interest. In such cases, when they used colony materials, the shop foreman had the additional burden of accounting. The unity of the colony was in jeopardy because some received extra compensation for outside work and others did not. Undertaking large construction jobs for noblemen away from the Bruderhof presented a problem, for such undertakings were not considered to be in the best spiritual interests of the brotherhood. The effects of war were also demoralizing. Men refused to work over long periods of time for fear of an invasion. There were alterations in mores—the introduction of various forms of dishonesty, such as secretly keeping money and wearing new worldly styles of clothing.[51]

The revitalizing efforts of Andreas Ehrenpreis (Vorsteher, 1639–62) in assembling all the earlier Ordnungen and insisting on their observance were insufficient to accomplish by law what had formerly been done by spontaneous Christian love. In his farewell address shortly before his death, Ehrenpreis acknowledged this: "We know from the bitterest experience that the enemy is busily engaged in planting abominable weeds into the church of the Lord." The people were following their own inclinations, "having departed from the simplicity of Christ and the filial obedience which they owed to God and the church."[52] A common saying during this period was:

Die Gemeinschaft wär' nicht schwer
Wenn der Eigennutz nicht wär!

(Communal life would not be hard
If there were not such self-regard.)

Had the Jesuits not come to forcibly convert the Hungarian Hutterites and to confiscate their books, the question remains whether the Hutterite movement would not have disintegrated of its own accord. The chronicle speaks of the complaints of the many "false brothers and stepsisters" (Horsch, *The Hutterian Brethren*, p. 72). A sermon of this period reprimands a brother who complained, "I shall work according to the food I am given" (ibid.). Another sermon mentions the *stinkfaul* (frightfully lazy) who scarcely did the work of children but were heroes in eating, drinking, and sleeping. Sleeping quarters were becoming living quarters with stoves and luxuries. There was too much wining and fraternizing with outsiders. The stewards were warned not to take any woman along to market except the housekeeper, and flirta-

51. Horsch, *The Hutterian Brethren*, p. 73.
52. Ibid.

tion with the cooks and other women was condemned.[53] In this state of moral decay, colony work was performed only for promises of money or wine; the foremen were not turning their profits over to the Bruderhof, and everyone was looking after himself first.

A law forbade Hutterites to compete with the local Saxons in the production of pottery. Nevertheless the Hutterite potters did not refrain from secretly selling their wares and keeping the proceeds, thus contributing to the downfall of the economic life of the Bruderhof. Before migration took place there were three factions among the Transylvanian Hutterites: a group that had turned Catholic, another that was steadfast in its faith, and a third group that refused to associate with the other two.

The Habaner. Today in Czechoslovakia and Romania there are vestiges of the former Bruderhofs; some well-constructed buildings made by the Hutterites, remnants of their pottery and crafts, and a few family names similar to modern Hutterite family names. Of the eighty-five or more former Hutterite Bruderhofs thus far identified,[54] the best preserved are at Grosschützen, Sabatisch, and St. Johann, all in Slovakia, now a part of Czechoslovakia. (See figure 15.) These places still have solidly built dwellings which date from the sixteenth century. In each case the buildings are arranged in a square around a central courtyard. In many other places in Moravia, especially Selowitz and Damborschitz, there are large underground cellars and dwellings known to have been built by the Hutterites. (See figure 16.)

Families in these villages with early Hutterite family names are Albrecht, Baumgartner, Bernhauser, Čederle (Tschetter), Kleinedler, Kuhr, Müller, Pullman, Schultz, Walter, Wolf, and Wollman.

Today in Czechoslovakia the Hutterites and their descendants are called *Habaner.* (See figure 17.) The origin of the name is obscure. It may be an alteration of *Haushaben*, another name for Bruderhof. Robert Friedmann states that Habaner was "originally a nickname for the Hutterites in Slovakia, used by the Slovakian peasants" and "later the general name for those Hutterites who after about 1760 turned Catholic and as such were permitted to continue to live in their existing Bruderhofs on a semicommunal or cooperative principle."[55]

53. Zieglschmid, *Das Klein-Geschichtsbuch*, p. 534.

54. Robert Friedmann, *Hutterite Studies* (Goshen, Ind.: Mennonite Historical Society, 1961), pp. 50–53. For a thorough study of Hutterite place names in Moravia, see Jarold K. Zeman, *The Anabaptists and the Czech Brethren in Moravia, 1526–1628: A Study of their Origins and Contacts* (The Hague: Mouton and Co., 1969).

55. *M.E.*, s.v. "Habaner." Robert Friedmann visited these places and reported his observations in "Die Habaner in der Slowakei," *Wiener Zeitschrift für Volkskunde* 32(1927): 1–11. Bertha Clark believed that *Habaner* was a contemptuous term meaning "lubber," or "awkward person" ("The Hutterian Communities," *Journal of Political Economy* 32[1924]: 477).

Figure 15. *Top*, house in Altenmarkt Bruderhof, founded in 1545, today near Břeclav, Slovakia (Photograph, 1970); *bottom*, gable of Hutterite dwelling at Grosschützen (Velké Leváry), Slovakia. (Photograph, 1970)

Figure 16. Scenes from Selowitz (Židlochovice, Czechoslovakia), where a Bruderhof was founded in 1536. (Photograph, 1970)

Figure 17. A Tschetter Hutterite descendant at St. Johann, Slovakia. (Photograph, 1970)

That *Habaner* no longer has a derogatory meaning is clear. From Beck we learn that it used to be a libelous invective, and after complaints were made a law was passed in 1780 forbidding its use.[56] By this time the Jesuits had already completed their work of forced conversion, and so the law merely lifted a stigma from those who did not want to be dubbed Hutterites. Despite this law, *Habaner* is widely used today in speaking of the places, people, and industries of the Hutterite movement. Of course, in historical and theological circles, the people are generally spoken of as *Wiedertäufer, Täufer,* or *Anabaptists.*

Little is known of the Bruderhofs that were entirely Catholicized. The chronicle mentions the remorse and pain of conscience of those who turned Catholic. These accounts have great didactic value for Hutterites today. An apostate brother, Jacob Stutz, encouraged several of the persecuted ones "to be faithful," for ever since he had denied the faith "he had no peace in his soul; but constantly the gnawing worm of an accusing conscience" (Horsch, *The Hutterian Brethren,* p. 97). Fines

56. Beck, *Die Geschichts-Bücher der Wiedertäufer,* pp. 564, 620.

were levied against the parents of a child who was allowed to die without baptism. The first parents to go against their consciences and permit their children to be baptized "heard the rooster crowing, and their hearts trembled within them."[57]

From a Moravian visitor we learn more about the Hutterites who turned Catholic. Having heard of the persecution of the Hutterites by the Jesuits, the Moravian Church in Saxony sent a representative, Schoolmaster Czolsch, to visit Grosschützen in 1783. He sought out the brother of Jakob Walther, whom he had met on his way to Russia, and having found him, spoke privately with him in the potter's shop. Walther said, "We now have peace, and all the trouble is over since we all became Catholic. We promised under oath to remain Catholic, and to ever confess that we all have accepted this religion of our own free will and not by compulsion."[58] Furthermore, all had promised to report any person suspected of anti-Catholic tendencies.

Asked whether they would not have done better to adopt the Augsburg Confession of the Lutheran Church, Walther said that it would be very dangerous for any person to suggest such a change and that he himself was risking imprisonment to come and talk about these matters. He reported that two wagon loads of Hutterite books had been taken to Pressburg and that conditions were the same in all the other Hutterite villages. The interview was abruptly interrupted. In his report to the Moravian Church in Saxony, Czolsch concluded: "I cannot describe how sad I feel to have found this folk in such a situation, and to leave without accomplishing anything."[59]

Contacts between the European Habaner and the Hutterites in Russia, and later in America, were minimal. In 1893 a Hungarian Habaner, Ignatius Pullman, visited the colonies in the United States, bringing with him some old books. He declined the invitation to join a Bruderhof. After his visit to Slovakia in 1925, Friedmann reported that many of the Habaners continued to live communally long after they had become Catholic.[60] Some of the fields were parceled out to individuals as late as 1863. But the Habaners themselves had but a faint knowledge of their earlier Anabaptist history.

Aspects of communal life continued throughout the nineteenth century, according to the Hungarian scholar Béla Krisztinkovich.[61]

57. From a handwritten manuscript (codex) located in the Bishop's library at Esztergom, Hungary [identified as Cod. III, 133 (n.d.)], p. 289. Microfilm in the possession of the author.

58. Horsch, *The Hutterian Brethren*, p. 112.

59. Ibid., p. 113.

60. Friedmann, "Die Habaner in Slowakei."

61. Béla Krisztinkovich, "Glimpses into the Early History of Anabaptism in Hungary," p. 138.

He reports that in 1847 the inhabitants of three villages sent a petition written in Hungarian to the Hapsburg emperor, Ferdinand V, stating that since olden days they possessed "noble privileges" and claiming exemption from war duty and taxes.

Two Hutterite preachers, David Hofer and Michael Waldner, made a tour of the old places in Europe in 1937 and recorded their observations in an extensive diary.[62] They found forty families at Sabatisch who were descendants of Hutterites, and thirty-nine Habaner dwellings, most of them with thatched roofs. In 1968 two more preachers, Paul Gross and Paul Walter, revisited the European homesteads.[63] When two Manitoba Hutterites, Jacob Kleinsasser and Jacob Hofer, were on a mission to England (to the Society of Brothers at Darvell) in the summer of 1974, they visited many of the old Hutterite places with Hardi Arnold as their guide.

Two world wars and the shifting of political borders played a major role in scattering the German-speaking people of Moravia and Slovakia. The situation also greatly affected the descendants of the Hutterites. Reactions against German-speaking people in the new political states after 1945 again changed the character of these villages.[64] Those who did not declare themselves native Slovakian and repudiate their German origins were forcibly removed from these areas.

62. Robert Friedmann, ed. and trans., "Hutterites Revisit European Homesteads: Excerpts from the Travel Diary of David Hofer," *M.Q.R.* 33(October 1959): 310–11.

63. Paul Gross, "On the Trails of Our Anabaptist Forefathers, Summer 1968," *M.Q.R.* 44(January 1970): 85–99.

64. See Max Udo Kasparek, "Habanerhöfe in Südmähren," *Südmährisches Jahrbuch*, 1957, pp. 92–94; Kasparek, "Zur Tracht der Wiedertäufer in Mähren und der Slowakei," *Südostdeutsche Heimatblätter* (Munich), 1956, series 2, pp. 91–95.

chapter four

Life in Russia

The Hutterites lived in Wallachia for only three and one-half years. The land was rich and sufficiently productive, but there were threatening problems, such as much sickness and the constant fear of being plundered or of being taken as slaves by the Turks. Realizing the dangers from the war between Russia and Turkey, the Hutterites sought the advice of the Russian army commander in Bucharest. There was no hope that the war would soon come to an end and no hope that the Bruderhof could survive "this thievish and marauding class of people."[1] There was "great deviltry and little justice in the land. Therefore we definitely decided to leave this country if God would only show us where to go." The general showed great interest in their welfare and proposed that they emigrate to Russia. He advised them to go to Kiev; at the Polish border the field commander, Count Peter Alexandrovich Rumiantsev, would provide them with particulars. After taking counsel among themselves, they cast the lot whether to go or remain. The sign was that they should go. The general gave them a letter of protection to safeguard their passage through occupied territory.

1. Zieglschmid, *Das Klein-Geschichtsbuch*, p. 316. The short quotations in this paragraph are from the same source and page.

The Move to Vishenka

A group of about sixty persons left Wallachia on April 10, 1770, and did not arrive at their destination until August 1. With them they took five wagons, each of which had a pair of oxen, and several cows, calves, and sheep. They traveled around Bucharest and headed northward, passing through Buzau, Roman, Bozosami, and Chotin. At the Pruth River was the Polish border and, nearby, the headquarters of the Russian field commander, Rumiantsev.

The journey had been extremely hazardous. The Hutterite refugees were robbed of their best garments, and seldom were they able to sleep under a roof at night. They were sustained by fresh milk and *Balukas*;[2] the chance to buy venison or Turkish wheat provided a rare delight. Often they had to camp in a forest to await the outcome of a pitched battle before moving on. On two occasions they arrived in villages whose inhabitants had been taken into slavery by the Turks only days before. A pestilence had taken its toll of lives among the populace. The migrants saw empty houses and dead bodies lying in the fields. By the time they reached Chotin, they were a destitute group of people.

After many delays Joseph Kuhr and Paul Glanzer were able to negotiate a contract with Rumiantsev (through his undersecretary General Weiss) to settle on his private estate at Vishenka (or Wishchenka) in the province of Tchernigov one hundred twenty miles northeast of Kiev. The twelve-point contract provided for the free exercise of religion, freedom to develop trades, permission to live communally, and exemption from military duty, the swearing of oaths, and appearances in court. The settlers were to be exempt from taxes for three years and were promised an advance with which to build houses. After three years they were to pay ground rent in cash. If the location did not prove satisfactory, they would be free to move after repayment of their loan.

The field marshal assigned a captain with ten Cossacks to escort the Hutterites to their destination. Their most urgent food problems were solved. When the time came for the noon and evening meals, an escort would ride ahead to the nearest village and notify the judge that warm food was to be prepared for a group of "field marshal people." Thus, "by divine guidance," the remnant of faithful Hutterites arrived in the Ukraine.

The manager of the estate advanced immediate necessities, including fifty sheep pelts. The Hutterites were permitted to select their

---

2. *Balukas*, mistakenly defined as fish by Zieglschmid (ibid., p. 711), was a gravy sauce made from flour and milk. The dialect term and the method of preparation are still remembered by Hutterites.

own building plots and were offered the services of an engineer for the construction of a large house that would contain the dining hall, kitchen, pantry, and carpenter shop. On July 27, 1771, the first worship service was held in the newly built house. Farming was the main subsistence activity, but orchards were planted and all the traditional enterprises were established, including pottery-making, weaving, metalworking, and blacksmithing. There was a distillery, a mill run with water power, a windmill, and ice and storage rooms. In 1778 "large" and "small" schools were built, and in 1779 a separate meetinghouse for worship was constructed. The Brethren were content, happy, and grateful to God that once again they had a place where they could live together safely in peace.

The group now became deeply concerned for the brethren who remained in Hungary and Transylvania. Some were apostates and others were in prison. Seven different journeys were made by representatives from Vishenka to their brethren in the Hapsburg domains. The distance from the Bruderhof residence in Wallachia to Vishenka, according to modern estimates, was about 740 miles. On their return visits to Hermannstadt (Sibiu) and nearby Alwinz, the distance covered one way would be about 850 miles, and to Sabatisch in Hungary, well over 1,000 miles.

Rescuing Kinsmen and Apostates

Paul Glanzer was sent back to Romania in 1771 to visit the Hutterites who remained in prison. He accompanied a member of Rumiantsev's staff who was returning to Wallachia and informed those in prison at Hermannstadt of the location of the new settlement. Although Maria Theresa had decreed that religious prisoners were to be freed if they would leave the country, Delpini refused to release the Alwinzers. Glanzer's wife, a daughter, and a brother were still being held captive, but Glanzer was able to return to Vishenka with Anna Wipf and her daughter Gretel, who managed to escape. Two years later a small group of prisoners were released and escorted to the border. They were brought to Vishenka by Rumiantsev's staff, using his equipment. This group included Matthias Hofer, a poet who had written over thirty hymns during his sixteen years in prison (and who later proved to be a troublemaker), and five Glanzers—Martin, Christian, Barbara, Maria, and Margaret.

The seven return journeys between 1771 and 1795 to points in Romania and Hungary, to Vienna, and to Carinthia provide touching accounts of Hutterite kinsmen attempting to regain their own family members and of devout believers trying to rescue apostate members.

Instead of going by way of Romania, the delegations often took a northern route, which brought them into contact with Mennonite communities in Lemberg (in Galicia), in Poland, and in Prussia.

In 1781 Joseph Müller and Paul Glanzer were delegated by the Vishenka group to visit all those locations where Hutterites still had kinsmen. Letters were sent in advance. The two delegates went all the way to Carinthia. For the most part they met with indifference, for in the long period of persecution the former members had lost their courage. Johannes Waldner writes of their relatives in Carinthia: "The pure teaching of the Gospel had become a strange thing to most of them, and they could not appreciate or understand that children should not be baptized, . . . but only adults, . . . for the epithet Anabaptist was still violently hated and the common man still supposed that there can be no worse heretic in the world than an Anabaptist."[3]

When they reached Grosschützen, the resident Jesuit hurried them away as fast as possible. In nearby Sabatisch there was great excitement at the news that there was a brotherhood in Russia, but the two visitors from Russia were prevented by the Jesuits from going there. Jakob Walther, the preacher at Sabatisch who had not even gotten to see the visitors, quickly sent several books, two Hutterite coats, two Hutterite breeches, and two pairs of shoes to them at Pressburg, "so that the brotherhood in Russia and their children might see and know the manner of clothes which our forefathers had been accustomed to wearing."[4]

Not many months afterward, Walther sent a letter to Russia asking for help, saying that as many as thirty persons in Sabatisch wanted to join the group in Russia. Two men, Joseph Müller and Christian Hofer, were sent to Hungary to assist in any way possible. At Sabatisch there was great outrage when several families refused to attend the Catholic services and openly expressed their intention to join the group in Russia. Six of the men most outspoken in favor of leaving were bound by the authorities and taken to Nitra to a rotten, stinking prison. Letters were sent to the women and children, threatening them with prison terms if they did not adhere to the Catholic faith.

In the spring of 1782 Joseph Kuhr and Elias Wipf went to Romania. Kuhr succeeded in bringing two of his three children back with him. A third mission was made by Joseph Müller and Christian Hofer. On their return to Russia they visited three different Mennonite churches, telling of their faith and way of life. Mennonites, they observed, were "pretty much dressed up" and wearing buttons. But the

3. Ibid., p. 356.
4. Ibid.

group at Gruningen wore hooks and eyes, and they collected Bibles and books for them. Their hospitality led to deeper ties and a few converts to the Hutterite faith. They brought fifteen Mennonite persons (Decker, and Knels families) to Vishenka with them. The account which the Hutterite visitors gave of the religious privileges and living conditions in Russia may well have influenced other Mennonites in their decision to migrate to Russia beginning in 1789.

Late in 1782 Jakob Walther of Sabatisch found his way to Russia. Joseph Müller and Christian Hofer had been unable to bring any Hutterites back with them. However, in 1783 eleven families, totaling forty-seven persons and including Jakob Walther's wife and two children, escaped from Hungary and joined the Vishenka group. Others who attempted to escape from Sabatisch were apprehended and forced to return. A total of fifty-six persons from Hungary succeeded in joining the Vishenka Bruderhof in Russia.[5] Several times delegations from Sabatisch went to Vienna seeking recognition under the Edict of Toleration issued by Emperor Joseph II in 1781, but without success. The emperor did, however, release the Hutterite prisoners at Nitra, where they had been held for one year.

Waldner's chronicle records an interview between Christian Hofer, one of the Vishenka representatives, and Joseph II in 1782. Disappointed in their efforts to take former Brethren back with them to Russia, Joseph Müller and Christian Hofer had come to Vienna where they made an attempt to recover the assets of the property of the Carinthians who had been deported to Transylvania thirty years earlier. The Russian consulate assisted them in the preparation of a petition. Their account of the interview follows:

As the Brethren came again to the imperial place to inquire about the matter, it happened that the Emperor was just descending from an upper room. He noticed brother Christian and called, "Come in." Christian went with him into a room, where they were alone together, and conversed for about a half hour. First the Emperor asked him what he wanted. The brother replied that he had sent him a petition and did not know whether it had reached him or not. The Emperor asked whence they came, whether they were not of those folk in Hungary. The brother replied that according to religion they were, but that they were natives of Carinthia, and were of the number who had been banished and forced to migrate to Transylvania in 1755. The Emperor replied, "I know, I know."

Brother Christian thereupon begged the Emperor most humbly concerning their property and inheritance which they had left behind them in Carinthia.

5. Ibid., p. 373, for the names of the fifty-six persons. There were no missions from Russia to the Hapsburg lands after 1795.

The Emperor replied, "Come back to your fatherland to your house and home and you shall have everything again." The brethren said, "They will not tolerate us but persecute us." The Emperor said with earnest words, "Who persecutes? Who persecutes? No one persecutes now."

Then the brother said, "Just this summer in Hungary six men lay more than a month in prison for their faith's sake." Then the Emperor was silent for a while and finally said, "Well, what of it? That is but a small thing. One must adopt some recognized religion, Catholic, Lutheran, Calvinist, or Greek." The brother replied, "We cannot be convinced in our heart of any teaching differing from that which Christ the Lord and his apostles themselves gave, namely that one should abide in the pure evangelical doctrine, and follow him, and live a pious Christian life."

Thereupon the Emperor asked many questions. What we are named. How it went with us in Transylvania. Whether we were allowed to have property in that country. Whether we had been given land. Whether the priest who had persecuted us in Transylvania was not named Delpini. How we fared in the persecution. How we came into Wallachia and where we lived there. Whether it was a good land. How we fared there. Why we had gone into Russia. Where we live at present. Whether the Count had given us enough land. Whether our houses were of stone or wood. Whether we had a priest and whether he was married.

All of these questions Brother Christian answered to his best knowledge, and the Emperor listened very attentively. Then Christian pleaded once more for the property which we had left in Carinthia. The Emperor did not reply with yes or no, but asked how we had been able to get out of Russia. When Brother Christian told him that we had secured a passport from our Count to visit our Friends in Austria, he permitted him to leave. The Emperor accompanied him to the door.

Some years later word was received from Hermannstadt, that our property left behind in Carinthia, amounting to 2,151 Gulden, had had to be sent in haste to Vienna, but what disposition was made of it, no one was able to discover. At least nothing of it ever came to the Brotherhood.[6]

Internal Problems

All of the Brethren met together for the first time in 1773. The Kreuz, Stein, Alwinz, and Hermannstadt groups, heretofore scattered in Transylvania, gathered together to live in one Bruderhof in Russia. Some of the converts from Carinthia who were imprisoned for years had never seen the others. Persecution had prevented the people from meeting as one group. There was great rejoicing in the new religious freedom, and the group praised God for their new-found unity. But soon a mighty struggle was to arise from within.

6. John Horsch, *The Hutterian Brethren, 1528-31: A Story of Martyrdom and Loyalty* (Goshen, Ind.: Mennonite Historical Society, 1931), pp. 110-11.

Matthias Hofer, who had spent sixteen years in prison, began to exert a strong influence in Vishenka. He knew the Bible thoroughly and was outspoken in his views. He could repeat the Psalms from memory, and he had memorized all the chapters in the Bible which contained prayers. At first it appeared that Hofer was invigorating the group, but it soon became obvious that for the majority of the members, he was too fanatical. He believed the Lord's coming was imminent and demanded that all prayers be audible, declaring that silent prayers by the individual were a means of serving Satan. Even while he was in prison he had carried on lengthy arguments with other Hutterites on the subject of audible prayers. Although the brotherhood deliberated these questions and voted down many of his proposals, he kept introducing innovations. He had scruples about singing at work, declaring that one must either sing or work and not carry on both activities at the same time. He demanded group prayer meetings before breakfast and work on Sunday afternoon, and he forbade greeting any person who was not a brother or sister.

Hans Kleinsasser, the spiritual leader, usually took Hofer seriously. Some members of the colony followed Hofer's teachings, but the majority found his influence disruptive and unacceptable. The Bruderhof earnestly sought a way to deal with him. They searched the writings of the forefathers, especially the old chronicle, which had only recently been recovered. The old book had come into the possession of the Alwinz Vorsteher's son, who had turned Catholic, and it was sold to the prisoners in Hermannstadt, who brought it to Vishenka.[7] The great chronicle became an authoritative source for settling disputes and it was on its precepts that most of Matthias Hofer's innovations were voted down.

Hofer advocated most of these scruples before his own baptism—a fact that indicates how great his charismatic influence must have been. But neither baptism, nor marriage in 1773, nor being elected to the council in 1778 mitigated his scruples. When Joseph Kuhr became Vorsteher, succeeding Hans Kleinsasser, who died in 1779, Hofer's influence was greatly diminished. On several occasions he wandered from the Bruderhof and was returned by Russian neighbors. One day he wandered into the forest. Several brothers went to look for him; should he be found dead, at least they could give him a decent burial. But he was found alive. The Bruderhof consented to take him back if he would agree not to mislead and agitate the others and if he would be willing to be treated as a guest. This he found intolerable, and finally he took to the road. When a Russian traveler far from Vishenka questioned him, he

7. Zieglschmid, *Das Klein-Geschichtsbuch*, p. 347.

denied any connection with the Vishenka Hutterites and pretended that he was a Quaker. One day the colony received a letter from Gerhard Wiebe, the Mennonite pastor in Elbing, Prussia, saying that Hofer had arrived there and told his whole story. Wiebe pleaded in Hofer's behalf for reconciliation with the Vishenka group. Hofer went on to Holland, intending to sail for America to join the Ephrata Colony in Pennsylvania.[8] How he learned of either the Quakers or the Ephrata Cloisters is unknown. For lack of funds, however, he did not make the journey. He died among the Prussian Mennonites in 1786.

A second troublemaker for the brotherhood was Hans Hofer, a gifted man of twenty-one, who read the Bible incessantly and, like Matthias Hofer, composed hymns. Not only did he read and study the Bible but he began to interpret it, often staying up all night with others discussing these matters. During the day he was too tired to keep up his share of the work in the blacksmith shop, which caused friction between his foreman and himself. He argued that concern with spiritual matters was more important than working with material things. He advocated sending out missionaries, preaching repentance to those outside the colony, and founding a church as the forefathers in Moravia had done. "We sit here in our houses," he said, "like a goose on her nest of eggs, ignoring the command of Christ to spread the Gospel, and we will be brought to judgment for this."[9]

Hans Hofer left Vishenka as a self-appointed missionary in 1784 and went directly to Sabatisch. There he found many who would have returned to their former faith if only they had been permitted to leave. With this in mind he went to Silesia and began negotiations with the government, promising new settlers and a Bruderhof like the one that had existed in Moravia, if the king would grant freedom of religion. The king was so pleased that he offered a group of thirty-two houses free of charge and permission to settle there immediately. Young Hofer was delighted. He returned to Sabatisch and wrote a letter to Vishenka requesting a preacher and a small group to come and start a Bruderhof. In a short time he hoped to have a community of four hundred persons located in Silesia. No one among the Vishenka Hutterites felt any sympathy toward Hofer's proposal, and his plans came to naught. For eleven weeks he hid in a small room at Sabatisch. Eventually he was asked to leave. No one heard from him thereafter.

This experience and other incidents made the group very wary of introducing changes. Materially the Bruderhof prospered, but there was one profession that was dying out—the barber-surgeon or physician.

8. Ibid., p. 354.
9. Ibid., p. 379.

In Moravia the Hutterite physicians had been famed and many had practiced the medical arts, but for many years following the severe persecutions there had not been a really good physician in the group. Now there were only one or two practitioners. In 1780 a French physician came to the estate of Count Rumiantsev and expressed his willingness to take a Hutterite as an apprentice. The Bruderhof chose young Christian Wurz, one of their most faithful and promising young men. He was married and the father of three children. The group felt relatively secure in permitting him to leave the community for apprenticeship. But Wurz lost interest in his family and community. The Bruderhof tolerated his trimmed beard and fashionable clothing in hopes that he would return, but after he became recalcitrant and asked permission to wear his hair in a braid, he was excommunicated. He died twelve years later in Moscow without ever having returned to his home.

The reaction of the colony to losing three young men—two who leaned toward the "right" in their interpretation of the Bible and Wurz, who leaned toward the "left," the world—was increased conservatism. The chronicle says, "The Brethren took the position that there shall be no innovations, but a steadfast determination to remain with the discipline of the forefathers."[10] Following Hans Kleinsasser's death and Joesph Kuhr's election as Vorsteher in 1780, there was a "mindset" to stay with the time-tested forms and discipline of "the old Brethren."

Russia and Turkey went to war in 1787, and the government imposed both a recruiting quota on all landowners and a universal head tax. The Hutterites' refusal to supply recruits or pay war taxes caused considerable friction. Finally the colony agreed to pay a higher annual rent, but they stated emphatically that they were not paying war taxes. The count purchased slaves or serfs to fill the required quota.

The Hutterites' beliefs were tolerated in the Ukraine, and for the first time the Brethren were not being harassed or persecuted by the church or state. Although much more isolated than ever before, they were not totally cut off. Rumiantsev brought some of his distinguished visitors to the Bruderhof, and through government channels the Hutterites were enabled to travel and make contact with kinsmen in Hungary and Transylvania. There were occasional visitors from the Mennonites and from the Moravian Brethren, who had established a colony at Serepta in 1765.[11]

10. On this point, see especially ibid., pp. 343, 350, 381. The tendency toward rigidity is given full thrust in German: Also ist vom mehresten Teil der Brüder erkennt worden, dz man in allen Dingen, soviel man kunnt, sich nach dem Form und Ordnung der alten Brüder richten soll (p. 350).

11. Correspondence between Johannes Waldner and John Wygand of the Moravian Brethren in Serapta has been preserved in the archives of the Moravian Brethren in

Some of the Amish Mennonites of Palatine origin who lived in the Polish regions of Volhynia and Galicia showed interest in joining the Hutterites. Six Amish Mennonite families resided in the Vishenka colony for a year with the intention of joining. Their leaders Jacob Müller and Jacob Burgthold were allowed to preach. Although there was general agreement on doctrinal matters (the Amish held out for footwashing), there were many practical matters on which they could not agree. The group returned to Lemberg.

Rumiantsev died in 1796, and his two sons, who were absentee landowners, attempted to reduce the status of the Hutterites to that of serfs. The great majority of the population in Russia were peasants, owned by the state, the church, or the nobility. The serfs cultivated the crown lands, but they also farmed land for their own livelihoods. There were in addition slaves who were employed in households and who could be sold or traded at will. But the Hutterites had not settled on crown lands; they had come on the invitation of a private landowner and had been granted various privileges, of which they were keenly aware. They appealed to Emperor Paul I, son and successor of Catherine II, to clarify their legal status. They were assured that their original agreement was valid and that in the future they would have the same legal status as the Mennonite colonists—who, incidentally, had migrated from Prussia to the Ukraine nineteen years after the Hutterites.

The new clarification of their privileges in a *Gnadenbrief* dated September 6, 1800, permitted the Hutterites to move off the Rumiantsev lands onto crown lands. For practical purposes they were now classed as Mennonites and put under the same supervision as foreign colonists. Under the law each family was eligible to receive 65 dessiatines of crown land (1 dessiatine equals 2.7 acres), and 13 kopeks per dessiatine were to be remitted annually to the crown as tax.[12]

On Crown Lands in Radichev

On the advice of a government representative who visited them at Vishenka, the Brethren decided to move to Radichev, 8 miles to the northeast along the northern banks of the Desna River. "Vishenka was our home for 32 years less 36 days," says the chronicle. "During

---

Herrnhut, Saxony (see Robert Friedmann, with the assistance of Adolf Mais, *Die Schriften der Huterischen Täufergemeinschaften* [Vienna: Hermann Böhlaus, 1965], p. 58). Wygand observed that "Johannes Waldner thinks much more literally than his congregation."

12. Zieglschmid, *Das Klein-Geschichtsbuch*, pp. 513–15.

this time many brethren, sisters, and children died, and 172 of them are buried there."[13] The entire group at Radichev consisted of 202 persons (99 men and 103 women).

The Bruderhof was laid out in 1802 in a 490-foot square and was enclosed by a hedge fence. Between May and November the group erected nineteen buildings. In addition to the living units and a large dining room and kitchen, there was a kindergarten building and a school building. The workshops occupied the ground floors of the buildings, and the second floors were used for sleeping quarters, similar to the pattern in Moravia. Families lived as units, but the older children were segregated by age and accommodated in separate quarters.

The lands and resources at Radichev offered woods, pasture, gardens, streams rich with fish, and pine trees from which to make building materials. The Bruderhof had access to almost two thousand acres (seven hundred dessiatines). At one time, as part of a former cloister, the lands had belonged to sixty separate owners. The Bruderhof invested heavily in livestock, raising "good Hungarian breeds." All of the traditional handicrafts were restored. The following productive activities were carried on in the Bruderhof, although there was not always a separate building for each: weaving, spinning, pottery-making, tailoring, tanning, dying, shoemaking, leatherworking, hat-making, broom-making, metalworking, blacksmithing, beekeeping, gardening, silk-growing, cabinetmaking, and carpentry.

Fifteen versts (about 9 miles) away, on the Assman (or Jessmann) River, the Brethren operated a water-powered mill that had been given to them by the government. They also erected a windmill on a hill beside the colony. On the other side of the Desna River at Föhrenwald, they operated a second whiskey distillery, which, together with the Bruderhof distillery, produced over twelve thousand liters of whiskey annually. Several thousand mulberry trees were planted to augment the silk industry.

John Wygand, the Moravian Brethren (*Herrnhuter*) preacher who visited the Bruderhof late in 1802, gives this interesting description of the physical aspects of the colony:

To the right of the entry into the village square, at the foot of a gently rising hillside covered with the most beautiful orchards, stands a not unattractive stone house with a thatched roof; it contains a spacious dining room adequate for the commune which now also serves as a chapel, and also a kitchen which is served by a regular cook assisted by two sisters who are changed daily. Beside the kitchen are various pantries and below them are arched cellars.

13. Ibid., p. 402.

Besides this building we found a blacksmith shop with coal sheds, further a tannery with a supply of leather, a cobbler's shop, a distillery with three boilers and the laundry beside a well six *Faden* (36 feet) deep; then the general bakery, where only one kind of bread is baked for all the inhabitants by a sister and her daily changing assistant; a temporary weaving-mill besides other temporary buildings; and finally the head teacher's house which consisted of a spacious room. On the left side of the square are two rooms which are now occupied by eighteen mothers, each with an infant. They remain in this room for the first year-and-a-half; their food is brought to them from the common kitchen. Finally there are two schoolhouses for larger and smaller children where the children of both sexes are taught together, but separated on the two sides, under the very careful supervision of the head teacher and his wife and several unmarried brethren and sisters; they are taught reading, writing, Christianity, and all of them are taught to knit, spin and sew until they are grown or receive baptismal instruction.

Of the unpleasantness one fears in such arrangements there was no evidence. Still it is noticeable that these children, generally quiet rather than wild or noisy, although free, have an unbroken, stiff streak—one would like to call it an unchristened streak.

Besides these schools are a shop for cabinet-making and several business buildings. A sisters' house is being built where all the sisters, single, married or widowed, will work when they are not otherwise occupied. That this is possible, indeed even suitable, results from their arrangement by which no woman conducts her own household, but man and wife and children are provided with all necessities; in return, each contributes what she is able to the community. In the same way all the men after learning their trade, work in shops, and have their sleeping quarters there. The unmarried boys, however, sleep in the room for brothers. The workshops of the potters, hatters, and dyers along one street form the fourth side of the quadrangle. Besides all these buildings, stables for the assigned cattle and several granaries are to be built.

The dress of the Hutterites in Radichev was described by John Wygand in 1802 as follows:

The men wear the beards unshorn, a round hat, a jacket similar to the Russian except that it has fewer pleats, does not overlap in front, is generally blue in color and instead of buttons has only hooks and eyes. Men and women have neither buckles or ribbons or buttons, or anything that is unnecessary, but confine themselves to what is absolutely necessary. Therefore, also no sugar, coffee, tea, tobacco, etc., are used. The women wear a black woolen cap [*Mütze*] with a simple linen band and in cold weather a coarse white head shawl, a cloth jacket and a skirt of homemade material with an apron of plain linen.[14]

14. Ibid., pp. 414–15. The passage was translated for the author by Elizabeth Bender.

The Bruderhof was visited occasionally by government officials who submitted reports to the ministry of the interior. Alexander Klaus, one of the more prominent, issued several reports in 1869 in a book in the Russian language. A German edition, *Unsere Kolonien*, appeared in 1887. These reports, together with the Waldner chronicle, which incorporates other documents and some letters by visitors, form the basis for our knowledge of Hutterite life in Russia.

A government inspector named Burin made extensive comments on the rearing of the young. He reported that before confinement a woman was placed in a special, warm room where delivery was to take place. She remained in these quarters, together with the other women who had given birth, until her child was one and one-half years of age. During this entire period she spent the nights away from her spouse. At the end of a year and one-half, the mother returned to her husband and the child was placed in another special room, usually in the care of an older widow. At the age of four the children were in the care of sisters in yet another room, where they remained until the age of seven. They were then separated according to sex; boys were assigned to male teachers and girls to female teachers. Parents were permitted to visit their children and to have them in their own homes (ibid., Klaus, p. 63–64).

The brotherhood in Radichev was resourceful. Soon there were real problems, however. Most of the first-generation members, who had been sorely persecuted, were no longer living. There was not enough land at Radichev to support the growing population, so that full employment could not be maintained. Their early experiences in Russia made the Brethren fearful of innovating or branching out. As factions and jealousies developed, the economy gradually became paralyzed. Instead of turning over funds to the treasurer, the foremen gave only an accounting to the Bruderhof. Those in charge of the shops bought and sold and were able to have more to eat and wear than the others. The membership was polarized between the two preachers. Johannes Waldner, of Carinthian origin, considered communal living a cardinal principle. "I would rather go to the martyr's stake than give up the old practice," he said. Jakob Walther, the young assistant preacher who had been reared among the old Hutterites in Sabatisch, where community of goods had been dissolved, took the opposite position, declaring that he would rather die than go back to communal living. Walther pressed for the dissolution of the Bruderhof. In 1817 he and his party of thirty families began to build family dwellings on land belonging to the Bruderhof. The faction cut across six marriages.[15]

15. Ibid., p. 418.

The Waldner party, consisting of twenty families, appealed to the ministry of interior. Fadyeev, the government inspector who went out to examine the situation, noted that many members were shirking their work and performing their trade poorly and that an unskilled Russian peasant could have done as well. Fadyeev proposed (1) that Radichev be divided among all colony members; or (2) that the dissidents be permitted to take their share of the property to a Mennonite settlement. The group decided on the second alternative and moved for a short time to the Chortitza Mennonite settlement about 350 miles to the south.

Those who remained at Radichev were demoralized. After a fire, which had started in the blacksmith shop and destroyed most of the buildings at Radichev, Johannes Waldner, then aged sixty-eight, gave his consent to the discouraged members to divide what was left. In the meantime Walther's group had difficulty in settling among the Chortitza Mennonites. When they heard that communal living had been dissolved at Radichev, they returned and worked out a compromise with those who had stayed. Several of the large buildings were to be used communally, but lands were parceled out among the various families, and each kept a few small animals and sheep. The group settled at two main locations: twenty-five families remained at the old location and twenty-four families moved across the Desna River. In 1819 religious and business affairs were placed in the hands of distinct and separate authorities, as was the case in Mennonite village life. Jakob Walther became the financial manager, and Johannes Waldner remained the recognized religious leader until his death in 1824.

Even though the Bruderhof had access to two thousand acres of land, less than one-third of it was arable; hence the amount of productive land, when divided among the families, was insufficient. The government official Alexander Klaus observed: "Under these circumstances the skills of the farmer are of little help, and the increase in population aggravates the situation."[16] The government was slow in deciding a course of action, perhaps out of fear that they would be financially responsible for what might happen. Hutterite life steadily deteriorated after 1819, when communal living was abandoned, until 1842, when the Hutterites moved to the Molotschna area; by then, the young had become illiterate.

Among the Mennonites in Molotschna

In 1834 the group petitioned to move to new crown lands. They were unsuccessful in their appeal and asked Johann Cornies, a trustee of the

16. Alexander Klaus, *Unsere Kolonien* (Odessa, 1887), p. 77.

government and an outstanding agricultural and educational leader in
the Mennonite colonies, for help. Because of his resourcefulness, he
had been comissioned by the government to supervise the settlement
patterns of several other minority groups, including the Molokans and
the Doukhobors.[17]

Cornies intervened on behalf of the Hutterites, and in 1842 the
Mennonites assisted in their relocation at the Molotschna Mennonite
settlement in the province of Taurida, a distance of 450 miles to the
south. Cornies named the new location Huttertal. It was located about
twelve miles from the city of Melitopol. There were at this time 69
families in a total population of 384: 185 males and 199 females.

The Mennonite settlers were of Dutch and Prussian background
and traced their spiritual origin to Menno Simons in the Netherlands
in the sixteenth century. The Mennonites began to settle at Chortitz in
1789 and in the Molotschna area in 1803. An estimated six thousand
were located on 424,000 acres of land by 1835. As Anabaptists they
shared many points of faith with the Hutterites.

Cornies required the Hutterites to model their community after
the Mennonite village pattern, with houses built on both sides of a wide
street and set well back in spacious orchards. Family units were
separated by ground space. The dwellings faced the street, and the
barns, shelters, and storage bins extended to the rear. The Hutterites
raised no objection to the Cornies plan. In order to acquaint the Hutterites with modern farming practices, Cornies placed their young men
and women on Mennonite farms. It was a radical change from Vishenka
and Radichev. Here they were brought into contact with German-speaking people and modern agricultural and economic practices. Huttertal
grew into a community almost indistinguishable from the surrounding
Mennonite villages. There were, however, differences in dress and
speech patterns. The Hutterite men dressed in plain dark clothes and
wore beards and long hair, which gave their settlement the nickname
"the bearded ones." The women wore dresses of dark blue or black
material. Homes were furnished very simply.[18]

Huttertal made such satisfactory economic progress that in 1852
a second village, named Johannesruh in honor of Johann Cornies,
who had died in 1848, was founded by twenty-one families comprising
seventy-two persons. The move away from Huttertal—which Hutterites refer to as a most regrettable split[19]—did not occur without difficult

---

17. D. H. Epp, *Johann Cornies* (Jekaterinoslav and Berdiansk, 1909).

18. Zieglschmid, *Das Klein-Geschictsbuch*, p. 441.

19. Ibid., pp. 565-67. The problems were complex. The young were taken from
Huttertal to the Mennonite villages to learn the various trades often against their own
wishes or the wishes of their parents. There were disagreements over economic questions
involving prices and land use between the Bruderhof and the authorities of the villages

economic, political, and internal problems. But whatever havoc the internal disunity may have brought, it seems to have taught the Hutterites a valuable lesson. The division of the Hutterites into five different villages in southern Russia from 1842 and 1868, separated by distances of up to eighty miles, helped them later, in America, to appreciate the necessity of branching out. Their basic economy and subsistence pattern was built on dairy and cattle farming, grain and vegetable (particularly potato) farming, and horticulture. The Mennonites grew, and also smoked, tobacco, but the Hutterites did not.

Not only did Cornies introduce innovations in agriculture, cattle breeding, and industry and train young Hutterites in these new methods, but he also influenced them to change some of their conservative social customs. Once, when a girl refused to marry an older widower, she fled to Cornies for help. He arranged a place for her to work in a distant village (Tashchenak) and then confronted the Hutterite leaders, demanding that they give up their unpopular old custom of having the church elders match the partners. "The young people must decide for themselves whom they will marry."[20] The principle of absolute obedience, even in marriage, had worked in Moravia. Courtship and romance did not exist, and once or twice a year the elders matched eligible marriage partners. A girl could choose between two or three boys, but if she elected not to marry any of them, she had to wait until the following year to marry.[21]

The entire history of the Hutterite settlements in Russia may be summed up as follows:

Vishenka was the original settlement and home of the Hutterites from 1770 to 1802. They lived on the estate of Count Peter Alexander Rumiantsev along the Desna River. Radichev, located 8 miles north of Vishenka, became the home of the Hutterites from 1802 to 1842. Here, as in Vishenka, the Brethren built a new set of Bruderhof buildings. Communal living was abandoned in 1819 and additional dwellings

---

in the Molotschna colony. The chronicle speaks of accusations, threats of imprisonment, and even beatings. A sixty-year-old man "was severely insulted and spit at, and was told: 'you have beards to your navels, brushes could be made from your beards, but you are all liars.' Such insults the Bruderhof had to bear from the village office" (ibid., p. 567). Within the Bruderhof there were also differences of opinion between the older and the younger leaders.

20. Ibid., p. 438. Following the ceremony, "when they were about to lock up the married couple together, the young woman managed to escape. She fled to the superintendent [Cornies] with the urgent plea that he rescue her from this relationship, to which she had not consented nor would she ever consent. He [Cornies] promptly, once and for all, put an end to compulsory marriage." There is also an account of this incident in Epp, *Johann Cornies*, pp. 146–52.

21. *M.E.*, s.v. "Marriage, Hutterite Practices."

were constructed across the Desna. Both Vishenka and Radichev were located in the province of Tchernigov, about 120 miles northwest of Kiev, in an area isolated from other German-speaking peoples.

Huttertal, 12 miles southwest of Melitopol, was founded as a Hutterite village within the Molotschna Mennonite Colony when Johann Cornies assisted the group to settle there in 1842. The Molotschna Mennonite settlement was located in the province of Taurida about 450 miles south of the two earlier Hutterite locations. Four additional Hutterite villages were formed: Johannesruh (1852–77), located 2½ miles north of Huttertal; Hutterdorf (1856–74), also called Kuchewa, 80 miles north of Huttertal and 30 miles east of the Dnepr; Neu-Huttertal (1857–75), or Dabritscha, located about 20 miles northeast of Saporoshje, across the stream from Lubimowka and 28 miles from Hutterdorf;[22] and Scheromet (1868–74), or Scherebez, 10 miles south of Hutterdorf. (See figure 18 and map 4.)

The Renewal of Communal Living

In Molotschna the Hutterites continued the practice of electing their own preachers, and they worshipped separately from the Mennonites. They lived in villages, as the Mennonites did. Their "Hutterisch" speech was distinct from the low German dialect spoken by the Mennonites. Hutterite sermons were read from the manuscripts of the forefathers. Some preachers struck out the phrases that emphasized common ownership, while the consciences of others did not permit such changes. The more sensitive Hutterite leaders were keenly aware that *Gemeinschaft* (mutual aid) as practiced by the Mennonites was not *Gütergemeinschaft*. Living in the midst of the Mennonites was a very different experience from the isolation at Vishenka and Radichev in the north. The threat of being assimilated by the Mennonites, the economic friction already mentioned, and the task of maintaining a separate identity were factors which contributed to the renewal of communal living. The details of this revitalization are broadly sketched in the chronicle, but greater insight comes from an Alberta colony document found by the author in 1964.[23] Michael Waldner, who was the strongest force in re-

22. D. M. Hofer, in his book *Die Hungersnot in Russland* (Chicago: K. M. B. Publishing House, 1924), p. 58, speaks of this location. Lists of families in these villages appear in J. J. Mendel, *History of the People of East Freeman, Silver Lake, and West Freeman . . .* (Freeman, S.Dak.: By the author, 1961), p. 14.

23. The document is entitled "Michael Walner's Account, 1858 to 1876 (as Related by His son).'' It was translated by Ilse and Don Reist, edited and introduced by Robert Friedmann, in Friedmann, "The Re-establishment of Communal Life among the Hutterites in Russia (1858)," *M.Q.R.* 39(April 1965): 147–52.

Figure 18. Sketch of Scheromet, a Hutterite village in Russia, from the diary of Peter Janzen, 1874.

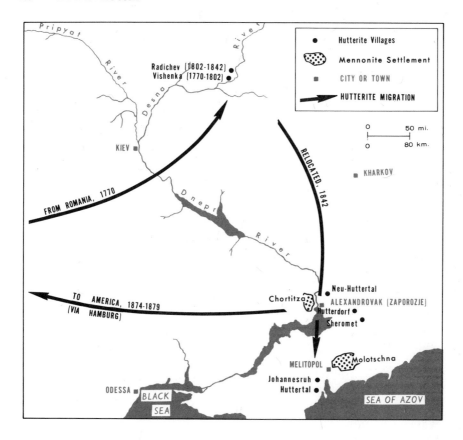

Map 4. Hutterite Villages in Russia, 1770–1879

organizing communal living, was given to psychic experiences, trances, and visions, which played a significant role in restoring the communal pattern.

A small group made plans for a Bruderhof in 1845 but was told to wait until the government approved their petition to buy separate land. George Waldner, the preacher at Huttertal for thirty-three families, attempted to reinstitute communal living in 1857. The attempt failed and resulted in polarizing the Hutterites on the communal issue.

After George Waldner's death, three preachers, Michael Waldner, Jakob Hofer, and Darius Walter, were elected. Although further attempts were made at communal living, Waldner says they "did not last very long; somehow the grace of God was not with them." When they met together for prayer, Waldner and Hofer "read the beautiful teachings of our forefathers." "Both prayed much to God for inner strength and help to enable them to do the right thing and to be faithful to the teaching of their forefathers. Eventually God showed them the way and the means to accomplish this great purpose."[24]

Even before his election as preacher, Waldner had experienced trances. Once his family thought he had died, "for he seemed no longer to breathe. He was not dead, however, but rather in a state of trance where God gave him a great vision." A guide in the form of an angel appeared to him and "showed him the heavenly host, a multitude of angels, who praised God with indescribable songs. Then he was shown hell and the company of the damned. It was a terrible picture to behold, with anguish and pain, which no mortal can imagine."

Waldner asked his guide about his own place in what he had seen. The angel answered in the form of a question: "Can you tell me whether any person was saved from the great Flood besides those in the ark? Now you know your place. The ark is the *Gemeinschaft* of the Holy Spirit to which you no longer belong" (p. 150). Waldner began to weep, but the guide told him to go back to his Brethren and establish a Gemeinschaft "after the pattern of Jesus and his disciples." The guide assured him: "I will be with you and will not leave you until death." Waldner felt himself flying through the air when his guide disappeared. From this point on Waldner himself said he was a new man. On regaining consciousness he saw his family around his bed weeping, supposing him to be dead. Turning to his family, he said, "Don't you hear the angels sing?" for it seemed to him that they were still singing.

The two men, Waldner and Hofer, often retreated "studying the Word of God and imploring the Almighty for strength and help to carry out his ordained work." One day as they retreated for prayer, "one said to the other that whoever finished his prayer first was to arise and ordain (or accept) the other" into the new Gemeinschaft. They began to pray "from their innermost heart to God that he might help them by his grace to carry out the intended enterprise [*diesen Handel zu vollenden*] in the right fashion and with the right spirit" (p. 151). Hofer finished his prayer first, then arose "and by the laying on of hands ordained and accepted [*einverleiben*, or incorporated] Michael Waldner into the new

---

24. Ibid., p. 149. Unless otherwise specified, the quotations in this section are from the Michael Waldner account in ibid.

Gemeinschaft. Hofer then knelt and was ordained by Waldner, and the two men accepted their wives into the newly-formed Gemeinschaft and began to set up the rule . . . under the guidance of the Holy Spirit. They went out to preach to the Brethren and to invite them to join them, for nearly all of them had been ignorant about communal living and its practice. And thus, with the blessing of God, the new *Gemeinschaft* grew and increased daily."

This renewal took place at one end of the village of Hutterdorf in 1859. In the following year preacher Darius Walter established communal living at the other end of Hutterdorf. In the center of the village were those who remained uncommitted to communal living. Michael Waldner was called "Schmied-Michel" because he was a blacksmith, and his group, therefore, acquired the name of *Schmiedeleut*. In 1868 his group sold their property in Hutterdorf and moved to Scheromet, about eight and one-half miles away, where they were joined by others from Johannesruh. The Schmiedeleut practiced communal living for fifteen years before they came to South Dakota in 1874, having lived nine years in Hutterdorf and six years in Scheromet.

The Schmiedeleut were a congregation distinct from the Darius Walter group, which soon took on the name *Dariusleut* after the given name of their leader. The Dariusleut lived communally in Hutterdorf for fourteen years before they immigrated to the United States. The third branch of the Hutterite movement, the *Lehrerleut*, was formed after the arrival of its members in South Dakota.

Michael Waldner continued to see visions and have strange experiences which had a significant effect upon all groups reestablishing communal living. After his group had settled in Bon Homme County in South Dakota, Michael Waldner and Joseph Waldner were sent back to Russia, in 1875, to rescue not only relatives but "more souls from perdition and to bring them to America too—that wonderful country where everyone is free to believe what he wishes." Michael Waldner's son relates incidents experienced by his father on this journey:

The two returned crossing the ocean for the second time, going by train from Hamburg to Russia. As they approached the place where they were to get off the train (Michael Waldner's relatives lived not far from the railroad tracks), Waldner asked the conductor to have the train go very slow, "which the good man also managed." When he thought it was going slowly enough, he took his sack and his preacher's coat, went to the steps and jumped off the train. Unfortunately, he fell, hitting his head against a stone and apparently losing consciousness. In this state he suddenly saw his father, who had died several years before, coming toward him and asking: "Michael, why are you lying there? Come, get up, I want to take you to your home." His father took the coat in one hand and Michael in the other, and led him to the home of his relatives.

When his father opened the door and let him in, Michael asked his father, "Where are we now, in Russia or in America?" His father, however, did not reply, but laid the coat on the bench and disappeared.

When the relatives in the next room heard Michael Waldner's voice, they quickly came out. When they saw him they cried: "My God, what happened to you, man? You look as if bathed in blood." But on his coat there was not a drop of blood. They washed him and gave him clean clothes and let him rest. He soon recovered and went about his business.

When he had finished his task by taking several families into the *Gemeinschaft*, Waldner and his group soon headed back to America. On this whole trip "he very much felt the presence of God's guardian angels not unlike the experience of good Tobias on his way home." One incident stood out. At one place where the railroad ran between two mountains, Waldner looked out of the window and saw in the distance a huge rock on the tracks. Immediately he notified the conductor who thereupon had the train stopped. Waldner and his brethren removed the rock from the tracks. The conductor expressed his appreciation to Waldner, for without him there might even have been a serious accident (p. 151).

Visions and psychic experiences are of course nothing new in periods of revitalization. One sixteenth-century Anabaptist was known to have been subject to hallucinations,[25] but never before in Hutterite history had visions figured so significantly in the reformulation of the central teaching of communal living. The revelations and innovations of the poet Matthias Hofer sixty years earlier had been rejected. The Amish have had two so-called sleeping preachers who preached for hours while in a state of trance.[26] Michael Waldner's visions had sound consequences for the Hutterites because they motivated a return to the time-honored form of communal living. His was a message not of innovation but of return to the simplicity of a way of life that had been given up forty years earlier.

The Exodus from Russia to America

At the time the Hutterites were turning back to their traditional form of communal living and the nearby Mennonites were experiencing revivals, Russia was becoming nationalistic. In 1864 the Primary Schools Bill made Russian the language of instruction in the schools. When compulsory military service was introduced in 1871, Mennonite and

---

25. *M.E.*, s.v. "Liebich, Jörg."

26. *M.E.*, s.v. "Sleeping Preacher Churches." See also Don Yoder, "Trance-Preaching in the United States," *Pennsylvania Folklife* 18(Winter 1968–69): 12–18, and Harry H. Hiller, "The Sleeping Preachers: An Historical Study of the Role of Charisma in Amish Society," in the same issue, pp. 19–31.

Hutterite leaders went to St. Petersburg for a meeting with the imperial council in order to have their privileges confirmed. When they had settled in Russia, the Hutterites and the Mennonites had been granted freedom from conscription. They offered to colonize undeveloped territories in exchange for continued "religious freedom," but the officials showed no interest. Thus the Mennonites and Hutterites decided to send delegations to various countries, including America, to look for colonization possibilities. The Hutterite representatives in the delegation to America were Paul Tschetter and his nephew Lorenz Tschetter. (See figure 19.) They left Russia on April 14, 1873, and returned on June 27, 1873. Paul Tschetter kept an extensive diary of his journey.[27]

The more expressive of the two Hutterites investigating North America was Paul Tschetter, aged thirty. Although he came from the village of Huttertal and was a preacher, he was not from a group that practiced communal living. He and his uncle traveled to New York City and then on to Elkhart, Indiana, to seek the aid of John F. Funk, a Mennonite publisher, who agreed to serve as their guide and interpreter.

27. J. M. Hofer, "The Diary of Paul Tschetter, 1873," *M.Q.R.* 5(April 1931): 112-27, and 5(July 1931): 198-220. Unless otherwise specified, the quotations in this section are from the Tschetter diary.

Figure 19. Paul Tschetter (b. 1842) and Lorenz Tschetter, noncolony Hutterites who investigated settlement in North America in 1873. (Photograph by H. Mertz, New York)

Together with Funk they traveled to Chicago and St. Paul, observing the areas around Duluth, Fargo, Moorhead, Pembina, Winnipeg, Sioux City, Council Bluffs, Omaha, Hastings, Lincoln, Plattsmouth, and other nearby points. They met members of the Russian Mennonite delegation along the way but traveled independently of them. The Tschetters were favorably impressed by the "fine orchards and pastures and beautiful fields of grain" of the Indiana Mennonites, but they were shocked to find that the Mennonites preached in English, hunted with guns (although they were pacifists), and had pianos in their homes.

In Chicago, Tschetter's head began to ache from "so much noise and tumult" (p. 198). The delegates spoke with pioneer settlers, occasionally finding some who could speak German. They saw marshy lands in Minnesota and dry prairie lands in Manitoba and the Dakota territory. They took note of the lumbering regions. In Canada they found streams and many beautiful trees but observed that "the people are lazy farmers of mixed Indian blood and are more cattlemen than agriculturalists" (p. 203). They ascertained the native pests, including grasshoppers, and the length of seeding for barley and wheat. South of Grand Forks, they traveled with the mail coach to get a better view of the land and found "very fine level land, black soil, and a good growth of grass" (p. 206), and "there was excellent hayland." Paul Tschetter was sufficiently moved to compose a song, "The New Jerusalem."

Although the Hutterite delegates were offered land at $3.50 and later, after they had returned to the East Coast, at $3.00 per acre, they declined. A formidable concern was "religious freedom"—exemption from military service and jury service and the right to govern their own schools. Paul Tschetter wrote a petition to the President of the United States, Ulysses S. Grant, and requested an audience with him. A railway representative, Mr. Michael Hiller, made the arrangements and the two Hutterites met with President Grant at eight o'clock on the evening of July 27 at Long Beach near New York City. The diary states that "the President received us in the most friendly manner and we presented our petition to him personally" (p. 217). Several weeks after they had returned to Russia, a letter from the President's office was received saying that their requests could not be guaranteed since some matters were under the control of the state legislatures. There was, however, a ray of hope, for the letter stated that "for the next fifty years we will not be entangled in another war in which military service will be necessary."[28] The Hutterites decided to migrate.

---

28. C. Henry Smith, *The Coming of the Russian Mennonites* (Berne, Ind.: Mennonite Book Concern, 1927), p. 72. See also Ernst Correll, "President Grant and the Mennonite Immigration from Russia," *Mennonite Quarterly Review* 9 (July 1935): 144–49.

When the Russian government realized that it was about to lose forty-five thousand of its best farmers, the emperor sent General von Todtleben as his representative to visit the Mennonites and Hutterites. Among other things he promised them alternative service under their own jurisdiction. The result was that only eighteen thousand of the forty-five thousand colonists emigrated, but this number included all of the Hutterites in Russia, both those who were living communally and those who were on individual farms.

The Hutterites lost no time in making preparations to leave Russia. Immigration took place in several stages. The property at Scheromet was sold to a Mennonite, Peter Epp. The first exodus of Hutterites consisted of both the Schmiedeleut and Dariusleut groups and their leaders. On June 7, 1874, 113 Schmiedeleut boarded the train at Alexandrovsk (Saporoshye) for Hamburg. There they were joined by a group of about equal size of Dariusleut, making a total of about forty families which sailed from Hamburg on the *Hammonia* on June 19. They reached New York on July 5, and after some immigration difficulties and an epidemic of dysentery in Lincoln, Nebraska, where thirty-six children died, they reached the Dakota territory on August 8, 1874.[29]

Michael Waldner's group settled in Bon Homme County along the Missouri River. The colony was named Bon Homme and is today looked upon as the "mother" of all the Schmiedeleut colonies.

The Dariusleut, under the leadership of Darius Walter, lived during the winter in sod houses on government grounds at Silver Lake and established their first Bruderhof, Wolf Creek, in 1875. This is the founding colony of all the Dariusleut colonies in North America.

The third group, consisting of thirteen families headed by Jacob Wipf, left Russia in 1877 and began to live communally at the Elmspring Colony (later called Old Elmspring) near Parkston, South Dakota, where they settled on 5,440 acres of land. Their attempt to form a Bruderhof in Johannesruh had never quite succeeded, but on coming to America they chose to live communally. Their leader, Jacob Wipf, had attended the Mennonite high school in Halbstadt and was an accomplished teacher (*Lehrer*); thus they were named *Lehrerleut*.

Between 1874 and 1879 all other Hutterites who were not living communally also left Russia. The majority settled as individual homesteaders on the prairie in South Dakota. These noncolony Hutterites became known as *Prairieleut*. They continued to speak "Hutterisch,"

---

29. The dates given in the chronicle (Zieglschmid, 1947, p. 458) as well as those given in the diaries of Paul Tschetter and Peter Janzen follow the Julian rather than the Gregorian calendar. Thus the date of arrival reported in Yankton's *Press and Dakotan* (August 20, 1874) was Tuesday, August 18, 1874 (Gregorian calendar).

The terms *Bruderhof* and *colony* are used interchangeably hereafter.

but their congregations eventually affiliated with the Krimmer Mennonite Brethren and the General Conference Mennonite church groups.

Only two families, according to tradition, are known to have remained in Russia.[30] This indicates an astonishing unanimity in favor of
migration in view of the fact that many Mennonites and other German-
speaking people did not leave Russia and that there were serious factions and "much quarreling on account of communal life." Counting
both colony and noncolony Hutterites, there was a total of at least 1,265
Hutterite emigrants.[31] The Hutterite literature states that about half of
the Hutterites settled in the three Bruderhofs and the other half were
noncolony people; the exact number is not known. From the United
States Census of 1880 we learn that there were 443 Hutterite
adults and children living in colonies. The seventeen most common
Hutterite family names on the ship lists were Decker, Entz, Glanzer,
Gross, Hofer, Kleinsasser, Knels, Mandel, Miller, Pullman, Stahl,
Tschetter, Waldner, Walter, Wipf, Wollman, Wurtz.[32]

The Century in Russia

The Hutterites lived in Russia for 104 years. From an estimated 120
destitute refugees, they increased to 384 persons by 1842 and to 1,265
persons by 1879. The first generation in Russia knew what it meant to
be persecuted and to find religious freedom. They were industrious and
built two Bruderhof sites during this time. At Vishenka and Radichev,
where they lived for seventy-two years, the group experienced neither

30. Hofer, "The Diary of Paul Tschetter, 1873," *M.Q.R.* 5(July 1931): 218. One of
these families (not living on a Bruderhof), the Andrew Wollman family, owned a factory
and was said to be worth millions. The other family that remained in Russia was a Stahl
family. See Mendel, *History of the People of East Freeman*, p. 20. D. M. Hofer (*Die
Hungersnot in Russland*, p. 136), mentions a John Wollman who hid himself on the day
of departure because he did not want to go to America.

31. This number is based on a count of typical Hutterite family names on eight
immigrant ships between 1874 and 1879. The ships carrying Hutterite immigrants departed from Bremen or Hamburg and docked in New York. For ship lists see Arnold M.
Hofer, Chairman of the Hutterite Centennial Steering Committee, *History of the Hutterite
Mennonites* (Freeman, S. Dak.: Pine Hill Press, 1974), pp. 64–96.

32. The first Hutterite immigrants came on the *Hammonia*, arriving in the Port of
New York on July 17, 1874. Of 826 passengers on board, 365 bore Hutterite family names,
represented as follows: Hofer 72, Waldner 59, Stahl 56, Walter 42, Kleinsasser 34, Wipf
21, Wolmann 19, Wurz 17, Tschetter 16, Decker 10, Walther 6, Knels 6, Gross 5, and
Janzen 2. The Bon Homme Bruderhof census on April 1, 1875, according to its own
records, numbered 123; 61 men and 62 women. Of course, not all of those on the *Hammonia* settled in colonies. The unpublished diary ("Reise nach America") of the Hutterite
Peter Janzen, which has recently come to the attention of historians, lists the daily activities and the route of the first Hutterite immigrants from June 6 to August 8. Also included is a sketch of the colony plan at Scheromet.

The distribution and survival of Hutterite family names is discussed by Robert
Friedmann in *M.E.*, s.v. "Hutterite Family Names," and by Mendel in *History of the
People of East Freeman*, p. 23.

persecution nor external threats to their identity. (See map 4.) There is no evidence of a lack of markets for their products.

A major problem of adaptation to the new Russian environment was the adjustment to geographic isolation and a world that was not hostile. Security, isolation, and the restructuring of communal living produced internal problems and divided leadership. Charismatic tendencies of individuals and deviance within the group could not be assimilated. The reaction of the Brethren was conservatism and a return to the old writings for solutions to existing problems. This gave rise to still other problems for the second generation.

After forty-nine years in Russia, communal living was abandoned. Hutterites attribute this downfall to the spirit of private property and individualism that crept into the thinking of the foremen and managers of the various income-producing enterprises. There is a traditional view among modern Hutterites that "the Russian markets were too close to the Bruderhof." Thus, individuals could weave cloth or make other products and, without the knowledge of Bruderhof officials, sell them at the local markets and pocket the money. Had the markets been farther away, requiring Bruderhof transportation, the products could not have been sold without the proceeds passing through the Bruderhof treasury.

What is significant from a sociological perspective is that the absence of persecution by the outside world tended to maximize internal problems. Many of the earlier, most capable leaders had passed on to their reward. The new generation did not have the same motivation or the same hostile experience of outsiders. Once the group adapted to individual homesteads and private property, the problem of land room was accelerated. Without the community functions of schools and industries, the dissemination of knowledge deteriorated and the children no longer learned to read. The Hutterites were rescued from disintegration by the Mennonites, who were successful large-scale agriculturalists in the Ukraine.[33] Thirty years of exposure to the Mennonites in Russia equipped the Hutterites with a vital knowledge of agriculture, which was essential to the development of their collective farms in North America.

After their resettlement in the Molotschna Mennonite area, the Hutterites began to prosper and recover their identity. Those opposed to communal living were able to find fulfillment within the Mennonite village pattern. Those who favored communal living forefeited that ideal for the time being. Factional differences were resolved constructively by forming new village sites, a practice that was to have great

33. C. Henry Smith, *The Story of the Mennonites* (Newton, Kans.: Mennonite Publication Office, 1950).

adaptive value in North America. Communal living was reintroduced in 1859.

Factors accounting for the renewal of communal living and the preservation of Hutterite identity were (1) the potential threat of absorption into the Mennonite villages, (2) the impending nationalization policies of the Russian government, and (3) the extraordinary revelations and capable leadership of Michael Waldner.

The primary source for this chapter is the Hutterite chronicle itself (Zieglschmid, 1947). The author wishes to acknowledge corroborating insights from others who have worked the German sources, especially Victor Peters in his book *All Things Common: The Hutterian Way of Life* (Minneapolis: University of Minnesota Press, 1965) and in his Ph.D. dissertation, "A History of the Hutterian Brethren 1528-1958," University of Göttingen, 1960.

chapter five

Adaptation to the North American Environment

The Early Dakota Years

In coming to the United States, the Hutterites began a new epoch, a period of population growth and prosperity that exceeded even the golden era in Moravia. After three and one-half centuries in war-torn Europe, their long pilgrimage—from Moravia to Hungary, Romania, and Russia—came to an end when they settled in the Dakota Territory in 1874, fifteen years before South Dakota was granted statehood. They now entered a country widely acclaimed for its freedom and economic opportunity.

The American West was still open to large-scale settlement. In 1861 Congress had created the Dakota Territory. In 1862 President Abraham Lincoln had signed the Homestead Act, and Congress had granted charters and enormous tracts of land to railway companies to encourage the settlement of the West. The stage was set for mass migration, and of course the Hutterites were but a small group of the many Germans who came from the Ukraine. Dakota was still occupied by many Sioux Indians. In the same year that the Hutterites arrived, Colonel George A. Custer led a military expedition into the Black Hills to investigate reports of gold. The violation of the Indian treaty by the many prospectors and settlers who occupied the area caused a series of

Indian uprisings. But in the plains in the eastern part of the territory, the situation was peaceful.

The plains states were anxious to attract Mennonite settlers, and in the period of mass migration the Hutterites were generally classed as Mennonites. The Yankton *Press and Dakotan* urged giving "this class of immigrants the best chance possible, for we have seen enough of their thrift and enterprise to convince us that they will make most desirable citizens." The paper pleaded for united action to secure as much as possible "of this most valuable tide of humanity."[1]

The Hutterites arrived in the United States not knowing exactly where they would take up settlement. Their uncertainty made them easy prey to competing railroad companies and unscrupulous immigration agents. They felt, as they had again and again throughout their history, totally dependent on God to lead them. Taking advantage of their helplessness, a smooth, German-speaking man, apparently posing as an agent of the Burlington Railway, met them in Chicago and offered them a free ride to Burlington, Iowa, to inspect some promising land.[2] When the train arrived in Burlington, they were warned, perhaps truthfully, of an epidemic and a lack of accommodations and were advised to go on to Lincoln, Nebraska, at the railroad's expense; if they were not satisfied with the railroad land there, they could proceed to Dakota.

The city of Lincoln provided immigrant quarters. Some of the men worked as day laborers, while a party of six searched for land around Lincoln. Meanwhile the group fell victim to a severe epidemic of dysentery, which claimed the lives of a seventy-eight-year-old man and thirty-six children during their four-week stay in Lincoln. Having found no suitable land, the group, as soon as it was able, boarded a train for Yankton, South Dakota, and arrived there on August 8, 1874. The Burlington Railway now repudiated the promises made to the Hutterites in Chicago and tried to collect their fares. The Hutterites refused to pay, and consequently the railroad would not release their baggage. However, outraged Yankton officials intervened in their behalf, as did the Volhynia Mennonites, who had arrived during the previous year.[3]

Homesteading was an easy way for most families to acquire government lands. By the Homestead Act each family living as a unit was eligible for 160 acres of land if they lived on the land, and by planting 40 acres of trees they were eligible for 160 additional acres and could purchase up to 160 acres more at $1.25 per acre. By homesteading, such

1. John D. Unruh, *A Century of Mennonites in Dakota* (Pierre: South Dakota Historical Collections, 1972), pp. 24–25.
2. Zieglschmid, *Das Klein-Geschichtsbuch*, p. 458.
3. C. Henry Smith, *The Coming of the Russian Mennonites* (Berne, Ind.: Mennonite Book Concern, 1927), p. 66. See also *M.E.*, s.v. "Volhynia."

families could collectively have acquired 12,800 acres of free land and 6,400 additional acres for only $8,000. But communal living ruled out individual or family ownership and the Hutterites were thus unable to take advantage of the act. Besides, they needed large acreages, pastures, and woodlands, preferably near streams. The Mennonites also wanted large reserves of land for organizing village life as they had done in the Ukraine.[4] In 1873 and 1874 there was an active campaign in Congress to permit the establishment of large compact communities on public lands.[5] But the petition failed after lengthy debate, and the Mennonites chose to form reserves in Manitoba, between Winnipeg and the United States boundary.

The Hutterites found a desirable site on the Missouri River west of Yankton in Bon Homme County. Walter A. Burleigh, a former agent for the Indians in the Yankton area, owned a large ranch which he had used for pasture; he sold 2,500 acres of this land to the Hutterites for the extortionate price of $25,000. On August 24, 1874, the Schmiedeleut paid $17,000 down and agreed to pay the balance in yearly terms.[6] The Dariusleut, temporarily settled near Silver Lake on government lands, bought a permanent site in 1875 at Wolf Creek, forty miles north of Bon Homme. The Lehrerleut organized their founding colony (Elm-spring) in 1877 near Parkston, a few miles west of the Wolf Creek colony.

From the original location in Bon Homme County beside the Missouri River, the Hutterite colonies expanded northward along the James River. Located near them (in Hutchinson, Hanson, and Turner counties) were three other German-speaking groups; in the northern part of this German settlement were the low Germans. South of them were the Swiss who had immigrated from the Province of Volhynia in Russian Poland.[7] To the west of these two groups were the noncolony Hutterites, whose language, religion, and ancestry were identical to the colony Hutterites. Each of these regional settlements had its own dialect and distinctive family names.

The noncolony people (or Prairieleut, as the colony people called them) were homesteaders. All of them settled in Dakota near the three original Hutterite colonies. During the pioneering years there were many interchanges; some marriages took place between colony

---

4. See Frank Epp, *The Mennonite Exodus* (Altona, Man.: D. W. Friesen and Sons, 1962), for a thorough review of this migration.

5. Smith, *The Coming of the Russian Mennonites*, pp. 77–91.

6. Norman Thomas, "The Hutterian Brethren," *South Dakota Historical Collections and Report* 25(1950): 272.

7. J. J. Mendel, *History of the People of East Freeman, Silver Lake, and West Freeman . . .* (Freeman, S. Dak.: By the author, 1961), pp. 8–13.

and noncolony groups, and there were some who joined and others who left the colonies.[8] But the lines between colony and noncolony people were soon drawn, and they began to grow apart. The homesteading Hutterites affiliated themselves with Mennonite conference bodies and adopted Protestant forms of organization. Their congregations joined the Krimmer Mennonite Conference (later Mennonite Brethren) and the General Conference Mennonites. Today in South Dakota, typical Hutterite family names are common among the farming population. David Wipf served as secretary of state for South Dakota from 1905 to 1909, and persons with the name of Mendel, Kleinsasser, and Waltner have served in the state legislature.

The early years, from 1874 until about 1917 (with the outbreak of World War I), were difficult pioneering years. Hutterites attracted little attention. These years were devoted to dealing with the basic matters of subsistence and colony organization. The letters between the colonies during this era were concerned with organization and unity. The colonists experienced the whole gamut of pioneering hardships. There were crop failures, prairie fires, grasshoppers, locust ravages, Dakota blizzards, spring floods, and transportation problems.[9] The James River area, on which are located most of the colonies, was part of the Great Plains area in the geological region known as Young Drift Plains. The land is flat except for river valleys, moraines, and occasional heaps of earth and stone. There is a wide differential in temperature between summer and winter, and although the loamy, nearly black soils are fertile, the rainfall (including melted snow) is still relatively low—from 17 to 24 inches annually.

After four years, Bon Homme colony organized a second location, the Tripp colony, which made a historically interesting contact with other communal societies. Facing financial problems, the new colony was able to borrow some money from the Amana Society in Iowa. But this was apparently insufficient, for at about this time contacts were established with the Rappites (Harmony Society) in western Pennsylvania. Visits were exchanged. The Rappites, a German communistic group founded by John George Rapp in 1804, were by this time extremely wealthy, but they were suffering from the problems caused by aging and celibacy. They therefore negotiated an agreement with the Waldner group in South Dakota whereby the entire group was to settle on grounds owned by the Rappites. The Tripp colony, numbering nine-

---

8. Zieglschmid, *Das Klein-Geschichtsbuch*, pp. 466–67, 489. Scarcely more than ten noncolony families joined the colonies before 1895 and parts of seven families left the colonies before 1918.

9. *M.E.*, s.v. "South Dakota." Harold E. Briggs, "Grasshopper Plagues and Early Dakota Agriculture, 1864–1876," *Agricultural History* 8(April 1934): 55–60.

teen families, sold its land and arrived at Tidioute, Pennsylvania, on May 1, 1884. Three families had preceded them in 1883, one of whose members was Elder Michael Waldner.

By Hutterite standards, the terrain and wooded area (located four miles south of the city of Tidioute in Warren County) was too difficult to convert into suitable farmland. But the Rappites had shown genuine interest in the Hutterites. In 1875, the year after the Hutterites arrived in South Dakota, the Rappites had loaned them $3,000 for the construction of a flour mill and had made additional funds available. The head of the society, Jacob Henrici (George Rapp had died in 1847), was favorably impressed with the hearty appearance, simplicity, and dedication of the Hutterites. Except for their rejection of celibacy, the Hutterites were considered to be fellow believers. Opinions and advice were interchanged. To the Hutterites' objection to musical instruments, the Rappites answered: "Our voices are too weak to hold singing in the right harmonious tune, [so] we use instruments to support us."[10]

The Rappites received many excellent offers for their lands, which contained rich oil deposits, but they consistently refused to sell. Karl J. Arndt, an authority on the Harmony Society, believes that the Harmonists wanted to make the Hutterites their heirs. Finding the Pennsylvania location unsuitable for making a living, the whole group of Hutterites returned to South Dakota on July 2, 1886. Michael Waldner died three years later, on October 13, 1889, at the age of fifty-six. The Pennsylvania venture was a move Hutterites today regard as economically unsuccessful.

In letters from Pennsylvania to his community at Bon Homme, Waldner had given much practical advice about unity and organization and taking care of the young livestock. He also reported several dreams. "One of our sisters here had a dream," he writes. "She saw three wells. One belonged to us, one to Darius [Walter] and one to Jacob Wipf of the Lehrerleut. When they tried to draw water from the well, the water started to flow together."[11] To Michael Waldner, who had worked hard in the revitalization of communal living, the dream was prophetic— there was to be unity among the three Hutterite groups. He says of the dream, "I was very glad about this, for I saw in this a true union. I pray that God in Heaven will let me have this sweet joy." Although the three founding colonies developed into distinct "people" (*Leut*), each having its own discipline, senior elder, periodic preacher assembly, and means of settling disputes, they are remarkably uniform in their patterns of communal living. The three groups share a common body of

10. Karl J. Arndt, "The Harmonists and the Hutterites," *American-German Review* 10 (August 1944): 26.
11. Colony documents, Riverside Colony, Arden, Man.

doctrine, language, and social patterns, but there are very few formal relationships between them. They formed a single corporation in 1905, making the Hutterische Bruder-Gemeinde invulnerable to any legal attack by dissatisfied members.[12]

The resources in South Dakota closely resembled those in the Ukraine. There was one significant change, however. Craft production for the market was significantly reduced, although the Hutterites still made many of their own tools and household articles. They responded to the growing specialization of modern agriculture and gave correspondingly less time to small industry and home manufacture. At Bon Homme the colony buildings were constructed of yellow chalkstone found along the Missouri River. (See figure 20.) From this material they built sturdy houses, barns, shops, granaries, ovens, a communal kitchen and dining room, a schoolhouse, and a steam-powered flour mill two and one-half stories high. The best machinery available was secured. The dwelling houses were two stories high, with wall furnaces in which hay, dung, and wood were burned as fuel. The productive enterprises included seeding and farming, and on every colony there were sheep,

12. Zieglschmid, *Das Klein-Geschichtsbuch*, pp. 613–18.

Figure 20. Original chalk stone Hutterite dwelling, Bon Homme Colony, South Dakota.

cattle, and hogs.[13] By 1897 there were five water-powered flour mills, and the colonists engaged in spinning, weaving, carpentry, shoemaking, tanning, blacksmithing, and bookbinding. The colonies were distinguished by their flocks of geese and ducks, their pigeons, icehouses, and tall flour mills. Waterfowl were an indispensable source of feathers for bedding and meat for the table. Pigeons were grown for the squab market in Chicago. Broom-making was a winter occupation, and many brooms were sold to nearby merchants.

Wolf Creek was a prosperous colony in 1899, with 400 head of cattle, 21 teams of horses, 2,300 sheep, 200 hogs, 700 geese, and 200 ducks. The colony had 27 families, with a total population of 160 people. A sorghum mill manufactured 40 barrels of sorghum yearly. The colonists made their own harness, boots, shoes, and clothing. Visitors to the colonies were impressed by the modern equipment in the shops, by the use of gasoline engines to power cream separators and churns, and by the flowing water piped from artesian wells. By 1912 the colonists were plowing with large tractors, and they had not only steam boilers and water wheels that operated the flour mill but also a dynamo that provided electric lights and power.

The grist and flour mills of the colonies were patronized widely by their South Dakota neighbors. Farmers made long journeys to obtain flour and cornmeal which the Hutterite mills produced. Some mills along the James River were in operation until recent years.

Colony records for the early period in the United States have not been systematized, for until about 1951 scholars paid little attention to the Hutterites. Periods of crisis invariably produced a flow of documents. From their original settlement until World War I, however, there is no record of any serious conflict between the Hutterites and their neighbors. Most colonies were isolated from the principal roads, and the main buildings then as now are typically hidden in ravines or a valley, usually near a river or lake. The dam at Jamesville, which was a source of water power for the mill, brought protests from neighboring farmers when damage was done to their crops. Several times the dam was torn out, and once the mill was burned; finally, the colony installed a gas engine to replace water power.

The Hutterites remained extremely sensitive to the involvement of their host country in foreign wars. When the Spanish-American War broke out in 1898, the Dariusleut established a colony near Dominion City in Manitoba with the intention, in the event that military conscription became an issue, to move to Canada. The Canadian authorities visited the Hutterite colonies in South Dakota and were favorably im-

13. Ibid., p. 468.

pressed with their farms. The privileges granted to Mennonites were extended to the Hutterites by an order-in-council in 1899.[14] The Canadians were eager to have all the colonies move to Canada. But there was no conscription in the United States, and the Hutterites found the Canadian lands to be poor and subject to flooding. The colony returned to South Dakota in 1905.

There were nineteen Hutterite colonies in 1917, when the United States became involved in World War I. Seventeen were in South Dakota and two were in Montana. The Hutterite population was nearly two thousand.[15] The growth pattern of the colonies in 1918 shows a major disturbance, with sixteen new colonies being formed in Canada. The South Dakota Hutterites were now confronted with a fervid, irrational, nationalist-patriotic spirit leaving in its wake the most flagrant violations of civil rights in American history.[16]

The Dispersion during World War I

In the early years of the Dakota settlement there was plenty of land, and state authorities had been eager to get settlers to farm it. The Hutterites, generally thought of as a special group of Mennonites, were largely ignored except by the occasional visitor who wanted to see colony life. The colonies had become rather prosperous, but they were generally isolated from the towns and villages of the area. When the United States entered the war, the attitude of the public quickly shifted from indifference to hostile intolerance. Suddenly a people were discovered who spoke German, who refused to lend money to a benevolent government, and who withheld their young men from military service.

The Selective Service Act, passed by Congress on May 18, 1917, presented the colony leaders with their first important confrontation with the United States government.[17] Men between the ages of twenty-one and thirty-one were now liable for military service. There were no provisions for conscientious objectors except for noncombatants within the military; this meant that even men who claimed conscientious objector status would have to become members of the armed forces and wear the uniform. Long before the first men were drafted, the colony leaders agreed among themselves that their men could register and report for their physical examinations, but having arrived at the induc-

14. Ibid.; for the Mennonite privileges and the order-in-council, see pp. 628–30.
15. Ibid., p. 471.
16. Paul K. Conkin, *Two Paths to Utopia: The Hutterites and the Llano Colony* (Lincoln: University of Nebraska Press, 1964), p. 55.
17. The author is indebted to John D. Unruh, "The Hutterites during World War I," *Mennonite Life* 24(July 1969): 130–37, for an excellent summary of the subject.

tion center, they should cooperate no further. They would not wear the army uniform, nor would they obey orders to work, for aiding the military effort in any way violated their principles. The officers were determined to pressure the men into military service by any means in their power, psychological or physical. By means of argument or casual observations, they tried to detect inconsistencies in the Hutterite position. The Hutterite youth were regarded as stubborn and obstinate; in all likelihood, they were less able to express their beliefs tactfully than were those objecting to the war on political grounds.

At Camp Funston some of the men were brutally handled in the guardhouse. They were bayonetted, beaten, and tortured by various forms of water "cure." Jakob S. Waldner, who retains an extensive diary of his experiences in the camp, was thrown fully clothed into a cold shower for twenty minutes for refusing a work order.[18] After such cold showers, the men were often thrown out of a window and dragged along the ground by their hair and feet by soldiers who were waiting outside. Their beards were disfigured to make them appear ridiculous. One night, eighteen men were aroused from their sleep and held under cold showers until one of them became hysterical. Others were hung by their feet above tanks of water until they almost choked to death. On many days they were made to stand at attention on the cold side of their barracks, in scant clothing, while those who passed by scoffed at them in abusive and foul language. They were chased across the fields by guards on motorcycles under the guise of taking exercise, until they dropped from sheer exhaustion. In the guardhouse they were usually put on a diet of bread and water. Such experiences were common to all sincere conscientious objectors, including Mennonites and those of other religious faiths.[19]

Typical of the Hutterite objection to performing work in the army camp is the following statement by Jakob Waldner: "I am against being persuaded to take part in any of the military services that President Wilson has outlined as noncombatant service. The reason for this is because I am a member of the Hutterian Brethren Church whose creed forbids taking part in any form of military service."[20] Other objectors

18. From an unpublished colony document of 231 pages in German script, translated into English by Ilse Reist (hereafter cited as Jakob S. Waldner, diary). The treasured diary contains not only eyewitness accounts but dreams and several songs composed at the army camp. Parts of the diary were recently published; see Jakob Waldner, "Diary of a Conscientious Objector in World War I," ed. Theron Schlabach, trans. Ilse Reist and Elizabeth Bender, M.Q.R. 48(January 1974): 73–111.

19. Of 554 "Mennonite" conscientious objectors, it is estimated that about 50 were Hutterites. See Smith, The Coming of the Russian Mennonites, p. 274. For a general treatment of conscientious objectors, see Peter Brock, Twentieth-Century Pacifism (New York: Van Nostrand Reinhold Co., 1970).

20. Jakob S. Waldner, diary.

who accepted work orders (menial tasks around the camp) received more considerate treatment than did Hutterites. The Hutterites felt that the Mennonites had compromised too much. When asked why Hutterites did not bend just a little, Paul Kleinsasser said, "Our whole case would be broken down."[21]

Paul Kleinsasser, along with three other Hutterites who arrived at Camp Funston after conscientious objectors were being assigned to farm work, received no less harassment. They were denied the privilege of eating in the mess hall and instead were given daily rations of bread, some raw beans, raw bacon, and coffee and directed to a ravine about a quarter of a mile from the mess hall. They were given no utensils except two pails in which to cook the raw food, and they had to improvise cooking facilities by using empty cans from the dumping grounds. This was done from September until mid-November. They were then put in the guardhouse for disobeying an order to build a sidewalk out of stones leading from their tent to the mess hall. They were courtmartialed and sentenced to the disciplinary barracks at Leavenworth for five years.

The Hutterite men resented the frequent physical examinations requiring them to appear nude for inspections for venereal disease. They were unhappy when their books, mostly German devotional books, were taken from them. At Fort Dodge they were forced to witness the hanging of three Negro men who had been charged with attacking a white girl. Waldner observed that there were many more Negroes than whites at the scene and that all the whites had firearms while all the Negroes were unarmed.

The Hutterites had sent a delegation of their ministers to Washington in August 1917 to present their concerns to President Wilson.[22] They were given an audience by Secretary of War Baker, who simply advised them to let the men go to the respective training camps and do what their consciences would allow them to do. Until near the close of the war no provision whatsoever was made for service outside the military jurisdiction; Americans were as yet totally unprepared to comprehend sincere conscientious objection to war and consequently all conscientious objectors were dismissed as cowards. The Hutterites staunchly endured ridicule, persecution, and malicious harassment; all of which simply strengthened their historic faith. But then a major incident occurred that finally convinced them to migrate to Canada.

---

21. John D. Unruh, "The Hutterites during World War I," p. 134.
22. Zieglschmid, *Das Klein-Geschichtsbuch*, pp. 478–80. In the petition, the Hutterites identify themselves as "We, the Hutterian Brethren Church, also known as Bruderhof or Communistic Mennonites, comprising about 2,000 souls, who are living in eighteen communities in South Dakota and Montana. . . ." The petition was signed by David Hofer, Elias Walter, and Joseph Kleinsasser.

Four Hutterites—Jacob Wipf and three Hofer brothers, Joseph, David, and Michael—were summoned to Fort Lewis, Washington.[23] As was customary, they refused to sign admission papers, put on army uniforms, or take up any kind of duty. After two months in the guard house, the four young men were sentenced to thirty-seven years in prison. They were taken to the notorious military prison on Alcatraz, attended by four armed lieutenants who kept them handcuffed during the day and chained by the ankles to each other at night. At Alcatraz they again refused to put on military uniforms. They were then taken to a "dungeon" of darkness, filth, and stench and put in solitary confinement out of earshot of each other. The guard placed a uniform in each cell and said, "There you will stay until you give up the ghost—just like the last four that we carried out yesterday."[24]

For several days the young men slept on the cold, wet concrete floor wearing nothing but their light underwear. They received half a glass of water every twenty-four hours but no food. They were beaten with clubs and, with arms crossed, tied to the ceiling. After five days they were taken from the "hole" for a short time. Their wrists were so swollen from insect bites and skin eruptions that they could not put on their own jackets. For the remaining months at Alcatraz, they were allowed one hour of outdoor exercise each Sunday afternoon.

After four months at Alcatraz the men were transferred to Fort Leavenworth, Kansas, by six armed sergeants. They arrived at their destination at 11 P.M., after four days and five nights of travel, chained together two by two. From the railway station to the military prison they were marched on foot through the streets and prodded with bayonets. Although they were handcuffed, they managed to carry their satchels in one hand and their Bibles in the other. On arrival at the prison, soaked with sweat, they were compelled to remove their outer clothing. Two hours later, when they received their prison clothing, they were chilled to the bone. In the early morning hours they stood outside and waited in the cold. Joseph and Michael Hofer collapsed and were taken to the hospital. Jacob Wipf and David Hofer were sent to solitary confinement and placed on a starvation diet. They were made to stand nine hours each day with hands tied and their feet barely touching the floor.

When Joseph and Michael became ill and were hospitalized, Wipf managed to send a telegram to their wives, who, accompanied by a male attendant, boarded the earliest train. The station agent insisted that

23. The much publicized account is recorded in ibid., pp. 477–89, and C. H. Smith, *The Coming of the Russian Mennonites*, pp. 272–93. Three of the men were married when they reported at the camp. Jacob Wipf, aged seventy-eight in 1965, stated in correspondence with the author that all four men were members of the Rockport Colony.
24. Smith, *The Coming of the Russian Mennonites*, p. 278.

the telegram had come from Fort Riley rather than from Fort Leavenworth and issued tickets to the wrong destination. After losing a day, the
women arrived at midnight to find their husbands nearly dead. When
they returned in the morning, Joseph was dead. The guards refused his
wife, Maria, permission to see the dead body. In tears, she pleaded
with the colonel and was finally taken to the casket only to find that her
husband's body had been dressed in the military uniform he had so
adamantly refused to wear. Michael Hofer died two days later. The
wives and a few other relatives accompanied the bodies to their home
community, where their enormous funeral seared Hutterite minds with
the price of true apostolic faith.

This was without question the experience that motivated the
migration to Canada, but there were other unendurable incidents that
contributed to the decision. While the men in camp were undergoing
this treatment, the colonies at home were suffering severe trials as well.
Newspapers were hostile to all German-speaking people, and they
spared no pity in ferreting out the unpatriotic, the cowards, the pro-
Germans, and the "Kaiser supporters." They condemned the Hutterites
for lack of patriotism and for profiting from high wartime prices. All
were harassed to buy Liberty Bonds, while Mennonite churches,
German-speaking or not, were painted yellow, and young men were
forced to kiss the American flag. The State Council for Defense, a
voluntary, semiofficial but dictatorial group, forbade the use of the
German language anywhere in public, in schools and also in churches.
Yankton high school students were highly praised when they threw all
their German textbooks into the Missouri River as they sang the Star-
Spangled Banner.[25]

Although willing to contribute money for the relief of war suffering, the Hutterites refused to buy Liberty Bonds. Most also refused
to contribute to the Red Cross. When a local bond committee assigned
the Hutterites a quota, and they refused to buy any bonds, a group of
patriotic enthusiasts visited the Jamesville colony and without opposition drove away a hundred steers and a thousand sheep. These were
shipped to the livestock market, the proceeds to be invested in war
bonds. The packing houses, however, refused to take the stolen cattle,
and they had to be sold at auction in Yankton for about half their value,
or $14,000.[26] In June of 1918 someone stole eighty-two gallons of wine

25. Conkin, *Two Paths to Utopia*, p. 59.
26. The War Loan Committee refused the funds, and the Dakota National Bank
in Yankton apparently held them in trust. The *Sioux Falls Press* (May 10, 1918) condoned
the work of the raiders: "If the Mennonites do not like the idea let them pack up what they
can carry away and return to that part of Europe whence they came. We should ask them
to be so good as to leave behind the land this nation practically gave them." At a later

from the Jamesville colony. Although the thief was found, no charges were brought against him. Local officials then raided the Bon Homme colony, confiscating the colony's wine under the Prohibition Act. The confiscated wine was distributed at the county seat in an Armistice Day Parade.

The Hutterites took immediate action to migrate to Canada. Ottawa officials assured the Hutterites that the exemptions granted them in 1899 were still valid.[27] The colonies bought land in both Alberta and Manitoba. Some formed branch colonies while others sold their South Dakota lands at sacrificial prices. Fifteen colonies were founded in Canada in 1918: six by the Schmiedeleut in Manitoba, and five by the Dariusleut and four by the Lehrerleut in Alberta. By 1920, eleven of the fifteen colonies had sold their South Dakota lands. The South Dakota State Council for Defense insisted that 5 percent of the sale price of the land be invested in war bonds and 5 percent be given to the Red Cross. The Hutterites simply lowered their price by the required amount but left the responsibility for purchasing bonds with the buyers. Not satisfied with this and hoping to completely destroy the communal system, the State Council for Defense persuaded the state attorney general to use legal action to revoke the 1905 articles of incorporation. The state argued that the Hutterite corporation, instead of serving religious purposes as called for in the charter, was really used for economic gain and that the Hutterites had amassed a fortune without dedicating any of it to the worship of God. Hutterites, they pointed out, did not even have a church building![28] They were further described as a menace to society, depriving children of the right to attend county fairs and mingle with the outside world and punishing members who contributed to the war effort. Although the lengthy legal proceedings finally resulted in the technical annulment of the Hutterite corporation, the Hutterites were allowed to hold their property as an unincorporated organization. The court did not demand receivership or the liquidation of Hutterite assets asked for by the State Council for Defense.

Only Bon Homme colony remained populated in South Dakota. Some colony sites were vacant for twenty or more years. Windows were broken in the substantial stone buildings and weeds grew over the roads and paths. They were "ghostly blots" on the landscape.[29]

---

date a land agent persuaded the Jamesville colony to use the funds as partial payment on Canadian lands. A photograph of local officials with sheep forcibly taken from the colonies is shown in Robert F. Karolevitz, *Yankton: A Pioneer Past* (Aberdeen, S. Dak.: North Plains Press, 1972), p. 156.

27. Zieglschmid, *Das Klein-Geschichtsbuch*, p. 632.

28. Conkin, *Two Paths to Utopia*, p. 62.

29. Nanna Goodhope, "Must the Hutterites Flee Again?" *Christian Century* 57(November 12, 1940): 1415.

After 1920 pacifism was no longer an issue. The farm population was now confronted with severe economic hardships, and county governments were concerned with farm foreclosures and shrunken tax revenues. During the great depression years some of the Manitoba colonies began to move back to South Dakota. To date all but three of the sites have been repossessed. The Lehrerleut and Dariusleut colonies which still owned land in South Dakota sold out to the Schmiedeleut. Today, all colonies in South Dakota and Manitoba are Schmiedeleut colonies.

To prevent the farm population from deserting the area, South Dakota passed a communals act in 1935 which granted the same tax privileges to communally owned farms as were granted to cooperatives. Hutterites were eligible to return to the state. They paid local taxes but were exempt from state and federal corporate taxes. Under the act each colony acquired a separate charter, and as in the 1905 incorporation, the colonies were protected from the claims of individual members. This inducement, combined with the threat of restrictive legislation in Manitoba in 1944, was effective in attracting the Hutterites to South Dakota, for at least fifteen colonies were chartered in South Dakota under the act. However, after a period of expansion, South Dakota in 1955 ceased to grant corporate privileges to the colonies. Existing colonies were prevented from purchasing or leasing additional lands, but there has been no restriction on the formation of new colonies.

The fifteen colonies which settled in Canada in 1918 located in grain-growing, dry-land farming areas resembling those in South Dakota and the Ukraine. The four Lehrerleut colonies in Alberta were given the same names as their South Dakota counterparts—Old Elmspring, New Elmspring, Rockport, and Milford. The Dariusleut gave entirely new names to their five Alberta colonies, choosing local names—Standoff, Raley, East Cardston, Rosebud, and Springvale. The six Schmiedeleut colonies in Manitoba were named after their South Dakota predecessors —Bon Homme, Jamesville, Maxwell, Milltown, Huron, and Rosedale.

The Manitoba colonies experienced productive crop yields during the first harvest season. The seven colonies in southern Alberta had a complete crop failure the first year. Two of the colonies (and a third, Stahlville, in 1919) situated farther north near Rockyford, which had good crops, assisted the southern colonies during the first year. Instead of building with stone as the colonies had done in South Dakota, most now used wood with stone and cement foundations. The Canadian prairies were suitable to Hutterite methods of large-scale agriculture. They expanded regularly so that by 1940 there were fifty-two colonies.

During World War II the Hutterites again were conscientious objectors. Attitudes toward conscientious objectors were less hostile than previously, and the government had made more adequate provisions for religious objectors. Instead of sending them to army camps, the United States permitted them to be assigned to work of national importance under civilian direction, a program called Civilian Public Service. Hutterites contributed to the cost of operating the church camps. Altogether in the United States and Canada, there were 276 Hutterite objectors serving in some type of public service work.[30] Twenty-six joined the armed forces of the two countries.

In Canada the camps for conscientious objectors were administered by the Department of Mines and Resources and were very isolated, often lacking adequate health facilities. Each draftee in Canada was paid fifty cents per day and was required to contribute a monthly stipend to the Canadian Red Cross. Many members of the Canadian colonies objected to this solution for conscientious objectors. Some preferred jail rather than alternative service. There was little overt discrimination against German-speaking populations, and no migrations resulting from harrassment as in 1918.

Land Restrictions

An awareness of continued Hutterite growth combined with the covert hostility toward the colonies during and after World War II led to legislative restrictions on the purchase of land. The Hutterites were willing and able to pay higher prices than most farmers; this provoked charges of unfair competition and the fear of land monopoly.

Alberta passed the Land Sales Prohibition Act in 1942 preventing the sale of land to "enemy aliens, Hutterites, and Doukhobours."[31] The Honorable Solon Low, who introduced the act, argued that the legislation was designed to allay public feelings which had been aroused to the point of threatened violence. The act was to expire one year after the war. By its provisions the Hutterites could neither buy nor lease any additional lands. The act was amended in 1947 to exclude only enemy aliens; Hutterites were permitted to buy up to 6,400 acres if the site was 40

30. Melvin Gingerich, *Service for Peace* (Akron, Pa.: Mennonite Central Committee, 1949), pp. 415-21.

31. Solon Low was a Mormon from southern Alberta. Hutterites pointed out that Mormons owned even larger contiguous acreages of land in the province than did Hutterites.

Sources and discussions on the legal restrictions appear in Zieglschmid, *Das Klein-Geschichtsbuch*, pp. 638-53; Douglas E. Sanders, "The Hutterites: A Case Study in Minority Rights," *The Canadian Bar Review* 42(May 1964): 225-42; Dorothy Griffen, "The Hutterites and Civil Liberties," *Canadian Forum* 27(1947): 125-29; *Report of the Hutterite Investigating Committee*, Province of Alberta, Edmonton, September, 1959, and *Report on Communal Property, 1972*, by the Select Committee of the Assembly, Province of Alberta, Edmonton.

miles from an existing colony. The reference to Doukhobours was no longer relevant since no such colonies existed in Alberta.

The Alberta law was amended again in 1960, eliminating the 40-mile clause and prohibiting land sales to Hutterite colonies without hearings before a communal property control board and approval by the legislative cabinet. The board was to recommend in each instance whether or not it was in the public interest to permit the sale of land. Though some new colonies were recommended by the communal property board and approved by the province, the Hutterites began to form new colonies instead in Montana (in 1948) and Saskatchewan (in 1952). Finally, in 1972 the Communal Property Act was repealed when the Conservative government succeeded the Social Credit Party. The new government issued a comprehensive *Report on Communal Property, 1972* that dealt with economic aspects of communal land use and the relations between the colonies and Alberta communities.[32] The government of Alberta formed a liaison office to deal with information and public relations aspects of Hutterite land purchases. The Dariusleut and Lehrerleut were each asked to appoint three members to the liaison office, through which land acquisitions were to be channeled.

When the Alberta colonies branched into Saskatchewan, there was immediate local opposition. In response to the agitation, the provincial government conducted a survey to explore the nature and extent of the problem and concluded that the colonies presented no threat and that future clashes could be alleviated by disseminating proper information.[33] A Provincial Committee on Minority Groups established a liaison officer to assist in a Hutterite settlement program which would free communities from the fear of being overrun by the colonies.

In Manitoba a similar attempt was made to introduce restrictive legislation, but a legislative committee urged that no restrictions be placed on "the fundamental right" to purchase land.[34] Accordingly, all attempts to enact such laws in Manitoba have failed, but in 1954 the Union of Manitoba Municipalities demanded restrictions on the acreage

32. *Report on Communal Property, 1972.*

33. The survey was entitled *The Hutterites and Saskatchewan: A Study of Intergroup Relations* (Regina, Sask.: Canadian Mental Health Association, 1953). See also Vernon Serl, "Final Report: The Hutterite Program," Provincial Committee on Minority Relations, Regina, Saskatchewan, 1959, and by the same author, "Stability and Change in Hutterite Society," (Ph.D. dissertation, University of Oregon, 1964). Intergroup relations and Hutterite settlement form a significant aspect of John Bennett's penetrating analysis of Hutterite agricultural economy and strategy in *Hutterite Brethren: The Agricultural Economy and Social Organization of a Communal People* (Stanford, Calif.: Stanford University Press, 1967) and *Northern Plainsmen: Adaptive Strategy and Agrarian Life* (Chicago: Aldine Publishing Co., 1969).

34. Relations with the Manitoba government are given extensive treatment by Victor Peters, *All Things Common: The Hutterian Way of Life* (Minneapolis: University of Minnesota Press, 1965), pp. 51-71.

and location of colonies. In 1957 this culminated in an informal agreement in which the Hutterites consented to locate no more than two colonies in large municipalities and one colony in small ones, to limit new colony acreage to 5,120 acres, and to keep colonies at least ten miles apart.[35] The threat of restrictive legislation affected the land-buying pattern of the colonies in some instances long before any formal agreements were reached. Some colonies in Manitoba responded to the threat by establishing daughter colonies in South Dakota. Attempts to enact restrictive legislation in Montana and Minnesota have failed.

The consequence of Canadian land restrictions on the colonies has been a dispersion of their settlements into wider geographic areas. To facilitate their representation to the government, the three Leut formed a single legal entity. With the aid of legal advisers, a charter was granted to the Hutterite colonies of Canada by the Canadian Parliament in 1951. Each Leut is defined as a church conference and elects three members to a nine-member board of directors of the Hutterian Brethren Church. The board elects a chairman, or senior elder, and meets annually, usually with a legal representative. The formal organization allows more unified representation to government, encourages discussion and anticipation of problems among the colonies, and facilitates greater consensus among the Leut. The Canadian charter specifies that property rights belong to the individual colonies and that disciplinary functions are the prerogative of each Leut. The charter protects the colonies against individual members who might desert the colony and make a claim on the corporate property.

The belief that Hutterites would purchase unlimited acres of land to add to their present holdings if they could or that they would exercise no voluntary restraints on either the location or pattern of settlement is unfounded. That they will eventually outnumber the rural farm population, a fear expressed by some farm organizations, has no empirical basis. The eighty-five colonies in Alberta own or lease an average of 8,792 acres per colony, or about 1 percent of the agricultural lands in the province.[36] The ratio of land to persons in Hutterite colonies is 58 acres per person. Among non-Hutterite farm families in the same counties, the ratio is 122 acres per person.[37] The farm population displaced by new colonies is usually minimal.

35. In 1971 the Hutterites purchased the land and buildings of a former airbase owned by the government. Since Premier Schreyer's government sold the land over the objection of the Union of Manitoba Municipalities, the Hutterites now consider the "gentlemen's agreement" with the union to be null and void.

36. *Report on Communal Property, 1972*, p. 17.

37. P. G. Davies, "Submission to the Agricultural Committee of the Legislature of the Province of Alberta on behalf of the Hutterite Colonies," (mimeographed), March 29, 1960.

The steady growth of the Hutterite population and the difficulty of acquiring land forced the colonies to develop submarginal lands and northern frontier areas in Alberta. This is true for all of the states and provinces where they live. Such lands are made productive by highly efficient agricultural methods. When the number of persons to be supported on the land is relatively large, new methods of agricultural production become necessary. The Hutterites have been very successful in the development of an agricultural economy that is well suited to the natural environment of the great plains.

part two

CONTEMPORARY SOCIAL AND CULTURAL ORGANIZATION

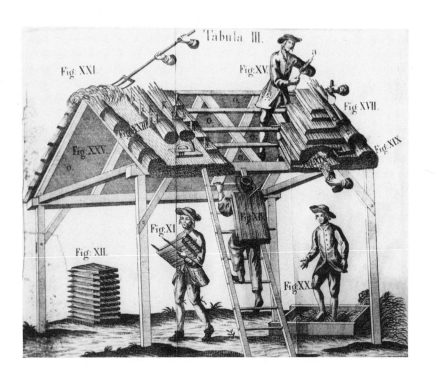

chapter six

World View
and Language

Beliefs and culture patterns which come to govern the life of a people differ from one society to another. The distinctive approach to life, that which colors the entire view of existence in a given society, is known as *Weltanschauung*, or "world view." Explanations of life and its meaning in a society are relevant and satisfying to persons who have absorbed the world view of their society. To outsiders, the same explanations seem strange and unnatural. In this chapter we present, by quotation and paraphrase, the world view of the Hutterites gleaned from the original sources.

The Hutterites derive their beliefs from the Hebrew-Christian Bible and from the Apocrypha. Many of their professed beliefs are similar to those of other Christian groups; yet the Hutterites differ sharply in their application of these beliefs, or charter.[1] Although there are

1. The concept of "charter" has been found useful for understanding the relation of belief to practice. See Bronislaw Malinowski, *A Scientific Theory of Culture and Other Essays* (Chapel Hill: University of North Carolina Press, 1944), pp. 48–52. Malinowski defined an institution as "an organized system of purposeful activities" and the charter of an institution as "the recognized purpose of the group" or "the system of values for the pursuit of which human beings organize. . . . " Although the Hutterite charter embodies codified conceptions of reality (world view), it also provides guidelines for carrying out beliefs in life situations. This chapter is a statement of the Hutterite view of reality and, to

discrepancies between belief and practice in all societies, beliefs play an important function in directing the behavior of a society. This is particularly true of the Hutterites, who engage in extensive indoctrination. Without a thorough understanding of the religious motives, we would be ill-prepared to appreciate the Hutterites' commitment to communal living and their genius for survival.

World View

The central Christian doctrine as understood by Hutterites is remarkably well summarized in a sketch drawn by an imprisoned Anabaptist, Leonard Schiemer, in the year 1527 (see chart 1).[2] Schiemer made a sincere attempt to explain his faith to others, including his interrogators. According to this diagram, human beings were created by "the Will of God" and were placed in the Garden of Eden. They disobeyed God and fell away from His will and, by acquiring the disobedient nature of "Adam," became helplessly "carnal." In order to be restored to God, a person must have an intermediator, Christ the Savior. The explanation thus far is common to the major Christian faiths. The difference for Hutterites is that a person is not saved by his professed faith or right beliefs alone but by living in a proper social relationship in a Christian community. Communal living, in their view, is essential to the process of salvation.

Additional perspective on the Hutterite world view can be gained from a detailed study of their historical documents. (See figure 21.) Their preserved writings, most of them in manuscripts, reveal their beliefs about the origin of the universe, the nature of the deity and of human beings, the proper relation of the sexes, the uses of property, the concept of community, and the proper worship of God. Summarized below from the original sources are some of the distinctive ways in which the Hutterites view themselves and the world around them.[3]

a large extent, Hutterite ideals. I am indebted to anthropologist Laura Thompson for assistance in the analysis of the Hutterite charter.

2. From a manuscript in *Epistel Buech* of 1566 (folio 240), discussed in Robert Friedmann, *Hutterite Studies* (Goshen, Ind.: Mennonite Historical Society, 1961), pp. 286–98.

3. The principal source for this analysis is Rideman, *Account of Our Religion*. The short quotations on pp. 141–48 are from Rideman unless otherwise indicated. Other sources used were Peter Walpot's "Great Article Book" of 1577, in Robert Friedmann, "A Notable Hutterite Document: Concerning True Surrender and Christian Community of Goods," *M.Q.R.* 31 (January 1957): 22–62. For a discussion of the methods of analysis, see Laura Thompson and John A. Hostetler, "The Hutterian Confession of Faith: A Documentary Analysis," *The Alberta Journal of Educational Research* 16 (March 1970): 29–45. Anthropological works helpful to the study were Ethel M. Albert, "The Classification of Values: A Method and Illustration," *American Anthropologist* 58 (1956), and Ethel M. Albert and Clyde Kluckhohn, *A Selected Bibliography on Values, Ethics, and Esthetics in the Behavioral Sciences and Philosophy, 1920–1958* (Glencoe, Ill.: Free Press, 1959).

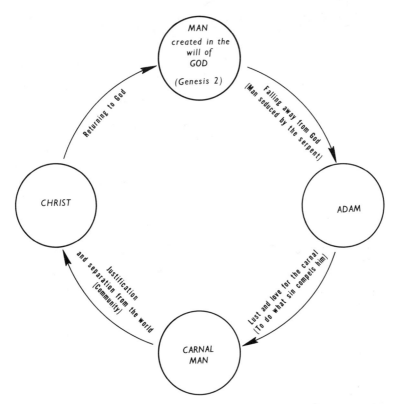

Chart 1. Epitome of Anabaptist Doctrine (Leonard Schiemer, 1527, in Prison at Rattenburg-on-the-Inn, Tyrol; from a Manuscript of 1566)

The universe, nature, and supernature. Hutterites believe that absolute authority resides in a single omnipotent God who created the universe and placed everything in a divine order and proper hierarchy. All events are ordered by God and nothing happens without the knowledge of God.

All that is of God is considered to be spiritual, unchanging, and eternal, while all that is classed as material, or created, is conceived as transitory, changing, and temporal. A dichotomy between spiritual and material phenomena is characteristic of the universe and underlies a fundamental dualism in Hutterite thinking.

The universe is conceived spatially as composed of two parts. An upper part, called "heaven" (*Himmel*), is sometimes described as including many subdivisions. The uppermost heaven is called the Throne of God, while the lower heavens are known as the abodes of the angels who occasionally serve as messengers of the deity to earth. The lower part of the universe comprises the earth (*Erde*), now inhabited by

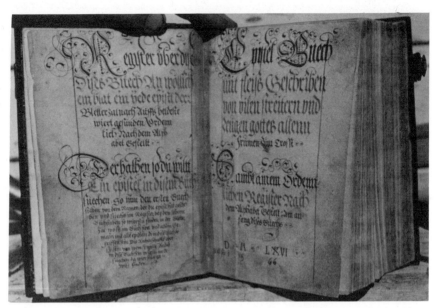

Figure 21. Handwritten Hutterite codex of 1566. A North American colony document.

people, and hell, a physical place of captivity (*Ort des Gefangniss*) that is the abode of those who lived wicked and disobedient lives while on earth.

Time is regarded as an endless, unchanging duration called eternity (*Ewigkeit*). Within the timeless duration, that which is temporal and changing becomes manifest, briefly, in material form.

Man was made to worship God, the Creator, and not to worship the creation, or things made by God. The orientation of the Hutterites is toward life after death (the spiritual, the eternal) and not toward the enjoyment of the present life. Thus, children are taught in their morning and evening prayers to acknowledge an "eternal God who has wonderfully created all things in Heaven and on earth." When baptized at the age of about twenty, the young adults "establish a covenant with God and all his people" to "give self, soul, and body, with all possessions to the Lord in Heaven."

A divine order and hierarchy. By the act of creation, God established a single law, or divine order, in the universe wherein He put each part or unit into its "right" place. The divine order is conceived as right and good. Any digression from, or transgression of, the divine order is conceived as evil and sinful. Good is believed to come only from God;

"evil" is the term used to designate any breach in the divine order or any transgression of God's law.

The divine order is believed to have been established through God's will. This order expresses a fixed relationship between God, on the one hand, and material, or transitory, things, on the other. Respect for hierarchy and authority pervades Hutterite thought and practice. The right, or divine, order requires a hierarchy of relationships. The superior cares for, directs, and uses the subordinate; the subordinate serves and obeys the superior. God is Lord over man, man over woman, parent over child, and the older person over the younger. Human beings have power over animals and are "lord of the same." Human beings may rule over material things, inventions, and machines and use them as long as the proper relationships and functions are observed, but they may not change the order of God—for example, no man may kill another man, or interfere with the process of natural conception.

Human nature and the relationship of carnal to spiritual nature. Since the first man, Adam, sinned, urged on by Eve who was "deceived and beguiled by the counsel of the serpent," all men have inherited sinfulness and have an "inclination to sin." In this "fallen state," human beings desire self-recognition, private ownership, and carnal, or "earthly," pleasure. Human nature is helpless and can never completely overcome its carnal tendency. God gave each person a conscience by which he can recognize sin and feel guilt. The individual can attain eternal life after death only by believing the Word of God, by repenting, and by receiving the grace of Christ through continual submission of the self to the will of God as expressed in communal living.

According to the divine order, only man's spiritual nature is good and pleasing to God. All that pertains to his carnal nature (*die Weltlichkeit*) is displeasing and evil. Therefore, to please God and thus acquire from him the gifts of grace and faith, man "should not be carnally minded but spiritually minded."

The carnal nature is temporal and passing and brings death to man. By contrast, all who are "born of Christ" are ruled by the spiritual nature, which is eternal.[4] The two kingdoms are separate, and each must go its separate way. It follows that Hutterites aim to live separated from the (carnal) world with their loyalties rooted in the spirit. Separation is ordained by God, says Ridemann. "Many tribes call themselves Christian but they do not wish for the kingdom of God and Christ. The Kingdom of God is the cross, tribulation, suffering, and persecution, to drink the

---

4. For the recurring theme of the second birth in other religions, see Mircea Eliade, *The Sacred and the Profane* (New York: Harper and Row, 1961).

bitter wine of suffering and to help Him carry His cross. They [other professing Christians] neglect such suffering. They do not like to be hated by the world."[5]

Although children are born in sin and with a tendency to sin, this condition can be mitigated if they are brought up "in the nurture and admonition of the Lord." The Hutterites say, "It is our endeavor to bring up the children in divine discipline, and to plant in their hearts the right morals and commandments of God."[6]

Before the individual is old enough to voluntarily acknowledge his own sinful nature, he is taught to obey God and reverence Him as the "Almighty Father." Children are not permitted "to carry out their own headstrong and carnal practices, but from the beginning are taught the divine discipline." According to the seventeenth-century elder Andreas Ehrenpreis, "Just as iron tends to rust, and soil nourishes weeds if not cultivated, so children require continuous care to keep them from their natural inclinations toward injustices, desires, and lusts."[7] Baptism is postponed until the threshold of adulthood, when the full implications of the denial of private property and the acceptance of suffering are understood.

The individual. Since "God worketh only in surrendered men," the individual will must be "broken" and fused with the will of the community. Just as the grain of wheat loses its identity in the loaf of bread and the grape is lost in the wine, so also the individual must lose his identity in one corporate body. Self-surrender, not self-development, is the divine order. The individual must at all times be submissive to the will of God, which is explicitly manifested in the believing community. Since man is endowed with both a carnal and a spiritual nature, he can overcome his carnal tendency only by submission to the community and with the help of his brothers.

The individual is believed to have no power over his destiny unless he receives grace as a gift from God. Indeed, he is not only helpless in the sense of not possessing any real power, but he is sinful and debased. By true humility and repentance of sin, the individual may receive the gift of grace and thereby be extended beyond death into eternal life. Only unconditional obedience (*Nachfolge*) and self-renunciation (*Gelassenheit*) permit the gifts of God to take effect in man.

5. Rideman, *Account of Our Religion*, p. 3. Texts documenting the concept of separation from the world are found on pp. 112, 139, 140, and 187.

6. For answers to accusations of Lutheran theologians that Hutterites neglected their children, see Wilhelm Wiswedel, "The Anabaptists Answer Melanchthon: (I) The Handbuechlein of 1558," *M.Q.R.* 29 (July 1955): 222 ff.

7. Andreas Ehrenpreis, *Ein Sendbrief, 1652* (Scottdale, Pa., 1920).

The soul of the individual, which is created by God at conception, has a spiritual character and hence will live forever—either in heaven or in hell. Only those who die as children or who repent and receive the gift of grace may enter heaven. Although the meaning of eternal life has not been "properly and fully" revealed, it is believed that at the day of "last judgment" God will appear to man "face to face," and man shall "know God, who is eternal and who maketh man eternal and to live eternally." The soul will be reunited with God. Then those who know him will be resurrected in body and "shall rejoice with Him with eternal joy."

Since human nature is sinful from birth, Hutterites value education not for self-improvement but as a means of "planting" in children "the knowledge and the fear of God." The consequences of original sin are moderated by intensive teaching from an early age. "We should let the Heavenly Gardener implant such fruit that will bear everlasting life," explained a contemporary Hutterite preacher.

The individual will is broken primarily during the kindergarten years. The child is taught self-denial, humility, and submissiveness. After approximately twenty years of rigorous indoctrination, the individual is expected to accept the teachings of the colony voluntarily. When he is able to express remorse, abasement, and the loathing associated with the sinful self, he will receive baptism.

But even though the individual is "grafted into the divine character or nature," he is never free from temptation by his carnal nature. His security in the divine order depends not on his verbal affirmation or the rite of baptism but on his "proven works," or daily behavior. In practice, this means adherence to the rules of the church community. The individual may not conform to his own interpretation of the Word or his own notion of obedience; he must submit to the will of the community, because community is the will of God.

The relation of the sexes. Parental authority is rooted in the creation of the universe and must be observed in the relationship between the sexes. Man, in contrast to woman, is the leader in righteousness and example, for it is he who is made in the image of God and "reflects some of God's glory." The divine order requires that woman be submissive. She neither votes nor participates in any way in the formal decision-making.

The marital relationship also proceeds from the divine order. Within marriage man is ordained by God to be "lord" and "head of the woman" as the spirit is head of the body and God is head of the spirit. He, "as the one in whom something of God's glory is seen, should have compassion on the woman as the weaker instrument, and in love and kindness go before her and care for her, not only in temporal but also and still more in spiritual things; and faithfully share with her all that he hath been given by God." Man should go before woman "in honesty, courage and all the Christian virtues that in him she may have a mirror of righteousness, an instigation of blessedness and a leader to God."

The purpose of marriage is to instruct and lead mankind to God. If the marriage is not rightly regarded and observed, it will lead mankind away from God and bring death. A husband must be the head of only one wife as Christ is the head of only one church. A marital union can be broken by transgression of the marriage promise, but a broken marital bond does not lead to divorce; reconciliation is possible through repentence and restoration of the broken covenant. To achieve marriage "one should ask not his flesh but the elders that God might show" through the community "what God has provided from the beginning." Man and woman come together not through their own action and choice but in accordance with God's will and order, and in fact, obedience to God and community are above obedience to one's spouse. Thus, if one partner forsakes the faith, the other remains bound to the community.

Sexual relations are justified for the sake of procreation. Ulrich Stadler explains, "if man had remained pure and good as he was created by God, then also conception [*Besamung*] would have functioned without lust and evil urges. But now it is no longer this way. God, however, winks at our marital work [*Gott sieht durch die Finger in ehelichen Werk*] for the sake of our children, and he does not incriminate against those who act in fear and discipline."[8]

Community, property, and the proper worship of God. Community (*Gemeinschaft*) in the Hutterite charter means a group of members of the church who are united in the fellowship of the Holy Spirit under the leadership of the spirit of Christ. This body is called the "community of the church of Christ," the "communion of saints," or the "children of God." The community is conceived of as a foretaste (*Vorhof*) of life after death. The Hutterites reject a purely "spiritual" community which does not bring property under the control of the body of Christ.

Community of goods (*Gütergemeinschaft*) is the will of God, who from the beginning created all things for common use. Through disobedience, man brought disorder into the world. By his grasping and greedy spirit, he has taken private possession of the things of God.

Carnal man is viewed as living in perpetual covetousness by making property, food, land, and "created things" the objects of private gain. The sun, the moon, the air, and all material things are for the good of all men and to make them private property is to ignore God's order. "There-

8. In Ulrich Stadler's *Sendbrief* of 1536, published in Lydia Müller, *Glaubenszeugnisse* (Leipzig, 1948), p. 228.

fore, whosoever will cleave to Christ and follow him must forsake such things." As the Father and the Son in Heaven live in common and hide nothing from each other, so His children should live. In his "Great Article Book," Peter Walpot lists 148 arguments for communal living.

Material goods as well as capital earnings are for the welfare of the community and are clearly at its disposal. Every member "shall give and devote all his or her time, labor, services, earnings, and energies . . . [to] the community, freely, voluntarily and without compensation. . . ."[9] The individual in turn, together with his dependents, will be "supported, instructed and educated" by the community.

Christians may make and use what is intended "for the benefit and daily use of man," such as bread knives, axes, hoes, and the like, "as well as plain clothes to meet their needs." Whatever "serveth but pride, magnificence and vanity," they should not make, in order that they may keep "conscience unspotted before God." Honest labor with the hands is honorable, but merchandizing (buying and selling for profit, without the contribution of labor) is "a sinful business."

The community of the church of Christ has been sought out, selected, and accepted by God through Christ to be "a people from himself," holy and without blemish, and it has been separated from all nations so that it might serve God "with one mind and heart." Its law is the law of God and "all temporal things are foreign" to it. Therefore, members of the community of the church should not go to law to settle civil disputes or accept appointments to government positions, such as judgeships or election as representatives of the people of their area. Government is a sign of man's departure from God. Warfare comes to an end in the church of Christ, for vengeance belongs only to God. Members must neither practice vengeance nor make nor bear arms. They should willingly pay taxes which are to be used for peaceful purposes; throughout their history, the Hutterites have refused to pay taxes specifically levied for purposes of war.

In the community of the church, where all are childlike and equal under the leadership of the Holy Spirit within God's law, such leadership roles as magistrate and policeman are unnecessary. Instead, each member is expected to watch over his fellows and admonish anyone who commits a fault. Those who commit a deadly sin, such as fornication, covetousness, idolatry, drunkenness, or robbery, are excluded from the church-community and from its common meals. In such cases, however, a distinction is made between deliberate sinning and sinning in haste through "weakness of the flesh." The former is judged more severely

9. E. A. Fletcher, *Constitution of Hutterian Brethren Church and Rules as to Community of Property* (Winnipeg, Man., 1950).

than the latter. Those who yield themselves to sin separate themselves from the church, and if they actually leave the community, they are considered lost and destined for hell. Murder has never occurred in Hutterite history. One colony preacher explained that the Brethren would not be able to deal with such an incident.

The church rather than any one individual has been given power by divine law "to exclude and to accept" as well as to forgive members. "Therefore, whatsoever she excludeth is excluded, but whatsoever she forgiveth is forgiven here and in eternity, and apart from her there is no forgiveness, no goodness, no healing and salvation, no true comfort or hope. For within her and not without her is and dwelleth the Father, Son and Holy Ghost who maketh all things good, and justifieth." Hence, according to the Hutterite charter, power may be delegated by God to Christ, and by Christ to the Church, but never by the Church to any one individual.

The community gathers daily for thanksgiving and prayer and annually at Easter for the Lord's Supper. They come together to give thanks, to pray to remain faithful and devout, and to "proclaim the Lord's word faithfully." They are forbidden to bow down to graven images or to meet in "temples of stone or wood," since temples "originated through the instigation of devils" and "are hated of God."

The spiritual kingdom is ruled by the spirit of Christ and is known by complete obedience in the sharing of all material goods. Only in a divinely created fellowship separated from the world can men succeed in living communally, and only in this way can God be properly honored, worshipped, and obeyed. It follows that not only is the community of love (the Hutterite Brethren Church) primary and central in the universe but its justification and continued existence are rooted in the will of God.

A knowledge of the way Hutterites view the world and their place in it helps us to obtain a perspective on their life patterns from birth to death. These basic postulates become the reference points that color the group's view of reality, giving them an orientation toward life which is distinct from that of other cultures. The manner in which the ideals are practiced varies in detail from one colony to another. The relation of the ideals (formal culture) to the solutions of day-to-day living (informal culture) is illustrated in Hutterite social organization. Before discussing contemporary colony organization, we will observe how important a role language plays in organizing the Hutterite view of the world.

Language

The Hutterites view the world through Germanic thought patterns and from a perspective common in medieval Europe before the dawn of modern science. After four centuries of limited contact with other language groups and isolation from intellectual changes, they still consider the German language indispensable. When discussing their most cherished beliefs with outsiders, Hutterite preachers not only prefer to speak German but are for the most part wholly dependent upon it. Those who believe that a language is not simply a neutral device for conveying experience but that its grammar and construction help determine the world view of a people have much to support their claim in Hutterite culture.[10]

In their formative years in Moravia, the Hutterite communities were enclaves of German-speaking peoples in an area where Slavic was spoken. The dialects represented among Hutterites were diverse, for the immigrants had come from Württemberg, Switzerland, the Palatinate, Hesse, Austria, and Tyrol. According to a contemporary writer, the Hutterite leaders saw to it that the Tyrolean dialect prevailed. Whether they succeeded permanently is not definitely known. The chronicle of this period was written in what philologists call "early new High German."[11]

The "Huttrish" dialect of today most nearly resembles that spoken in the province of Carinthia, Austria. The reason for this is not difficult to understand, for the Carinthians, who joined the Hutterite movement in 1762 in Romania, outnumbered the others fifty-one to sixteen.[12] A sprinkling of the present-day vocabulary reflects the Hutterites' stay in Slavic areas, in Transylvania (Romania), in the Ukraine, and in North America. The terms for in-law relationships (*Schwiegermutter, -sohn,* etc.) reflect the pattern of Carinthia. The word for "cucumber" (*Kratse-*

10. Benjamin L. Whorf, for instance, says, ". . . we dissect nature [the flow of experience] along lines laid down by our native languages." And again, "we cut nature up, organize it into concepts, and ascribe significances as we do, largely because we are parties to an agreement to organize it in this way. . . . " The quotation is from R. L. Beals and H. Hoijer, *An Introduction to Anthropology*, 2d ed. (New York: Macmillan Co., 1959), p. 587.

11. Catholic writers state that the Tyrolean dialect was imposed on everyone (see Claus-Peter Clasen, *Anabaptism: A Social History* [Ithaca: Cornell University Press, 1972], p. 271). The language of the great chronicle is discussed by Herfried Scheer, "Sprachliche Untersuchung der Ältesten Chronik der Hutterischen Brüder" (M.A. thesis, University of Alberta, 1962).

12. See Zieglschmid, *Das Klein-Geschichtsbuch*, p. 299. Speech patterns of modern-day Hutterites were compared with European German dialects by Alfred Obernberger (unpublished paper). That present-day speech is more like that spoken in the province of Carinthia than in Tyrol is born out in a recent study by Herfried Scheer, "A Lexicological Analysis of the Hutterian German Dialect" (Ph.D. dissertation, McGill University, 1972). He reports that the phonology of the Hutterian dialect is distinctly Carinthian and that Carinthian words appear three times more often than typically Tyrolean words. For English usage, see Jerome J. Holtzman, "An Inquiry into the Hutterian German Dialect" (M.A. thesis, University of South Dakota, 1960).

wets) apparently entered Hutterite speech in Transylvania. From the Slavic there is *dsainik* for "kettle," and the words for "teapot" (*cajinik*) and "cap" (*Xatus*) are Ukrainian.

Today Hutterites are trilingual. Children first learn to speak the native Huttrish dialect. Once they reach school age, they are taught to read and write German in the German school, English in the English school. In the German school, they learn to read and write in high German from the Bible and other religious texts. English is taught in the English school using the same textbooks that children in the public schools use, and English more than any language except German has influenced Hutterite speech patterns. German and English usage are symbolic of the two kingdoms, the colony and the world. English is spoken with outsiders; high German is used for all sacred and cere-monial occasions. The sermons read in church have been copied from seventeenth-century German texts. "We believe," said a preacher, "that our faith can be expressed more deeply, sharply and fully in the German language."

When a Hutterite preacher wants to know the interpretation of a Bible passage, he will rely on his old sermon books. Sermons are an un-challenged source of authority. No individual, not even a preacher, may interpret the Bible without the aid of the traditional sermons. They say that no one is spiritual enough today to preach without the written sermons; it would be very unsafe. Preachers do not embellish their sermons with contemporary illustrations, as this would be too distract-ing. The dedication to the gothic German handwritten sermons insulates the ideology from competing outside influences. Critical scholarship is considered unnecessary and is suspect. The biblical German used in their written sermons is equated with the Bible itself, for "sermons" and "scriptures" are terms used interchangeably.

Private interpretation of the Word of God is forbidden. No individ-ual Hutterite, no matter how mystical or saintly his behavior, has legiti-mate authority to interpret the Word of God. There is for Hutterites no "inner light" to challenge either the Word of God or the religious tradition of the community. Worn-out Bibles and sermon books are placed in the casket of a deceased person, where the pages of the books and the body decay together; but the Word of God and the soul are identified with the eternal and live forever.

Verbal and ritual sharing is supportive of the communal organiza-tion. Although the Hutterites are literate and capable of writing in both German and English, literacy is less important to them than verbal sharing. Oral sharing of words and phrases in ceremonial practices lends strong support to uniformity of thought patterns and communitarian values. In all colony schools from kindergarten through the rite of baptism, words and phrases are memorized and repeated in unison. Everyone memorizes the same (or similar) prayers, the same hymns, and the same vows. The right hymns must be sung in the right way "for the glory of God";[13] they must not be sung in a manner to make a "sweet sound" or for "carnal joy."

Ritualized prayers before and after meals, before retiring, and at rising are always considered necessary. A Hutterite is so thoroughly conditioned to ritual at mealtime and coffee time that his hands spontaneously form a posture of prayer before and after eating. Whether in the dining hall, in his apartment, or at a roadside restaurant, he makes virtually no exceptions. Thus, access to God, food, sleep, and a new day is provided through ritual prayer. Individual fulfillment is achieved by fusion with the group in daily oral recitation and singing and in the evening church service. The blending of words and phrases with the communal whole allows little place for individual assertion, and individual utterances are indistinguishable from the whole. In verbal sharing as in property ownership, the individual's voice is blended and lost in that of the group.

In Hutterite society material objects do not become sacred. Special importance is attached to words, language patterns, and oral tradition. There are virtually no religious relics. Ritual centers around words, not objects or property. Bibles and sermon books are the most valued property, but the contents (the Word), not the material object itself, are believed to be sacred. Even in baptism it is not the water but the Word of God that is holy. Passages from sacred writings are more easily shared than material objects. Group recitation and singing are the most common forms of sharing, which is so intensive that participants in the church service do not possess individual hymn books.

In a Hutterite colony the dialogue with the past is cultivated as ardently as the dialogue with those of good faith in the community. Continuity with those who have witnessed and suffered through the centuries is not just intellectually comprehended but emotionally reenacted. By the constant reliving and reappropriation of biblical events and their own early history, the Hutterite communities are saved from the "dehydration of Fundamentalism" with its purely individualistic relation to God.[14]

---

13. For the relationship between "the Word" and oral tradition in Christian history, see Walter J. Ong, *Ramus: Method and the Decay of Dialogue* (Cambridge: Harvard University Press, 1968) and *The Presence of the Word* (New Haven: Yale University Press, 1967). Peter Riedemann, like St. Augustine, saw danger in enjoying music for itself; see Rideman, *Account of Our Religion*, p. 123.

14. The phrase is borrowed from my colleague Franklin Littell, Professor of Religion, Temple University.

chapter seven

Colony Organization

Spatial Arrangements

The Hutterite world view leads to the creation of an earthly environment that is ordered spatially, temporally, socially, and symbolically.[1] Within this created environment the individual matures and ages. For the Hutterites, the colony is the center of the universe. Hutterites sometimes compare the colony to the ark of Noah in the biblical account of the flood. Only those in the ark (the colony) are prepared to escape the judgment of God and to receive eternal life. In the Hutterite view, "You either are in the ark, or you are *not* in the ark."

1. The analysis of contemporary Hutterite life is based upon research and observation in many North American colonies for a period of over fourteen years. Three specific colonies, fictitiously named Dariushof, Lehrerhof, and Schmiedehof, were studied in depth. Detailed, longitudinal case studies based on anthropological field guides yielded a broad variety of data. Each of the three colonies represents a different Leut but is not necessarily representative of other colonies within the Leut. Two are located in Canada and one in the United States. The three colonies are at least 500 miles apart. The aim was to observe and to participate in colony life among small rather than large numbers of people in order to learn more about cultural patterns and interpersonal relations.

Initially the research was part of a study of communal education in Hutterite society; see John A. Hostetler and Gertrude Enders Huntington, *The Hutterites in North America* (New York: Holt, Rinehart, and Winston, 1967). The conclusions in this volume are based upon the same research findings and upon revisions and pertinent observations since 1967.

Like religious men in all cultures, the Hutterites desire "to live in a pure and holy cosmos, as it was in the beginning, when it came fresh from the Creator's hand."[2] Only within a colony, they say, can man maintain God's order. The concept of order influences the layout of the colony: the buildings must be in proper relationship to one another, the angles determined by a compass. Time patterns reflect a right order, for everyone must have the right position in a hierarchical world. These ideals, although never completely achieved, are dominant in the organization of colony life.

Dariushof, one of the colonies that has been studied in depth, is located in the northern part of the Great Plains one hundred miles from a large trading center. Ten miles away is a small town which is its postal address. The colony is sufficiently near its parent colony (fifteen miles) that work and services can be exchanged but not so close that young people can walk between them. The colony buildings (numbering over sixty) are set back from the highway and can only be reached by a gravel road. The colony owns eight thousand acres and leases two thousand additional acres, about the average for lands owned or leased by other colonies in this dry-land farming region.

At the center of the colony site is a rectangle with long houses on either side. The kitchen complex is at one end and the kindergarten at the other. (Among Lehrerleut the kitchen is usually in the center; see figure 22 and chart 2.) The long houses run due north and south, for as a preacher put it, "They are squared with the compass. You don't walk crooked to the earth, you walk straight, that is how our buildings should be, straight with the compass and not askew." In each long house there are four apartments with separate entrances. In a normal-sized apartment there are three rooms. There is an entrance room containing a table, straight chairs, a wash basin, a cupboard for a few dishes, and the stairway entrance to the attic, or second story of the house. Off either side of the entrance room is a bedroom with two double beds, one or two day beds, and a crib. The attic is one long unpartitioned space where families store their out-of-season clothing and tools. Under some of the newest houses there are basements. Many of the other buildings in the colony are laid out parallel or at right angles to the long houses.

The colony people meet in the communal kitchen three times daily to eat their meals. Here the women prepare food for the colony and launder their family's clothes. The showers and bathtubs are also lo-

2. Mircea Eliade, *The Sacred and the Profane* (New York: Harper and Row, 1961), p. 65.

Figure 22. Center square of a Hutterite colony.

cated here. Adjacent to the kitchen is a large bell that signals most of the colony's communal functions.

The arrangement of the buildings reflects Hutterite orderliness: everything is classified; each part of the universe has its correct place, which in turn determines its correct function and proper use. The biblical passage "By their fruits ye shall know them" is interpreted to mean that one's appearance reflects one's attitude or the strength of one's belief. Or more succinctly, as one colony preacher said when discussing the dress of the women of his colony, "I don't care how frilly and frothy their underwear is, it's what shows that counts." What shows classifies the woman, just as it classifies the building. Her dress indicates to a Hutterite that she is an adult woman, a Christian, and a Hutterite and that she knows her position relative to men. Her clothing also indicates whether she is dressed for work, for evening church, or for Sunday.

Life on earth is transient, temporary. According to Hutterites, "We are always in strange lands under Jews and Gentiles." In these strange lands they create their own remarkably uniform physical environment. The colony is a concrete expression of the Hutterite belief system and the social environment in which the beliefs are transmitted to the children. It is not the place that gives the Hutterite identity; it is rather that the pattern of his life remains the same in spite of geographic moves and the passage of time, even to the floor plan of his house and its position in relation to neighboring houses. A specific place is not important—but specific social relationships are of utmost importance.

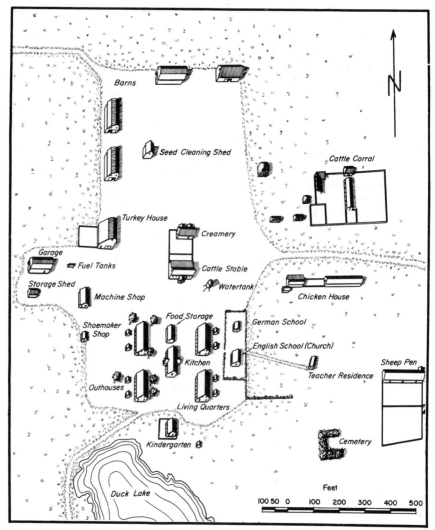

Chart 2. Layout of Rock Lake Colony (Lehrerleut) in Alberta

Time Patterns

Not only is there a preferred spatial order for human activity in Hutterite society, but time is used to structure social relationships. Time spent on earth functions as a means for establishing social order. Individuals are ranked by age and sex. Age determines both the group to which an individual belongs and, generally, his place within the group.

Traditional cultures have conceived of two classes of time—the sacred and the secular—and the Hutterites participate in both. Sacred time is related to their beliefs about creation and is nonflowing and eternal, originating with God. It partakes of the character of the Word of God, for God's words always remain an inseparable part of Him and are therefore eternal. The human soul has a beginning but no end.

Secular time has both a beginning and an end. It is the measure of events that take place on earth. The secular encompasses all material objects including the human body.

Between sacred and secular time, some place is given to history and dreams. History is important as a dimension of the presence of God in the world. Hutterites are interested in history not as so many dates on a secular time scale but as steps in the development of the church of God. Therefore, historical events which are unrelated to their own outlook on life have little meaning for them. Even their own history is remembered as a source of strength to their faith rather than as a dated sequence of events. This means that there is some fusion of the beginnings of Christianity (the historical period of Christ's birth and the writing of the Bible) with their own beginnings (the persecutions of the sixteenth and seventeenth centuries and the writing of the Hutterite sermons). Miracles of the sixteenth century are fused with those of the nineteenth, for the worldly time sequence is unimportant when compared with God, who "broke into history." History is a dimension of secular time that is recalled primarily because it illustrates eternity.

Every evening, between the end of the day's work and the evening meal, secular time in the colony is interrupted by sacred time, when the whole community gathers for the evening church service. Here the Hutterites symbolically return to the time of their origin. The renewing of motivation by daily ritual participation is of utmost importance. For the Hutterite it is the sacred time which makes secular time meaningful. As the preacher slowly reads the sermons and unhurriedly recites the prayers, and the congregation sings the long, slow hymns, time is suspended. There is no rush to complete this task, for the members are participating in a sacred time dimension. God's time is eternal, nonflowing, spiritual, and immaculate.

In their daily round of meals and work, the Hutterites are keenly aware of the passage of time. The day is broken into small units that form a tight, although not rigid, schedule. This severe patterning means that the individual members of the colony have little free choice and few decisions to make with regard to time. Just as material objects are not owned by a Hutterite, he also has little concept of private time. The time that is needed for the completion of an operation (for example, building a goose shed), not the time contributed by the various individuals, is given careful thought. The speed with which an individual works, however, gives him status. A woman knows how long it takes her to make an article of clothing, and both adults and children set up tasks in such a way that the speed with which they finish is obvious. There is little savoring of the moment, for the attitude toward almost everything in this earthly life is to get it over with. This applies to meals, to work, even to life itself, which is believed to be short, transitory, and of real significance only as it relates to eternal time.

The daily work patterns of all individuals mesh in such a way that the colony runs smoothly and efficiently. The basic schedule varies with the time of year. It may be modified by the weather on a given day or adjusted to accommodate special tasks or an emergency. When the men are busy haying, food is sent to them in the fields during the day and supper is fed to them when they return for the night, which may be as late as 10:00 P.M. If the women are not finished with their colony work, supper may be served late. When colony work is pressing, evening church may be canceled.

Each age group has its own daily schedule. Some parents are up an hour or more before the rising bell. The time of rising for married adults is determined by their special work assignments and by the age and number of their children. The woman who is baking mixes the bun dough at 3:30 A.M., the cowman starts milking at 4:30, the mother of a young baby nurses him at 5:00. During the busy season the rising bell rings at 6:15, and at 6:30 the bell for adult breakfast is sounded. At 6:45 the school children eat breakfast and the three- to six-year-olds go to the kindergarten for their breakfast. After eating, the school girls clean the children's dining room and kitchen. Before the children have their breakfast, the women clean the adult dining room, wash the colony's dishes, and gather food to carry back to the children under two years of age, whom they feed in the apartments. The men do their assigned chores, and the boys assemble informally to learn their job assignments for the morning. The day passes quickly, for it is divided into small blocks of time.

The colony bell has a number of important functions. It is rung to announce rising time and most of the meals, to call the women to work or to announce a wedding shivaree, and to summon the members to help put out a fire or cope with an emergency. The bell heralds events that involve large segments of the colony but is never used to call the members to church, as is the custom among "worldly" people.

The weekday pattern of activity builds up to a climax on Sunday. On Monday the women do the family washing at the community wash house at the time assigned to them. They wash in rotation, beginning with the oldest woman and ending with the youngest, moving up one turn each week. Ideally, a woman does all the washing for her family and finishes the ironing and the mending on Monday. In some colonies the women try to polish their floors every day, but if they are unable to do this, they polish them on Tuesdays and Fridays. During the summer the school girls pick peas for the kitchen on Tuesday morning. On Wednesday, Thursday, and Friday the women hoe the garden and pick vegetables. Women with small children wash again on Thursday. Friday is a major cleaning day. The kitchen and dining room floors are scrubbed with hot water and soap by all the women. The women clean their own apartments and wax and polish the floors. The cook, the baker, and the milking-woman clean their respective work areas because women's work assignments change on Sunday night and their places of work must be clean for their successors. One of the work teams makes noodles. Saturday morning all of the women roll buns, and the unmarried girls scrub the school house so that it will be ready for the Sunday services. On Saturday afternoon everyone bathes, hair is combed, and beards are trimmed. Everything must be in order and everyone must be clean for Sunday.

Food served in the colony conforms to a weekly pattern. In Dariushof during the summer months, bread is baked on Monday and Wednesday and rolls are baked on Tuesday and Saturday. (See figure 23.) From seeding time until after harvest time, when the boys are working hard, a treat is often baked for the people to eat in their homes. The meals have a pattern that varies somewhat with the season and from one colony to another. The sweetened orange pekoe tea that is served at Saturday supper is called "Saturday tea" to distinguish it from the medicinal or herbal teas that are drunk in the homes. A person with stomach trouble may regularly skip a certain meal because he knows that the food to be served does not agree with him. Sunday dinner consists of noodle soup and roast duck; if there is no duck, chicken or goose is substituted.

The Saturday evening church service marks the onset of Sunday. Among the Dariusleut the women and girls wear special Saturday afternoon dresses to this service and to supper. In the evening members usually visit one another and sing hymns informally. They discuss religion and retell Hutterite history. People tend to go to bed early on Saturday night so that they will not be tired for Sunday. The women wear nice dresses to Sunday breakfast, the school children wear clean clothes, and the kindergartners, because they do not attend church, wear everyday clothes. The kindergarten children are often cared for during this time by one of the school children in order to free the kindergarten teacher to attend church. After breakfast the women and girls change into "Bible clothes" and at 9:00 A.M. walk to the service. The

Figure 23. Hutterite women baking bread in the common kitchen. (Photograph by Kryn Taconis)

sermons, read from German script, are not spontaneous, nor are they intellectual discourses on contemporary concerns. The function of the sermons is to encourage the believers, to interpret the meanings of biblical passages, and to guide the Hutterites through the present, secular, "evil times." The rhythm of the preacher's voice differs from ordinary speech during this period of sacred time.

When the church service is over, at approximately 10:30, the women and girls change into Sunday afternoon dresses and proceed immediately to Sunday dinner. After the noon meal the adults take a long Sunday afternoon rest. Families are together on Sunday afternoon. If another colony is within easy traveling distance, there will often be an exchange of visits, with the visitors attending Sunday evening church and supper at the host colony. The leisurely Sunday schedule distinguishes this holy day from work days. In a Hutterite colony Sunday is long: the church service is long, the rest period is long, and there is almost no work done. Each person is reminded that God's time is measured by eternity in strong contrast to the swift flow of hours during the busy work week.

The strictness with which Sunday is observed varies among colonies. Some allow absolutely no unnecessary work. Other colonies are quite relaxed about observing Sunday and permit clothes to be washed, garden produce to be picked, and ducks to be plucked on Sunday afternoon. When the weather is unseasonable for harvesting during the week, a colony may decide to work in the fields on Sunday. Since goods and time all belong to God, no individual is benefiting from Sunday work and God is still being honored.

The liturgical calendar, punctuating the year and dividing it into definable seasons, begins with Advent (the preparation for the coming Christ) and ends with Pentecost (the establishment of the Christian Church).[3] During the long and uneventful winter the important colony events are related to the liturgical calendar. The liturgical cycle and the agricultural cycle are interrelated. Christmas, Easter, and Pentecost are each observed for three days, and special services are performed at the proper times. The Thanksgiving sermon is read the Sunday after the harvest is gathered. Specific sermons are read to meet colony needs, such as discipline or comfort for the sick; otherwise Hutterite preachers follow a traditional yearly pattern in selecting the sermon to be read aloud on a specific Sunday. The preacher and his assistant keep a record of the date and text of all sermons delivered, the preacher who read them, and the particular hymns sung at each service.

3. For Hutterite holidays, see appendix 11. Traditional sermon texts for the liturgical calendar appear in Robert Friedmann, with the assistance of Adolf Mais, *Die Schriften der Huterischen Täufergemeinschaften* (Vienna: Hermann Böhlaus, 1965), pp. 158–62. Texts used by Hutterites today are listed in appendix 12.

Authority Patterns

All authority, whether inside or outside the colony, is believed to originate with God. Governmental authority over the secular world is said to be ordained by God in his wrath to take venegeance on evil and to discipline the godless. Within the Hutterite colony there is order and harmony, but outside there is physical coercion. Baptized members are believed to have received the supernatural gift of the Holy Spirit through obedience and submission and to have more power and responsibility than those who have not been baptized.

The baptized members of the colony make up the *Gemein*, or "church." The corporate group has the power to exclude and to accept members. Women participate in the church service by their presence, by joining in the prayers and hymns, and by formally greeting newly baptized members; but they have no "voice" in church matters. Having no vote, they do not participate in formulating colony policy, nor are they eligible for church leadership positions. Only baptized men are eligible for church offices and colony positions, such as cattleman, pigman, shop mechanic, and shoemaker. Only they may vote to elect members to these positions and make decisions concerning the economic, social, and religious life of the colony.

A council of from five to seven baptized men, headed by the first preacher, is elected to serve as an executive body. The members of the council hold the key positions in the colony, including those of first preacher, second preacher, steward, and field manager. Often the German school teacher and one or two other men holding leadership positions in the colony, or men whose age entitles them to a position of authority, serve on the council. The council makes all major decisions. Members of the council initiate changes in jobs and departmental positions, execute discipline, and perform a judicial function. Almost never is there conflict between the council and the rest of the church. The actions of the council are directed by the church and are performed neither in the name of God nor for God but with the help of God. The head preacher has the highest leadership position, but his actions are constantly subject to review by the council. Authority is thus group-centered. The individual council member has learned to be submissive, for he has been taught that the individual never reaches a state of perfection. Ideally, group decisions are impartial and have higher priority than those made by an individual.

The preacher receives no formal training prior to his election. Elected by lot to the position of assistant preacher from nominations by his own colony (with the aid of delegates from other colonies), he is ordained to full power only after several years of experience and proven leadership. As head preacher he must combine conservative religious values and progressive ideas about work and economic planning. Good handwriting is an asset, since he must copy a set of sermons for his own use. (See figure 24.) The preacher is expected to exert authority wisely, since he must carry out the collective will as well as God's will. His role encompasses *total*, as well as very specific, responsibility. He must know when to refer weighty matters to the council. He takes turns with his assistant in delivering the sermon and lining out the hymns at the church services; he conducts funerals, marriages, and baptisms, hears personal problems and voluntary confession, and administers punishment for sins. The lifelong indoctrination of his people and the spiritual tempo of the colony depend on him. He must interpret the present in terms of the past. It is important that he oversee the colony schools, though his relation to the teachers is informal. The responsibility for smoothing over difficulties that may arise between colony members lies in his hands. He also records births, marriages, and deaths, and the travel records of members who go to town or visit other colonies.

The preacher is intimately concerned with the economic well-being of the colony. He supervises the activities of the steward to insure

Figure 24. The preacher acquires a set of sermons by copying them from generations past. (Photograph by Kryn Taconis)

that the colony is run efficiently and countersigns checks with him. The preacher is both guardian of traditions and spokesman for the colony in its "foreign affairs." He must remain vigilant against the *Weltgeist*, the "spirit of the world," and individualism when it creeps into the colony.

The organization of the colony may be summed up as follows:

The colony. The Bruderhof, or colony, consists of all persons of Hutterite parentage or persuasion residing on the premises. It is the domestic, biologic, economic, and self-sustaining unit within which the needs of the members are met by living communally.

The church, or Gemein. The church consists of all the baptized men and women. They observe holy communion as an exclusive unit, accept or reject new members, and welcome back into their midst repentant members. Baptized males vote on major colony policies and determine who will fill positions of leadership.

The council. The council consists of five, six, or seven men who are selected by the church to serve in an executive capacity. The first preacher, the assistant preacher, the steward, and the field manager are always on the council. Frequently, one individual will hold two of these offices, or in a small colony, there may be no assistant preacher. Generally, one or two older men serve on the council. They sit in order of rank, facing the congregation. The council makes practical day-to-day decisions, grants permission for travel, and judges minor disagreements.

The informal subcouncil. This is an informal group that functions when questions of procedure arise. It consists of the head preacher, the assistant preacher, the steward, and the field manager who generally meet after breakfast each day to lay out the day's work and assign men to the various tasks.

The head preacher. The head preacher, as indicated, is responsible for all aspects of community life. He must, as Hutterites say, "keep his hive in order." He is directed in this all-inclusive role by his own colony church and by the preachers of his Leut (his peers) who ordained him; his church and his peers also have the power to remove him from office should they see fit. The head preacher represents the colony in all its aspects to the outside world; he also interprets the outside world to the colony. The preacher is often called "elder."

The colony steward. The steward (*Diener der Notdurft*) often called the householder, or "boss," is in a trusted position, for under the direction of the council and the Gemein and with the help of the department managers, he is responsible for the economic well-being of the colony. In economic matters he represents the colony to the outside world. Other stewards, or managers, are the "farm boss" and the foreman of the farm enterprises.

Two informal subcultures in the colony, the men and the women, tend to support the corporate group. Women, as indicated in discussing world view, are believed to be inferior to men, intellectually and physically. Therefore they need direction, protection, guidance, and consideration. For although it is said that man was molded in God's likeness, reflecting something of God's glory, woman was taken from man and is weak, humble, and submissive. Hutterite men believe that "women just *are* inferior." When there is a marriage, the groom does not leave his colony. His bride, usually from another colony, is the one to move, and she must adjust to new people and a new colony pattern. Women, as has been mentioned before, do not formally participate in colony decisions; they do not even vote for the woman who is to become head cook. A man's job is assigned by the colony men regardless of his family obligations, except that married men do not work on the night shift during harvest time, and they are expected to help their wives with rotating colony work when that work is heavy.

Women are relatively free to voice their opinions when they or their families are affected by formal colony decisions. They cannot appeal their position on the basis of individual preference, but they can plead for the welfare of the group. Differences in behavior between the sexes can be observed with respect to child-rearing. Youngsters who are punished by the German school teacher (always a male) seek and receive comfort from their mothers. When hurt physically, the children seek comfort from their fathers (as the protector from the world and the environment). While the father tends to uphold the rules of the patriarchal system because of his own involvement in the structure, his wife may be more lenient in her attitude and more critical of the punishment. Wives are prone to making complaints, while husbands try to avoid confrontation with the colony power structure; thus, a husband would rather suffer unjustly than complain openly. A wife has little to lose by complaining. She may frequently be frustrated because her husband will not give her the support she wants. She mildly dislikes men as a group and often projects her annoyance. Women as a group support one another against masculine influence, and a dominating female will receive the support of the weaker ones. The cultures of men and women, as observed in earlier Hutterite studies, are different and at points may appear to the outsider or the psychological examiner to be opposed.[4]

The loyalties of the men are divided between their peer group (the colony power structure), their family of orientation (the family into which they were born), and their family of procreation (the family they establish by marriage). The women have a strong loyalty toward their family and children and are therefore more difficult for the colony to manage and integrate—especially when this attitude is coupled with ambivalent feelings toward the men. Thus one colony preacher said in all seriousness: "Our colony troubles would amount to very little if it were not for the women." This view is not necessarily typical of other colonies.

Community Integration

Central beliefs, the appropriate uses of space and time, and authority patterns must be harmoniously integrated into the lives of Hutterites if they are to achieve strong feelings of identity. Song, prayer, and worship are the predominant forms of community integration.

Toward evening when the day's work is suspended, the adults and school children follow the preacher to the school house for the evening service. The room is large, undecorated, and almost empty except for benches. The council faces the audience, and the two preachers sit directly behind the teacher's desk. All sit according to age and sex: the youngest in the front seats, the oldest on the back benches, the women to the right as they enter from the rear of the building, and the men to the left. (See chart 3.) A period of quiet ushers the group into the interval of sacred time. One of the preachers draws his chair to the desk and in a seated position announces the hymn. With his German hymn book open, he intones the first line. Only he has a hymn book; the congregation sings each line after him. After three or four verses have been sung, the leader sits back and the other preacher stands behind the desk. In a quiet, slow monotone, he beckons all to hear the word of God. The sermon consists of passages from the Bible followed by a seventeenth-century interpretation of each text, which are read in a stylized manner.

All are exhorted, for example, to "walk not after the flesh, but after the spirit. For to be carnally minded is death; but to be spiritually minded

---

4. Measures of psychological tendencies have shown striking differences in scores between men and women; see, for example, Bert Kaplan and Thomas F. A. Plaut, *Personality in a Communal Society* (Lawrence: University of Kansas Publications, 1956), pp. 34–44.

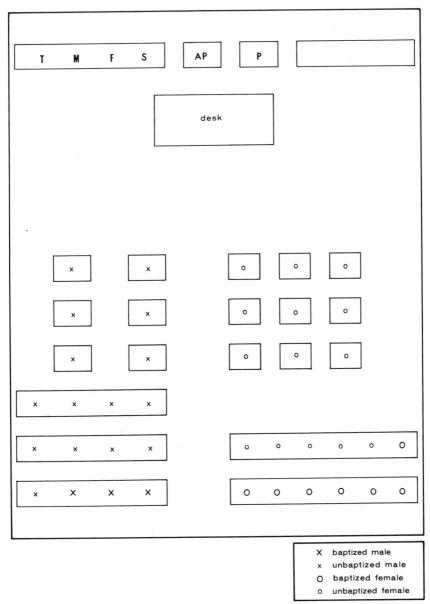

Chart 3. Seating Pattern at Worship Service in the Schoolhouse (P: Preacher; AP: Assistant Preacher; S: Steward; F: Field Foreman; M: Council Member; T: Teacher)

is life and peace."[5] A sermon typically states that under the rule of Moses, the people of God had to obey hundreds of laws, but Christ narrowed the rules down to two: "Thou shalt love the Lord thy God" and "Love thy neighbor as thyself." For a Christian, this is actually not a law, since he can meet this requirement without compulsion. Practicing love will do away with all enforced laws.

The sermon ends with an extraordinary descending intonation. An exhortation to prayer follows and all kneel forward with faces uplifted and hands folded at shoulder height. The preacher kneels on a small stool and audibly leads a memorized prayer which lauds the righteous acts of God the Father. He pleads for patience and steadfast faith so that all may withstand the trials of the earthly life. There is a short benediction, and all file out in the order in which they were seated. Thirty minutes have passed since the service began. The worshippers quickly proceed to the communal kitchen for the evening meal. The colony gathers daily (although the service may be canceled at the discretion of the preacher) and twice on Sunday. The Sunday morning service is from 9:00 to 10:30, and vespers is held in the late afternoon.

The manner in which the Hutterites worship and practice their religious life supports their world view. The specific place where the worship service is held is unimportant. There is no church building. Sacred space is not confined to one room or one building but encompasses all the central living space in the colony. It encompasses that area where God's order is respected. Most colonies worship in the school building, some in the dining hall, others in a room in the kitchen complex. The only requirements are that the room be large, orderly, clean, and unornamented and that there be enough seats to assign everyone his place.

The church service contrasts with and supplements daily life. Special clothes are worn to special services, and only clean, neat clothes with long sleeves may be worn to "church." Men must never attend without their Sunday jackets. Women, who seldom raise their voices when men are present, sing the hymns loudly and lustily, almost drowning out the men's voices. The tempo of the service is restful and unhurried: the hymns are sung slowly, the sermon is read in a stylized chant, and the long prayer is recited softly. The community is symbolically returning to the time of its origins (to Jakob Hutter, to the twelve Apostles, and to the spiritual source of its power) so that it may recreate its existence beyond secular time.

---

5. The quotation is translated from a colony sermon. For more about sermons, see Robert Friedmann, "Hutterite Worship and Preaching," *M.Q.R.* 40(January 1966): 5–26.

The church service makes visible the authority pattern of the community and emphasizes its supernatural rightness. The service stresses the importance of right order both in the seating of the members and in the sequence of the service. The women's seating is arranged by age, separate from the men. (Families do not sit together.) In the congregation men sit according to age, but on the council bench at the front of the room they sit by rank. When the service is ended the oldest man in the rear of the assembly leaves first. The oldest woman follows the youngest boy, and finally the council files out behind the youngest girl. The first minister leaves last, shepherding his flock. If anyone is absent his place is left empty and the community is incomplete. Every member knows that his absence is conspicuous and that he is missed. Thus the church service supports the hierarchical structure of the colony and reaffirms the God-given place of each individual in the church, in the colony, and in the universe. Only he can fill his place; he is an indispensable part of the larger whole.

The worship period not only is a means of community integration but also has a didactic function. During this period the members are instructed in their discipline, their faith, their history, and the reason for their existence. The evening service is followed immediately by a community meal, by breaking bread together. Temporal bread immediately follows spiritual sustenance.

The church service reinforces the basic pattern of Hutterite life and simultaneously gives relief and depth by setting the sacred against the secular and thus permitting behavior and responses on a different plane. Within the service—protected, surrounded, and observed by every other colony member—life becomes predictable, time is no longer fleeting, each individual is essential. The words of the sermon are believed to flow from God and to remain part of God. The message teaches anew the values adult members have internalized. The church gathering is a symbolic integration of community, an emotional ingathering of souls; it encompasses and gives meaning to all of life.

Ritual Integration

Singing and the observance of holy communion are two powerful integrative rituals. The first is practiced daily, the second yearly. These rituals have a sustained emotional appeal in Hutterite life. Here individual sentiments are fused with the experience of the group.

Of all communal groups in existence, the Hutterites are probably the most vigorous singers. They sing in religious services, in their homes (especially on long winter evenings, as a pastime), and at festive and informal settings. Since many recreational activities are shunned by the culture, singing becomes a major outlet for emotional expression. Dancing, playing musical instruments and cards, attending movies and concerts—all are considered disruptive. The primary function of Hutterite music is to inculcate Hutterite values of self-surrender, communal living, and obedience in times of trial, and to form a psychic unity with the forefathers.

Hutterite singing suggests a hypnotic, emotional catharsis. To the young it is a cataclysmic force impossible to resist. The shrill, overly loud nasal singing presents an insurmountable wall to the outsider. Every Hutterite can sing dozens of songs from memory. Singing is a major source of identity with the present and the past. The songs contain the drama of their lives and their world view—paraphrases of great Bible stories, songs of the martyrs, and touching experiences of the faithful.

Throughout the centuries the hymns have been learned by memory and, with the melodies, passed on to each new generation. The standard hymnal, printed for the first time in 1914, contains but a portion of the number of hymns in codices still in existence in the colonies and in European archives (see figure 25).[6] The songs are long, some having over one hundred stanzas. Many anonymous song writers have been identified by acrostics—a technique frequently used to convey a message or a name by the brethren in prison.

The singing in church is slower than the singing in school or at home. The loud, penetrating quality of the singing was introduced intentionally by the imprisoned brethren, who sang for those in distant cells. Singing was also a means of missionizing by giving personal testimony. In singing there was mutual comfort, a means of overcoming agony. To this day singing is intended solely as praise of God and is not regarded as folk music or as art. Loud singing persists, though the function has changed from boosting prisoner morale to providing group catharsis—an emotional release, a form of purification, a "high," an authentic expression of a people emptied of the burden of sin and guilt. This dimension of group pleasure, which defies quantification, seems to have eluded the social scientists who have studied Hutterite personality and mental health.

The vigor of the singing tradition is authenticated by recent scholarship on Hutterite melodies.[7] The melodies come from a wide variety of

6. *Die Lieder der Hutterischen Brüder* (Scottdale, Pa.: Die Hutterischen Brüder, 1914). Many of the songs predate the *Ausbund*, the Amish Hymnal. The contents are discussed by Robert Friedmann in *M.E.*, s.v. "Lieder der Hutterischen Brüder"; see also *M.E.*, s.v. "Singing, Hutterite." Among Hutterites this large song book is called "Väterlieder" to distinguish it from the *Gesangbüchlein* (first ed., 1919) used in home and school and the *Gesangbuch* (first ed., 1880) of Lutheran and Mennonite background.

7. See Helen Martens, "Hutterite Songs: The Origins and Aural Transmission of Their Melodies from the Sixteenth Century" (Ph.D. dissertation, Columbia University, 1968).

Figure 25. Page from Hutterite hymnal written by Andreas Ehrenpreis, 1642. (Courtesy of the Austrian National Library)

sixteenth-century sources: from court songs, meistersinger songs, Lutheran chorales, hymns of the Reformed Church, Gregorian chant, and secular folk songs. The Hutterite hymnal contains songs by at least ninety sixteenth-century song writers. Contemporary Hutterites sing approximately forty different melodies, all of which originated over four centuries ago. Because of the aural transmission, the rhythms of the melodies vary from colony to colony. The texts, however, have not changed.

In their informal singing, Hutterites demonstrate a remarkable ability to incorporate new texts and themes in support of their religious and communal ideology. The standard book for home and school use is the *Gesangbüchlein*, but in addition each pupil has his own notebook containing many songs which he has copied and committed to memory. Weddings and funerals are festive occasions for long hours of singing. Singing may be requested by a person suffering from terminal illness. In one difficult case, families in the colony, joined by families from a nearby colony, took turns singing day and night until "the steadfast soul was ushered into the banquet of the redeemed." Occasionally a Hutterite poem will be sung for a fitting occasion.[8] Songs of tragedy and melodrama—including Westerns—have great appeal to the young, though *Buhlenlieder* and *Fleischesgesänge* (songs expressing carnal affection) are forbidden.

The yearly high point of spiritual renewal is holy communion. This major event is observed the day after Easter by all the baptized members in good standing. The Hutterites understand and interpret fasting, almsgiving, and footwashing differently from other surviving Anabaptist groups such as the Amish and the Mennonites.[9] Communion is not preceded by fasting, for the Hutterites teach that the correct fast is "when man refrains from all sin and unrighteousness." Christians should fast continually, they say, and not just at appointed times. Nor is communion associated with almsgiving, for the Hutterites believe that true alms are given "when man proves all his abilities in his work." The communion service does not include ceremonial footwashing although a sermon on footwashing precedes Easter. Footwashing for the Hutterites means serving one another in daily life. As a ceremony communion is symbolic of brotherhood in Christ, of colony life. "As the bread is made a loaf by the bringing together of many grains, even so we, many human beings, who were scattered and divided, of many minds and purposes are led by faith into one, and have become one plant, one living organism and body of Christ."[10] The communion cup containing wine is

8. Eduard Hartig (died 1937), a former member of the Amana Society in Iowa who was displeased when the traditional forms of communal living were abandoned, went to live among the Hutterites. He composed a song that has been incorporated into the Hutterite singing tradition.

9. For a discussion of "Fasting," "Alms," and "Footwashing" as practiced by other Anabaptist groups, especially the Old Order Amish, see articles under these headings in the *Mennonite Encyclopedia*. During the early period of breaking away from the Roman church, the Hutterites rejected these practices as "relics of the Pope." The Amish retained them, incorporating them into symbolic acts of brotherhood.

10. Rideman, *Account of Our Religion*, p. 86.

symbolic of the shed blood of Christ. Just as grapes grow in clusters, so the colony is many people, and as the grapes lose their identity to become wine, so the members of the colony lose their individuality to become one church.

The deemphasis of material objects is demonstrated by the Hutterite attitude toward the bread and wine and their method of serving it. The bread is baked in the colony kitchen from a special recipe that is rich in eggs and sugar. The Hutterite women are careful to bake extra amounts so that there will be some left for the children. Although the children do not participate in the high ritual of communion, they are given some of the bread in the more secular ritual of their own dining. The carry-over is obvious; the bread is not sacred but is good food suitable for physical nourishment. During the communion service the bread is not served on plates but is passed from hand to hand; the first preacher takes two half-pieces from the loaf, breaks a couple of pieces off (the bread is broken as Christ's body was broken) and eats them as he hands the broken loaf to the second preacher, who repeats the process and hands the remaining pieces of bread to the steward on the council bench. Then the second preacher distributes half-slices to the congregation. Each person breaks off a piece and passes what remains to the next person. The fragments are returned to the table. The wine is usually made in the colony, but if there is no homemade grape wine on hand, some is purchased. The wine is served in four ordinary white pottery table-pitchers. The first preacher drinks from a pitcher and then the same pattern of distribution is followed as with the bread.

Neither the bread, nor the wine, nor the containers are holy; they are articles from daily life that are being used symbolically. Following the serving of the bread and wine, the congregation is reminded that Miriam made a loud noise and sang praises. They also sing loudly happy that they, imperfect individuals, can form a perfect group and through their identification with the community become a part of God.

Hutterite Identity Symbols

As in all distinctive culture groups, the sense of belonging is enhanced by signs and symbols that distinguish member from non-member. For Hutterites, the whole colony and its pattern of living become symbolic; the symbols include not only the use of space, time, authority, and ritual in preferred Hutterite ways but also the manner of dress, gestures, leisure, art, and nonverbal forms of communication. The signs and symbols distinguish *unser Leut* ("our people") from *Welt Leut* ("worldly people"). The symbols of colony life provide the basis for a common consciousness—a community that constitutes a real world, teaching members how to live, what to avoid, and what to imitate. The following discussion considers some of the more important identity symbols.

A Hutterite man wears black denim trousers with suspenders and a black coat or jacket. Blue denim is the dress of the worldly person and is scrupulously avoided. Shirts may vary in color, but only white shirts are worn for the Sunday service. Felt caps and hats are black. All colony clothes are made according to a distinctive Hutterite pattern. Men never appear at a church service without coats. Beards must be worn after marriage, a practice that is strongly defended on biblical grounds.

A Hutterite woman wears an ankle-length gathered skirt, a long apron, a blouse, and either a vest or a jacket with long sleeves, depending upon the Leut to which she belongs. The dress material is typically plaid or speckled with flowers. Women wear black polka-dotted kerchiefs on their heads at all times. All women wear their hair long and combed in the prescribed manner.

The three Leut are differentiated from one another but accepting of the other's differences. Each Leut devises its own discipline for member colonies, although within the same affiliation there are slight variations from one colony to another. Differentiations between or within the affiliations do not necessarily bespeak progressive or conservative tendencies: minor differences in customs can be attributed to leadership patterns and family traditions. Groups of colonies originating from a single founder colony are considered to be related. Within the Lehrerleut, for example, Rockport colonies are distinguished from the three other founder colonies. (See appendix 16.)

The Schmiedeleut occupy a common geographic region: South Dakota, North Dakota, and Manitoba. Lehrerleut and Dariusleut colonies often consider them to be the most liberal of the Hutterites. Their dress styles are more relaxed than most; the women wear elbow length blouses and men's trouser pockets resemble contemporary styles. The men have lapels on their coats and collars on their shirts. The Schmiedeleut no longer require hooks and eyes on the men's Sunday coats as the Dariusleut do. The Lehrerleut wear buttons.

Both Lehrerleut and Dariusleut colonies are located in Saskatchewan, Alberta, and Montana. Although many are adjacent to one another, the three affiliations do not intermarry. Such marriages are not forbidden, but they are not preferred. The Lehrerleut have had a tradition of thorough schooling in the German language. Their spoken German resembles high German more than that of the other affiliations. Having been the last to re-form communal living, the Lehrerleut were most influenced by the educated Mennonites and wealthier noncolony Hutterite families in Russia. The Dariusleut federation of preachers is in some respects not as cohesive as those of the other two affiliations. If a colony wishes to branch out, for example, the consent of all other Dariusleut colonies is not always required. When the Lehrerleut congregations assemble for Sunday worship, the preacher is the last to enter. Among the Dariusleut and the Schmiedeleut, the preacher is the first to enter the place of worship.

In the preaching service itself, gestures are subdued and severely limited. The preacher does not motion with his hands or walk about. Hutterites generally disapprove of body gestures that express relaxation or personal idiosyncrasies. When seated on a chair, a Hutterite will sit upright. Kneeling for the long prayer is a strenuous exercise all Hutterites learn at a very early age. Work is taken seriously and any attempt to minimize the physical effort is generally frowned upon.

In their leisure time, Hutterites are inclined to conversation. Modesty and restraint are characteristic of conversational patterns. The young are expected to show respect, take orders, and avoid reference to personal opinions. The conversation among men, as members of the same fraternity, is very different from that involving women. In public men generally address women as inferiors, even though husbands may have a high regard for their wives.

Generally, the culture frowns on meaningless talk, and unnecessary or foolish remarks bring reproach. Humor varies greatly among individuals. (Hutterites are more apt to laugh and jest with outsiders who are friends of the colony than among themselves.) At weddings, the young gather in a room and tell amusing stories. Mishaps or inappropriate role playing form the substance of much of the humor. Obscene, or "dirty," stories are rarely a subject for jokes among the men.

Hutterites are a serious people. Sports are not regarded as a proper activity for adults. Singing, reading, visiting, and going for long walks are acceptable forms of leisure. Dancing is strictly taboo. There are no musical instruments except an occasional unobtrusive harmonica played by an adolescent. The young unbaptized people may go swimming in a nearby pond or river. Vacations take the form of extensive visiting in other colonies. Weddings and funerals have a relaxed atmosphere and serve as holidays. Sundays are days of rest and relaxation which break up the heavy routine of the week. There are no food taboos and no ceremonial fasting. Some of the men and women have developed hobbies in their leisure time. Young men in their spare moments may learn how to wire electric motors or make leather goods, and women how to embroider or copy sermons. Hobbies generally suit a person's age and status and serve a utilitarian function. Hunting and fishing have little or no tradition among Hutterites. Guns, with few exceptions, are taboo; when permitted, they are used for shooting coyotes intent on destroying the sheep. Hunting, as in Europe, is considered a sport, a pastime for the worldly person. Wild meat is not considered a delicacy.

Decorative arts are sparse among the colonies. Although there are some older samplers, kerchiefs, and pillowcases in their chests, Hutterite women no longer make these beautiful pieces. The acceptance of labor-saving devices and mechanization has influenced this change. There is no oil painting, but a few women make drawings from picture postcards and calendars. Love of the beautiful as expressed in material goods appears to be muted, retained largely in the varnished natural wood finishes on chests, cabinets, and floors. Today there is nothing comparable to the decorative pottery of the sixteenth century, although penmanship and bookbinding remain a viable aspect of Hutterite culture.

chapter eight

Subsistence and Economic Patterns

Community Resources

In contrast to the diversified economic activities pursued by the Hutterites in Moravia, all colonies in North America now depend upon agriculture for subsistence. The number of acres operated by the colonies varies according to the climatic and geographic conditions of the region.[1] Colonies begin with a minimum acreage and expand their holdings as population and productive capability increase.

The founding and growth process is exemplified in Dariushof, a small colony in Alberta. This colony started with a population of only

---

1. The average number of acres operated per colony was 8,792 in Alberta, 9,816 in Saskatchewan, 3,687 in Manitoba, 5,387 in South Dakota, and 10,929 in Montana. See *Report on Communal Property, 1972*, by the Select Committee of the Assembly, Province of Alberta, Edmonton, pp. 11–12; Marvin Riley and Darryll R. Johnson, *South Dakota's Hutterite Colonies, 1874–1969* (Brookings: Agricultural Experiment Station, South Dakota State University, 1969), p. 21; and Hans D. Radtke, *The Hutterites in Montana: An Economic Description* (Bozeman: Montana Agricultural Experiment Station, August, 1971), p. 27.

For specialized studies of Hutterite economic practices, see John W. Bennett, *Hutterian Brethren: The Agricultural Economy and Social Organization of a Communal People* (Stanford, Calif.: Stanford University Press, 1967); for comparative studies of Hutterite and family farm economic practices in Saskatchewan, see Bennett's *Northern Plainsmen: Adaptive Strategy and Agrarian Life* (Chicago: Aldine Publishing Co., 1969).

forty-nine persons and leased four thousand acres with the option to buy. There were hog and cattle barns and one dwelling house, which had been used by the previous owners. The annual rainfall there ranges from fourteen to seventeen inches. Droughts and frosts, late as well as early, are common. The vegetation consists of grasslands and bluffs of silver leaf bush. Soils range from black to brown to sandy loam and are usually well supplied with nitrogen and organic matter, though deficient in phosphorus. With good management, rotation of crops, and use of fertilizers, arable lands produce modest-to-good grain yields. Lands which are not cultivated are used for pasture. The terrain is uneven, varying from moderate hills to sloughs and water holes. The colonists say, "It is good cattle country. If the loam can grow poplars and red willows, it can also produce grain."

Gophers, beavers, muskrats, bobcats, lynx, coyotes, and badgers threaten the colony's productive enterprises. The gophers eat the seeded grain and roots, the coyotes disturb the sheep, and the lynx kill the poultry. There is danger that cattle will fall into the holes made by badgers and muskrats, and cropland may be flooded by the dam-building of beavers. Clearing, a seasonal activity, is an added burden for a small colony. The Dariushof clears from two to three hundred acres of bush land each year. In winter when the ground is frozen, a tractor with a bulldozer is used to break off the underbrush, which is heaped into windrows and left to dry for a year and then burned. The soil is broken with a large two-ton colony-made plow. It takes three years to convert a parcel of virgin land to crop land.

The colony adapted the ranch buildings to their own uses. The buildings included a dairy barn, two hog barns, several grain bins, a horse barn, a chicken barn, a repair shop, and two small dwelling units. In addition, long houses and a communal kitchen were erected. An abandoned schoolhouse was moved to the colony site, and a kindergarten building and a seed-cleaning plant were transported from the parent colony. The colony also constructed a root cellar, a smokehouse, a shoe shop, a storage building with a refrigeration unit, and additional buildings for poultry.

The new colony began with a loan of $8,000 from the parent colony, a modest amount of livestock, and the use of machinery and services from the parent colony. In four years the total assets of Dariushof were evaluated at $360,000. The land was worth $70,000, the balance representing the worth of the buildings and machinery. The annual cash intake after four years was slightly more than the expenditures of approximately $74,000. Twelve years after its inception, the colony numbered seventy-eight persons and 8,300 acres of land and had an annual expenditure of $190,000 out of an income of over $230,000. The greatest profit was made from raising and fattening cattle and from the sale of whole milk, pigs, eggs, grain, honey, geese, turkeys, and sheep, in that order. After twelve years the colony was able to pay off its major debts, which included legal settlement of a dispute that had arisen over the option to buy the colony land.

Within a six-mile radius of the colony there are six neighboring households (twenty-four persons) headed by small farmers who own or operate from a quarter- to a half-section of land. The colony often assists neighbors who have limited machinery and manpower in planting and harvesting their crops. The local and county officials have appreciated the positive influence and stability which the colony has contributed to the community, which stands in contrast to a general anti-Hutterite sentiment in Alberta.

Lehrerhof, in Montana, was founded thirty years ago by ninety people. Of its 16,000 acres of land only 4,500 are arable, and since summer fallowing is practiced, only 2,250 acres can be seeded each year. The remaining acres consist of grazing land and hay fields. Whenever possible, the colony farms additional acreage belonging to absentee farm owners in the surrounding area. The soil is light and shallow, yielding only 15 to 20 bushels per acre in contrast to 50 bushels in more fertile regions. The colony's land is located on the eastern slope of the Rocky Mountains within the chinook wind belt, which has a marked effect on the area's climate. Strip farming is essential, as wind erosion is a serious problem.

In a typical year, Lehrerhof harvested 28,000 bushels of barley, 12,000 bushels of wheat, and 9,000 bushels of oats. The hay crop yielded 36,000 bales, which was stored for winter feeding. Much of the grain raised is consumed by the colony's livestock. Surplus wheat is sold for cash during the fall and winter. The colony's federal acreage allotment is limited to about 700 acres for wheat, 900 acres for barley, and 600 acres for oats. If the crops are hailed out or yield poorly the colony is eligible for a subsidy. All crops, including several hundred acres of alfalfa hay, are sprayed for weeds by a colony-made, self-propelled sprayer.

The colony owns five hundred head of cattle. A dairy herd of forty cows provides dairy products for colony consumption, and the sale of cream supplements other cash income. Five teams of horses and five saddle horses are maintained for working with range cattle and for hauling supplies in snowy winter months. About one thousand ducks, fattened during the summer, are consumed by the colony. An equal number of geese, most of which are marketed in nearby towns, are also raised and processed each year. Hog production is organized on a mechanized, continuous basis. One barn contains the brood sows and their young, while another is used for fattening the hogs. These barns are equipped with running water, a chain drag to carry out the manure, a system of ventilation, water heaters, and a heating unit with infrared lamps to keep the young pigs warm.

The colony raises about a thousand lambs each year. Lambing takes place during February, March, and April. During this time the sheep require almost constant care, thus providing work for the young men of the colony at an otherwise slack time. The marketing of wool and lamb brings in a significant portion of the colony income, and mutton is an important source of meat in the colony diet.

Lehrerhof was founded in Montana with the aid of real estate agents who showed colony representatives five possible sites. Its proximity to a good road and its reasonable distance (sixty-five miles) from a large trading center were main considerations. However, the disadvantages of the present site have now become apparent. The land is too poor and the rainfall too limited to produce the desired yields.

When it was formed thirty years ago, Lehrerhof was considered "modern" because of its trucks and electricity. In comparison with its own daughter colony, it is now old-fashioned. "We work with outdated facilities," said the steward, "and if we had the capital we would install a modern poultry barn and a new hog barn, put gas heating in the homes, make a larger kitchen, and buy better tractors." Since capital is lacking for such improvements, and present facilities suffice, improvements will be modest in the years ahead.

Schmiedehof in Manitoba has many of the agricultural characteristics of the two colonies already discussed, but it is distinguished by a greater degree of mechanization. Although its acreage is approximately five thousand, it is more productive than the other two colonies. Hog, egg, and turkey production are facilitated by the most modern equipment. Several chicken barns, housing up to ten thousand laying hens each, are automated with feeding, egg-gathering, egg-grading, and ventilating equipment. Mechanization appears to be more characteristic of the newly formed colonies than of the older colonies. As a rule, funds for modern machinery are allocated to the newly formed colony, and newer types of machinery are acquired in preference to older and less efficient models. New colonies generally have a limited supply of labor and need labor-saving equipment.

Oats, wheat, barley, and hay production are the main crop resources of the Manitoba colonies. A few other crops raised on Manitoba farms, such as flax, rye, field peas, rapeseed, and sugarbeets, are important to the colonies. The major income-producing items in order of importance are hogs, chickens, grain, turkeys, cattle, geese and ducks, custom work, vegetables, and honey. Hutterite colonists make more intensive use of their land resources than does the average Manitoba farmer, according to a study by John Ryan.[2] In terms of volume of output, the colonies are more productive in every major agricultural enterprise except cattle feeding. Because of the shortage of land for pasture, the Manitoba colonies do not specialize in this enterprise. Hutterites had about 74 percent of their farmland in crops as compared with 46 percent for other Manitoba farms. The colonies had higher yields per acre for grain crops than did other farms. On a per acre basis, the colonies had seventeen times as many hogs as the average for Manitoba. They had a higher turnover of market hogs per year than did the average Manitoba hog producer. The chicken enterprise focuses on egg production, with broiler raising a secondary pursuit. With less than 1 percent (.87) of Manitoba's arable farmlands, the colonies produced 17.9 percent of Manitoba's laying hens and 15 percent of Manitoba's hogs.

The Manitoba farm population had 118 acres per capita, or about 500 acres per family, in 1968. The Hutterites by contrast had 36 acres per capita, or 250 acres per family. Ryan observes that if colonies had land available to them at the same ratio as the rest of Manitoba's farm population, the average colony size would increase from 3,696 to 7,400 acres.

The various economic enterprises are carefully considered by each colony at the yearly meeting. Whether to expand, mechanize, or diminish one enterprise, such as hog or turkey raising, is an important question affecting the welfare of the whole colony. Certain factors enter into decision making with respect to the productive enterprises, such as the extent of agreement between the old and young men (the younger tend to support more mechanization), the ability of the person in charge of a given enterprise, and the ability of the group to arrive at an amicable consensus. Colony members have learned that consensus is more important for "the good of the colony" than sheer efficiency. They generally avoid speculative production. Their strategy is to maintain a wide diversity of agricultural enterprises so that there will be work for everyone throughout the year. Having many enterprises with a small margin of total profit is often considered better than maintaining only those enterprises which yield the largest margin of profit.

With their settlement in the Ukraine and later in North America, the colonies ceased their production of crafts for the markets (for example, pottery) and became agricultural producers. In America they responded to the growing needs for mechanization and intensive agri-

2. John Ryan, "The Agricultural Operations of Manitoba Hutterite Colonies" (Ph.D. dissertation, McGill University, 1973). This thorough study of land utilization practices should go a long way toward dispelling major distortions and stereotypes of the colonies.

culture. There remain, however, several manual skills and handicrafts. Important to the economy are bookbinding, clock repairing, tinsmithing, furniture making, shoemaking, tailoring, and perhaps less important economically, rug making, wool spinning, knitting (socks), quilting, and the making of traditional toys for the colony children.

Work Patterns

Work is important as a unifying and integrating element in colony life. Individualized conceptions of time, money, and man-hours are deemphasized in a colony. Work patterns are clearly defined within age and sex groupings and by formal authority patterns that are firmly supported by informal associations in small groups. Every person capable of working is expected to perform work assigned to him. Men, rather than women, are directly engaged in the income-producing phases of colony operations. Women as a rule are assigned to family, domestic, and food preparation jobs (for an exception, see figure 26).

The productive capacity of a colony varies with the size of its population, acreage, and the number of adults in the labor force. In one average-sized colony, there are 101 persons: forty-eight men and fifty-three women. The labor force (persons aged fifteen or over) consists of twenty-four males and twenty-four females. The married men have the most important positions of leadership. All major decisions, whether they pertain to work or to religious activity, are made by the whole colony and are implemented by the council. The preacher has an influence over the economic life and activity of the colony. He is always the president of the colony corporation. The second preacher is always his assistant. Normally, on Sunday evening after supper, the steward comes to the preacher's house with a summary of the work that needs to be done during the coming week. Together they formulate a plan and make assignments. Specific orders are given daily for jobs that are not routine.

Colony work is patterned according to the seasons. The leaders plan ahead and provide enough work for all males during the entire year. Lack of work could mean the breakdown of harmony. In summer there is a greater need for manpower than in winter, when the colony absorbs the surplus labor by giving each department additional younger apprentices. Most men have two jobs in which they have achieved a degree of specialization. The preacher may look after the geese in summer and concentrate on bookbinding in winter. The gardener may be the caretaker of honey bees. The pigman may have an extra boy assigned to him, the carpenter may have two extra helpers to make household furniture (see figure 27), and the shop mechanic additional help for overhauling machinery.

Figure 26. On butchering day men work in groups processing meat for sausages. This traditional method has been displaced by machines in most colonies. (Photograph by Lawrence Strang, 1948)

The constant need to improve and expand colony facilities absorbs some of the off-season labor. A newly formed colony with a small kitchen must build a larger complex as its population expands. Additional buildings must also be planned. During slack work periods, the colony may decide to remodel, a task that usually begins with the search for a supply of lumber. Old buildings may be secured from a neighbor, carefully dismantled by colony labor, and transported to the building site. Bulldozing underbrush when the ground is frozen is a part of one colony's winter work activity. In another, hunting foxes with a snowmobile and hounds is part of the winter work schedule. (Geese and ducks are vulnerable to these pests in summer.)

Competition and experimentation are desired and encouraged in work and productive activity. Competition between department managers plays a part in the healthy growth of a colony. It does not involve direct competition between individuals or their assigned statuses but

Figure 27. Apartment furniture is made by skilled colony carpenters and cabinetmakers. (Photograph by Philip Garvin, 1974)

between income-producing phases of the operation. For instance, the foreman of the chicken-raising enterprise may accumulate a great deal of knowledge about the best methods of building, ventilating, feeding, and processing and about the exact cost of producing a case of eggs. The dairyman learns all he can from farm magazines, agricultural experimentation publications, neighbors, and salesmen about livestock and the prevention of disease. Borrowing skills and techniques from the outside is deemed essential. Inventions in one colony will spread to others, often in a very short time.

The work tempo varies with the seasons. In winter the pressure to complete any particular job is not as great as in summer, the growing season, which in many colonies is relatively short. (See figure 28.) Work is not done in an erratic manner; the work pattern is predictable, regular, and satisfying. There is no effort to make work last. There are times of relaxation and a minimum of physical exertion. When work assignments are completed before the end of the day, men tend to gather in the central shop. By gravitating to the unfinished tasks of others, the individual is in effect showing cooperation. Boys will run errands and older men will voluntarily offer assistance.

Figure 28. Lunch time during the busy harvest season. (Photograph by Kryn Taconis)

Patterns of Colony Expansion

The viability of Hutterite culture is nowhere more ably demonstrated than in its strategy of growth. Effective use of land resources, a high birth rate, disciplined work patterns, austerity of personal consumption, and motivation for community rather than individual fulfillment all contribute to what Hutterites call "branching," or "branching out." The formation of new colonies, or "cell division," is the response the Hutterites make to biological growth, thereby enabling them to maintain small, manageable, face-to-face domestic groups. (For a graphic overview of branching in each Leut for a century, see appendix 16.)

The characteristics of social organization and expansion are basically alike in each Leut. Each colony forms its own new colony by a planned method of splitting. A growing colony deliberately plans a new daughter colony in advance. This process requires delicate management of capital assets and investments, redistribution of colony authority, and careful attention to kinship factors and work patterns. When the population of a colony reaches a maximal size, from 130 to 150 persons, the leaders begin to have management and supervisory problems, problems of increasing inefficiency caused by affluence. The growth span between branchings varies, but the average is about fourteen years. During this time a colony may well increase from about 70 to 130 persons.

The growth pattern of a colony can be classified in several stages from the time it is formed until it forms a daughter colony. First, the new colony must work hard to pay off 50 percent of its indebtedness; the parent colony is responsible for the other half of the debts. When this is accomplished, the debt-free colony will expand its land holdings and obtain more equipment to provide more jobs for its growing population. The third stage is the period of affluence during which a colony is able to save money for expansion, loan money to other needy colonies, and make and install many labor-saving devices. Each of these stages has distinct capital, management, and labor problems.

Before branching, savings of about $200,000 are needed for the initial investment in land and equipment. To accumulate this amount of capital, a colony must average $10,000 of savings annually for twenty years, although some colonies are able to branch out after only twelve years. The decision to branch out is not just an economic proposition; ease of obtaining land, population pressure, and how well the "politics" of the colony are managed are all factors in making the decision. Each new colony must be formed in such a manner that the age and sex distributions of the population are maintained. In the small colony of approximately sixty persons, about half are under the age of fifteen. Of the adults, about fifteen are males who carry on the major work and managerial responsibility. The minimum number of positions in a new colony include those of preacher (who may temporarily serve also as steward), field manager, cattleman, schoolteacher, and council member-at-large. Five of the fifteen men are normally aged twenty-five or older. Only married men are eligible for foreman positions. The remaining ten men may be unmarried, and most of them will be unbaptized. Their work requires careful supervision. Several positions may be combined and held by a single foreman until younger men become eligible. Thus the new colony is characterized by much work, many potential jobs and status positions, and a minimum of struggle for the more important roles.

In a new colony both men and women tend to be overworked. The shop mechanic has more work than he can do himself. He needs young helpers who show aptitude for a number of skills, such as electrical work and welding. The cattle herd may require two men to tend it, depending on its size. During the seeding and harvesting seasons, great demands are made on the entire colony. Four or five combines are necessary to harvest the crop in the short time before winter sets in. The combines are operated on a twenty-four-hour basis. Several truck drivers are necessary to haul the grain. Others are required to swathe, and the mechanic is often busy with emergency repair work. Tractor fuel is transported to the fields. In case of a breakdown, a mobile welding unit is brought out into the fields.

New colonies are formed within a few miles of existing colonies and rarely as far as five hundred miles away from the parent colony; about thirty miles distant is considered ideal. (See figure 29.) New colonies usually acquire from 3,000 to 4,000 acres and increase their acreage as opportunity and need arise. They seldom start with the maximum number of acres desired or the maximum number set by law— 6,400 acres in Alberta in 1947. Legal restrictions on buying land, particularly in a bulging colony where there is competition for roles and a need to expand the work program, have intensified internal problems. New land is secured, preferably land adjoining the colony property, but other nearby lands are also purchased as the colony approaches its maximum size.

The ratio of qualified persons to available positions is reversed when a colony reaches maturity. (Changes in population from founding to branching are shown in table 1.) The thirty or more men who are over the age of thirty hold all the important positions. Another five to eight

Figure 29. Apartment dwellings in a new colony in South Dakota. (Photograph by Philip Garvin, 1974)

Table 1. Changes in Schmiedehof Colony Population from Founding to Branching

	Colony population			
			After branching in 1969	
Age group	At founding (1954)	Before branching (1969)	Parent colony	New colony
75 and over	0	0	0	0
70–74	1	2	0	2
65–69	0	2	1	1
60–64	0	1	0	1
55–59	3	0	0	0
50–54	2	1	1	0
45–49	1	7	2	5
40–44	0	8	5	3
35–39	1	8	4	4
30–34	7	6	1	5
25–29	8	7	6	1
20–24	6	11	2	9
15–19	8	20	11	9
10–14	4	31	17	14
5–9	8	35	18	17
Under 5	19	26	15	11
Total	68	165	83	82
Percent male	50.0	53.3	49.4	57.3
Percent under age 15	45.4	55.7	60.2	51.2

persons typically are between the ages of twenty-five and thirty and expect to be assigned to important positions soon. Since all appointments tend to be permanent, the opportunities for younger married men become increasingly limited. The upward mobility that normally comes with age is thwarted by the lack of foreman positions. When the labor force is large, the division of labor becomes more specific, overlapping jobs are eliminated, and competition tends to develop between family lines. Fathers who hold positions of influence have a slight advantage in getting their sons into favored jobs. Thus, competition tends to become personalized and reaches a stage that is conducive to social unrest. In a young colony there is a pronounced age difference between the leaders and the followers, while in a mature colony the age differences between those eligible for the important jobs tend to be slight, making the rules increasingly difficult to maintain. Factionalization and the formation of cliques anticipate the need for branching, which mitigates disruptive tendencies and channels competition into productive enterprise.

Among Lehrerleut and Schmiedeleut a colony must have the consent of all other colonies within the Leut before forming a new colony.

This procedure is not only a formal courtesy but a check on the credibility of the communal system as a whole. Successful communal living depends upon the well-being of every newly formed colony. Should a new colony run into difficulty with crop failure or suffer financial reverses, all are obliged to come to its aid. Among the Dariusleut, a colony may branch without formal consent of the others, and their practices permit one of two factions in a colony to "volunteer" to move to a new location. But this volunteering, some say, works against the goal of impartiality, since it is usually a kinship group that does the volunteering. A colony that branches without the consent of others and then experiences financial reverses will have difficulty borrowing money from other colonies. Population growth is not the only impetus toward branching. If the colony is divided into two factions, if the preachers, or the preacher and the steward, do not get along too well, colonies may branch years before their numbers are optimum. Branching tends to resolve the usual conflicts between sibships.

Following the decision to branch, a suitable site must be agreed upon by the whole colony. A preferred site has the following features: availability of a good water supply, good soil and drainage, an adequate growing season, sufficient rainfall, a record of productivity, and a location several miles from any town but having access to roads and markets. Potential fire hazards and hailstorms are also taken into consideration. The colonists prefer the buildings to be located near the center of the acreage. The women like a reasonable amount of space between living houses, the communal kitchen, the schoolhouse, and the kindergarten. They are permitted to view the prospective new location and to express preferences. As soon as the land is leased or bought, it may be farmed and the construction of dwellings begun. As a colony grows, more buildings are added to the over-all layout. Frequently the colony buildings are also hedged in with trees and shrubs for protection against the wind and the gaze of worldly traffic. Although branching practices differ in detail among the three Leut, the following account of a division in a Lehrerleut colony is fairly representative.

Thursday was to be moving day and many trucks from the nearest colonies (up to three hundred miles away) came to help. All members packed their belongings on Wednesday. Since no one knew who was going to move, everyone had to be prepared, even though half of the families would remain. The cattle were divided into two herds and a lot was drawn to determine which herd would go. The lot system was also used to divide certain kinds of small equipment. It was agreed that the new colony would purchase additional new equipment, including tractors. The parent colony provided the capital for branching, and the two colonies decided to remain a single corporation until the debts were paid.

The parent colony was to retain the older machinery. The milking equipment was not to be removed, for the new colony would obtain its own equipment as assets permitted. Some benches and desks were removed from the school, since the group staying behind would not have need of them.

The division of the colony population is always a matter of great concern. The preacher, with the aid of his assistant, listed families on the blackboard in two groups, each of which was headed by the name of one of the preachers. Family heads were permitted to choose between the two preachers. Older people were grouped according to their known preferences, but a balance between the two groups was worked out that took into account age, sex, family size, and kinship. On Wednesday afternoon, all the baptized men gathered in the school to consider the plan of their leaders. The women anxiously waited at home to hear the outcome. After the evening meal, the lot was drawn between the two preachers to see which of the two groups would move. The older of the two preachers drew the first slip of paper from a hat. It indicated that he was to remain. On Thursday morning the loaded trucks rolled away with the assistant preacher and his group. Those remaining on the colony quietly unpacked their belongings, sad to be separated from friends and family but happy that they were allowed to remain in familiar surroundings.

Branching is supported by religious teaching and by the authority patterns. Only the will of God is strong enough to separate family members—parents from older children, brother from brother—and break personal and sentimental ties. The individual will must be subordinated to the will of the community. If the level of spiritual dedication is high, branching can be achieved with few problems; otherwise, long-standing grievances may result. The highest ideal to be achieved in branching is impartiality in personal relationships and in the division of property.

The Distribution of Goods

The natural, or carnal, desires of the individual (as discussed in the section on world view) are considered so strong that the help of the community is essential if life is to be lived according to the divine order. "Needs" within the colony are therefore defined by consensus and reflected in the way the colony distributes its resources. Equality and need are two professed ideals.[3] Equality, however, does not imply that all

---

3. "Each was given what he needed according to the measure . . ." (Rideman, *Account of Our Religion*, p. 88).

persons have the same needs. In practice there are differences in the amount and kind of food, furniture, and clothing that are distributed.

There are two dining rooms, one for the adults and one for the children, where the people in the colony receive their food. (See figure 30.) The only adults who do not eat in the dining hall are the two preachers, who eat in the apartment of the head preacher. The reason for this practice, Hutterites say, is that God-fearing people hold their ministers in high esteem.[4] In practice it allows the leaders the necessary privacy for counsel, and it also gives members the opportunity to bring needs and complaints to the leaders' attention. Each family apartment has a few dishes reserved for feeding preschool children and for serving snacks at coffee time.

Distribution of clothing illustrates the Hutterite concepts of need and equality. Clothing can be saved, modified, and exchanged. The head tailoress of each colony keeps a record specifying the kind and amount of clothing allocated to individuals and family heads. Allotments and specifications are determined by the rules of each Leut. Most rules have been modified from the old allotment book in some way. Each mother usually keeps a record of what her family has received. A certain quantity of material is distributed several times each year from the store room. A family is not obligated to use it for a specified purpose, and it need not be used by the person for whom it was allocated. There is some trading of material between families and even between families in different colonies.

In Lehrerhof the following allocations go to a newly married couple: a groom receives one bed with mattress and pillow, a table and two chairs, a closet, cupboard, stove, wall clock, and sewing machine, and a set of Hutterite books; a bride receives from her colony 7 yards and 8 inches of bedspread material, 10 yards of comforter cover, material for a mattress pad 60 inches wide, six pillow cases, 12 yards of material for a feather comforter, an enamel dish, one cup and saucer, a kettle, spoon, knife, fork, soup pail, scissors, and large chest. Clothing and bedding are homemade. The pillows and feather bedding are usually made by the bride's family before the wedding day. Feathers for making comforters were allocated in years past at the rate of sixteen pounds per person, but now a couple has the option of taking a mattress and only twelve pounds of feathers. Eight pounds of feathers are permitted for each new baby.

The number of children determines the number of beds and amount of bedding: with the first child the family gets a crib, with the second a

4. Zieglschmid, *Die älteste Chronik*, p. 363.

Figure 30. *Top*, main dining room in a Hutterite colony; *bottom*, in a separate dining hall for children, every child learns table manners and approved colony behavior. (Photographs by Philip Garvin, 1974)

Schlafbank (a settee that opens into a bed for two children), with the fourth child a second Schlafbank, with the sixth child a second bed, with the eighth child a third bed, with the tenth child a third Schlafbank (or a fourth bed), and with the twelfth child another bed.

For every baby, the family receives 2 yards of material for shirts, 4 yards for two little dresses, 2 yards for aprons, 2 yards (of flannel) for underwear, and 4 yards for diapers. Obviously this is not enough for a year, but with gifts from relatives, the supply is ample. A mother may always draw upon her regular allotment of yard goods for the family.

The rule book specifies to the inch how much yardage each person shall have on the basis of his age. Ten-year-old boys are allowed 3 yards and 6 inches of material for a jacket annually, eleven-year-old boys are allotted 3 yards and 12 inches, and men over fourteen receive 4 yards. When someone is overweight, he is given 9 additional inches. Clothing allotments change most dramatically when boys and girls become adults. The rule book allows 9 yards of material for a girl's dress. It takes only about 5 yards to make a woman's dress today, but the traditional allotment is still distributed. (See figure 31.)

The colonies buy yard goods from salesmen who frequent the colonies in spring and fall. The tailoress knows how much the colony needs and will inquire about the price and quality. The steward must consent to the cost, and the preacher must approve the colors. After a clothing salesman visited the colony, one preacher said: "The women have so much material, they don't know what to do. They are just like children

Figure 31. Hutterite girls in everyday dress. (Photograph by Larry Porteous)

who don't know what they should have and who don't realize what it costs." Women admit that the material is stronger than it was years ago, and the men say they cannot possibly wear out everything in such a short time. Women will often buy the less durable material, so as to be able to get another new dress sooner. Some boys are finicky about colors and the fit of their shirts and trousers.

Each household is assigned sleeping rooms according to the size of the family. At Lehrerhof one additional room is provided for every six children. But should the colony have spare rooms, use is made of them. Frequently brothers and sisters sleep in the same room until they are twelve. Younger members of the family sleep in a room with their parents. Every family has a box in a root cellar for storing the vegetables, fruits, and beverages that are allocated regularly to them. The amount of beer and wine distributed to each family varies with the colony. In one colony each person over fourteen years of age receives twelve bottles of beer quarterly. Wine is frequently made by the colony from grapes and rhubarb, and each adult receives one quart per month. Rhubarb wine is usually regarded as "a poor colony's wine." Beverages served at weddings and at butchering time are in excess of the family allotment. Twelve bottles of soft drink are allocated to school children quarterly; persons over fourteen who prefer soft drinks to beer may obtain twice that number of bottles.

Equality in the distribution of goods is generally established on the basis of age and sex. Socially sanctioned needs, not individual wants, are satisfied. Impartiality and sharing are emphasized. Abuses of the system do exist, but what matters to the colonists is not that there are abuses but that there is a standard from which exceptions can be granted. Respect for the system is thereby maintained.

Consumptive Austerity

The principle of community of goods governs not only the production and distribution of resources so that "one person must not have abundance and another suffer want,"[5] but also the control of the natural appetites. Carnal desires are believed to express themselves in the adornment of the body and in activities that cater to gratification—"the lusts of the eye"—such as movies, television shows, dancing, recreation in public places, excessive drinking, and worldly music. Curling, a common form of recreation in Canadian towns, and skiing are also viewed as a great waste of time and money and are forbidden. Such manifesta-

---

5. Rideman, *Account of Our Religion,* p. 88.

tions are not legitimate "needs" and are not part of the consumption pattern of either the individual or the colony.

The strategy of limiting consumption in the colonies has been described as the "culture of austerity—a way of living with less, and doing so with dignity and purpose."[6] The Hutterites do not live at the poverty level, although the colony income on a per-family basis is well below $3,000. Austerity as a way of life results in enormous savings by prevailing American and Canadian standards.

The consumptive needs of the colony are reflected in the buying practices and recorded in the annual fiscal statements. The buying pattern of Schmiedehof, a colony of eighty-eight persons, showed cash expenditures of $320,289 in 1971. The major expenditures were for underwriting the productive enterprises of colony life, for feeds, building supplies, machinery, repairs, gasoline, seeds, and insecticides. More was spent for livestock medicines, taxes (property and school), and seeds than for groceries. Although this colony spends more than most colonies for groceries, only 2.5 percent of the total cash expenditure was for food. Only about 1 percent of all cash expenditure was for clothing.

The widespread belief among outsiders that Hutterite colonies ignore local merchants, buy only from wholesale sources, and are responsible for introducing economic hardship into rural regions is unfounded. Recent studies made by economists show that although the colonists do not buy luxury items in the small towns nearby, they buy building supplies, hardware, machinery, groceries, trucks, fuel, feeds, fertilizers, repairs, seeds, and other supplies wherever they can obtain them.[7] They sell produce locally wherever there is a market, and they patronize local merchants who price competitively and give good service. "In total spending a colony will contribute more per acre to the economy of Montana than the average farm or ranch."[8]

The yearly income and profits of the colonies vary from year to year and with the climate and crop yields. The annual receipts over expenditures in Schmiedehof for 1971 showed a balance of $23,700. When allocated to individuals, this balance amounts to $270 per person, or $2,154 for each of the eleven family heads. This figure does not include a share of the colony's capital investments. The average colony income for Manitoba colonies in 1968 was approximately $31,000.

Hutterites are able to offset many of the high costs of large-scale farming. Massive tractors and large trucks are repaired in colony repair

6. Bennett, *Hutterian Brethren*, p. 173.
7. See ibid., pp. 228-41; Bennett, *Northern Plainsmen*; Radtke, *The Hutterites in Montana*; Ryan, "The Agricultural Operations of Manitoba Hutterite Colonies"; and *Report on Communal Property, 1972*, pp. 15-19.
8. Radtke, *The Hutterites of Montana*, p. 46.

shops. The labor force is trained by practical experience and by limited exposure to outside industrial plants. Occasionally colony men will take a short course in electrical wiring, welding, and veterinary training in technical schools outside the colony. The shop absorbs labor when idleness would threaten the cohesion of the colony, thus keeping the system efficient at minimum cost. These shops utilize scrap iron and steel, often available from city dumps at low prices.

Colony repair shops provide an inexpensive way of mechanizing operations. Used equipment is bought, and skilled Hutterite mechanics adapt it to colony needs. They modernize hog and poultry barns and install feeding and egg-gathering equipment; they improve the existing brands of farm machinery or adapt them to new uses. Plexiglass cabs for grain combines were constructed by Hutterite mechanics before farm implement companies sold them commercially. Cultivators adapted to dry-land farming are made by colonies in Canada. Specialized machines such as hydraulic rock pickers and tractor cabs are manufactured by colony shops. The Noble Blade, widely used by Canadian colonies, acts like a gigantic knife, slicing the soil at a depth of about five inches. This method of cultivation, an alternative to disc plowing, reduces wind erosion. The Rosedale capping knife for extracting honey from honeycombs was made by a colonist in the Rosedale colony; it was later patented and produced by an outside firm. Potential patents and royalties from such inventions have not been seriously pursued. Neither individuals nor colonies have accumulated wealth from royalties.

By outside standards Hutterite austerity results in savings, in the accumulation of colony capital wherever possible, sometimes in unusual ways. Colonies as far away as Canada pool their orders for watermelons from a Texas dealer each year. Large petroleum tanks discarded by oil companies are converted into grain storage bins. Damaged canned goods are bought at reduced prices from chain stores. Grain damaged by fire is often purchased from elevators at half price and fed to the livestock. Used electric motors and generators are secured from discarded equipment, then rewound and repaired by colony mechanics. One Montana colony drove its trailer truck to the East Coast to obtain earthmoving equipment from Army surplus stock. Colony foremen frequently receive courtesy gifts from stock dealers and salesmen who seek the business of the colony. Such favors might include free subscriptions to farm magazines that directly benefit the colony. Although the colonies do not solicit repair work, one mechanic earned $70 per day for the colony by repairing upholstery on trucks for outsiders.

Such are the communal patterns of austerity. Any inclination to overspend reveals itself in the work world of men rather than among the women. The men may be tempted by expensive farm equipment and ingenious labor-saving devices.[9] In the most mechanized colonies, there is greater incentive for work and pride in the communal system; personal indulgence would be a more direct threat to colony cohesion than would colony indulgence.

In keeping with their belief in the necessity of civil government, Hutterites pay all taxes levied against them except war taxes.[10] Local property and school taxes are imposed on colonies, as on all landowners. Systems of taxation vary within the states and provinces where the colonies are located, but in most places the colonies are taxed as corporations. At one time colonies were exempt from federal taxes as "religious and charitable" institutions, but this is no longer true in either the United States or Canada. Since individuals do not receive any income, no individual tax returns are filed. Instead, colonies file federal tax returns as corporations, reporting gross as well as net income. Taxes are determined by the number of men, women, and children in the colony and are levied on any income over a standard deduction.

The "tax problem," as the Hutterites call it, has been a foremost concern of all Canadian colonies in recent years. Colonies have had to acquire tax accountants and lawyers not only to meet legal requirements but to protect themselves against oppressive and discriminatory laws. Anti-Hutterite politics could have drastic consequences in the form of tax discrimination. Even with the corporation tax, there remain many forms of inequity. In making parity payments, school tax rebates, and acreage grants—hog and egg deficiency payments, for example—colonies in Manitoba are treated as a single family unit. Thus, when a $50 school tax rebate went to each Manitoba family living on the land, each colony was eligible for only $50 even though there were from eleven to twenty families in one colony. The colonies do not draw welfare, old age, or unemployment compensation. Most do not accept the family allowances available to them in Canada.

The Individual and Property

Colony austerity is one thing, and individual conformity is yet another. The individual Hutterite, as in any society, is inclined to want more than the colony will permit him to have. Throughout their history, from the beginning of the sixteenth century to the present, the major warning in all Hutterite literature and sermons has been to curb the

9. Bennett makes this observation in *Hutterian Brethren*, p. 173.
10. Rideman (*Account of Our Religion*, p. 109) says, " . . . Where taxes are demanded for the special purpose of going to war, massacring and shedding blood, we give nothing. This we do neither out of malice nor obstinacy but in the fear of God, that we make not ourselves partakers of other men's sins."

desire for private possessions. Modern Hutterites are realistic; they admit their human desires and recognize that without the help of the colony they could not live in such a state of submission. There is, then, a delicate balance between the colony standards of consumption and the desires of the individual. The rule against private property is relative and contextual rather than absolute.

Personal property to an adult Hutterite means: "Something given to me from the colony for me. Once it has been given, it is mine to use." Property is defined as the right to use but not to possess. Personal belongings include those items that are formally given to the individual by the colony plus anything acquired by the individual with money from his small allowance. Typically, for a man, this consists of wallet, watch, pocket knife, small tools, flashlight, writing materials, technical or general books (in addition to Hutterite books), magazines, small souvenirs, and personal articles of clothing such as slippers. Belongings that a person may retain are kept in a chest under lock and key. Personal belongings are passed on to children and relatives before or after a person dies. Yard goods which have not been utilized for clothing are returned to the colony storehouse at the time of death. Ideally, all personal gifts from neighbors or outsiders are reported to the steward. In practice, individuals are permitted to keep some of these gifts, which they may have earned in return for work or favors. Some gifts benefit the colony. In one colony several men had been given a pair of binoculars. They were used by the sheepherder and cattle foreman in their work. There is little sentimental value attached to old clothing, dishes, or furniture. Books are an exception to the general rule of indifference to personal property. A book may be valued if it is old or if a relative has copied it. The sons of preachers who are themselves elected preachers are privileged to use certain books, especially sermon books. Although having one's picture taken is taboo, possessing a photograph once it has been taken (by an outsider) carries little negative sanction.

From the perspective of children growing up in a colony, there are two kinds of property: things under lock and key to which access is forbidden, and materials that are not locked up. The latter are accessible to all and available for use. The practice of using padlocks in the colony "is necessary to keep children from getting into everything." There is a widespread expectation that children will get into everything; one preacher said, "Opportunity makes thieves, and we have to keep things locked up." School girls at Lehrerhof from grades three to eight keep their chests locked, "or else our brothers would take everything," they say. Each girl carries her own key to guard her own little secret world containing chewing gum, perfume, coins, scarfs, pictures, letters, and keepsakes. Young people learn the appropriate restraints against taking property that is not locked up.

In some colonies, members receive small monthly allowances for which they need not give an accounting. Traditionally, a small amount of spending money was given to those individuals who went to town with the colony officials when they conducted their weekly business. Even though these persons usually went to town for a specific reason, such as seeing a doctor, the numbers wanting to go increased, a practice that was unfair to those who rarely left the colony. To correct this, some colonies began giving a monthly allowance to all persons in the colony whether they went to town or not. The amount of the allowance varies from colony to colony. In Lehrerhof, adult men receive one dollar per month and adult women receive one dollar every six months. Dariushof discontinued the allowance system altogether after several years, making sure that all needs were adequately provided for instead.

Sharing is normative in a colony. But there are additional forms of voluntary sharing, such as informal friendship pacts and agreements and reciprocal exchanges between siblings and relatives within the colony. Equality within the peer group is the norm, so that when a whole roast duck is served on Sunday noon, it must be shared at the table in an equitable manner. One duck is for four persons—always the same four, since persons are always seated at the same table in the same position. Courtesy requires that the two persons who eat the breast and better pieces one Sunday give the same privilege to the other two persons the following Sunday.

Individuals as well as families may exchange goods and favors. One family will exchange some of its feather allotment for a particular pattern of cloth from another family. Gift-giving among friends and relatives takes many forms and is made possible by the modest monthly allowances. Gifts are given to a newborn baby. Candy is exchanged on many holidays. Gifts of food are prepared on short notice by a family to be given to relatives in another colony. Greeting cards at Christmas, Valentine's Day, and Easter are exchanged by young people. Unmarried men and women may exchange gifts about five times a year on major holidays. Because boys have more opportunity to obtain pocket money than girls, they often give their girl friends money with which to buy gifts.

In summary, Hutterite society is modern in its technology and generally efficient in its agricultural enterprises. The adherence to religious authority prevents the maximizing of individual wants. Austerity and simplicity are consciously accepted by the individual as necessary to a way of life in which carnal desire must be subjugated to man's spiritual well-being. Hutterite society is communal not only in production but also in consumption and distribution. Food is consumed in a communal, not a family, setting. Clothing and most other necessities are distributed through resident household units. Profits realized from the marketplace are held by the corporation for the welfare of the whole colony.

chapter nine

Schooling and Preparation for Life

When the fathers and mothers in the colonies we studied were asked, "What is the greatest or highest good you want your children to achieve in life?" typical answers were "That they be honest and faithful Christians and learn to love God and the communal way," and "We want our children to be good born-again Christians, strong supporters of the Hutterite faith—not only to be able to talk about being a Christian but rather to show it in works and deeds by following the footsteps of our Dear Lord and Savior; to give their time and strength, and if need be, their blood and very life." In reply to the question, "Do you worry much about how your children will turn out?" most parents said that they were "very seriously concerned but not worried."

Self-Surrender

Vital to an understanding of Hutterite education is the group's conception of the individual and of the "self."[1] The Hutterite view of human nature contrasts sharply with that of contemporary American society. It is generally assumed in American society that what is good for the in-

1. Discussed under "World View" in chapter 6; see pp. 144–45.

dividual will be good for the community. The secular conception of man in American society leads to the belief that "a person with developed rational powers has the means to be aware of all facts of his existence. . . . He can enrich his emotional life and direct it toward even higher standards of taste and enjoyment. . . . He can free himself from the bondage of ignorance and unawareness. He can make of himself a free man."[2]

To the Hutterites such a goal is anathema, for individual human nature is inclined toward evil. Apart from the community and without the restraint of fellow members, the self is considered a liability. Children are taught from the beginning "not to carry out their headstrong will and carnal practices. We teach them . . . to bring the flesh into subjection, and to slay and kill it."[3] By learning first obedience and then faith, children can overcome their carnal nature and receive the spiritual nature, a nature that will live eternally.

The English language usage of "self" is undoubtedly functional in the individualistic American way of life. We, speaking modern English, conceive of the self as something extremely personal (individualistic). We can even speak of the self in a way that excludes the physical body. The self is assertive, able to control an independent body and, to some extent, the surrounding world. Our thought patterns recognize a dichotomy between a self and a nonself. The individual may habitually think of himself as apart from his society. Communitarian societies and many primitive societies do not recognize such a dichotomy. The Wintu Indians do not have an exclusive concept of self and therefore do not alienate the self from the society.[4] The Dakota Indians made self and society coextensive, for they strove not for self-expression or self-development but to achieve the experience of relatedness to all things.[5]

The Hutterites also strive to make the self and society coextensive. They have succeeded, in that one cannot remain a Hutterite outside a Hutterite colony. The Hutterite self-image demands identification with the colony. The usage of "I" reflects the intimate identification of the individual Hutterite with his society. He will use it in the typical sense referring only to himself, but he will also use it when referring to the action of a group with which he identifies, even though he was not present when the action took place.

    2. *The Central Purposes of American Education* (Washington, D.C.: Educational Policies Commission, National Educational Association, 1961), p. 8.
    3. Rideman, *Account of Our Religion*, p. 130.
    4. Dorothy Lee, *Freedom and Culture* (Englewood Cliffs, N.J.: Prentice-Hall, 1959), p. 132.
    5. Ibid., p. 63.

The Family and Socialization

The Hutterite family lives together in an apartment in one of the long houses. The long houses are built on a sixteenth-century floor plan, usually 100 feet long and 36 feet wide, running north and south, with four entrances. (See chart 4.) Each entrance leads to a middle room with two adjacent bedrooms. There is a stairway in the middle room leading to the attic, which is often one large room in which all the families in that long house store their out-of-season clothing and furniture.

When a couple marries, they are given a room and if possible an entrance of their own. As their family increases, they are given additional rooms. The apartment is the center of the universe for the tiny child under two and a half. or three, but for the older members of the family it is primarily a place to sleep and to store things. All meals are eaten in the central dining room. Food preparation takes place outside the long house, clothes are washed in the colony laundry, and baths are taken in the colony bath house.

There is little privacy. Children run around in the attic and into one another's apartments through the attic entrance. Colony people do not knock when they visit one another, nor do they hesitate to enter if no one is at home. Not only is privacy deemphasized; the constant surveillance of the colony is valued.

The function of the family is to produce new souls and to care for them until the colony takes over the major responsibility of training the children. The family performs those functions that cannot easily or efficiently be performed by the colony. Child-rearing is not thought of as a private enterprise; children are not extensions of the parents' egos but gifts of God who belong to the colony and potentially to the church, which is the body of Christ. There are no limits to the number of children a couple may have except those set by nature. Having children is supported by the world view, and birth-control practices are forbidden. The prohibition of sexual relations before marriage is firmly adhered to—a practice not inconsistent in a society that lives by absolute values in many aspects of life. A demographic study of the Hutterites covering the period from 1874 to 1950 shows that in 1950 the median age at marriage was 22.0 years for women and 23.5 years for men. Few persons remain unmarried; only 1.9 percent of the men and 5.4 percent of the women over the age of thirty had never married. Only one divorce and four desertions were reported since 1875. The median size of the completed family was 10.4 children.[6]

6. Joseph W. Eaton and Albert J. Mayer, *Man's Capacity To Reproduce: The Demography of a Unique Population* (Glencoe, Ill.: Free Press, 1954), pp. 16, 18, 20.

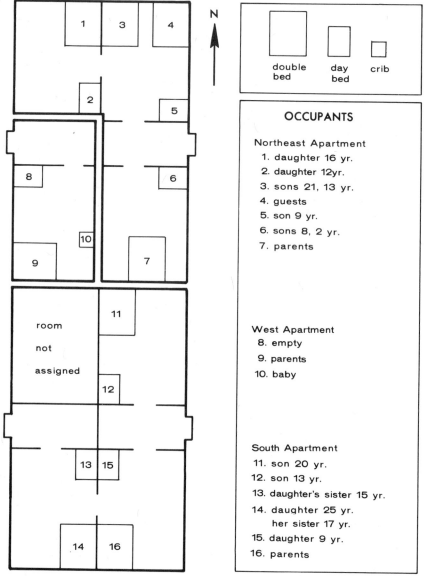

N

| double bed | day bed | crib |

OCCUPANTS

Northeast Apartment
1. daughter 16 yr.
2. daughter 12yr.
3. sons 21, 13 yr.
4. guests
5. son 9 yr.
6. sons 8, 2 yr.
7. parents

West Apartment
8. empty
9. parents
10. baby

South Apartment
11. son 20 yr.
12. son 13 yr.
13. daughter's sister 15 yr.
14. daughter 25 yr.
   her sister 17 yr.
15. daughter 9 yr.
16. parents

Chart 4. Winter Sleeping Pattern, Typical Longhouse

The Hutterite colony functions in many ways like an extended family. Because Hutterite society has institutionalized a continuing relationship between parents and children, the family is emotionally less demanding and less exclusive than is the rule with middle-class Americans.

The relationship between generations continues throughout life. The sons marry and settle down in the colony of their parents. The girls typically leave the home colony when they marry, but with the birth of every child a girl's mother goes to her and cares for her. Once each year a wife may return to her home colony for a visit; thus, the "line" is maintained. In other words, there is an emotional identification with the family of origin that is not unlike the identification and sense of loyalty that individuals living during the Middle Ages felt for their "line."

In the Middle Ages there was the "line" to which nobles owed allegiance, and there was the village which provided peasants with an orientation superior to and more meaningful than the family. The individual identified more closely with his line or his village than with his nuclear family. There were many reasons for this. A husband and wife could own property separately and buy and sell without much interference from each other. Marriage was arranged and considered an alliance of fiefs and not of hearts. In fact, the rules of courtly love decreed that although a husband and wife could be "bound to each other by a great immoderate affection . . . everybody knows that love can have no place between husband and wife."[7]

In the Middle Ages a child entered the adult world almost as soon as he was weaned. Similarly, one of the earliest Hutterite statements proclaimed that "as soon as the mother hath weaned the child she giveth it to the school."[8] In a society that severely limited the functions of the nuclear family, the family's unique role was finished when the child was weaned. Thereafter, any responsible person could take over the care of these small, dependent adults. However, in most of society during the Middle Ages the child remained with his family until he was about seven years old, for until that time he was so dependent that no one else would take him. A thirteenth-century jingle says:

Thus the child six summers old
Is not worth much when all is told.[9]

Children had no rooms of their own. In the same room, visitors were received, meals were served, business was transacted, and couples and children slept. Poor families lived adjacent to a manor house or in one- or two-room hovels that served as shelters for sleeping and sometimes, though not always, as a place to eat. After the age of about seven, children lived in families other than their own, where, as ap-

7. John J. Perry, ed. and trans., *The Art of Courtly Love by Andreas Capellanus* (New York: Columbia University Press, 1941), p. 100.

8. Rideman, *Account of Our Religion*, p. 130. Educational ideas of the Hutterites compared to other German-speaking Protestants are discussed by Mary A. Harada, "Family Values and Child Care during the Reformation Era: A Comparative Study of Hutterites and Some Other German Protestants" (Ph.D. dissertation, Boston University, 1968).

9. Philippe Ariès, *Centuries of Childhood: A Social History of Family Life*, trans. Robert Baldick (New York: Alfred A. Knopf, 1962), p. 22.

prentices, they learned manners and skills. While living with their masters, children might attend "little schools" where they were taught to sing, to memorize prayers by reciting them in unison, and to read a little. In order to have more education, a child of ten might travel with an older scholar to a university town where they would attend classes and support themselves by begging in the streets, from house to house, and at the churches. The family was a moral and social reality, but it had less claim on its members' emotions and was less important as a source of personal identity than the trade of the father, the land owned by the family, or the village in which the family lived.

Early Hutterite child-rearing practices were more humane and modern than those that obtained in the general society around them. In contrast to the practice of giving their children to outsiders to acquire manners and skills, the Hutterites kept their children in the Bruderhof. By twentieth-century standards Hutterite parents still had little control over their children, but in contrast to sixteenth-century practices, they kept their children close to them and maintained contact with them at all times. During their early history, when Hutterite children slept at the school, the school regulations mention that parents might visit the school and take "their children home to themselves for a visit." The emphasis on discipline, care, and concern for the child and his family is made very clear in the Hutterite School Discipline of 1568.[10]

Age Patterns and Formal Schooling

Acquiring the appropriate colony attitudes and values begins informally in the family and is reinforced, formally and informally, in all age groups until death. Unlike folk and peasant societies, Hutterites do not depend entirely on informal associations for rearing children; schools and formal instruction are greatly valued. Schooling is not, however, emphasized to the exclusion of informal group interaction. The daily and constant association with peers, between leaders and followers, and among persons of all ages contributes greatly to colony solidarity.

The world view, requiring a proper hierarchy for every activity, is projected onto the ordering of social relationships. The human life span is divided into a series of discrete age-sets that serve as impartial means not only for maintaining social order but for teaching the young how to become responsible adults.[11] Age determines both the group to which an individual belongs and, generally, his place within the group. One of the secrets of Hutterite survival, it is maintained, is that there are clearly

10. For "The Hutterite School Discipline of 1568," see appendix 4.
11. For the number of persons in the various age-sets, see table 2.

Table 2. Population of Three Colonies by Age-Group and Sex

Age-group	Schmiedehof			Lehrerhof			Dariushof		
	Male	Female	Total	Male	Female	Total	Male	Female	Total
Over 55	2	3[a]	5	1[b]	0	1	1	1	2
35–55	8	6	14	7	8[c]	15	2	3	5
Married, under 35	6	8	14	5	5	10	5	4	9
Baptized, un-married	1	1	2	1	4	5	1	2	3
Youth, 15 to baptism age	9[d]	4	13	10	7	17[e]	4	3	7
School children, 6–15	16	23	39	17	16	33	11	7	18
Kindergarten children, 3–5	12	13	25[f]	4	7	11	3	0	3
House children, under 3	7	5	12	3	6	9	5	3	8
Total	61	63	124	48	53	101	32	23	55
Married couples		18			12				8

[a]One widow
[b]Widower
[c]One widow
[d]Includes one single male over 30 who is mentally retarded
[e]Includes 14-year-olds
[f]Includes 17 "runabouts" (Schulela group) ages 5–6; 7 boys, 10 girls

defined goals and rewards within each age-sex group. Although the individual is subservient to the colony, the rules of conformity that apply are those of his age-sex affiliation. Deviation of an acceptable type is permitted within each age category. Dependency upon the peer group is maximized while at the same time the individual is motivated to accept communal responsibility.

The goals of socialization are principally two: preparation for adult life (initiation into baptism) and preparation for life after death (initiation into eternal life). Examined in the remainder of this chapter (and in chapter 10) are the age-sets of the Hutterite life cycle and the relation of each stage to colony goals. Particular attention will be given to the role of formal instruction.[12]

12. Informal socialization patterns are discussed in greater detail in John A. Hostetler and Gertrude Enders Huntington, *The Hutterites in North America* (New York: Holt, Rinehart, and Winston, 1967), pp. 57–90.

House Children

House children are children under two years of age. There is no institutional recognition of pregnancy; it is generally ignored by everyone. Many babies are born in the parents' apartment, especially in the United States where hospital costs are high. In Canada, childbirth usually takes place in a hospital. The mother is relieved of all colony responsibility and assigned the help of a mature woman, usually her mother. She is cared for and mothered at the same time that she cares for and mothers her baby. When the baby is four weeks old, the mother's helper leaves. For two more weeks the mother is relieved of colony work. Most babies are nursed for about a year or until the mother becomes pregnant again. Pacifiers are widely used.

Religious training begins with the introduction of solid food into the baby's diet, often before the baby is a month old. The mother folds the baby's hand in hers and prays with him before and after feeding. Religion is intimately associated with food and at this early age is already a ritual, a formal activity, and a social activity. When the child is put into his crib at night, his parents repeat a child's prayer aloud to him. Toilet training frequently begins at three months but always by the time the child can sit alone. Many do not wear diapers after they are six months old.

A baby is loved by everyone in the colony. (See figure 32.) When adults are not at work, babies are always held. Children will crowd around a baby and vie for the privilege of holding or playing with him. After the evening meal, when the men gather informally to discuss colony affairs, one or two can be seen holding babies on their laps. All of the adults in the colony, including Hutterite visitors, commonly give a young child cheerful attention. He is picked up, tickled, played with. When it is time for the adult meal or time for church, however, the child is placed in his crib and the parents disappear. Thus from the time that he is seven weeks old, he alternates between being in a socially stimulating environment and being completely alone. After he is old enough to climb out of his crib, he is watched by a baby-sitter.

The ideal baby sleeps a lot and, during his parent's work periods, responds to anyone. In other words, he adapts to the colony time schedule and accepts all other colony members. The child is considered innocent until he is observed to hit back. When he hits back or knows what a comb is for, his level of comprehension is believed to be sufficiently developed that he may be disciplined; he has both self-will and understanding. When small children quarrel over an object, the object is removed. The older house child may be disciplined quickly and frequently, but he is also petted, played with, and desired. Mothers do not take their young

Figure 32. Everyone loves a baby in a Hutterite colony. (Photograph by Kryn Taconis)

children with them when they do colony work. In summer the children have a great deal of freedom to wander about the colony grounds. They often play near where the adult men are working. There is a concerted effort to wean the house child away from his parents and into the group.

By the time a child is three and ready to enter the kindergarten, he has learned that the colony takes precedence over the individual, that he has little control over his environment, that punishment is usually physical and unpredictable. He has learned to respond positively to every person who comes within sight, not to complain when he is handed from one caretaker to another, and to be happy when he is with people. (See figure 33.)

Kindergarten Children

Three- to five-year-old children attend Kindergarten (*Klein-Schul*).[13] The experiences of the child in kindergarten differ among the three Leut and among different colonies. When the practices in the three colonies are observed in depth, they reveal differences not only in schedule, equipment, and kinds of punishment but also in the range of individuality permitted (see table 3).

Parents look forward to the child's entrance into kindergarten. But with this first major transition, the child plummets from a desirable position to a very low one, within both his family and the colony. The kindergarten child is expected to be more obedient and quieter than a house child. Adults rarely spend time with a kindergarten child, and visitors from other colonies do not exchange greetings with him. His low status is reflected by the quality of the food served to him in the kindergarten and by the fact that adults and older children usually banish him from any gatherings, partly because he has not yet learned to be sufficiently quiet. The preschool child is considered to be willful and useless, unable to contribute any labor to the colony.

The small kindergarten building, which ideally is located near the colony kitchen, consists of two or three rooms surrounded by a fenced-in play area. (See chart 5.) One of the rooms can be darkened, and here the

13. Although *Klein-Schul* is translated into English as *kindergarten*, it more closely corresponds to what we in this country call *preschool*, or nursery and kindergarten classes combined. The Hutterite child-rearing institutions evolved during the second quarter of the sixteenth century and have remained almost unchanged since then. During the eighteenth century, Hutterite colonies in Europe maintained day nurseries to care for weaned babies (ages fifteen to eighteen months to two and one-half years). From these day nurseries children entered the Little School (*Klein-Schul*), which at that time was a boarding school. Since their immigration to North America, the Hutterites have discontinued the day nurseries and boarding schools.

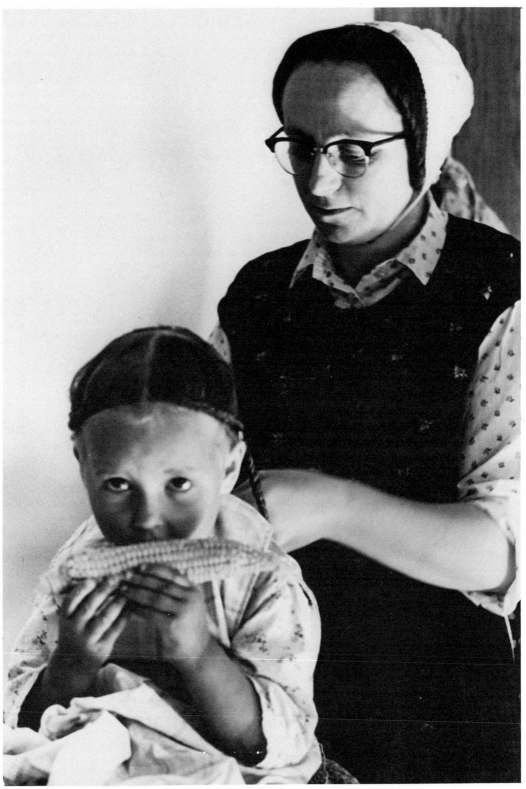

Figure 33. The tedious weekly combing. Hutterite women are skillful in teaching patience. (Photograph by Kryn Taconis)

Table 3. Characteristics of Kindergarten in Three Colonies

Item	Lehrerhof	Dariushof	Schmiedehof
Number of children	13	4	25
Age span (years)	2 ½ to 5th birthday	3rd to 6th birthday	2 ½ to 5th birthday
Months attended	9; Aug. to May	12	7 ½; May to Dec.
Stated reasons for kindergarten	To learn to obey and sit properly	To learn to obey, pray, and keep out of way	To learn to pray, share, and get along together
Number of meals	2 and snack	2 and snack	3
Toilet facilities	Outdoors	Outdoors, plan to install indoors	Two flush toilets indoors
Length of day	7:00–2:30	7:00–3:30	7:30–6:00
Play equipment	None	Minimal	Indoor and outdoor play equipment
Toys	None permitted	Small toys from home tolerated	Toys provided in school
Indoor play	Limited to sitting position	Limited to sitting position and class-room	Permitted in separate indoor play room
Memory work	Each learns 8–10 prayers and 6–12 hymns	Each learns 15–20 prayers and 26 hymns	Each learns 13 prayers and 24 hymns
Punishment	Firm punishment for all; use of willow	Firm punishment for all; use of strap and ladel	Older ones pun-ished, younger ones diverted from mis-deeds; use of rod
Sleeping arrange-ment	Blanket and heavy cardboard	Padded surface	Regular bed mat-tress, four children to each
Outdoor play	No adult super-vision	No adult super-vision	Adult supervision
Leaving age	5th birthday to enter *Schulela*, to learn to read and write German	6th birthday	5th birthday, some tutoring until age 6
Range of individuality	Minimal	Limited	Not stressed but greater variation permitted

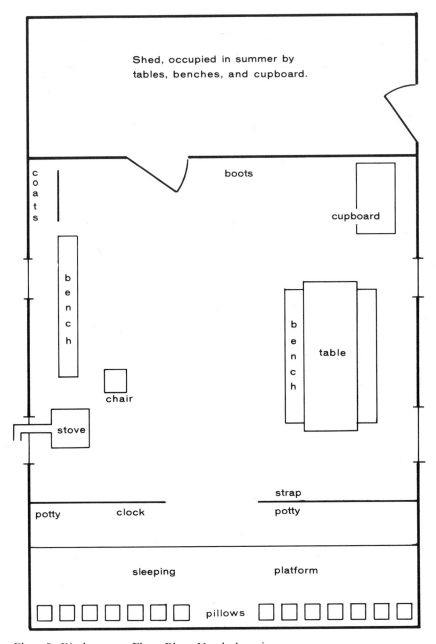

Chart 5. Kindergarten Floor Plan, North America

children take their naps. Each may bring a pillow from home. Another room functions as a dining room and to a limited extent as a play room. Traditionally, the kindergarten is supervised by the oldest women in the colony who are still able to work. The kindergarten mothers alternate, each woman taking responsibility for one full day. A school-age child supervises the kindergarten on Sunday so that the adults may attend church services.

The kindergarten children arrive before breakfast; led by the teacher, they recite prayers before and after the meal. Gradually these prayers are memorized. During their kindergarten years children learn numerous prayers and hymns by rote. At this age little effort is made to explain the meaning of what is memorized. In some colonies children return home about midafternoon, but in others they remain until after supper at about six o'clock. Despite variations in schedule among individual colonies, a major function of the kindergarten is to free the mothers for colony work.

Social misbehavior is quickly punished by scolding or switching, or a threat of some kind. The children may not quarrel, hit one another, call one another names, or disobey the person in charge. The kindergarten mother does not take any aspects of the children's misbehavior personally, nor does she inflict punishment vindictively. Rather, she regards the children almost as her own and believes that they need punishment to help them learn correct behavior. She also uses encouragement, praise, and rewards to modify their behavior. Hutterites feel that children of this age have stubborn wills that must be broken, an end the kindergarten helps to attain.

The kindergarten helps wean the child from his family. It introduces him to his peer group and teaches him how to function within this group. At an age when the child in North American society is expressing his emerging individuality and developing a concept of self, the Hutterite child is being placed in a setting that minimizes his individuality and maximizes his identity as a member of the group. The kindergarten teaches the child to respect the authority of the colony in addition to that of his parents and baby-sitters. The kindergarten teaches the child to tolerate a limited, restricted environment and rewards him for cooperative, docile responses to correction and frustration.

The colony's impact on the individual is maximal during his stay in kindergarten, for these are the most restricted years, having the least variation in program. Having fallen to the lowest position within the colony, he must now begin the steady climb toward full colony membership.[14]

14. In most colonies children leave kindergarten on their fifth birthday but do not enter the English school for another year or more. These "runabouts" attend German school when it is in session, eat in the children's dining hall, and attend church. Among

School Children

School children (ages six to fifteen) are taught unquestioning obedience to Hutterite authority: to parents, teachers, adults, and to Hutterite traditions and teachings. Self-discipline is not taught but rather obedience to those in authority who will supervise, punish, and protect. If in weakness the child fails to obey, he is taught to accept punishment meekly. The Hutterite child does not develop a strong sense of guilt. Because it is considered natural for a child to sin, he does not internalize the responsibility for his misbehavior. His actions must be directed by means of the praise and punishment of those in positions of authority.

The school child masters the basic rituals of Hutterite life. He abides by the rules because of the strong sense of obedience that has been instilled in him. Although he learns the verbal expressions of the belief system by rote, he is not expected to understand its more difficult aspects until adulthood. He learns to adjust to his designated position in the society, to accept many frustrations passively, to interpret teasing as positive attention, to enjoy hard physical labor, to begin to appreciate a life uncluttered by material objects, and to accept with a kind of pleasure the cleansing processes of pain and punishment.

Hutterite children attend three schools: German school, English school, and Sunday school.

German school. All children are taught German before English. At about the age of five children enter the *Gross-Schul*, or German school. (See figure 34.) German school is taught by a married man selected by the colony. His role is defined by tradition, and his work is supervised by the council members. Often, but not always, the German teacher is a member of the colony council. The German school mother is either the teacher's wife or an older woman appointed by the council. She has no responsibility for teaching religious subjects, nor does she give permission for, assign jobs, or punish. She helps supervise the children's meals, including serving the food and teaching manners.[15] Her other functions include assisting the German teacher and instructing the girls in patterns of work rotation that will be part of their colony work for the remainder of their lives.

Children over six meet in the schoolhouse before and after English school and on Saturday. Here they learn to read German, recite passages from Hutterite hymns and the Bible from memory, and practice writing in German script. (See figure 35.) During these meetings the German

Lehrerleut there is a special school for these children called *Schulela*; it is a transition school where they learn to read and write German before they are introduced to instruction in English.

15. See appendix 5 for the table manners memorized by the children.

Figure 34. Teacher and pupils in German school. (Photograph by Kryn Taconis)

Figure 35. Page from a Hutterite pupil workbook: "We must obey God rather than men." Acts 5:29. Darius P. Tschetter.

teacher admonishes them about their beliefs and their behavior. He teaches the children to accept punishment without resistance or anger. Usually three straps on the palm of the hand are given for a first offense or minor infringement. If a child lies about his misbehavior, two more are added. A more serious transgression warrants being turned over the bench. Milder punishments (being scolded, or ordered to stand in the corner) function primarily to remove the child from the group and to shame him in front of his peers. Work is never used as a punishment, for no colony work is categorized as unpleasant. Privileges are not withheld from a naughty child, nor is he punished by being deprived of food. Misbehavior is punished as soon as possible after it occurs.

German school is ungraded in the modern sense, and children progress at their own speeds. Material is assigned in terms of a child's ability. Instead of grades or formal levels, there is an accepted sequence of material to be learned. All children learn to read and write medieval German script. Throughout their school years they practice handwriting and memorize prayers, hymns, Bible stories, the catechism, and episodes of Hutterite history. They also learn the directions of the compass, measurement equivalents, and how to count and write to ten thousand. Children are taught to work efficiently.

The primary purpose of the German school is to teach Hutterite children the ritual of life. This ritual has two essential functions: to insure the smooth social functioning of the group and to reduce the fear of death and physical injury. The German school emphasizes the first function, although the second is by no means neglected.

Psychological studies of Hutterite adolescents show that they are not frightened by physical threats.[16] Children's play is vigorous, often rough, and sometimes even dangerous. Adults ignore it, considering the children's play to be the German teacher's responsibility. School children play many games that are exercises in discomfort and endurance. Free play reinforces community values: the physical nature of their play teaches them to ignore discomfort and fear of injury.

Children identify closely with their peer group. Everyone in the group is rewarded for a successful group endeavor, and everyone is scolded when most of the group members misbehave. Transgression may go unnoticed if no one in the group reports it.

English school. All children from the age of six attend the colony English school and complete the elementary grades. Normally the colony supplies the building, the heating, and the maintenance costs. The school board selects and pays the salary of the teacher.[17] Many colonies provide a small house, for the teacher and his family. The colony makes a point of not interfering with the living pattern of the teacher, who may have a radio, a television set, and even a separate mailbox. The teacher becomes an informal source of worldly knowledge to colony people and, if not properly controlled, a disruptive force. Teachers who have never taught in a colony are typically given a "lecture" by the preacher when they begin or with their first offense. The preacher will outline the limits for practices which are "against our religion." The use of projected audio-visual materials, radios, phonographs, and tape recorders is forbidden in the classroom. Since the school building in most colonies becomes a church every evening, the walls must be bare. The blackboard must be erased and pictures must be removed or turned to face the wall at the close of each school day.

English school is considered important. One leader said: "We expect our children to learn math, reading, and science as required by

16. John A. Hostetler and Dennis Kleinsasser, "A Cross-Cultural Investigation of Adolescence in Hutterite Society" (unpublished paper, 1965).

17. See appendix 10 for a copy of "Agreement between a Divisional School Board and a Colony, Alberta." Of thirty colonies in South Dakota, only six operate private schools at the present time. Twenty-four are operated as Public Attendance Centers and are staffed and supported by the state.

the Department of Education. We must learn English to understand the people around us." Hutterites insist that discipline be maintained in English school. Teachers are expected and often encouraged to "lay down the law," and if they cannot maintain order, they are considered failures. A German teacher advised a new English teacher to "use the willow, for it's the only language they understand." Greater respect for colony authority can be maintained if the English school also supports the prevailing authoritarian pattern.

Hutterites accept the English school but restrain and bridle its influence so that it will serve colony ends. Emotionally, the English school is outside the colony. The colony time patterns, schedule, and holidays suggest superior loyalties. German school is more important in a child's day than is English school, as is evident from the scheduling of classes. German school is held at the start of the day. English school comes after it. In effect, the English school is held in the invisible presence of the elders, the council bench remaining in the front of the schoolroom and the pews in the rear.

The farther the child goes in English school, the less he is said to learn. From the colony's point of view this is correct, for once a child has mastered the basic skills, much of the rest of the subject matter learned has little relevance to his way of life. German school teaches the Hutterite way; the English school teaches worldly knowledge. The functions of the two schools are clearly different, but both are regarded as necessary. In the ideal colony there is little conflict between the two schools, and from the viewpoint of Hutterite culture, the normal child receives an integrated learning experience.

Sunday school. Children start attending Sunday school, which is held every Sunday afternoon throughout the year and on every religious holiday, when they begin English school and continue until they are baptized. It is taught by the German school teacher. The instruction consists of singing, recitation, and recounting the Sunday morning's sermon text with explanation. The children are frequently allowed to choose a song. The teacher will line out the hymn as does the preacher in the church service. He may talk about the song, often reading it line by line and discussing the meaning of the words.

The Sunday school is essentially an extension of the German school, continuing the process of teaching the young people the verbal content of their religion. Those over the age of fifteen are essentially treated as adults in their work and family associations; but as long as they are not baptized, they are not considered to be fully grown-up.

The school-age children learn a great deal about the authority structure of their society and how to live comfortably within it. Although they have internalized the respect for hierarchy that gives precedence to age, they have also learned that each person's authority is limited. The individual knows when and whom he must obey and what orders can safely be ignored.

In summary, the socialization of school-age children includes the following significant aspects. Most of the child's day is spent under the supervision of an authority figure—the German teacher, a parent, or a work supervisor. There are, however, periods during the day when the child works with his brothers or sisters and when he is unsupervised in his peer group. The groups of brothers and sisters working together within the nuclear family develop patterns of interaction that continue into adulthood, when brothers will assume leadership positions in the colony and when sisters will marry members of the same colony or another colony.

During the school years children learn to function within both the sibling group and the peer group. They learn how to adjust their dual memberships as the two groups overlap, interact, and supplement each other. The two loyalties persist, with modification, until the peer group embraces the entire adult membership of the colony.

Childhood comes to an end with the fifteenth birthday. The young Hutterite leaves the children's dining room and is said to be *bei die Leut,* "with the people." The *mandle* ("little man") becomes a *buah* ("boy"); the *dindla* ("little girl") becomes a *die-en* ("girl.")

Young People

On reaching the age of fifteen, the colony immediately recognizes the new status of the young person. (See figure 36.) The symbolic significance of this transition is marked by his presence in the adult dining hall. Left behind him is the world of childhood, school, baby-sitting, and children's work. Although there is no ceremonial recognition, informally the person's new status affects his eating, working, religious observance, social life, discipline, use of possessions, clothing, and adult privileges.[18] All changes in status demand acceptance of sex roles and emphasize these roles.

Physically, the young person is considered an adult, capable of hard work in cooperation with other adults. Religiously, he is still a child and must attend Sunday school and memorize his weekly verses. Emotionally, he vacillates, and this period is sometimes called "the in-between years" or "the casual years," meaning that the individual's loyalties have not completely crystallized. Some disregard of colony

18. For "Rites of Passage from Childhood to Adulthood," see appendix 6.

Figure 36. Hutterite boy and chest received on his fifteenth birthday. (Photograph by Kryn Taconis)

mores is expected during this period, but moodiness or poor work performance is not tolerated.

For two years the young person is in an apprentice position. Boys and girls in this stage constitute a mobile labor force which is utilized throughout the colony as needed (in jobs suitable to their sex). They may be sent to other colonies to help during times of need or crisis. Boys in this age group do most of the hard labor and enjoy the opportunity to demonstrate their strength and stamina.

The young person is subject to the control and influence of the colony, his family, and his peer group. However, the influences exerted by these three groups are less well integrated than at any earlier period. Because the areas of control are more diversified, the young person has slightly more freedom than at an earlier age. His work is under the control of the colony, although there may be some tendency to let a son work with his father and a girl with her mother or a sister. In areas of religious development and moral and social behavior, the young person is primarily the responsibility of the German teacher or the preacher, depending on the colony.

The colony and the family expect a certain amount of deviant behavior from young people, much of which takes place within the peer group in the form of such forbidden activities as singing English songs and playing harmonicas. The peer group, however, will tolerate only certain activities, and the individual who deviates too radically is ostracized even by his peers. Relationships in the family are still completely hierarchical, and since the German teacher is no longer responsible for all of the child's waking hours, the parents take more interest in his or her free time.

Siblings support each other in various ways. A girl may sew clothes for her brother that depart slightly from the accepted pattern, or she may iron his clothes just the way he likes them. Boys have some opportunities to earn extra money which they may lend or give to their sisters or to a girl friend. Several brothers from one family frequently keep company with sisters in another family, and it is not uncommon to find marriages in which several brothers have wives who are sisters. The cooperative patterns learned in the family influence the selection of marriage partners. Colonies that visit frequently, exchange work and produce, and provide marriage partners for each other are usually ones that are related by kinship ties.

Boys and girls work with and under the direction of older colony members, but they also work in peer groups. For example, all the young men make hay together, and all the young girls paint as a group. Work and social life intermingle, for young people talk together as they work, especially when adults are beyond earshot. It is considered a privilege to go to other colonies to work, since in these settings the young people of both colonies work together and have a chance to establish new friendships. After supper the peer group expands to include both sexes and visitors of the same age group from other colonies. A sixteen-year-old girl explained boy and girl relationships:

"When boys or girls from other colonies come and visit, we all go together in the evening. If the visitors have never been here before, one of our group does the introducing (so the boys know what the girl's name is when he wants her for a date). Then we sit and talk or play. If a boy wants a date, he goes out with one of our guys and tells him; then he calls out the girl he wants. If she wants, she goes along with him. If not, she says no. Sometimes the boys don't like it if we refuse, but you can't tell a girl to go along if she doesn't want to. It's only in leap year that the girls call the boy for a date. Otherwise the boy has to do the calling. In winter time we really get a lot of visitors because there's not much work to do. In all the colonies each boy gets a two-week vacation. Then they can go and visit whenever they please. When it comes to dates, I think sometimes we have too many. (What would the boys do if we girls all went on strike? What a heartache for the boys—ha, ha.)"

Hutterite preachers assert that "courtship" and "dating" are not allowed on the colony. These terms connote for them romance and carnal pleasure. Nevertheless, the young use these terms freely and find associations between the sexes that are sanctioned by the colony. Though young Hutterites find their marriage partners voluntarily, parents have almost complete veto power over a child's choice. If a young person is keeping company with someone of whom the colony disapproves—for instance, a first cousin or the English school teacher— the German teacher or the preacher will speak to him about it. If a person is "courting" someone whom his family dislikes, the family, not the colony, must resolve the situation. Whether or not a young person has formed a friendship with a person of the opposite sex, he or she is included in the mixed peer group activity and remains absolutely loyal to this group.

Exclusive cliques may develop in large colonies or with the young people of nearby colonies, but all young people present a united front to those who are not included in their age-set. Adults conveniently overlook mild transgressions, and the young people enjoy some escape from adult surveillance.

The young person eventually rejects the world and chooses the colony way of life. Yet the "casual years" are a time for testing boundaries; there is some flirtation with the world, some investigation of that which will be rejected. Most young people have their photographs taken, and some have wrist watches. One young girl said, "We have no cameras, but when people from the city come to tour the colony, they take some pictures and send them to us." A few boys own transistor radios on which they listen to western songs; some trap during the winter or "moonlight" to earn extra money; occasionally boys smoke secretly. Girls may use colored polish on their toenails, which are hidden by their heavy shoes. They buy perfume, dime store jewelry, and sometimes fancy underwear. The in-between years are a period of limited self-realization. A young man may temporarily leave the colony, knowing he will return to marry and raise his family.

Girls in particular may create a secret world. As long as this make-believe does not interfere with work, it is tacitly accepted by adults. The secret world may be confined to a locked wooden chest or to a corner of the attic where bits of the temporal world are kept— photographs, sheet music, suntan lotion, souvenirs. They represent the world outside the colony; they represent the self in its indulgent, vanity-pleasing aspects. The young person continually measures these trinkets and indulgences against the full life in which he is involved. He generally finds that the satisfactions received from participation in colony affairs far outweigh those of self-indulgence.

The young person's status within his nuclear family is quite high. During the later years as a young person, he is expected to demonstrate by his daily behavior his ability to adhere to the colony rules. When he has displayed by his actions that emotionally and intellectually he is no longer an irresponsible child, he willingly and humbly requests baptism in order to become a full member of the colony. After baptism a young man is permitted to visit colonies for the specific purpose of finding a wife if he has not already made up his mind.

Adolescent Personality Patterns

Are there differences between Hutterite and non-Hutterite personality patterns? During the course of our field work several kinds of questionnaires were given to Hutterite children and to a sample group of non-Hutterite children. We wanted to know whether there were differences in aspirations, perceptions, fears, and ways of thinking about the self and whether our general observations of the culture could be supported by psychological data. Since Hutterite cultural goals are very different from those of the surrounding culture, standardized tests used in public schools were not appropriate. We found most of them unreliable as measures of Hutterite personality traits and capabilities. Instead, Hutterite children were given simple sentence completion exercises. The results were very different from those of public school children. Some of these findings are reported here.[19]

Hutterite children are socialized to obey their parents and are not treated as equals by adults in their culture. Thus, in exercises eliciting attitudes toward parents, Hutterite children tended to be neutral in their responses, whereas non-Hutterite children showed many more positive as well as negative attitudes. They expressed strong likes and dislikes. Hutterite girls tended to respond more positively toward their mothers than toward their fathers. The response of the Hutterite boys was primarily neutral toward both parents.[20]

Punishment was perceived differently by the two groups of children. The non-Hutterite children responded primarily in terms of *how* they were punished, not *who* punished them. These differences were striking (see table 4). Hutterite children mentioned the punitive figure (father, teacher, or elder, in this order) with greater frequency. (In Hutterite culture it is important who punishes, not how one is punished, for Hutterites learn to accept punishment as chastisement from God.) When non-Hutterite children mentioned a punitive figure it was more frequently the mother than the father.

19. Abstracted from Hostetler and Kleinsasser, "A Cross-Cultural Investigation of Adolescence in Hutterite Society."

20. The several studies of adolescent Hutterite role perception by Shirin and Eduard Schludermann generally support our findings; see "Adolescent Perception of Parental Behavior (CRPBI) in Hutterite Communal Society," *Journal of Psychology* 79 (1971): pp 29–39. Boys and girls described adults in more favorable terms than did the teenagers. Also reported was a low degree of social role differentiation after the age of sixteen. Thus, what counts among Hutterites is not position but qualities of character: whether a person is friendly, mature, selfless, and loyal.

Table 4. Perceptions of Punishment by Hutterite and Non-Hutterite Children (in Percent)

Category	Hutterites (N=70)	Control Group (N=100)
Punitive Figure	81.4	43.0
Form of Punishment	8.6	54.0
Nonclassifiable response	10.0	3.0

To discover whether children thought of *how* they were punished or *who* punished them, they were asked to answer the question: "Because Kathy (or Dick) was bad, she (he) was punished by   ." The responses were grouped according to the presence or absence of a punitive figure and the method of punishment.

The exercise was given to seventh- and eighth-grade pupils in South Dakota. There were 70 Hutterite pupils from 36 colonies and 100 non-Hutterite children from nearby public schools in rural regions.

That the differences are due to chance is doubtful. A chi-square test of significance yielded the following: $X^2 = 32.5$; d.f. $= 1$; P $= .001$

The wishes expressed by the children on sentence completion exercises were different in the two cultures. Hutterites wished for material possessions and for adventure and travel more frequently than did non-Hutterites. From the viewpoint of the culture, the elders are right: the children have a strong desire for property, material possessions, and self-indulgence. This age group must still achieve a mature Hutterite attitude toward possessions. An indirect method of discovering aspirations, through the recounting of dreams, tends to substantiate the desire for material possessions. Themes on "the best dream I ever had" centered on material possessions and candy.[21] Also high on the list of responses were trips and visits. The trips were usually described as outings to the home of relatives in other colonies or to nearby cities. Many dreamed of trips to the nearest village post office. Some who dreamed of visiting other colonies wished never to return.

Examples of "best" dreams are these:

A boy and I went down the hill. I ran ahead of him, and I lifted up a plate and saw a big hole of money. The boy with me ran for a pail while I watched the hole. We carried it home to the preacher's house.
(Boy, aged eleven)

I once got a camera for a present. The camera was quite big and could develop pictures in two minutes. I was very glad, but then just as I was going to take a picture, I woke up, but I was happy anyway.
(Girl, aged fourteen)

I dreamed we went to Saskatchewan. It took us a couple of years to get there. The dream was happy because I have a sister down there.
(Girl, aged twelve)

The predominance of dreams about material possessions must be viewed in the cultural context. Toys, money, and candy are not denied but are strongly controlled. It is not uncommon for children to receive candy and gum from adults who return from town. Sweets are used as tokens of love and approval by the parent, and since children strive desperately for any token of affection, sweets are occasionally withheld by parents when they are provoked or used as a substitute for personal attention. Toys are given in recognition of work well done, and thus sweets and toys have social meaning in relation to superiors. The desire for material possessions is by no means absent in the preadolescent Hutterite, but it is channeled into socially tolerated forms.

Fears are indicators of personality patterns. The children were asked to write answers to the question: "What are some things that

21. Hostetler and Kleinsasser, "A Cross-Cultural Investigation of Adolescence in Hutterite Society."

scare you, things that make you afraid?" The answers given by the Hutterite and non-Hutterite groups were very different (see table 5). Hutterite children regarded animals as a source of fear far more than did the non-Hutterite children. The fears of non-Hutterite children centered largely on other persons, including teachers, members of the opposite sex, and other adults. Hutterites were more afraid of supernatural phenomena than they were of other people. Children in the control group feared unpredictable happenings more than Hutterites did. Hutterite children were less afraid of bodily injury that were the non-Hutterites.

These findings substantiate what is known about the culture from observation. Hutterite children live in a colony environment that is secure and predictable. They know every person in the colony and have no apparent need to fear the adults in their immediate environment. Not knowing many people well or intimately may make non-Hutterite children more afraid of adults and may make their environment less predictable. Children who attend public school in American society are taught to avoid contact with adults who are strangers.

Table 5. Fears of Hutterite and Non-Hutterite Children by Category (in Percent)[a]

Category	Hutterites (N=70)	Control group (N=100)	Chi-square P value
Mediators of threat			
Animals	55.7	16	.001
Other persons	4.3	29	.001
Parents	0.0	0	
Teacher	0.0	8	.05
Opposite Sex	0.0	8	.05
Peers	0.0	5	
Adults	0.0	3	
Siblings	1.4	0	
Other people	2.9	13	.01
Natural phenomena	7.1	15	
Supernatural phenomena	10.0	2	.05
Threats: psychological, social, and biological			
Loss of affiliation	0.0	2	
Exposure	4.3	5	
Punishment	1.4	1	
Unpredictable experiences	1.4	10	.05
Injury, illness, and death	1.4	8	.05
Dreams/fantasy	2.9	4	
Nonclassifiable	11.4	8	

[a] Children were asked to write answers to the question: "What are some things that scare you, things that make you afraid?" The pupils were seventh and eighth graders in South Dakota: 70 Hutterites from 36 colonies and 100 non-Hutterites from nearby public schools.

An indirect method of ascertaining fears was to ask the Hutterite children to describe "the worst dream I ever had."[22] The most frequent responses were in the category of "strange and threatening animals." Snakes, bulls, and bears were the animals alluded to most frequently. Such encounters were often quite vividly described and involved animals attempting to bite or devour the child or animals intent on attacking the child while he was in bed. The category "threatening or strange people" did not include any colony adults but only robbers and criminals.

Here are examples of the "worst" dreams:

There was a ladder in our house. Some snakes were crawling up and down. Then they came to me and bit my foot. I couldn't sleep the whole night through. I was very frightened.
(Girl, aged twelve)

I dreamed that my mother and all my relatives died and I was left alone and had nothing to eat or anything at all. Then I awoke.
(Boy, aged eleven)

We were playing behind the shed and we heard a loud mooing sound. We went to the corral to see what happened. The wild bull was fighting with the other bulls. The wild bull looked up at us and pushed us around on the ground. Finally we got into the cow barn. Then I awoke.
(Boy, aged eleven)

The predominance of threatening animals in the children's dreams may reflect two aspects of Hutterite culture. First, parents often use threats as a coercive measure for the purpose of attaining conformity to Hutterite mores. Threats such as "a bear will eat you" are not uncommon in parent-child interactions. This kind of parental threat is intimately related to the Hutterite world view. Animals in the Bible are often equated with the instinctual, or "id," components of the human personality. For the Hutterite, animals, in addition to posing a threat to physical well-being, symbolize a parallel threat of consumption by the lusts and evils of the flesh. This association is most clearly seen in the use of the snake as a symbol, the referent being the id impulses of man as depicted in the Genesis account of the Garden of Eden. Hence the threat of animal attack carries with it the threat of expulsion from the community of the chosen people.

A second reason for the prominence of animal responses is simply that animals are a part of the group's environment. In spite of the many fears involving animals, the colony does have adequate control over threatening animals. Hutterite children do not, as a rule, readily ex-

22. Ibid.

press fear of bodily injury from any source, even though our observations indicate that with the constant movement of heavy machinery and trucks, children are in fact often in danger of being injured.

These findings are suggestive, but certainly not conclusive. The reliability of these generalizations for the Hutterites, particularly for anyone doing psychological or educational research, depends greatly on the awareness of the field worker and on the colony's acceptance of him. Hutterite youth, like the adults, are sensitive to the probing questions of the outsider. They are often very free in talking to the visitor, but they know how and when to withhold information or to confuse him. In some of the dreams, there are undertones indicating their opinions of researchers who come to study the colony and how they should be dealt with. For example, a boy of fifteen wrote:

I had a dream that a man came into the colony to try and find out why we live in a community. The first day he asked every one in the colony he met if they knew why. He didn't find out very much. He was so angry and impatient for not finding out anything that he left. He was so ashamed . . . that he went and joined a church.

This dream supports the ego structure of the culture—that investigators who come to study the colony are disappointed or confused about their findings—and in this case the outsider is so conscience-smitten that he joins a church.

Asked about his worst dream, a boy of sixteen expressed resentment at the question:

I can't remember anything. Maybe it is nice or ugly, but I couldn't care less.

The same boy, in answer to the question about his "best dream," wrote:

I sleep so good I never have any dreams. The last dream may have been a couple of years ago, but I can't remember any. Once I remember that Miss [the field worker] landed in a mental institution.

Dreams not only reflect moral attributes in real life but also the manner in which the young learn to deal with outsiders. The following dream by a boy of eleven reveals some of the ambivalence of the young in a closed community:

Once I dreamt I went in the woods and I had a pleasant time. Some other people were camping nearby. One day they were missing some tools. They called the police and the people looked for the thief. The police asked if I had stolen the tools and I said "No." I sure was telling a lie. I had stolen the tools. So the police looked for two weeks and asked again if I had stolen the tools. I said "No," but he really found out that I had stolen the tools. He put me in prison. There I had nothing to eat. They put some lions in the place. The lions just sat. All at once the lion jumped at me and hurt me very much. So the police put me in the hospital. When I was well they put me back in jail and there I stayed for forty years.

The perceptions children have of outsiders must certainly be taken into account by researchers. Experienced teachers know that when they attempt to introduce greater competition by appealing to self-interest and to self-importance (which works well in middle-class, individualistic American culture), they meet resistance. There are differences between Huterrites and non-Hutterites in terms of motivation, time patterns, work skills, and the priority of values. Hutterites are not motivated toward scholastic achievement but know a great deal about getting along with others, both young and old.

What conception does the communal person have of himself in contrast to the person who is reared in an individualistically oriented culture? To discover how persons conceive of the self, two groups of children were given the W-A-Y (Who Are You?) exercise, with these instructions: "Ask this question of yourself, 'Who Am I?' Give three answers to this question that are different." This method allowed the person to structure his responses along lines that were expressive of his needs, with virtually unrestricted freedom. The responses were tallied in several categories (see table 6).

Hutterite children differed from non-Hutterite children in their responses in respect to age, family, occupation, group membership, and personal description. Hutterites tended to respond according to their age category more noticeably that did the others. This supports empirically what we have observed, that age (within the appropriate sex group) is the single most important determinant of an individual's placement in the colony hierarchy.

Occupation (work) is very important to the Hutterite self-image. Hutterite youngsters, in contrast to non-Hutterites, thought of themselves in terms of work responsibilities assigned to them by the colony. That this particular image of self is so strong in the adolescent period, while the youngsters are still in school just prior to the assignment of adult responsibility, attests to very successful socialization. Most American young people of this age have minimal work responsibility and do not identify with an occupation.

Hutterite children identify themselves as part of a group more readily than do non-Hutterites. Being part of a group is important to

Table 6. Responses by Hutterite and Non-Hutterite Children to the Question "Who Am I?" (in Percent by Category)[a]

Response Category	Hutterites (N=70)	Control group (N=100)	Chi-square P value
Name	5.71	3.66	
Age	7.14	1.33	.01
Sex	7.14	6.00	
Family	9.05	5.33	
Occupation	10.00	1.66	.001
Group membership	18.57	7.33	.001
Religious affiliation	(4.76)	(1.60)	.05
General	(13.81)	(5.66)	.001
Personal description	18.81	48.33	.001
Positive effect	(10.00)	(19.33)	.001
Negative affect	(1.91)	(16.00)	.001
Physical attributes	(4.76)	(2.66)	
General	(1.91)	(10.33)	.001
Metaphysical (religious affirmation)	8.10	3.33	
Interests and special ability	10.48	14.00	
Nonclassifiable	10.48	6.33	

[a]Children were instructed: "Ask this question of yourself, 'Who Am I?' Give three answers to this question that are different." For source, see J. F. T. Bugental and S. L. Zelein, "Investigations into the Self Concept: The W-A-Y Technique," *Journal of Personality* 18 (1950): 483–98.

them, and their answers indicate that a wide range of groups was included in their thinking. They thought of themselves not only as members of a religious group (Hutterites) but as members of a family, a state, and a country. This way of thinking is essentially a nonindividualized identification and supports the ideology of "self-surrender."

In their personal descriptions of themselves, which included observations on height, dress, maturity, and happiness, Hutterite children tended to be neutral. While non-Hutterites offered more colorful and affective descriptions, they were also more disparaging and possibly less accepting of themselves. Affirmation of belief or of a religious (metaphysical) position was greater among Hutterite children. (See figure 37.)

Finally, Hutterite children think of themselves as belonging to a particular colony group by virtue of their place in the recognized social order, their age, sex, and work responsibility. The cleavage between male and female subcultures is affirmed by these limited studies. Boys can learn a farm job they may retain for the better part of their life, whereas girls are not thought of in terms of colony positions. The desire to remain a Hutterite is a persistent undertone. Contentment with one's peers is a dominant theme. Hutterites emphasize the positive aspects of physical endurance. The appeal to bodily comfort made by modern

Figure 37. Hutterite girl and copy of an old chronicle. (Photograph by Kryn Taconis)

advertising is effectively smothered by the culture. Self-descriptions are linked to industriousness and contrast with the more hedonistic identifications among non-Hutterite children. The evidence from these measures of personality underscores the general effectiveness of Hutterite socialization patterns.

chapter ten

Adult Life Patterns

Admission to Adulthood

Admission to the adult world of the Hutterites is through baptism. Prior to baptism the young Hutterite has been socialized and generally motivated to believe that the collective will is more important than the separate individuals who compose it. From infancy he learns to fit into the group pattern and is treated as a member of the group rather than as an individual. He first identifies with his family, then with his peer group in school, and finally with his work group. With each stage of growth the number of people above him in status decreases and the number below him increases. He is taught to serve and obey those above him, to care for and direct those below him. Although there is some competition within his peer group (primarily in work performance), the group is cohesive and provides strong support.

When the Hutterite voluntarily requests baptism, he expresses a desire to devote his whole life to the colony and its members. Baptism signifies submission to the spiritual community and acceptance of adult responsibility. In Hutterite society baptism and death are the two most important rites of passage. Baptism is essential to the adult's participation in the ritual of daily life; death leads the true Hutterite into life everlasting. Both rites of passage stress dying as an essential step to life. Baptism requires that the natural man die so that the "spiritual man" may be born. Similarly, the human body must die so that the spiritual man may enter into eternal life.

The colony decides months or even a year in advance when to have baptism. Girls are about nineteen and boys are between twenty and twenty-six years of age when baptized. In all colonies baptism is requested in a highly stylized form, and generally with the support of the peer group. If there is only one person who requests baptism, he may receive instruction with a group of applicants from a neighboring colony. The baptismal service usually takes place on Palm Sunday or, occasionally, at Pentecost.

Everyone in the colony generally knows who will request baptism and who will wait. If there is a question about any candidate, all aspects are discussed so that the colony is in agreement; often a young person is advised to postpone his request for baptism. During the six- to eight-week instruction period, applicants must demonstrate that they have humbled themselves, are devoid of self-will, and are completely obedient to the community. They are admonished as a group for three hours every Sunday afternoon. Each applicant must realize that he is about to make the greatest commitment of his life.

All of the candidates memorize the standard *Taufspruch* ("baptismal recitations"), including the Apostles' Creed. The emphasis on a great number as well as on "good" recitations enhances the solemnity of the occasion and provides a legitimate form of competition among applicants. The three important baptismal sermons (*Taufreden*), which originated with Walpot during the Moravian period, are delivered a few days prior to the baptismal service. They are solemn explanations of repentance, rebirth, and the church and its discipline.[1] The baptismal vow includes the promise "to consecrate, give and sacrifice self with soul and body and all possessions to the Lord in heaven."

The ceremony consists of two parts. On Saturday afternoon the candidates are examined with respect to their beliefs, and on Sunday, after the last of the three baptismal sermons, the preacher baptizes the candidates. He lays his hands on the head of each one, and with the aid of an assistant, sprinkles them with pure water, praying that they may be preserved in piety and faith until death. After baptism, men are given voting privileges, and they become eligible for more responsible work assignments, but there is no change in the work status of young women.

---

1. Published in Robert Friedmann, *Glaubenzeugnisse oberdeutscher Täufgesennter* [*Österreich*, pt. 2], Quellen zur Geschichte der Täufer, vol. 12 (Gütersloh: Gerd Mohn, 1967), pp. 59–124. For the baptismal vow, see appendix 7.

Baptism is considered a preliminary step to marriage since commitment to God must precede commitment to a spouse. Ideally the interval between baptism and marriage is not long, especially for a young man. A young man is frequently not baptized until he is contemplating marriage. The baptized but as yet unmarried person participates only marginally in the young people's social life. He has made his choice and is prepared to reject the immature aspects of the casual years. He prefers to use his energies in the interest of the colony.

Baptism produces a closer relationship between parents and child. Parents now treat their child as a colony member as well as a family member. With the help of God and the colony they have accomplished their task of raising this child "in the nurture and admonition of the Lord." Baptized children and parents identify very closely with one another.

Marriage

The present practices with respect to courtship, marriage, and divorce must be distinguished from those of the early period. Courtship and romance scarcely existed among early Hutterites. Married men spoke of their wives as married sisters (*eheliche Schwester*) in a manner that suggests monastic marriage. Couples were matched by the leaders. Men and women worked separately, sat at different tables, and were separated during religious services. They were seldom seen together. Marriage was accepted as a necessity for the sake of procreation and to avoid fornication. In finding a spouse one was not to follow the inclinations of the flesh, the allures of youth, beauty, or money, but to choose in accordance with the will of God as made known through the servants.[2]

Those wishing to marry informed the servant of the word and at the appointed time in spring and fall were called to one of the principal Bruderhofs. Here the matching followed the religious service. Many of the prospective couples had never met each other. Men and women lined up on opposite sides of the room. A man would choose one of three women. The woman could refuse, but if she did she could not marry until the next matching.[3]

Although there was some discontent with this procedure even in Moravia in the sixteenth century, it remained in effect until Johann

2. Rideman, *Account of Our Religion*, p. 100.
3. It appears that in some cases matching was done entirely by the elders who informed the man of his wife's name and the woman of her husband's name. Erhard and Fischer, who were Catholic theologians, claimed there was much discontent with the pairing procedures. See Claus-Peter Clasen, *Anabaptism: A Social History* (Ithaca: Cornell University Press, 1972), p. 265.

Cornies put an end to the practice in Russia. A matching Ordnung in 1643 affirmed the old practice, declaring that it eliminated competing loyalties. If love resulted from marriage and family, it should be supportive of the community.

Divorce for personal reasons is not sanctioned among present-day Hutterites. In the sixteenth century, divorces and separations were permitted when refugees had to choose between the Hutterite faith and an unbelieving spouse. Many who fled Tyrol, Hesse, and Württemberg left their marriage partners behind. Zealous missionaries encouraged the believers to forsake unsympathetic married partners. Some women left and took their children with them, without telling their husbands.[4] Those who did not accept the faith were allowed to accompany their spouses if they did not make trouble. They were told to leave Moravia if they did not want to be divorced. However, if they grumbled, shouted, or maltreated the believing one, they were left behind. Hutterite missionaries were accused of being divorce mongers and kidnappers. Governments feared that, among other revolutionary activities, the Hutterites would undermine the institution of marriage.

Early Hutterites took the position that where a woman "is endangered in her faith or is hindered by the unbelieving husband in the training of her children in the true faith, she may divorce her husband, but must remain unmarried as long as her husband lives."[5] It would be much better, they said, if the unbeliever would accept the faith. Present-day Hutterites concur with the early Brethren and might quote an old saying that "the union with God weighs a thousand times more than the union of marriage between men."

Mate selection among modern Hutterites is not forced or formally arranged: a young person is expected to make up his own mind when and whom he will marry. The influences which have a bearing on mate selection are peers, parents, and kinship preferences. Courtship, as explained in chapter 9, plays a more significant role in mate selection than in former times. The young people have opportunities to meet one another during the visits between colonies that are brought about by marriages, funerals, work exchanges, and the visiting of relatives. The Hutterites prefer sibling exchange marriages in which two brothers marry two sisters or a brother and a sister marry a brother and sister.[6] Hutterites also prefer to marry one of their kinsmen rather than a person

4. Ibid.
5. Zieglschmid, *Die älteste Chronik*, p. 308; trans. Robert Friedmann in *M.E.*, s.v. "Divorce from Unbelievers."
6. See Arthur P. Mange, "The Population Structure of a Human Isolate" (Ph.D. dissertation, University of Wisconsin, 1963). Mange reports that of 812 Schmiedeleut marriages there were 82 double, 16 triple, and 4 quadruple sibling marriages.

who is unrelated. An individual tends to choose a mate related to himself in the same degree as his parents are related. Sibling marriages tend to support strong kinship ties.

No formal acknowledgment is made of the intention of a young couple to marry until the prospective groom, accompanied by his father or other close relatives, makes a trip to the girl's colony and seeks her permission and the consent of the colony. Following the affirmative response of the girl and her parents, the colony members are summoned to the church and an engagement service lasting about fifteen minutes is held.[7] Afterward, the suitor and his bride-to-be serve wine to her parents in their apartment. They then proceed to each of the other apartments, serving wine to the people and receiving good wishes for their marriage. In the evening, colony members gather in the dining room for *hulba* ("festivity"), where they enjoy refreshments and sing wedding songs. After the children and old people retire, the singing goes on, often until midnight.

After two days of festivity, the suitor arranges for the departure to his own colony, taking with him his bride-to-be, her relatives, and her belongings. There are personal gifts from colony members and the allotted goods from the colony: bedding, a sewing machine, and extra cloth for dresses. Meanwhile the groom's colony has been informed that a wedding is to be arranged for Sunday. On arriving at the colony, wedding guests are introduced and treated to an evening meal. The singing and festivity continue every evening until the day of the wedding. The marriage ceremony follows the Sunday morning sermon. The bride and groom come forward at the bidding of the preacher and return to their seats following the ceremony. The young man promises that in case he should lose his faith and leave the colony, he will not cause his wife to follow him. After the service the colony meets in the communal kitchen for a simple wedding meal served with beer, wine, and soft drinks, followed by singing. Throughout the afternoon snacks are served and drinks replenished. Everyone receives an allotment of sweets to take home. The formal wedding festivity ends at vespers. The bridal couple visits with the guests in the evening, then goes to a newly prepared apartment.

The season for marriages today is determined by both the liturgical and work calendars. Weddings may not take place immediately before Christmas or in the period from just before Easter until after Pentecost. Forty-nine percent of all Schmiedeleut marriages occur in November and December.[8] Fewer than 4 percent of all marriages occur during the

7. For the engagement and marriage vows, see appendix 8.
8. Mange, "The Population Structure of a Human Isolate," p. 34.

spring planting season (March and April), and fewer than 5 percent occur during the harvest season (August and September).

A wedding provides an occasion for the gathering of relatives and friends. Old friendships are renewed, relatives visit one another, and young people court. Since the wedding entails considerable work and expense for the colony, double or triple weddings are encouraged, and often as many as five couples are married at the same time. Multiple weddings also enhance the festivities of the day, as the crowd is much larger and gayer.

In contrast to the long, rigorous ceremonial preparation for baptism, preparation for marriage is casual. The groom has only minor adjustments to make. Often he retains his former room in or adjoining his parents' apartment; his brothers move out, and his bride moves in. Emotionally, the husband is in a strong position and becomes eligible for work assignments which entail greater responsibilities. He maintains all his primary ties and in addition acquires a wife. He is completely familiar with all aspects of colony life and with every colony member.

Marriage involves greater social adjustment for the bride than for the groom. Usually she moves to a new colony, sometimes one she has never visited. She must leave her parents, siblings, and peer group and come under the direction of her mother-in-law. Her work patterns are altered because of her married status and also because things are done in slightly different ways in the new colony. However, the bedroom is referred to as hers and becomes her niche. The bedroom belongs to the wife and mother, the colony to the husband. Compared with her husband, a new wife is in a vulnerable position. He is her main source of support and information. The Hutterite marriage patterns function to maintain the husband in his dominant position and to emphasize the dependency of his wife.

Education for pregnancy and childbirth is even more rudimentary than formal preparation for marriage. These topics are rarely discussed among Hutterite women and never in the presence of girls. When she becomes pregnant, the young wife is generally living in a different colony from the one in which she grew up. Her mother does not come to care for her until after the baby has been born. Most young women know little about the details of labor. However, they have grown up in a society that has a high birth rate and a positive attitude toward babies. They have been taught to ignore discomfort and to accept their lot without complaint. The attitude toward pregnancy and childbirth is one of either passive acceptance or mild annoyance when there are already many children.

Kinship and Naming Patterns

Hutterites have a saying—*Blut ist kein Wasser* ("blood is not water")—meaning that blood ties are not to be taken lightly. Intra-family relationships are very important to the individual, for these are the first relationships learned by the child and will remain the primary ones throughout his life. The individual's primary relatives are his parents, his brothers and sisters, and his grandparents, uncles, aunts, and cousins.

Recognized kinship units are (1) the nuclear family (married pairs and their offspring), (2) the patrinomial family (family members with the same surname), and (3) clans (family lines that tend to intermarry).[9] Since each Leut is virtually endogamous, each is, strictly speaking, a closed kinship group. However, the Brethren do not consider the Leut as kinship groups; they are regarded as historical branches of the same brotherhood with different customs. Family genealogy is not a preoccupation with most Hutterite persons. There are individuals who take special pains to trace family lines, and this task has been aided by geneticists who have nearly constructed the complete genealogy of the Hutterites.

Hutterites trace their descent bilaterally. Although some women may feel closer to their maternal relatives, especially their mothers' sisters, there is a pronounced tendency for both men and women to identify with the paternal line. The patriarchal patterns of authority and the patrilocal residence patterns lend support to patrilineal loyalty. In a single colony there may be only one family name, or there may be several.[10] Typically there are two or more. Where there are many family names in a single colony, some Hutterites say there are also many problems of maintaining colony harmony.

Naming practices have great significance in colony life because the means to express individual identity are so limited. The fifteen traditional Germanic family names existing among the colonies are Decker, Entz, Glanzer, Gross, Hofer, Kleinsasser, Knels, Mandel, Stahl, Tschetter, Waldner, Walter, Wipf, Wollman, and Wurz. Only five of these surnames—Gross, Hofer, Waldner, Wipf, and Wurz—are common to

---

9. The clan is intermediary between the colony and the Leut, although the term is given no special recognition by Hutterites. The clan is a group of intermarrying patrinomial families deriving from a founder colony. The Lehrerleut, for example, have four main founder colonies (see appendix 16) whose descendants are referred to as Old Elm Leut, Rockport Leut, New Elm Leut, and Milford Leut.

10. For diagrams of kinship and colony organization, see John W. Bennett, *Hutterian Brethren: The Agricultural Economy and Social Organization of a Communal People* (Stanford, Calif.: Stanford University Press, 1967), pp. 114ff.

all three Leut. The chronicles contain many other family names which no longer survive. Decker and Entz can be traced to a few Mennonite converts in Russia. Entz occurs only among the Lehrerleut, Walter only among the Dariusleut, and Glanzer and Knels only among the Schmiedeleut. Knels is about to disappear, for the only married male with this name has no male descendants. The names of Janzen, Pullman, and Miller have disappeared among American colonies but survive among the noncolony Hutterites. In America some new surnames have been added through conversions—Alexander, Baer, Dorn, Randle, Seuss, and Teichroeb—but they constitute a small proportion of the total Hutterite population.

Married couples name their children first after themselves (indicative of a strong family bond) and then after the grandparents, uncles, and aunts (a generational bond). Typical masculine names in the three colonies in our study were Benjamin, David, Jacob, John, Michael, Paul, Peter, and Timothy. Common feminine names are Annie, Barbara, Elizabeth, Katie, Susanna, Magdalena, and Mary. Though most first names are biblical, and certainly traditional Hutterite names, there is a trend toward giving the girls non-Hutterite names in a few of the liberal colonies. Older people call this practice *auslandish* ("alien"). Examples are Dora, Judy, Linda, Frieda, Lillian, and Helen.

Any confusion arising from similar first names is minimized by the use of middle initials and by the use of a prefix. Normally the newborn child of either sex is assigned as a middle initial the first letter of the father's first name. This changes at marriage when a boy takes as his middle initial the first letter of his wife's first name. The girl changes her middle initial to the first letter of her husband's first name. Then when Susie J. (from her father Jacob) Tschetter married George Wollman her name changed to Susie G. Wollman. Middle names are looked upon with disfavor.

The selection of a prefix (either the first or last name of the father) is somewhat flexible, depending on the frequency of already existing names. In a colony where there are eleven Annas, Joseph Anna is distinguished from Peter Anna, Michael Anna, Jacob Anna, etc. Unmarried girls take the name of their father as a prefix and married women, the first name of their husbands. When father and son have the same name, the last name will often precede the son's first name in colony conversation. Thus Jacob Wipf's boys are called Wipf Jake, or Wipf Joe.

In Hutterite dialect the naming patterns manifest many fine distinctions not apparent to those unfamiliar with the dialect. This is especially true of honorary titles and nicknames. Although *Vetter* designates a cousin relationship, it also is a title of respect for all men when combined with a person's first name (viz., Jacob-Vetter, or John-

Vetter). *Alt-Vetter*, the name for grandfather, may be used in referring to an old man in the colony. *Basel*, or "aunt," is used in speaking of any older woman in the colony. It may be combined with first names: Anna-Basel, or Susanna-Basel. *Ankela* (or Angela) is used in speaking of grandmothers.

The practice of nicknaming varies considerably from one colony to another. In some, the preachers forbid all nicknaming. Many more men and boys have nicknames than girls. Children are often designated by their father's nickname until they, especially boys, acquire their own. Some nicknames are used consistently by nearly everyone in a colony, while others are rarely heard.

Most nicknames are unknown to outsiders, and some are deliberately kept from outsiders. (When elected preacher, a man automatically loses his nickname.) As in other societies, Hutterite persons derive their nicknames from physical traits and idiosyncratic behavior patterns. Frequently the origin of a name is obscure and has no known meaning whatever. Most acquire their nicknames when they are very young.

"Big Jake" was named by outsiders to distinguish him from others with the same name. The colony has known him as "Jakela" (little Jake) from the time that he was a small boy.

"Sturtz" is short and stubby in physique.

"Six," a man over six feet tall, was so widely known in the colony by his nickname that some members did not know his real name.

"Wooly" carried this name long before he was assigned the task of sheep boss.

"Red" is a man with a bushy red beard.

"Fat John" (Dicka Johannes) is distinguished from "Thin John" (Kleina Johannes).

Other nicknames, not necessarily typical, are "Porky," "Much," "Shep," "Toys," "Speedy," "Chamber," "Guss," and "Windy." Occasionally these names are used as prefixes to the real names.

Dialect names and nicknames also apply to the names of colonies. Until a new colony has an official name, it may be given a nickname. The nickname may continue long after the colony has been given a proper name. Though many colonies take the name of their local post office, they are frequently named after their former owner. They are never named after individual Hutterites.

In small, homogeneous, self-contained communities, nicknaming is frequently a widespread and complex custom. As an essential and vital part of interpersonal relations, it serves important functions besides differentiating individuals from one another. Nicknaming is both a means and a manifestation of solidarity. It is a legitimate means of private indulgence, of permitting ingroup knowledge and intimacies in a society that otherwise requires conformity in property ownership and use. Informal naming is a group's way of evaluating individual idiosyncrasies, role, status, and position. It is both a form of indulgence and a means of community censure.

Adult Life

The adult Hutterite receives constant social reinforcement. The Sunday and daily religious services are part of his continuous formal socialization. These group ceremonies function both to teach the young and to reinforce beliefs which the adults have internalized. All adults must be good examples to others at all times. Virtually all their activities are carried on within the age-set hierarchy and the same-sex group. In work situations both men and women constantly participate in patterns of decision making that enable the group to reach a consensus. A single individual does not try to persuade the group; rather, a subject is discussed by most members, and the final result is a group decision.

The youngest adult men may still have onerous labor assignments. Older men occupy leadership positions such as the departmental heads of various economic enterprises. The men with greatest seniority tend to hold executive positions as council members. The young men are highly motivated to obtain the more important jobs, and although there may be muted intragroup competition for various positions and fairly obvious competition among those holding the different positions to demonstrate maximum efficiency in their particular operations, the individual generally progresses automatically to higher status positions as he grows older. Within the well-integrated colony there are no contests for place (which is determined by age and sex) or for office (which is determined by vote of the church). Hutterites do not seek the satisfaction that may accompany a position of dominance. They have been well socialized against self-assertion. Power, authority, and influence are expressed as group action.

Biological brothers cooperate closely among themselves and with their father in all areas of life, but this is not necessarily disruptive to the colony as a whole. These men have learned to handle feelings of jealousy and competition and to work smoothly together, depending on one another's strengths and compensating for one another's weaknesses. Early identification and constant interaction with the peer group have taught Hutterite men to work well with their spiritual brothers. Groups of brothers are functional in making colony decisions. News spreads informally among them and they freely argue the relative merits of various alternatives. One set of brothers may discuss the problem further with another set, each individual knowing that he has some support in the group. A decision can often be reached rapidly. The men have been socialized against stubbornness. They have also been taught that, when a colony issue reaches the voting stage, church members must vote as spiritual rather than biological brothers. Biological brothers thus function as a closely cooperating subgroup within the larger cooperative.

As in most cultures, social control is achieved primarily by the individual's fear of rejection. The adult Hutterite has identified with the group since childhood, and his self-esteem depends on his complete acceptance by the group. Cautioning represents the simplest form of social control. An individual who is disturbed by the conduct of another person will reprove him. If this approach is not effective, the preacher will speak privately to the erring member. If misconduct persists, such a member may be approached privately by one or more council members or asked to come before the council and the church. In the case of continued transgression, for example, persistent drunkenness, a person may be placed in excommunication. Such a person is deprived of his church membership and may neither eat with others nor participate in work and colony life until he shows humility and is reinstated. Most excommunicated individuals soon reunite with the church, but a few remain under the ban and eventually leave the colony. No person under the ban is ever asked to leave the colony. Usually he is required to stay in a room apart from his family and allowed to speak only with the preacher or persons designated by the preacher. While in the state of excommunication members may show love for the one who is "cast out," including giving the kiss of affection, but they may not offer the hand (the Hutterite symbol of peace). Other than the shedding of blood, which the church cannot forgive (no murder has ever occurred among Hutterites), deserting the colony is the worst possible offense. There is no hope of heaven for anyone who dies outside the church.

A successfully socialized adult Hutterite gets along well with others and, submissive and obedient to the rules and regulations of the colony, is a hard-working, responsible individual. He is taught never to display anger or to precipitate quarrels. Intensity and imagination are not admired; rather, quiet willingness coupled with hard work is considered desirable. The constant "pruning" which adapts each individual to the group results in a minimizing of differences. The individual is not believed to have unlimited freedom, as illustrated in the Hutterite saying; "No man with rights has a right to all of his rights." The elimination of extremes and the respect for order enable members to find satisfaction in the "narrow way" that leads to salvation.

Adult responses to attitudinal questions reveal few doubts, a hardy ego structure, willingness to change for the good of the group, strong beliefs about sharing, and general agreement on questions of morality. A selected number of Hutterite adults (thirty-six) were asked: "How many close friends would you say you have?" Most replied that they had several hundred (see table 7).

In terms of personality type (Myers-Briggs type indicator) Hutterites are decidedly ESFJ—extraverted rather than introverted, sensing rather than intuitive, feeling rather than thinking, and judgmental

Table 7. Responses by Adult Hutterites to Attitudinal Statements

Item number	Statement	Percent responding *yes* (N=36)[a]
1.	Sometimes I feel all alone.	16.7
2.	Sometimes I have the feeling that other people are using me.	19.5
3.	I often wonder what the meaning of life really is.	52.8
4.	People are just naturally friendly and helpful.	86.1
5.	I always try to keep my political beliefs to myself.	67.7
6.	With so many religious beliefs today, one doesn't really know what to believe.	27.8
7.	Property is something which should be shared.	91.7
8.	A true friend is one who says, "what's mine is yours."	94.4
9.	The problems of our country are man-made, and man can solve these problems.	52.8
10.	I like a job where I know that I will be doing my work about the same way from one week to the next.	77.1
11.	When I get used to doing things in one way, I don't like to change.	55.5
12.	We should be as helpful to people we don't know as we are to our friends.	94.4
13.	Everyone should think the same about what is right and wrong.	77.8
14.	Children should be taught that there is only one right way to do things.	77.8
15.	I find it easier to follow rules than to do things on my own.	86.1
16.	Having the chance to make up my own mind is very important to me.	80.6
17.	Do you like to spend money?	97.2
18.	Health experts say adding certain chemicals like chlorine or fluoride to drinking water results in less tooth decay. If you could add these chemicals to your water, without cost, would you be willing to do so?	69.4
19.	Do you think a person who does not believe in God can still be a good American?	36.1
20.	There are many things about me I'd like to change.	58.3

[a] The 36 adults consisted of 18 married couples under the age of 35 in three colonies.

rather than perceptive.[11] This measure of personality is concerned with the way people perceive and judge. A person of this type (the following description is not comprehensive) is talkative, popular, conscientious, interested in everyone, a born cooperator, an active committee member; he has little capacity for abstract thinking but works hard to master facts in a lesson and to win approval; he works best with a great deal of praise and encouragement and always expresses friendly feelings toward others in a practical way. A need for strong support from the group, a willingness to abide by the standards of the group, and few doubts about what is right and wrong appear to go hand in hand with these personality features.

The Elderly

The elderly constitute a small minority of the population in any colony because of the large number of children in virtually all the colonies. The aged are neither segregated within a single colony nor moved to a separate colony or old people's home. Hutterite culture requires that the aged be respected by all younger persons. The pressure to move upward in the age-set is invariably present from kindergarten through the final rite of passage, death. Older people are believed to deserve "rest," and work is optional for them. They may spend more time traveling, going to town, and talking with neighbors and visitors.

There is no arbitrary age of retirement. Women between forty-five and fifty are usually relieved of their rotating colony jobs, although women who hold the positions of head cook or kindergarten mother continue in these jobs until they are too old to fulfill their responsibilities. The first jobs women give up are milking and hoeing, usually followed by full-time cooking and baking. Most older women, however, continue to assist with food preparation, for they prefer working to being alone in their apartments. When an older person loses a spouse he often moves in with one of his children. A grandchild is assigned to run errands for and even to sleep with him, and his meals are brought to him when he becomes too infirm to go to the dining room.

Retirement is more difficult for a man to accept than for a woman. An elderly man is frequently removed from a foreman position and simultaneously elected to a position on the council. By this means his conservative influence is used constructively, and the economic develop-

---

11. For a description of the indicator, see Isabel Briggs Myers, *The Myers-Briggs Type Indicator* (Princeton: Educational Testing Service, 1962). The scope of our findings is limited to one colony. Of 41 persons who took the test in one colony, 40 percent were ESFJ and over 70 per cent were SFJ—sensing, feeling, and judgmental personality types.

ment that requires constant change is put into the hands of a younger man. Once elected, a man remains on the council indefinitely. Often the most difficult person to relieve of responsibility is the colony steward. Conservatism is a disadvantage in a steward, for the economic success of the colony rests on its willingness to risk capital and remain dynamic in its economic practices. Several years may be required to change stewards. Gentle persuasion rather than coercion is the rule.

The Hutterites emphasize good health, and older people who are ill consult physicians in nearby towns. But utilization of outside medical help is influenced by the view that the body is important only because it houses the eternal soul. Hutterites go to great lengths and expense to obtain special treatment for chronically ill members, but it is often difficult for them to reach the best physicians because of their relative geographical isolation. Their famed sixteenth-century tradition of healing, bathing, and surgery has almost disappeared, although they still train midwives, masseurs, and bonesetters.[12] Women are especially fearful of poor health, for a loss of status accompanies the inability to work.

Age is no secret in Hutterite society, and the denial of aging or falsification of one's age is uncommon. Hutterite security in old age is part of the total pattern of economic and ideological security. There is no decline in the standard of living. The colony pays for all medical care. All older people are cared for in the home with their children and grandchildren. They eat in the community dining hall as long as they are able. No elderly person is forced to choose between the extremes of doing nothing or holding a full-time job. Loneliness is unknown among the Hutterites. The high value placed on marrying and having a large family is ample "grandchild insurance" against loneliness in old age. Those who never marry and those who are widowed live in quarters next to a close relative.[13] At the daily church services and at mealtimes the older adults mix with those of all ages. The nature of colony life insures that a person will live his life among relatives and friends, those he has known from his youth.

The psychology of aging and the preparation for death is unique and consistent with the culture. Old people are not forced to exert themselves, nor are they denied active participation. They can reduce their work load without being excluded from the policy-forming group.

12. The healing arts during the Moravian period were discussed in chapter 2. There is virtually no "powwowing" among modern colonies. The general Community Ordnung of 1651 states that "witchcraft, magic and fortune-telling, whether pronounced on man or beast, are absolutely forbidden in the community." A contemporary preacher said, "If it comes up, we don't fight it, for it will die out of itself."

13. Only about one in one hundred Hutterites aged forty-five and over has never married. In 1950, 55 percent of all widowers but only 5 percent of widows had remarried. See Joseph W. Eaton, "The Art of Aging and Dying," *Gerontologist* 4 (1964): 98.

An old man's contribution to the colony is limited economically, but his strong identity with colony tradition and the respect he is accorded by younger members exert a stabilizing influence. Intergenerational communication is maintained and provides older persons with a means of keeping abreast of changing times. Occasionally the oldest active man is given the honorable position of *Brotschneider* ("bread cutter"); he cuts the fresh loaves and keeps every table in the communal dining hall supplied with bread. In this capacity he acts as a symbolic father figure for the community.

Death

Death is the culminating stage of socialization. All of life has been a preparation for death, which to Hutterites means the termination of the earthly struggle and the beginning of paradise for those who have lived faithfully. Attitudes toward death and the appropriate final rite of passage are conditioned by communal values and world view. The time of death is believed to be controlled by God. Suicide is equated with murder and is an intrusion upon God's prerogative.

From the days of the early Hutterite martyrs to the present, bedside accounts of dying men and women, occasionally set in verses, have reinforced the values of faithful communal living.[14] "We prefer slow deaths, not sudden deaths," explained a Hutterite. "We want to have plenty of time to consider eternity and to confess and make everything right. We don't like to see a grownup go suddenly." Deaths typically occur in the context of colony life, in the midst of young and old, and the interchanges between the dying person and the other colony members validate all that everyone believes and practices. The dying person is supported by praying, singing, and by conversation with persons of his choosing.

Children who die in their innocence are envied by adults, for they have been spared many temptations and the struggles of self-denial. Following a death by scalding, it was said of a child of seven, "She will sure be a beautiful angel." A mature father said: "When these little ones die we know they are in heaven, but we never know what will happen to them if they grow up. I sure wish I would have died when I was a kid."

The announcement of death reaches other colonies by telephone. Colony work is dropped; relatives prepare for mourning and funeral activities. Normally only those who are baptized are permitted to come to the colony where the death has occurred. The girls and women pre-

---

14. See, for example, appendix 14, "Last Words of Michael Waldner, 1823-1899."

pare quantities of food, including several thousand "funeral buns." The body of the deceased is normally embalmed by a nearby undertaker. If the deceased was a male, the body is dressed in a white long-sleeved shirt, black trousers, and white knitted socks. It is then draped in a white sheet, and with the face, chest, and hands exposed it has an apostolic appearance. A deceased woman is dressed in plain black or blue. The body stays in the home of the deceased until the day of the funeral, usually the third day after death. On the morning of the funeral, the body is placed in a coffin made by the colony carpenter.

The wake, held in the room of the deceased for two nights preceding the funeral, is a large gathering of friends and relatives. Hymn-singing alternates with periods of silence, short spontaneous remarks about the deceased, and gestures of mourning. There is much coming and going from the scene of the wake to the kitchen and to groups of people in other rooms. Refreshments of food and wine are interspersed in the mourning activities. After a midnight lunch all guests leave, but family members keep watch until morning.

The funeral of Michael Decker on June 30, 1973, was larger than most. As steward of the Tschetter Colony in South Dakota, he had been well known in all the colonies in South Dakota and Canada. The service was to be held in the dining hall, because it accommodated more people than the schoolhouse. The pallbearers, who were nephews of the deceased, carried the casket from the home to the service at three o'clock in the afternoon. Some of the older persons had already gathered together when the casket was brought in and placed in the center of the large dining area, encircled by chairs for the close relatives. The full-length lid of the coffin was removed for the service. Seated at the head of the coffin were all the preachers; the women and men sat separately on rows of benches on either side of the deceased. The one-hour service began and ended with a hymn led by the oldest preacher. The sermon, read by one of the several elders present,[15] took the frailty of life as a predominating theme: "Today we are fresh, healthy, and strong; tomorrow the body withers and health and strength are gone. When God takes to Himself again what belongs to Him, what is left but a dead corpse—a stinking abode for worms which you cannot preserve, be it ever so dear to you. We must soon rush to the grave, else we must guard the nose from its stench."

After completing the sermon, the preacher sat down briefly. He then arose and in a few short words committed the body to the earth for burial. All who wished could take a last view of the deceased by

15. Sermons at funerals are typically based on the texts of Genesis 3:19 and Psalms 90:10.

rising to their feet. No line was formed to walk past the coffin. After the mourners had left the room, the casket was placed on a truck, which the procession followed to the colony cemetery on a nearby hill. Without ceremony the body was lowered into an open grave and immediately covered with earth. When the earth formed a slight mound all of the men removed their hats. The preacher issued a short statement of thanks in behalf of the bereaved family. The burial was complete.

The dress of the men is normally black and is no different for a funeral. The women, however, in contrast to their patterned dresses of every day, wear black skirts, jackets, and aprons. There is mourning and weeping by some individuals. Observers have noted that weeping follows a pattern at wakes and funerals, for when one person begins to weep and shake, others follow one by one down the long aisle.

In Europe Hutterites buried their dead in white cloth without a coffin, according to colony informants. Hutterites believe that funeral services were begun in America. Why were there no funerals in Hutterite tradition? For the Hutterites, funeral services were associated with the world they had rejected—elaborate state and church rituals, eulogies of the dead, and the rite of extreme unction. Today, all but the newest colonies have cemeteries. Most are fenced in and, except for the older graves, most are marked with tombstones.

The emotional acceptance of death is supported by many aspects of the culture, specifically by the lack of sentiment attached to property. There is no property to divide among the survivors. Funerals permit the integration of the society on all levels. Persons from distant colonies participate in the religious and burial services. Funerals provide one of the principal opportunities for young people to make new friends; they provide an ideal time for finding prospective marriage partners, as there are few occasions when large gatherings of young people are possible.

Individuality, which is denied and carefully guarded against throughout life, is to be completely abolished in heaven. The vision of dying Hutterites emphasizes likeness, uniformity, and unity, for all personal tendencies and idiosyncrasies are to be dissolved. There is little speculation about heaven or the kinds of enjoyment or activity it will provide. What matters most is preparation through submission to the divine and right order. There is to be more perfect communal living in heaven.

part three

THE PROBLEMS
AND TECHNIQUES
OF SURVIVAL

chapter eleven

The Social Problems
of Communal Living

The essential conditions for human and social survival are ably met in Hutterite society. Through offspring, new members are produced for the group. The colony socializes the young into functioning adults, produces and distributes goods and services necessary to life, maintains order within the group, defines the meaning of life, and maintains motivation for all ages. These basic human needs are met by the system, but not without also producing threats and social problems from the surrounding society. Some distinctive external as well as internal problems of Hutterite communal living are discussed in this chapter.

Hostility

Direct hostility against the Hutterites was most intense during the formative period in the sixteenth century.[1] Although such cruel persecution does not exist today, the members are deeply conscious of the price they pay for being Hutterite. Modern forms of persecution have consisted of restrictions on buying land, refusals to recognize the conscientious objection to war of young men of draft age, coercion to buy war bonds, and various forms of economic discrimination. These subtle

1. See chapter 3.

forms of persecution are a constant reminder to Hutterites that hostility may erupt at any time and that they are completely dependent upon God for security.

The Hutterites are not nationalistic in their loyalties and with few exceptions do not vote. They generally comply with local civic, school, and tax laws, and their beliefs enjoin them to pray for their government. However, to pay special war taxes, called "blood money" (*Blutsteur*), is expressly forbidden by their beliefs.[2] In the past, when goods have been forceably taken from them for special war taxes, they have offered no resistance. Today, Hutterites have not seriously questioned the sizeable allocation of general taxes used for military purposes.

Vandalism by unsympathetic gangs is unpredictable and harrying for some colonies. "The townspeople often call to tell us to come and get our geese which are roaming the streets," said a Hutterite woman. "We know who the teen-age boys are that let them loose but their parents don't care and the police do nothing about it." Other intrusions range from broken windows to pilfered tools and supplies to armed robbery. Cattle thievery occurs in some of the sparsely populated areas of the prairie country. One colony suffered the loss of thirty head of fattened hogs. Pranks such as putting harmful substances into gasoline tanks are disruptive and costly.

Hostile acts by carnal, jealous, unbelieving outsiders are taken for granted and support Hutterite expectations. When such acts do occur, the Hutterites tend to function as a cohesive force, thereby integrating the structural relations of the society. Persecution is turned to constructive ends. When there is no persecution, Hutterite leaders acknowledge a tendency toward internal decay. While publicity is not shunned, favorable articles about them are disturbing to some of the more sensitive leaders, who say: "We don't like horn tooting. It makes people jealous, and creates hard feelings." Writers and reporters who visit colonies and hear individuals unburden themselves of their grievances often assume naively that relations with outsiders can be helped by the right kind of publicity. But the fact that their neighbors have more information about the Hutterites does not necessarily assure that they will have a more tolerant attitude toward them. (See figure 38.) One Hutterite elder told the writer that "the worst and the best publicity does us no good."

Today the disappearance of the family farm and its related way of life is keenly felt in rural society. In some areas where Hutterites live, they have become the target of the ranchers and farmers. When there

2. Peter Rideman, *Rechenschaft unserer Religion, Lehr und Glaubens, von den Brüdern, so man die Hutterischen nennt, ausgangen 1565* (Ashton Keynes, Wilts., England: Plough Publishing House, 1938), p. 117.

Figure 38. Members of a South Dakota Hutterite colony. (Photograph by Philip Garvin, 1974)

have been formal meetings to discuss the "Hutterite problem," the participants have demanded measures to restrict Hutterite expansion and to involve Hutterites in the affairs of the world. The confrontations have usually been hostile, with few or no Hutterites attending. When community representatives want to force certain changes on the Hutterite colony which they think are necessary to preserve their local community, the Hutterites interpret the pressure as persecution. They are determined not to change their community life or to become involved in worldly things.

Fraternization with Outsiders

Hutterite leaders must have constant contact with outsiders in order to operate their colonies as commercial enterprises. There are many channels of contact with outsiders on both formal and informal levels. Formal contacts involve colony leaders with local, state, and provincial governments and with professional and community organizations. Many informal contacts bypass the preacher and the steward but are not, for that reason, threatening to the colony, for through contacts with visitors and business firms, new ideas are introduced which the colony can use. Colony produce and vegetables are commonly traded for privileges or goods, and gifts are frequently used as a means of cultivating friendly relations. Peddling chickens, ducks, or turkeys is another valuable source of contact with individuals and firms.

Outsiders, it appears, tend to be either hostile or sympathetic to the Hutterites. In their formal contacts, Hutterite leaders are adept at humanizing their relations, or making them seem informal. This practice usually evokes a sympathetic response, and throughout their history the Hutterites have always had a few defenders and advocates in and out of government. In Moravia their advocate was Fredrick Žerotin, the nobleman who rented his lands to them and whom they called informally "Unser Fritz." Catholic priests who were attempting to halt the spread of Hutterite teachings maintained that, by pandering to high officials, the Hutterites always got what they wanted. After leaving Romania, the Hutterites found an advocate in General Rumiantsev, who settled them on his estate in Russia. In their move to south Russia, Johann Cornies aided them in finding lands and developing agricultural skills. Today the Hutterites also have their "Fritzes."

Prolonged, intimate, primary relationships with non-Hutterite neighbors can be a serious threat to colony harmony unless properly managed. Segregation as the Hutterites practice it is perhaps one of their most intolerable vices in the eyes of society at large. An outsider can maintain only a partial friendship with a Hutterite, and at best, a guarded one. The problem posed by "neighboring" was expressed by one colony official in this way:

> We have a number of neighbors with whom we exchange work and machinery. In winter when the roads are snowed shut we loan our teams to them. The more contact we have with neighbors, the more chance our boys have to buddy up with them. We don't mind favoring them with help, but when they want to favor our boys by taking them into their homes, letting them listen to the radio and television, and taking them to shows, then our colony rules are broken. When we tell our neighbors not to do this, they just get mad, and then there is friction.

Some colonies have a good reputation as neighbors and others have a poor one. Some of the most self-sufficient colonies tend to display the most conspicuous ethnocentric patterns and therefore to have the poorest public relations. The smallest colony in our study, which had the smallest number of people and was the most geographically isolated from other colonies, was deliberately cultivating favorable public relations. The colony had a good reputation in an area where no colonies had previously existed. Neighboring farmers came to the colony for specialized tractor repair services, to have their seeds cleaned in colony plants, and to get machines for spraying their crops. These services, often combined with additional assistance in planting and haying, were seen by the Hutterites more as gestures toward cultivating good neighborly relations than as means of increasing colony income. "We have to be accommodating, and we will not turn anybody away," said the colony preacher. The same colony also "loaned" a young man as a tractor operator to the municipal road building crew for a few weeks.

Some colonies permit groups to visit by appointment. After a tour of the grounds, lunch is served, and the visitors are seated in the church for a "lecture" by the preacher. A discussion period follows. One colony receives so many visitors and inquiries from persons interested in communal living that it has devised a questionnaire to screen the prospective visitors and discourage curiosity seekers.

Attitudes toward the Hutterites prior to their moving into a new area are often very different from those that prevail once a colony is established. Fears that a colony will not contribute to the local economy are often expressed by the local people. Such assertions have proven to be without foundation. Hutterite colonies do make substantial purchases and economic contributions to the community.[3]

There is an element of vexation caused by a colony's refusal to mix socially in the local community. The many symbolic ways in which Hutterites isolate themselves give rise to a variety of myths and falsehoods about their communal life. Although some of these falsifications do little direct harm to the colony, in the long run they are distortions that add to the already burdened public relations of the colonies. Dislikes and discrimination expressed by outsiders tend to strengthen the internal cohesion of the colony.

Sustained, intimate friendships may be more frequent between colony leaders and businessmen than between Hutterite young people and outsiders, but some dating with outsiders does occur in colonies that are not on guard. Although friendship with outsiders is possible, such intimate relations are discouraged because of their potentially adverse influence on the colony. Through investment sharks, one colony lost a half-million dollars in spurious oil reserves. The steward in another colony was induced to gamble a large sum of money at Reno. There are

---

3. Attitudes toward Hutterites before and after a colony is established in a given area are discussed by Vernon Serl, "Stability and Change in Hutterite Society" (Ph.D. dissertation, University of Oregon, 1964), pp. 111–29. In his excellent study of economic organization (*Hutterite Brethren: The Agricultural Economy and Social Organization of a Communal People* [Stanford, Calif.: Stanford University Press, 1967], pp. 78–88), John W. Bennett finds the Hutterite contribution to the economy of the wider area to be substantial.

reports of investment agents who induce fathers, without the knowledge of the colony, to turn their family allowances over to stock companies. These deceptions, from the viewpoint of the colony, occur when there is too much fraternization of members with outsiders.

Compulsory State Education

Hutterites desire a basic education in reading, writing, and ciphering in the English language, but they do not want the English (public) school to disrupt colony life. Keeping the English school "in its place" is crucial to Hutterite survival, for it is there that the ideologies of the world and the colony vie for the loyalty of the young. The English school can become an important influence toward future desertion for a child who does not respond properly to communal indoctrination. It is from the English school teacher and his school books that children learn about the world outside the colony. (See figure 39.) Intimacy between teacher and pupil can lead to defection; in one case a colony girl eloped with the English school teacher. Some teachers have helped young Hutterites find jobs and leave the colony. Young and single public school teachers are a greater risk than older ones who are married and have children of their own.

The influence of the teacher is carefully delineated, and he is given moral encouragement in ways that aid the colony discipline; but the colony has little veto power if he proves unsatisfactory. A teacher is

Figure 39. Elementary schoolchildren. (Photograph by Philip Garvin, 1974)

seldom allowed to encroach on the colony time pattern by asking a child to stay after school, stay during lunch hour, or do homework assignments. Discussion of a teacher's shortcomings in the presence of children limits his or her influence. Some of the colonies complain about receiving poor teachers; indeed, some teachers are inferior. Mediocre academic teaching is tolerated, and teachers are virtually free from the informal supervision of superiors. There is little pressure from parents for excellence and almost no parental interference in teaching. The formal relations between colony adults and the teacher are generally cordial and are typically enhanced by gifts of food and help. Low-cost housing and eating privileges are available to many of the teachers. Those with cooperative attitudes, including the poorer teachers, are more readily absorbed into the environment of the colony than teachers who are truly competent by outside standards and who demand independent thinking of their pupils. Even then, there is little danger that the teacher will become a model for the children. When the teacher emulates the colony pattern, for example, in his dress or by wearing a beard, the children tend to show him greater respect.

Attempts by Hutterites in the past to provide their own teachers by permitting their young men to enter college and acquire teacher training have largely failed. In both the Ukraine and North America some of the young men deserted the colonies. Although there are presently a few college-educated Hutterite men teaching in colony English schools, the practice is not favored with unanimity by the leaders. The reason as given by one spokesman is: "It is better to have the worldly school taught by a worldly person so that we can keep the lines straight."

Laws requiring children to take formal schooling through grades 9 or 10 have affected colonies in some states and provinces. Some take correspondence courses from state colleges to satisfy the requirements. Teachers who are assigned to teach in the colony are often willing to tutor or give instruction beyond the elementary grades. Manitoba has made exploratory efforts to establish high schools for Hutterite young people in regions where there are many colonies. However, all efforts to take the pupils from the colony grounds run counter to the Hutterite religion and to Hutterite conceptions of child training. Cases brought against parents for not keeping their children in school after their fifteenth birthday have proven unsuccessful. The consequences of having to attend school beyond the time when a child is accepted as an adult in his society (age fifteen) adversely affect the pupil's self-esteem. At this age young people are given adult work privileges and serve as apprentices to skilled adults under close supervision. Young Hutterites feel deprived of their status as growing persons when forced to attend formal schooling beyond the age required by their culture.

On the whole, Hutterites have been successful in utilizing the English schools for acquiring the skills needed for the management of colony life. They restrain its influence and, by counterindoctrination, provide adequate motivation for the children to become adult Hutterites. The occasional recommendations of state and provincial investigating committees that Hutterites be integrated or assimilated into courses in agriculture, industrial arts, and home economics have not come to fruition.

Mental Health and Medical Care

The high level of economic security and apparent absence of anxiety among Hutterites has prompted scientists to study their mental health.[4] Except for brief periods of diagnosis and treatment, Hutterite members are not found in hospitals for the mentally ill. Contrary to widespread belief, however, colony life is not free from neuroses and psychosis. The Hutterite people have graciously cooperated in mental health and medical studies.

Among 8,542 Hutterites (in 1951), the researchers discovered a total of 199 who had active symptoms of mental disorders or had recovered from such illnesses. Of these illnesses, 53 were diagnosed as psychoses. This rate (1 in 43) is much lower than that in the United States generally, where scientists estimate that 1 person in 10 suffers an incapacitating mental illness at one time or another in his life.

To their surprise, however, the researchers found that the distribution of types of mental illness was the reverse of that in the mainstream of society. Only 9 Hutterites had ever shown symptoms of schizophrenia, manifesting such behavior as delusions and hallucinations. Their rate (2.1 per 1,000 persons aged fifteen or over) is one of the lowest on record. In society at large, schizophrenia is one of the most common psychoses.

The proportion of manic-depressive reactions, on the other hand, was unusually high. Of the 53 persons diagnosed as psychotic, 39 were suffering from manic-depressive reaction; of these, 25 were women and 14 were men. They suffered such afflictions as depression, irrational guilt feelings, and withdrawal from normal social relations. The rate was 9.3 per 1,000 persons aged fifteen or over. A few of these patients

4. For a knowledge of mental illness among Hutterites, we are indebted to Joseph W. Eaton and his research team, which included Bert Kaplan, Robert J. Weil, Thomas F. A. Plaut, and William F. Pratt. The findings are largely contained in two works: Joseph W. Eaton and Robert J. Weil, *Culture and Mental Disorders* (Glencoe, Ill.: Free Press, 1955), and Bert Kaplan and Thomas F. A. Plaut, *Personality in a Communal Society* (Lawrence: University of Kansas Publications, 1956).

had suicidal tendencies. Hutterites were found to have the highest proportion of manic-depressive reactions in ten studies in which patients were compared. As in many other societies, Hutterite women have much higher rates of manic-depressive reaction than men. Psychologists believe that manic-depression is most common in societies with a high degree of social cohesion or group-centeredness. Women are more closely identified with family, kinship group, and infant care than are men within the same culture. Hutterites intensify cohesiveness not only by sharing property and having large families but by restricting the roles of individuals, especially women, in the society.

The unusual distribution of symptoms of mental illness among Hutterites suggests that cultural factors have some influence on the manifestation of psychoses. The educational and religious values of the Hutterites teach them not to use physical aggression and not to blame others for their shortcomings. In psychological tests Hutterites, like other people, show strong aggressive impulses. In their daily lives they apparently repress these tendencies very effectively. Personal violence among adults is uncommon, and their history reveals an unusual record of conformity. Adultery, promiscuity, homosexuality, murder, arson, and severe physical assault are unknown or rare. Chronic marital discord and desertion are also very rare. No homicides and only one suicide have been reported in the colonies.

A specific, restricted cultural environment apparently can prevent the manifestation of certain malfunctions that are prone to occur in the mainstream of society. But the reverse might also be true, that certain symptoms will occur more frequently in some cultural groups than in others, because of the values that are stressed. Hutterites, for example, have a recurring, persistent illness known as *Anfechtung*. All but a few of the thirty-nine cases which were diagnosed as manic-depressive reaction had the symptoms of Anfechtung. The symptoms of this illness center on the feeling of having sinned. "The sick person withdraws from those around him and ruminates on his religious unworthiness," says Bert Kaplan.[5] A preacher defined Anfechtung as occurring "when a person feels that he is guilty, that he has committed some crime or sin and can't get rid of it." Another said Anfechtung is "when they start worrying about their sins and they get a nervous breakdown. Or when they do something they know they shouldn't do. It is not a case for the doctor. You help the person by talking to them."

Hutterite culture not only produces the symptoms of Anfechtung; it also provides an effective means of treatment. The individual is not isolated or admitted to a "strange" hospital or excommunicated from

5. Kaplan and Plaut, *Personality in a Communal Society*, p. 67.

the church. Rather, the colony preacher talks to the person, or very often the sick person voluntarily talks to the preacher or another colony member. The preacher has an important role in the treatment, for if the sick person is carrying on a struggle with the devil and is tempted to reject the Hutterite morality, the preacher becomes an ally in the battle against evil. He is in some sense the psychiatrist. His tools are prayer and confession and emotional support. When the affected person confesses his feelings, the preacher, in the presence of all assembled members, reads a sermon for the occasion at the evening service. In this manner the person is helped to overcome the depressive doubts and is restored to normal life.

Hutterites accept Anfechtung as a form of deviance. They do not punish the sick person or regard him as either dangerous or hexed but instead recognize the problem and often support him with their solicitude. Hutterites are repulsed by the harsh treatment given to mentally ill individuals in the mainstream of society when they are removed from their family or locked in a room with strangers.

From the viewpoint of psychology, the demands for conformity and unquestioned adherence to absolute values impose a great strain on the individual. Compliance is achieved at the cost of renouncing important impulse satisfactions. The Hutterite goals may be too high and too difficult for some members, and "the disparity between what people feel they are supposed to be like and what they actually are like is too great for psychological comfort."[6] At any rate, the effective psychotherapy devised by the culture buttresses the Hutterite value system.

Hutterite attitudes and treatment of the mentally ill differ in two major ways from those common in American society. First, the patient is not socially isolated from his family and his normal social ties. Second, the patient is not stigmatized for life, and persons who recover from mental disorders can achieve any position available to a normal person in the colony. Hutterites accept physicians and surgeons as technicians in the healing process. Outsiders, however, are not trusted in matters affecting the soul or conscience. When it comes to the mind and spirit, Hutterites have considerable confidence in their own methods of healing. These methods include a wide variety of practical social therapies.

Mental patients are cared for by their families. They live at home and are encouraged to participate in normal life as they feel able. Such persons are protected from the major sociopsychological stresses. The colony permits the mentally ill person to see doctors or undergo surgery, even though it may appear that the sick person has no more than a hypochondriac complaint. Occupational therapy, chiropractic treatment

6. Ibid, p. 69.

by Hutterite "doctors," visiting, travel, prayer, confession, and compassion are all socially supportive forms of Hutterite "psychiatry."

The authors of the mental health study hinted that "genetic and social factors have reinforced each other to produce a highly unusual distribution of functional psychoses."[7] Did the four-century movement attract individuals who were more inclined to be group-centered rather than persons who tended toward individualism? The unanswered questions led to a series of genetic and medical investigations.[8] For human biologists, the Hutterites provided an ideal setting for population and genetic studies. Here limited studies of microevolution were possible among clones (descendants from a family in a founder colony) within each Leut, among the colonies, and within family lines. Conditions making this possible were literacy, high fertility, good vital statistical records and pedigree data, uniform living conditions, small residential groups, and virtually no in-migration or illegitimate offspring.

Studies of inbreeding (among Schmiedeleut) revealed that the average husband and wife are more closely related than second cousins but not as closely related as first cousins once removed.[9] Inbreeding had no noticeable effect on family size or on the birth rate. Of 667 marriages only 6 couples were as closely related as first cousins. Several curious findings emerged. A man whose parents were first cousins tended to be heavier (by an average of 18 pounds) than a man whose parents were "unrelated."[10] The more inbred a father, the heavier he tends to be, but his children tend to be significantly lighter than average.[11] These correlations do not hold for women. Studies of body measurement and weight

7. Eaton and Weil, *Culture and Mental Disorders*, p. 92.

8. Arthur G. Steinberg of Case Western Reserve University initiated an extensive field study of health and genetics. W. W. Howells of Harvard University supervised the research in physical anthropology. Those who assisted included Arthur P. Mange, Hermann K. Bleibtreu, Eugene Giles, Frank P. Saul, Daniel Asnes, David Horr, and others. Research studies stemming from these investigations include Arthur P. Mange, "The Population Structure of a Human Isolate [Schmiedeleut]" (Ph.D. dissertation, University of Wisconsin, 1963); and also "Growth and Inbreeding of a Human Isolate," *Human Biology* 36 (May 1964): 104–33; Arthur G. Steinberg, "Dependence of the Phenotype on Environment and Heredity," in *The Genetics of Migrant and Isolate Populations*, ed. Elisabeth Goldschmidt (Baltimore: Williams and Wilkins Co., 1963), esp. pp. 137–38, 193–94; Hermann K. Bleibtreu, "Marriage and Residence Patterns in a Genetic Isolate [Lehrerleut]" (Ph.D. dissertation, Harvard University, 1964); W. W. Howells, "Variability in Family Lines vs. Population Variability," *Annals of the New York Academy of Sciences* 134 (February 28, 1966): 624–31; Arthur G. Steinberg et al., "Genetic Studies on an Inbred Isolate, in *Proceedings of the Third International Congress of Human Genetics*, ed. James F. Crow and James V. Neel (Baltimore: Johns Hopkins Press, 1967), pp. 267–89; and W. W. Howells, with the assistance of Hermann K. Bleibtreu, *Hutterite Age Differences in Body Measurements*, Papers of the Peabody Museum 57, no. 2, 1970.

9. Mange, "The Population Structure of a Human Isolate," p. 85.

10. Ibid, p. 35.

11. Ibid, p. 57.

showed Hutterites generally to be on the heavy side.[12] The average fifty-year-old man who is 5 feet 6 1/2 inches tall weighs 180 pounds. [13] Hutterite asceticism and austerity clearly do not extend to fasting or austere food consumption.

The serum cholesterol level among Hutterites was found to have a pattern similar to noncommunal populations. In American society, cholesterol levels are generally higher among men than women. In Hutterite society the pattern of serum cholesterol level for females is like that of males. The absence of a sex difference in cholesterol levels may have some relationship to life expectancy, which in the population under study was the same for both men and women.[14]

In the study of blood groups, the Lehrerleut were found to be more inbred than the Schmiedeleut.[15] Gene frequency as determined by blood type was found to vary greatly from colony to colony. In spite of this, the genetic composition of Hutterites is believed to be more homogeneous than was the case fifty years ago.

Body measurements, however, do not indicate any observable tendency toward reduced variation. Interfamily variation in physical types is much greater than intrafamily variation, and "these interfamily differences may be looked on as essentially genetic in origin."[16]

Does inbreeding adversely affect the health and stability of the Hutterite population? In spite of much basic genetic research, no thorough survey has been made of the kinds of hereditary diseases existing in Hutterite colonies. On the basis of the studies made thus far, there is little evidence to suggest that Hutterites have more hereditary diseases than other human groupings not living in a closed society, and perhaps they have fewer hereditary diseases than other isolates, for example, the Old Order Amish.[17] There are at least six dwarfs and perhaps as many as twenty-four albinos among the Hutterites.[18] Hereditary heart disease has been observed.[19]

---

12. Howells and Bleibtreu, *Hutterite Age Differences in Body Measurements*, p. 23.

13. Mange, "The Population Structure of a Human Isolate," p. 35.

14. Steinberg, "Dependence of the Phenotype on Environment and Heredity," pp. 137–38.

15. Steinberg et al., "Genetic Studies on an Inbred Isolate," p. 271.

16. Howells, "Variability in Family Lines vs. Population Variability," p. 630.

17. Victor A. McKusick and Harold E. Cross, of The Johns Hopkins University School of Medicine, Baltimore, Maryland, have published extensively on Amish genetic diseases.

18. Victor A. McKusick and David L. Rimoin, "General Tom Thumb and Other Midgets," *Scientific American* 217 (July 1967): 103–10. The albinos were observed by Victor McKusick and the author in field work from 1965 to 1969.

19. Richard V. Lee and Richard S. Buker, Jr., "Congenital Heart Disease among the Hutterite Brethren," *The New England Journal of Medicine* 280 (May 8, 1969): 1061–62.

Mentally retarded persons are not baptized, for baptism is reserved for those who are mature and capable of making a spiritual vow. Persons with mental and physical disabilities generally do not marry.

Alcoholism has been a minor but persistent problem in Hutterite history. Hutterites argue that wine is permitted by God but must be taken in moderation. Many a teetotaler has been laughed out of the colony. Not all will abide by the old rule of not frequenting taverns. The ideal of moderation is often lost sight of in disorganized colonies and among those who have unequal access to transportation, money, seclusion, or the colony supply of wine. This is most likely to occur among men who have a privileged position and who have little prospect of further upward mobility in the occupational hierarchy. They manage to escape the punishments meted out to the younger men, although several preachers have been silenced for excessive drinking. In the sixteenth century, drunkenness seems to have been a problem for several persons, for colony rules dating from that era warn leaders not to have the smell of brandy on their breath in the morning.[20]

Smoking is taboo and the rules against it are strictly enforced. A member who suffered asthma was advised by his doctor to smoke. He refused. "Rather he inhaled tobacco vapor out of a dish of hot water. Then it was no sin."[21]

Sickness and disease are considered normal malfunctions of the body. Attitudes toward illness and its treatment are utilitarian and remarkably free from divination and demonology. Hutterites are not parsimonious in spending money for health care. On the advice of physicians they will submit to surgery, including heart surgery, and hospital confinement. A hospitalized patient is accompanied by a close relative or two, who usually remain in the city. The use of home remedies is minimal, though the use of teas and herbs does exist. Bonesetters, chiropractors, and dental workers are found in the colonies, and these healing gifts, according to Hutterites, are hereditary. The Hutterite chiropractors are also patronized by non-Hutterites. A few members have acquired a rudimentary knowledge of medicine and know how to give injections and anesthetics.

Eyeglasses are worn by a large proportion of persons of all ages in some of the colonies. Women especially seem eager to get glasses if

20. The Gemeinde Ordnung of 1651 acknowledges that "many formerly esteemed members of the brotherhood have miserably perished by drowning in wine, and have become objects of shame and mockery."

21. Cited by Samual Kleinsasser, in "Report of a Preachers' Conference, Held at the Ibate Community of the Society of Brothers in Primavera, Alto Paraguay, on October 9 and 10, 1950" (duplicated in the original German at Poplar Point Hutterian Community, Poplar Point, Man., 1950; portions translated into English by the author).

they are needed, and they wear them more consistently than do the men, who tend to wear them only part of the time. Perhaps this is because women need them more for sewing than men do for agricultural work.

Cleanliness is highly valued, though Hutterite and non-Hutterite conceptions of what is clean and what is dirty may differ. At the least, each person washes his face and hands daily and bathes every Saturday. Hutterite girls were among the first to insist on toilet soap instead of the traditional brown colony-made laundry soap. Cleanliness, polishing floors, and varnishing in some of the larger Lehrerleut colonies appears to be an obsession, perhaps a hobby or a pastime, or a way of "keeping up with the Joneses." The interiors of the dwelling units, the kitchens, and the school floors are immaculate. The chests and furniture must have a light glossy finish, and when the varnish turns dark after three years or more, it must be removed and new varnish applied. In addition to the daily and weekly cleaning, all women must houseclean in spring and fall. Spring-cleaning is done on four consecutive Tuesdays, ending before or no later than the Tuesday after Pentecost.

Affluence

The dangers of Hutterite affluence are twofold: it adversely influences the colony as a corporation, and it tempts individuals to acquire some economic independence. The major function of colony wealth is to provide capital to keep pace with the population growth. Saving is characteristic of all colonies, and the major incentive is to save for the time of branching. A debt-free colony with additional accumulations of money in the bank may be inclined to spend it for certain "extras," such as new farm machinery, tractors, or combines. Additional machines make more positions available to younger men who are eligible for the important jobs. Too much money, however, has certain dangers for the welfare of the colony. Wealthy colonies that obtain many labor-saving tools tend to be envied by other colonies. This type of expenditure is particularly evidenced in a high degree of mechanization of women's work, usually the last area to be modernized. Automatic coffee makers and electric floor polishers are examples. A limited amount of consumer goods can be permitted if all share equally, but there is a danger that the wants of individuals will be increased.

A wealthy colony may be tempted to develop a policy of exclusivism and delay its branching out. This can prove disruptive to the communal way of life. Excessive wealth with unresolved conflicts between informal factions can lead to disruption. The Hutterites might say that the reason for not branching is that "the colony becomes too content" with its reputation for financial prosperity and with its "luxuries." There is frequently the added complication that members may be unable to agree to branch or to resolve polarization between sibships.

A high standard of living tends to have a strange influence on marriage patterns. With colony affluence, there emerges what Hutterites call "girl power"—the tendency for girls to put off marriage for a number of years in order to enjoy the conveniences of their own colony. Most girls are not fortunate enough to obtain a husband in their own colony, and patrilocal rule requires that girls join the colony of their husbands. The prestige of an affluent colony reaches a point that is rather atypical for the colonies as a whole. The restraints on consumption are modified to allow for the enjoyment of small luxuries. The girls say, "Why should we get married, we have it so good here." Thus marriage is put off until the late twenties, just short of the "old maid" stage. A colony of poor reputation, whether through chronic drought or poverty or mismanagement, also has marriage problems. A boy receives no encouragement from his parents to marry a girl who belongs to a colony with a poor standing, and a girl does not want to marry into an inferior colony.

Through privately owned wealth the individual can be drawn away from his proper spiritual status. Thus, luxury must be avoided. The temporal life of the individual must be controlled by the spiritual order. While material goods are necessary for the body, they must not become objects of pleasure. The human body itself is important only because it houses the soul that is capable of establishing an eternal relationship with God.

Private income beyond the small allowances given by the colony is a threat to the ideals and practices of the colony. Unauthorized money can be obtained in several ways, and it is a perpetual problem for the colony leadership. Laboring for a nearby farmer during evening hours is a potential source of private income, as is selling or trading colony property—a duck, a turkey, a chicken, or a bottle of colony wine—with outsiders. If caught, the offender will of course be punished.

A tempting and occasionally profitable private enterprise for adolescent boys is trapping. Boys of school age trap rabbits, which can be caught with little effort, while older boys catch the more cunning animals or those with more valuable pelts. Frozen rabbits can be accumulated during a very cold winter until an older and abler boy offers to take them to town for a cash price. In a single season, one boy trapped 150 muskrats, and he also caught several beavers and mink. Suspicious mail that comes to the colony is opened by the preacher or the parents. To overcome this barrier, boys who are assigned to prolonged jobs away from the colony buildings—jobs like sheepherding or bulldozing—will rent a personal post-office box in a town not usually patronized by the colony. Furs may be shipped to faraway places, and through mail order houses the boys can secure transistor radios and other private, but forbidden, property. The small, secretive adolescent clique can often do an effective business until the subversion is discovered. All of this in the Hutterite view attests to man's natural, selfish desire, and before baptism all such subversiveness must be confessed. The consequences of not confessing all previous sins can be disastrous. One man who had left the colony in his youth but had returned to it before baptism was ordained as preacher. He was highly respected by most colonists. After several years, secret sins began to bother him. He confessed that he had earned money while outside the colony and that he had invested it and was still collecting interest on it. He was excommunicated for one week and permanently relieved of his position.

Young men in some colonies are permitted to accumulate savings with which to buy furnishings for the home after marriage. In still other colonies, money earned by working for neighbors is accumulated by family heads. This practice leads to serious consequences for the colony since it introduces a basis of differentiation between families.

Affluence can help to undermine the basic motivations for work, thrift, and austere consumption. The "narrow path" allows no pursuit of pleasure for its own sake. Ideally, the purpose of wealth getting, as emphasized by Riedemann during the precapitalistic age, is that "men should labor, working with their hands what is honest that they may have to give to him that needeth."[22] Even though hog barns are equipped with automatically controlled heat, running water, feed, and equipment to remove the manure, as long as members have denied themselves conveniences in their dwellings, affluence has not destroyed the system. There are constant pressures to change. Affluence is one of several factors that must be balanced in the delicate management of communal living.

Colony Failure

Since the goal of Hutterite life is Christian communal living, the vitality of the system depends upon the success of every single colony. The failure of one colony reflects on the reputation of the system as a whole. A "poor" or a "bad" leader may cause a colony to fail. Poor leaders lack native ability sufficient to the task; bad leaders lack integrity, fall into temptation, and use colony resources or their own position for personal or family gain. Rivalry for leadership between the preacher and

---

22. Rideman, *Account of Our Religion*, p. 126.

the steward is a possible source of difficulty, but through long experience, the chronicle has defined very clearly the role and relationship of each. Stewards especially are warned against the temptation of selfishness, the desire to dominate, and the tendency toward laziness. The steward is subject to the church and the preacher, and all of the foremen are to guard their work and resources carefully. In modern times it is unlikely, but possible, for a steward to squander the money of the colony through excessive drinking and unwise investments made without the consent of the colony. All such offenses are reviewed and punished by the assembly of elders. A steward is often the son or brother of the preacher, and thus on the informal level, any tendencies toward rivalry or extortion are few and unlikely.

If there is mismanagement within a colony, any member may "complain to the elders," the assembly of preachers. The preachers will conduct an investigation and intervene where a leader is believed to be guilty of misconduct. A preacher can be deposed from office. There is little a colony can do to remove a weak leader if he does not commit a flagrant transgression. When a bad leader cannot be restrained, there is invariably a factionalization of the colony into dominant family lines that vie for power. Often the latent elements of this factionalization have culminated in the selection of a bad leader in the first place. If a colony is already factionalized into competing families, there is little a strong, capable leader can do to correct the situation other than attempt to lead with a firm hand and plan for an early branching. If an incapable leader is selected, the total structure of a healthy colony may carry it through this period of weak leadership. Similarly, most cohesive colonies can survive the tenure of a poor steward if the other members of the council are capable leaders. In some cases, the assembly of preachers will step in to mitigate the situation. This is supportive and corrective.

Natural disaster, crop failure, floods, or drought are not the chief problems that lead to colony failure. When one new colony could not make its land payments, it was discovered that the leaders were excessive drinkers. Merchants and bankers no longer gave them credit. The assembly of preachers brought the pressure of patient censure to bear on the colony, eventually silencing the leaders and giving the key positions to younger men. Often, economic problems are overcome with the financial assistance and remedial advice of other colonies. Several colonies will cooperate to raise the necessary collateral to help a needy colony branch to a new location.

Colonies that appear to the outsider to be cohesive and well-managed may actually be suffering from chronic internal troubles. Informal power struggles between groups of families can lead to disruption. When formal power is wrested from the colony by a nuclear family, a group of families, or usually, a group of grown brothers, deep divisions can result. Other problems arise from the tendency of colonies to rank each other by such factors as wealth, degree of mechanization, managerial ability, amount and kind of defection by individuals, reputation of the preacher, and degree of conformity to rules, although variations in these characteristics are normal.

A colony may be polarized between two or more sets of older brothers who hold key positions. Their mothers, more than their wives, are important in the informal leadership pattern. The role of women is crucial in maintaining the balance in colony power on the informal level. Women must be socialized to "accept their place." Since they are believed to be inferior to men physically, intellectually, and emotionally, they must obey and follow their husbands. Through marriage, women unite (or form a link between) different family lines. This introduces an extended set of loyalties into the husband's family, which checks the exclusiveness of blood brother relationships. The woman is bound more closely to her family of procreation than to her family of orientation (although she maintains a loyalty to and a relationship with her parents and her sisters and brothers), and she always supports her grown sons. The man tends to maintain a deeper loyalty to his family of procreation than to his family of procreation.

The differing loyalties of the husband and wife function to prevent the nuclear family from becoming too strong. Any aggression the wife may feel against her husband for his seeming lack of emotional support is channeled against men in general. The woman's loyalty to the female subculture also offsets the emotional importance of the nuclear family in much the same way as the man's identification with the colony as a whole supersedes and thus limits his personal identification with his wife and children.

When women become powerful in intracolony politics, it is usually through an emphasis on the consanguineal family rather than in terms of the interest of the colony as a whole. When a leader is said to be strict, it usually means that he is strict in keeping women in their place. This is said to contribute to the smooth functioning of the colony as a unit, protecting the society from self-centered, competing family groups.

A declining colony is plagued not only with intracolony conflicts but with one or more of the following symptoms: unequal job opportunities available to low and high prestige families, a demand for occupational positions greater than the colony can supply, a high rate of defection, slow population growth, the failure to produce a daughter colony, and colony poverty. Family loyalties tend to become stronger than colony loyalties when a colony is unable to satisfy the job aspirations of the younger male members of all families. The "normal" condition by Hutterite standards is equality of opportunity.

Apostasy and Defection

The Hutterites have a low overall rate of defection to the outside world. Only 106 men and 7 women permanently left the colonies between 1918 and 1950.[23] Among the Schmiedeleut, 98 men and 7 women had defected by 1960.[24] This is a rate of less than 2 percent of the total population and, for the male population, about 7 percent of those fifteen years of age or older. Not included in this rate are individuals (usually young, unbaptized men) who "try the world" for several months or weeks, perhaps by following the harvest, but who return. In fact, most of those who are "tourists" in the outside world return. The increasing tendency toward defection in recent years gives leaders reason to be concerned.

To desert the colony is a serious matter, and to do so after baptism is apostasy. The Hutterites believe that defection occurs in certain "weak" family lines. This view of defection has some validity. In interviewing as many dropouts as possible, the author found that, of 38 defectors, each had come from a "dying" colony (recognized by leaders as *ein sterbene Kolonie*) and over half belonged to the same five families. Two conclusions emerge from our study of defectors: first, those who abandoned colony life were deprived of the usual socialization process in a colony; second, discontent emerges in so-called dying, or declining, colonies.

When asked "What made you decide to leave the colony?" defectors gave many different reasons. Some responded with a long chronology of events, while others were either not capable of vocalizing their experience or were not sufficiently relaxed to do so. One admitted "I don't know myself." The immediate reasons were associated with curiosity and adventure, religious and personal conflict, mistreatment, dislike for colony customs and rules, desire for spending money or an automobile, and romances with outsiders.

A declining colony has chronic unresolved problems of internal leadership. The older colonies appear to have more structural problems than the newly established ones. Custom does not permit a member to move from his home colony to another colony. Thus, persons may not abandon a declining colony to join a more desirable one, and runaways must return to the colony they left. Many of those who defected permanently had experienced long-term disputes with the householder,

23. Eaton and Weil, *Culture and Mental Disorders*, p. 146.
24. Mange, "The Population Structure of a Human Isolate," p. 32.

the preacher, or the German teacher. Leaving the colony in most cases was premeditated and touched off by arguments or antagonisms with superiors.

The high status accorded to some families (usually those in leadership positions) and the low status accorded to others were also pronounced characteristics of declining colonies. Nepotism was common. Discrimination was invariably felt by the low-status individuals and families. The parents of many of those who abandoned the colony were atypical in some way: the relationship of the sons to their fathers was abnormal—either the father was very authoritarian or he showed favoritism toward one son. Out of a group of 38 defectors, 11 were the sons of either preachers or householders. In a family where the father had been deposed as householder, 7 children had defected from the colony.

Inequality of opportunity to obtain positions may occur when one family on the council dominates the decision-making process. When there is such an inequality of opportunity, there is some tendency for elitist positions (preacher, steward, and farm foreman) to be passed from father to son.[25] A son often acquires an intimate knowledge of his father's work. The cattleman, for example, must have the knowledge and ability to compete within the market conditions outside of the colony. Usually his son is his helper as he is growing up. It is important that the son learn everything his father knows about cattle, and he must improve upon this knowledge. If relations are strained between father and son, the economic efficiency of the colony will often be diminished. Discontent is intensified if the traditional roles are not equitably distributed among sibships.

When an adult or a leader flirts with alien values or is too lax in discipline, the effect on the younger members will be pronounced. The young, unbaptized man in a declining colony gets little support from his peers if he has an ambition to restore order and return to the earlier idealism of his colony. Since adolescents are believed to be naturally "young and unproven" and behave accordingly, there is a particular problem in such a colony to maintain the traditional respect for authority. The discrepancy that develops between belief and practice will, for example, allow a person to have a radio but not allow him to listen to it in public.

25. The observation is borne out by Peter Gordon Clark; see "Dynasty Formation in the Communal Society of the Hutterites" (Ph.D. dissertation, University of British Columbia, 1974). Using the Schmiedeleut data, Clark reports that colonies which produce an excess of positions tend to be equalitarian; colonies which produce too few tend to be dynastic (having a sequence of rulers from the same family). Defection was more frequent among offspring of the nonelite than the elite (p. 190). No large patronymic group was found to dominate an entire Leut, but there were localized instances of dominant dynastic families, primarily in poor colonies (p. 221).

Daughters have fewer opportunities to familiarize themselves with the outside world than do sons. They share the subordinate status of women. If a family has a good reputation, the daughter has a good chance of an early marriage and does not feel the need to be preeminent or to rebel. Even though few women leave the colony, there is evidence that daughters of leaders occasionally face atypical problems. If a daughter writes sermons, does bookkeeping, or serves the preacher in a special way, she may be willing to postpone marriage for several years out of respect for her father. All colony roles are psychologically marked by strong elements of dependency, but this is especially so for women. Any woman who cannot accept the definition of the role given to her will have more difficulty than a man in finding alternative avenues of expression. Several groups of sisters who abandoned a colony gave as their reason that the colony was no longer Christian; an underlying factor was that these sisters, who found company in each other's misery, rejected the submissive role assigned to Hutterite women. Their conversion to an individualistically oriented fundamentalist denomination permitted a way of escape.

Parents who show favoritism to a child or entertain ambitions for a child beyond those sanctioned by the colony introduce dissident elements and increase the probability of defection. The favored child, who obtains more attention and privilege than others in the family or the colony, acquires self-confidence beyond that of his peers. Interests are developed and needs are felt beyond those the colony can provide. A child who does not experience the same rejection as his peers will not be frightened by problems that require imagination and individual interpretation or solution. A father who wanted his son to become an engineer (a goal not attainable by others in the colony) entertained a noncolony goal for him. An able leader who exceeds the limits (usually intellectually) or engages in certain privileges may unwittingly pave the way for subsequent deviation by his children. When some of the children are treated as separate personalities in the formative years, the resulting individualism is likely to constitute a threat to the collective welfare.

Most of the defectors we interviewed were single when they left the colony. They found homes for themselves in predominantly rural areas and found work similar to that performed in the colony. Very few moved directly into urban centers. One took flight training and became a pilot on a transcontinental air line. Geographically they were scattered from Florida to Alaska. Several were welders, a skill they had acquired in the colony. Most were highly motivated in their job performance. The male defectors tended to be inactive or indifferent to religion and showed little interest in making distinctions among the vast numbers of denominations that are not Hutterite. The absolutist position of the

Hutterite religion continues to structure the thinking patterns of the dropouts. The religion taught to them in childhood is unconsciously respected by them in such statements as: "If I ever want religion, I know where to find it." One who had abandoned the colony forty years before said that during the intervening years "the little faith that you had was right there to sort of guide you. The guardian angel was always with you, it seemed like."

Hutterite leaders go to great lengths to retrieve their dropouts and runaways. Never is anyone asked to leave the colony. Persons who have permanently left the colonies may return to visit their relatives. Colony leaders exert great efforts to persuade the runaway to repent and return to the godly path. The father of a young man who joined the marines and served over thirty years wrote an acrostic poem of twenty-eight verses pleading for his son to return. In free translation four verses read:

Hark to the beckoning call,
"Oh weary soul come home."
Turn from your course in the world
Lest you should perish.

Seek after God's grace
And wait no longer.
God still calls; His light still shines.
Night comes, it's getting dusk.

Christ invites you to the feast
Prepare tonight for the Lamb.
You too may come—just as you are
Just come and turn away from sin.

Mere knowledge brings no healing
To your burdened soul,
But striving for righteousness
Can make you whole.

Legal Predicaments

The necessity for legal services has grown with the complexity of large-scale agriculture. There are the usual problems of incorporation, land acquisition, tax accounting, and representations at marketing boards. There are also special problems arising out of statutes that prevent colony expansion and suits brought by defecting members. Tax litigation is an ongoing problem for the colonies.

The colonies will defend themselves by legal means if necessary for the welfare of the colony. A few colonies have fallen prey to the advice of lawyers who have urged them to make exaggerated claims. The solution is to hire a single reputable law firm. To deal with provincial or national problems, the colonies have banded together. In Manitoba, the Schmiedeleut colonies have been represented for many years by E. A. Fletcher of Winnipeg, who obtained a charter for the Hutterites in Canada in 1951. In Alberta, P. G. Davies has represented the Dariusleut and the Lehrerleut before the Alberta Provincial Assembly and dealt with many of their legal problems.

Two legal cases have reached the Supreme Court of Canada. In one of them, the Rock Lake Colony contested the constitutionality of the Communal Property Act on the grounds that it was discriminatory and violated the Canadian Bill of Rights. The court ruled that the Communal Property Act of Alberta was essentially a law dealing with land tenure.

Suits brought against the colonies by defecting members for a share of the corporate property have not been productive. In those instances where courts initially ruled against the colonies, their decisions were overturned by a higher court. At baptism every Hutterite agrees to live communally and, if at any time he should give up his faith, he promises to make no claim on any part of the colony's assets. The constitutionality of this position reached the Supreme Court of Canada in 1966.

Two Hofer brothers at the Interlake Colony in Manitoba had begun to show an interest in the teachings of Herbert W. Armstrong, founder of the Radio Church of God. Despite colony rules against radios, they listened avidly to his program and subscribed to the literature of the Worldwide Church of God. The Hofers were fascinated by Armstrong's teachings, taken largely from the Old Testament and the book of Revelation. Armstrong claims to understand God's plan for the world, which enables him to predict major world events. The British and the Americans are descendants of the lost tribes of Israel, destined to fight the battle of Armageddon against Russia and China. Emerging from this battle will be a world government headed by the Messiah. Meanwhile, faithful believers who await the apocalypse are to observe the ceremonial practices of the Old Testament. They are to worship on Saturday instead of Sunday, observe kosher laws, celebrate the Passover, the Feast of Tabernacles, the Day of Atonement, and the New Year in the month of Ahib (April) rather than such holidays as Christmas and Easter. When the Hofers attempted to practice these beliefs the colony was polarized into two camps.

The Hutterite elders carefully defined their position to the Hofers and warned them of the consequences of their actions. After patient but unsuccessful efforts to regain the brothers to the Hutterite faith, the Schmiedeleut formally expelled them from the church. They refused to leave the colony and ate in the colony dining hall, thereby refusing the role assigned to apostates. They began to hold religious services on Saturday, eat specially prepared meals, dress in worldly clothing, and make pilgrimages to the headquarters of the Worldwide Church of God at Pasadena, California. With the support of their new religious association, they brought court action against the colony corporation. They held that their expulsion was invalid and that since the colony was in disharmony, the assets should be equally divided among the members. The Hutterites challenged the suit and came to the defense of their constitution.[26] Many witnesses, including children and Hutterite elders, were summoned in a long contested and widely publicized case. The highest court in Canada ruled that the plaintiffs could not lay claim to the colony property on grounds that they had abandoned the Hutterite faith. All four families, part of a total group of thirty-four persons, left the colony as apostates.

Encounters with Other Communal Groups

Fundamentalist preachers who visit colonies for the purpose of witnessing and converting Hutterite members are no match for the Hutterite preachers. All such proselyters are referred to the head preacher, who generally asks, "If you are a Christian, why don't you live communally?" "Here the argument stops," according to one Hutterite preacher.

Although the Brethren have a warm interest in groups which practice communal living, during most of their history in North America they have had little interaction with other communal societies. Both the Harmony Society of Pennsylvania and the Amana Society of Iowa assisted the colonies financially in their early period, and the colonies maintained a cordial but distant relationship. Before 1900, eighteen-year-old Michael Hofer of Bon Homme Colony went to the Amana Society in Iowa to receive medical treatment for his eyes. He remained in Amana and married there. Hutterites have had occasional informal contacts with the Old Order Amish. During the depression some Amish congregations gave financial assistance to a needy colony in Montana. Occasionally outsiders have joined the Hutterite movement and moved away with some of their members.

26. The Hutterite constitution reads: ". . . if any member of a congregation or community shall be expelled therefrom, or cease to be a member thereof, he or she shall not have, take, withdraw from, grant, sell, transfer, or convey, or be entitled to any of the property of the congregation or community or any 'interest therein." See Article 39 in Constitution of the Hutterian Brethren Church and Rules as to Community of Property. Winnipeg, Man.: [E. A. Fletcher, for the Hutterian Brethren], 1950. For the legal citation see "Manitoba Queen's Bench," J. Dickson, Hofer, et al. v. Hofer et al. 59 Dominion Law Reports (1967). The four Hofer brothers who were plaintiffs brought suit against two other brothers and a cousin who were the trustees of the colony.

Julius Kubbasek (1893–1961), a Hungarian communist converted to the Nazarene faith, came to North America in 1925 and attempted to establish "Apostolic Christianity" in his denomination.[27] After stormy but unsuccessful reform attempts in Ontario and Saskatchewan, his small group moved to British Columbia. He visited the Alberta Hutterites in 1936 and, returning with a full beard and Hutterite dress, insisted that his followers emulate the Hutterites. Soon the entire Kubbasek group moved to the West Raley Hutterite colony, where they lived for fourteen months in an attempt to adopt the Hutterite way of life. When differences began to emerge in 1939, Julius moved his group to Ontario. The Hutterites supplied the "Juliusleut" with three railroad cars of farm implements, horses, cattle, geese, and hogs. Joining the group were two of the Hutterite wives and some of their young children; their husbands refused to accompany them. The group purchased a farm near Bright, Ontario, in 1941, calling themselves the Community Farm of the Brethren. Since then the colony has attracted a variety of converts. In spite of internal factions and several different language groups, the colony has prospered financially by selling their produce in nearby farmers' markets. The Hutterites severed formal relationships with the Juliusleut in 1950, giving as their reason that Julius was too dictatorial and impulsive and noting also that he was an advocate of celibacy. The loss of about forty persons to the Julius group, all of them named Entz, was a great disappointment to the Alberta Hutterites.

Eberhard Arnold (1883–1935), founder of the Society of Brothers, was a German theologian who, as a result of deepening conviction, led a small movement in Germany in 1920 devoted to communal living.[28] He and his wife Emmy were interested in identifying with Anabaptism and primitive Christianity. After learning that the Hutterites had retained the practice of communal living in North America, he visited all of the colonies in 1930 and 1931. The Hutterites were greatly impressed with Arnold's devotion to the Chrstian faith, his interest in communal living, and his humility. He was well versed in the Bible and in history, he professed unity of faith, and he spoke good German. His manner of dress, including the wearing of a beard, undoubtedly helped to symbolize the unity which existed between them. The Hutterites readily accepted Arnold and his Bruderhof in Germany into the Hutterian membership. In December of 1930 Arnold was "confirmed in the service of

---

27. Peter Gordon Clark, "The Brethren of Early Christianity: A Study of a World-Rejecting Sect" (Master's thesis, McMaster University, Hamilton, Ontario, 1967).

28. *Eberhard Arnold: A Testimony of Church-Community from His Life and Writings* (Rifton, N.Y.: Plough Publishing House, 1964). For a sociological study of the Society of Brothers, see Benjamin Zablocki, *The Joyful Community* (Baltimore: Penguin Books, 1971).

the Word with the laying on of hands by the elders" to "proclaim the Word of God" and establish the faith in Germany. Arnold returned to Germany with the moral and financial support of the Hutterites in North America and began to publish and reprint basic Hutterite works.

Arnold died in 1935. His Bruderhof was suppressed by German National Socialism. Two Hutterite leaders visited the Bruderhof in Germany in 1937, just in time to see their property confiscated by the Nazis.[29] The survivors moved from Germany to Liechtenstein and then to England. Under heavy pressure from the British government, which feared the group would aid the Germans in a possible invasion, most migrated to Paraguay between 1940 and 1941. All attempts to migrate to the United States or Canada and locate near the Hutterite colonies had failed. In Paraguay there were three Bruderhofs with over five hundred members. Some Hutterite colonies supported the colonies in Paraguay in the hope that they would be faithful members of the traditional Hutterite movement. Visits between the Hutterites and the Paraguayan group, who called themselves the Society of Brothers, were infrequent.

The occasional reports Hutterites heard about the Bruderhofs in Paraguay did not please them. Exchange of letters did not suffice. A delegation of two Hutterite preachers was sent to Paraguay to engage in a "heart to heart talk." The differences between the traditional Hutterites and the so-called New Hutterites were openly examined and discussed at the Ibate Conference in 1950.[30] Distressing to the North American visitors were such practices as smoking, attending movies, picture-taking, and folk dancing; not folding the hands for prayer, singing instead of speaking the mealtime prayer, and omitting the use of the children's prayer from Moravia. They also objected to the presence of sisters in deliberations which among Hutterites take place only in the male council, the dress and uncovered heads of the young girls, and the dearth of weighty sermons—and they felt that the interpreter in the Spanish service should perforce be a preacher.

The Hutterite visitors then carefully listened while the "Arnold-leut" asked the questions. They wanted to know, "Is there a flag in your schools and do the children sing the national anthem?" (To Hutterites the flag "is just a piece of cloth.") The New Hutterites were also uneasy about a number of practices in North America: civilian forestry service

29. Robert Friedmann, ed. and trans., "Hutterites Revisit European Homesteads: Excerpts from the Travel Diary of David Hofer," *M.Q.R.* 33 (October 1959): 306.

30. "Report of a Preachers' Conference, Held at the Ibate Community . . . 1950." In discussing the issues that separated the two groups it is not my intention to expose intimacies unduly but to illustrate the differences in style, perception, and character between a traditional communal group and a charasmatic movement of similar value orientation.

in lieu of military service, the purchase of victory bonds (Hutterites had pasted a note on them saying, "Not to be used for war purposes but for the benefit of the poor and the suffering"), donations to the Red Cross, the use of small allowances or pocket money, the practice of permitting individuals or families to claim old books that have been handed down, the neglect of missionary work, the lack of unity and a common treasury for the three groups or leut, and the lack of a common sewing room.

A German-Paraguayan elder told the Hutterite delegates: "We are a different kind of people. We have only just now come out of the world. And we are not inspired to do so by Hutter but by the example of the early Christians and some other much older movements. Though we should be in agreement on the main issues, in some ways we must differ from you." The Paraguayans were dismayed by the simplistic ways of the Hutterites. Arnold, for example had begun the publication and editing of the old chronicles. The Hutterite elders, they said, were taken in by Zieglschmid, whom they felt was indiscriminate in the selection of documents included in their printed history.

The spokesman for the Hutterite delegation, Samuel Kleinsasser, said: "We cannot operate like you here. If we preachers would always sit around, with the householder in his office and a man at the telephone, we couldn't exist. I was a preacher and a householder and had to do all that work and was still out in the fields from morning to night."

The delegates returned home, sharing their frank discussions and their findings. The differences seemed so great as to be irreconcilable. There were exchanges of letters and admonitions, but both sides drifted apart. The Paraguayans were charged with worldliness, and financial support was terminated. The Hutterites were told that they had lost their missionary zeal, which, in part, they admitted.

The story does not end there. Forest River colony in North Dakota, which had more than its share of dissident members, was sympathetic to the Society of Brothers. Against the advice of the Schmiedeleut assembly of preachers, the colony invited the Paraguayans into their midst. According to one informant, "they invaded Forest River Colony like an army, bringing thirty-six people, including nurses, teachers, lawyers, and four ministers, and took command of the place from the first day on." The resident Hutterite preacher returned to the parent colony in Manitoba with forty of his people. The Schmiedeleut dispatched six preachers from Manitoba and five from South Dakota. For two weeks these preachers tried to persuade the Paraguayans to leave and the dissident ethnic Hutterites to change their attitudes. The Schmiedeleut preachers met in session on September 6, 1955, and excommunicated the Society of Brothers for causing disunity and divisiveness and for wrongdoing. The Forest River Colony was placed on probation.

Economic difficulties added to internal dissension caused the Paraguayans to move from Forest River to Farmington, Pennsylvania, in 1956. They were accompanied by thirty-six sympathetic Hutterites including fifteen baptized members. The leaders of the Society of Brothers felt that North Dakota was too remote and inaccessible for missionary contacts with the outside world. The seasonal demands of the farm and the inadequacy of accommodations were other factors in their decision to relocate. Some of these former Hutterites found their way to still other communal groups, such as Koinonia Farm in Georgia, and others became altogether worldly. As with the Kubbasek episode, the Hutterites were pained to lose their kinsmen.

Meanwhile the Society of Brothers had disbanded their settlements in Paraguay and most had moved to the United States. The Woodcrest Community at Rifton, New York, was formed in 1954 and began to manufacture educational toys under the brand name Community Playthings. The group at Farmington, Pennsylvania, founded in 1956 as Oak Lake Community, has changed its name to New Meadow Run Community. Two additional settlements are Evergreen Community, Norfolk, Connecticut (founded in 1957), and Darvell Community, Robertsbridge, Sussex, England, (founded in 1972). The four communities number somewhat over one thousand persons.

For twenty years relations between the Hutterites and the Society of Brothers were strained. Contacts were limited largely to letter writing and infrequent visiting. The hope of persuading relatives and apostates to return was still a viable point of contact. Heini Arnold, son of the founder, Eberhard Arnold, visited the Hutterite preachers in 1964 and made a personal apology for the division. Efforts at formal reconciliation were initiated by the Society of Brothers in 1973 and culminated in the following year.[31]

A delegation from the Society of Brothers, led by Heini Arnold and representing their four communities met with seventy-one preachers of the three Leut in Manitoba in January, 1974. The Society of Brothers offered a formal apology for the wrongdoing at Forest River and accepted the "punishments" required by the Hutterians. Those

31. The reconciliation to this date is discussed in three small pamphlets by Heini Arnold: *A Printed Sendbrief*, *A Second Printed Sendbrief*, and *A Third Printed Sendbrief*, all dated March, 1974 and issued by Plough Publishing House, Rifton, N.Y. It was agreed that no members would be permitted to move from Hutterite colonies to the communities of the Society of Brothers, or from the Society of Brothers to the Hutterite colonies, without permission on both sides.

members who had been baptized in Hutterite colonies were thereafter soon reinstated. A spokesman for the Society of Brothers said: "This is a great moment of God, something is happening which is beyond the Bruderhof or the Hutterians."[32] At this writing the coming together of both groups is considered a great spiritual culmination.

32. Johann Christoph Arnold, in personal correspondence with the author, January 26, 1974.

chapter twelve

The Strategy of Hutterite Survival

When the Hutterites came from the Ukraine in 1874, there were 8 communal societies in 72 separate colonies in the United States: Harmony Society, Oneida, Shakers, Amana, Bethel, Zoar, Saint Nazianz, and Ephrata. During the ensuing years all of them have vanished as viable social systems.[1] The Hutterite growth record—from 3 to over 225 colonies—speaks for itself. To account for this survival and pattern of expansion in terms of tradition, isolation, and selective migration is insufficient.

The Hutterite colonies have not survived by avoiding the troubles that plague other communal living groups. They are not free from crises and problems. The Hutterites have triumphed because they have had more than sufficient resources to weather the disasters common to communal societies. The early period of prosperity and growth in the sixteenth century, in which large numbers of refugees joined the movement, is very different from the twentieth century experience, which is

1. Lee Emerson Deets (*The Hutterites: A Study in Social Cohesion* [Gettysburg, Pa.: By the author, 1939], p. 22) points out that of 130 communal-type settlements, 4 endured a century or longer. For a study of communal longevity and success, see also Rosabeth M. Kanter, *Commitment and Community: Communes and Utopias in Sociological Perspective* (Cambridge: Harvard University Press, 1972), pp. 126–38, and *Communes: Creating and Managing the Collective Life* (New York: Harper & Row, 1973), pp. 493–98.

characterized by natural increase and unhindered expansion. When the wider society around them changed, they were able to adapt to the new environment and even to solve problems of their own making. How have the Hutterites managed this? What resources and wisdom have they brought to human experience that may be instructive for other human communities? The genius of Hutterite communal living, or what we believe to be the uniqueness of their strategy for survival and stability, is formulated in the following five categories.

Uncompromising Beliefs

Hutterite life is governed by a positive model for influencing human conduct. Central to Hutterite survival is an uncompromising ideology (vocalized by Hutterites themselves as *Der Glaube*) that defines and orders the entire system. The inclusiveness of the Hutterite way of life is very different from what is required of the individual in most Christian denominations. Uncompromising beliefs, which may not be challenged, provide the foundation for the Hutterites' willingness to die rather than change their social institutions. The central beliefs provide the basis of supernatural authority and a view of the world that is hierarchical and patriarchal, requiring social separation from the carnal world. The hierarchial order is projected into the social sphere in the sense that "the lower obeys and serves the higher." The higher directs and protects the lower. The incarnation of divine authority in the social arrangements governing the use of material goods and property is learned in infancy and vigorously supported throughout life. Thus, the colony is accepted as an expression of the will of God, a divine provision.

It is not simply "beliefs" which make a Hutterite. To be a Hutterite is to participate in a religious experience, a group-related experience in which the spiritual nature rules over the carnal. The efficiency, motivation, and material prosperity of the colonies would collapse without the mystical qualities generated in the experience of community.

The central beliefs about goals, subgoals, and norms of practice are explicit and have a high degree of internal consistency. The deification of societal unity on a subverbal level and the submission of the self to the will of God minimize arguments and speculations of a theological nature. Logical thought and reasoned solutions are applied mainly to the economic adaptations of making a living. The basic ideology is supported by constant teaching and appropriate ritual. There is a clear delineation between power that may be democratically managed by man and power that is exercised only by God. The shared beliefs appear to be sufficiently comprehensive to satisfy individual inquisitiveness within the scope of the colony environment.

The dualistic view of human nature, spiritual and carnal, is the reasoned basis for separation from the world. The activities of the colony, the training of the young, and the management of specific problems are grounded in the predetermined spiritual, rather than carnal, assumptions. Geographic isolation as well as symbolic isolation through language and dress are manifestations of spiritual separation from the world as required by the central beliefs. Isolation from external and competing beliefs effectively minimizes the problems of communal living as the Hutterites practice it.

The absolutism of their ideology has made it necessary for Hutterites to migrate to various countries where they have been able to live in isolation from their neighbors. (See figure 40.) The overriding ideology has not, however, forced the members to isolate themselves from biologic, economic, and technological solutions to living. Integrated central beliefs have minimized the problems of fragmentation, of individualistic and dictatorial leaders, and of defection. The basic beliefs are defined in such a way as to include the physical and emotional components of human need.

Comprehensive Socialization

Hutterite society does not require the individual to mortify himself because of the basic human drives but to subject himself to a community of love that is both human and divine. Every person acquires a knowledge of what is expected of him. The individual is socialized within a spatial environment that includes all the social institutions, activities, and resources he will need as an individual. Dependency upon other colony members is maximized while interaction with outsiders is minimized. The scope of socialization is truly comprehensive. Hutterite education embodies temporal as well as eternal time dimensions and prescribes an active participation by the individual in both. The ritualization of temporal and sacred activity is well proportioned and supports vital links between the generations.

The Hutterite appraisal of human nature is functional within the colony educational system. A child is regarded as having a carnal nature which must be supplanted by the spiritual. Personality is viewed as intrinsically good only insofar as a person gives up his individual will and conforms voluntarily to the will of the colony. Spiritual maturity is expressed within a social hierarchy that is based on graduated moral obligations.

The young child learns to enjoy people and to respond positively to many persons. In the colony kindergarten, he is weaned from his nuclear family and taught to accept authority in virtually any form. He

Figure 40. Evening scene in a Hutterite colony in Alberta, Canada. (Photograph by Kryn Taconis)

learns that aloneness is associated with unpleasant experiences, being with others with pleasant experiences. During the school years he moves farther away from his family, learns more about authority, and acquires a verbal knowledge of his religion. He acquires the ability to relate positively to his peer group and to respond to its demands. While a small child his universe is unpredictable, but as he matures in his peer group and takes part in colony life, his universe becomes increasingly predictable. He learns to minimize self-assertion and self-confidence and to accept dependence on the group. As a member of a categorically defined age-set, the young child learns explicitly when and whom to obey.

School-age children receive limited companionship and little indulgence from their parents; they learn how their peer group protects and punishes them; they learn to accept frustration passively and to enjoy hard physical labor. When the child becomes an adult, he is rewarded with responsibility, privileges, and greater recognition and acceptance from his nuclear family. After becoming a full member of the colony through the rite of baptism, his self-image expands to include the whole colony membership with whom he now identifies.

Training is consistent and continuous in all age groups. From early childhood to adulthood there is no relaxation of indoctrination within clearly defined age and sex groupings. Each person is subservient to the colony at every stage of his life. The goals of each stage in the social hierarchy are attainable by virtually all Hutterites. Individuals are well trained not to assert themselves, and each person is rewarded by important work and by the awareness that his contribution is needed.

Reconciliation of the Delinquents

The Hutterite system tends to be tolerant of deviance in its adolescent members.[2] Most deviance expresses itself within the peer group and therefore is manageable within the confines of the colony. All individuals have a peer group determined by their age and sex. Great stress is placed on voluntary conformity, for, as the Hutterites say, no person should be coerced. Since all human nature is carnal and inclined toward disobedience, patience must be exercised toward the young and the immature. The Hutterite position is simply that the individual is not perfect and cannot attain perfection without the aid of his brothers.

When a Hutterite youth transgresses colony rules, he is punished, not because he was "bad" (every child has a carnal nature) but because

2. The management of delinquency is discussed at length by Joseph W. Eaton, "Adolescence in a Communal Society," *Mental Hygiene* 68(1964): 66-73.

a wrongdoer must suffer the consequences of his behavior. Instead of being stigmatized as bad and pitted against his peers, he remains emotionally identified with them. Though he may be physically punished or shamed before the group, he is never deprived of food, work, or self-respect. Hutterite society makes it a point to forgive when true signs of betterment are observed; such manifestations are encouraged and rewarded. Not until the individual becomes a full member is he obligated to teach and uphold the morality of the colony. The colony people, the parents, and the kinship group expect that immaturity will be supplanted by responsibility. The net result is a view of human nature that encourages rehabilitation with a minimum of condemnation. The toleration of some deviance within each age-set relieves the system of stifling rigidity.

The typical Hutterite knows why he is alive, and how he should live, and he feels able to meet the standards of his society. The result is a firm sense of identity and a stable society. The individual Hutterite may exhibit what appears to the outsider as egocentrism or exaggerated pride. To the Hutterite, however, this appearance of complacency is not personal pride but the reflection of a state of mind that is free of doubts. The strong emotional appeal of the colony is evidenced by the high proportion of runaways who return after "trying the world."

Biological Vitality

The reproductive patterns in Hutterite society result in a high rate of natural increase. The family as a social unit, made up of a lifelong monogamous pair and their offspring, with firm patriarchal authority, constitutes no threat to the cohesiveness of the entire colony. The Hutterites have chosen neither celibacy, on the one hand, nor the communalization of sex, on the other.[3] Sexual intercourse is limited to pair-marriages. There is not the slightest inclination toward celibacy or interest in continence after marriage. In its socially sanctioned place, the practice of sex is distinguished from the "lust of the eye," which is illegitimate desire. Families are generally happy and supportive of the colony's superior power position.

During a century in Russia, Hutterite population grew tenfold, from 116 to approximately 1,265. The 443 Hutterites who lived in colonies in 1880 increased to approximately 21,521 by 1974, or about fiftyfold (see chart 6 and table 8). Demographers report that the average

3. See, for example, Kanter, *Commitment and Community*, pp. 287–307; and Sallie TeSelle, ed., *The Family, Communes, and Utopian Societies* (New York: Harper Torchbooks, 1971).

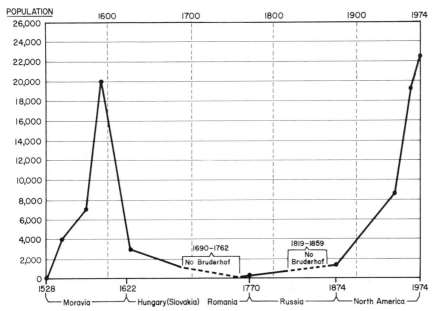

Chart 6. Hutterite Population Growth by Centuries, 1528–1974

family size (of completed families) is over ten children, even though the young people tend not to marry as early as in American society. The median age at marriage for girls (in 1950) was twenty-two years and for boys twenty-three and a half years. The average interval between births was under two years.[4]

4. The benchmark of Hutterite demography is Joseph W. Eaton and Albert J. Mayer, *Man's Capacity To Reproduce: The Demography of a Unique Population* (Glencoe, Ill.: Free Press, 1954), reprinted from *Human Biology* 26 (September 1953). Other specialized studies include Christopher Tietze, "Reproductive Span and Rate of Reproduction among Hutterite Women," *Fertility and Sterility* 8(1957): 89-97; Arthur P. Mange, "The Population Structure of a Human Isolate" (Ph.D. dissertation, University of Wisconsin, 1963) and "Growth and Inbreeding of a Human Isolate," *Human Biology* 36(May 1964): 104-33; Mindel C. Sheps, "An Analysis of Reproductive Patterns in an American Isolate," *Population Studies* 18(July 1965): 65-79; Gertrude Huntington and John A. Hostetler, "A Note on Nursing Practices in an American Isolate with a High Birth Rate," *Population Studies* 19(March 1966): 321-24; Arthur G. Steinberg et al., "Genetic Studies on an Inbred Isolate," in *Proceedings of the Third International Congress of Human Genetics*, ed. James F. Crow and James V. Neel (Baltimore: Johns Hopkins Press, 1967); and Sandra H. Hartzog, "Population Genetic Studies of a Human Isolate: The Hutterites of North America" (Ph.D. dissertation, University of Massachusetts, 1971). For interpretative discussions, see also Population Reference Bureau, Inc., "Pockets of High Fertility in the United States," *Population Bulletin* 24(November 1968), and William F. Pratt, "The Anabaptist Explosion; Adaptation of Pockets of Higher Fertility in the United States," *Natural History* 78(February 1969): 8-23.

Table 8. Hutterite Population, 1528-1974

Year	Place or circumstance	Population	Source of information[a]
1528	Origin, Nikolsburg (Moravia)	200	Wolkan (1923), p. 62
1545	Moravia	6,300	Hrubý. See Friedmann (1961), p. 105
1589	Moravia	20,000	Rideman (1950), p. 275
1622	Expulsion from Moravia	2,500	Estimate
1767	On moving to Wallachia, Romania	67	Zieglschmid (1947), p. 299
1770	On moving to Vishenka, Russia (60 persons, followed by 56 fourteen years later)	116	Zieglschmid (1947), pp. 403, 374
1802	On moving to Radichev, Russia	202	Zieglschmid (1947), p. 411
1842	On moving to Huttertal, South Russia	384	Klaus (1889), p. 79
1874	On migrating to Dakota Territory	1,265[b]	Ship lists
1880	Census of the United States	443	Eaton and Mayer (1954), p. 5
1908	South Dakota	1,500	Elias Walter (1908), p. 89
1950	Mental Health Study Survey	8,542	Eaton and Mayer (1954), p. 45
1970	Projection	19,200	Eaton and Mayer (1954), p. 45
1974	Colony census	21,521	Hostetler (table 10, p. 295 below)

[a]See bibliography for complete references.
[b]Includes noncolony Hutterite immigrants, 1874-79.

Hutterites place a positive value on having children. The colony assures the economic support of as many children as parents produce. Colonies are willing and able to pay for good medical care. Few adults fail to get married, and the sterility rate of Hutterite members is low. There are no divorces and virtually no migrations or occupations that separate husband from wife. In contrast to the experience of most contemporary industrial populations, men tend to outlive their wives; also in contrast to the general trend of industrializing societies, the Hutterite population has not declined with the increasing use and diffusion of modern technology.

The demographic patterns resemble those of a stable population model. The age-sex distribution for the past century has remained fairly constant. Compared with the rural-farm population in the United States, the Hutterites have proportionately more young people and proportionately fewer people over the age of forty (see chart 7 and table 9). The birth and death rates have remained almost constant.

The Hutterite population pattern differs from that of primitive peoples, who generally have a high birth rate and a high infant death rate. Adults have about the normal life expectancy of Americans in general, but old people form a small minority because of the successive waves of new children. The fertility rate resembles that of underdeveloped countries, but the mortality pattern resembles that of industrialized countries.

The high fertility rate of the Hutterites is accompanied by appropriate social adaptations. To maintain a continuous high rate of population growth, the society must be stable, it must have access to land resources in order to expand, and it must maintain a value system that supports the biblical instruction "Be fruitful and multiply." Keeping colony populations to a manageable size is essential for maintaining the Hutterian way of life. By adapting to large-scale agriculture and by firmly controlling the size and location of colonies, Hutterites have prevented urbanism and merchandising.

The general expansion pattern is similar for the three Leut. Each Leut founded colonies in Canada when the harassment associated with World War I began in 1918. Colony branchings for the three Leut are

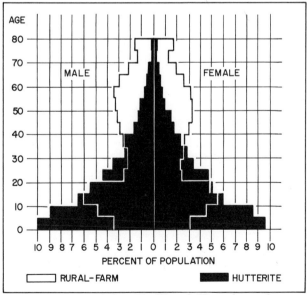

Chart 7. Age and Sex Profile of Hutterite and Rural-Farm Population, 1970

Table 9. Age and Sex Distribution of Hutterites and Rural-Farm Population in the United States, 1970 (in Percent)

Age-group	Hutterites		Rural-farm population in U.S.	
	Male	Female	Male	Female
75 and over	0.3	0.3	1.7	1.7
70–74	0.2	0.2	1.5	1.3
65–69	0.5	0.5	2.2	1.9
60–64	0.6	0.6	3.0	2.6
55–59	0.9	0.8	3.4	3.1
50–54	1.2	1.0	3.4	3.3
45–49	1.3	1.6	3.3	3.3
40–44	1.8	1.8	3.0	3.1
35–39	2.6	2.3	2.5	2.8
30–34	2.5	2.9	2.2	2.4
25–29	3.5	3.4	2.2	2.3
20–24	4.5	4.7	2.4	2.3
15–19	5.5	5.0	5.6	4.9
10–14	6.5	6.1	6.1	5.7
5–9	9.0	8.5	5.0	4.8
Under 5	9.6	9.6	3.5	3.4
Percent	50.8	49.3	51.0	48.9
Number	4,801	4,683	5,403,796	5,184,738

Source: The Hutterite population data are based upon the census of Steinberg et al. ("Genetic Studies on an Inbred Isolate," p. 270) of Schmiedeleut and Lehrerleut. The rural-farm population comes from the *United States Census of Population, 1970.*

shown in charts A-1, A-2, and A-3, appendix 16. (The list of colonies, dates of founding, and colonies of origin are shown in appendix 15.) The Schmiedeleut moved to Manitoba, and only they are located in Manitoba, North Dakota, South Dakota, and Minnesota. Both Lehrerleut and Dariusleut are located in Alberta, Saskatchewan, and Montana, and the two colonies in Washington belong to the Dariusleut. (See map 5.) The laws restricting the colonies from buying land also influenced the branching pattern. The Lehrerleut, for example, founded no colonies in Alberta between 1937 and 1950, but during this period they founded eight colonies in Montana. In South Dakota, colony sites were abandoned when the members moved to Canada. Later most of the Lehrerleut and Dariusleut colony lands were purchased by the Schmiedeleut. In a few instances colonies were moved because of economic problems and unsuitable lands. The largest Leut in terms of membership and number of colonies is the Schmiedeleut, followed by the Dariusleut and the Lehrerleut (see table 10). The average span between each branching is about fourteen years. During the past five years, colonies have been forming at the rate of six per year.

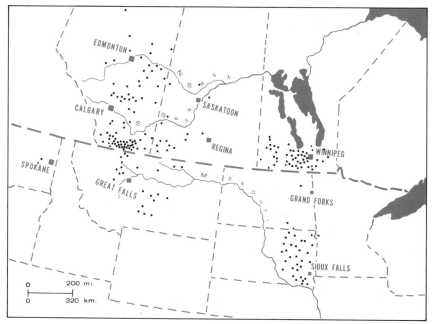

Map 5. Location of Hutterite Colonies in North America, 1974

Table 10. Hutterite Population in North America by Leut Affiliation and Location, 1974

Category	Schmiedeleut	Dariusleut	Lehrerleut	Total
Population	8,873	6,368	6,280	21,521
Number of colonies	91	77	61	229
Mean colony size	97.5	82.7	103.0	94.0
Location and number of colonies in U.S.				
South Dakota	34	0	0	34
Montana	0	7	16	23
North Dakota	4	0	0	4
Washington	0	2	0	2
Minnesota	1	0	0	1
Total in U.S.	39	9	16	64
Location and number of colonies in Canada				
Alberta	0	54	30	84
Manitoba	53	0	0	53
Saskatchewan	0	13	15	28
Total in Canada	53	67	45	165

Source: Report on Communal Property, 1972 (by the Select Committee of the Assembly, Province of Alberta, Edmonton) and the colony census supplied by each Leut. Colonies in the process of formation (frequently referred to as "farms") are included in this enumeration.

Growth through conversion of outsiders is minimal. During a century in North America, there have been scarcely more than fifty adult converts to the Hutterites. Some who joined during the hard years of the depression later left the colonies. Though Hutterites do not send out missionaries, they take seriously the responsibility to help the sincere believer who wants to join.[5] They do not force their views on others, and the prospective convert is expected to serve a period of probation. Outsiders who are divorced are not accepted as members. The small number of nonethnic converts to the colonies is conducive to a stable social pattern, for it eliminates the problems of assimilating large numbers of outsiders.

The Management of Innovation

The Hutterites have demonstrated a remarkable ability for adapting to natural, geographic, and agrarian environments. Their firmness of purpose and resourceful planning has allowed them to experiment with agricultural production and to develop sufficient capital to buy heavy agricultural equipment equal to the challenge of prairie farming.[6] Adaptability, efficiency, and reasoned technological innovation have been in their tradition since the sixteenth century when they managed Moravian estates. In this respect the Hutterites exhibit very different attitudes from their "cousins," the Old Order Amish and the Old Colony Mennonites, who feel they are compromising when they permit electricity, telephones, and agricultural modernization. A Hutterite colony is less threatened by such changes than are those groups that live as single-family farm units.

The Hutterites do not follow the normal pattern of tradition-directed societies with respect to social change. Most closed societies have been forced to modify their social structure as their population has

5. Hutterite preachers and other colony members are emphatic and often very competent in explaining their beliefs to seekers. In recent years a Christian communal group in Japan and one in the Philippines expressed unity with the Hutterite faith and sought affiliation. Persons from Japan have spent several months among the colonists. Several colonies sent financial aid to the Japanese and Filipino groups. Through the translation of basic Hutterite writings into Japanese by Dr. Gan Sakakibara (see bibliography), an admirer of the Hutterites, more Asiatic visitors may soon be learning about the Hutterite way of life.

6. We are indebted to John W. Bennett for an insightful analysis of Hutterite economic practices and change; see *Hutterian Brethren: The Agricultural Economy and Social Organization of a Communal People* (Stanford, Calif.: Stanford University Press, 1967), particularly chapter 11. For other treatments of social change, see Joseph W. Eaton, "Controlled Acculturation: A Survival Technique of the Hutterites," *American Sociological Review* 17(June 1952): 331–40; and Vernon C. Serl, "Stability and Change in Hutterite Society" (Ph.D. dissertation, University of Oregon, 1964).

expanded. With the coming of industrialization, some subcultures in North America disintegrated because they were unable to manage modernization and at the same time retain their social bonds. Many have been swept out with the broom of civilization. The Hutterites have not only fully accepted mechanized agriculture but have adapted their way of life to a high rate of natural increase. All of this has occurred without drastically affecting their identity and strong communal life. What is the Hutterite secret?

Social change in Hutterite society is best understood from the attitudes Hutterites themselves take toward it. In many respects Hutterites act as if changes were not taking place. They are not anxiety-ridden about impending social upheaval. They admit no discontinuity between the life they presently live and that lived by their forefathers. This feeling of continuity and identification with their ancestors is itself a by-product of a high degree of social security supported by unalterable religious beliefs.

Most colony leaders also fail to acknowledge any conflict between religious beliefs and technological improvements. "Nothing is too modern if it is profitable for the colony" is a typical attitude. "It doesn't matter what color we paint our buildings; there isn't anything in the book that says we have to have them white, or gray, or anything."[7] The uses of color in the economic sectors of colony life are virtually unrestricted, in contrast to the Amish Mennonites who, in changing from horse-drawn buggies to the automobile, are allowed to buy only black automobiles—and the "Black Bumper" Mennonites in Pennsylvania who paint the chrome on their new black automobiles with black paint. The Hutterites are careful to distinguish between changes that improve the economic viability of the colony and changes that result in personal convenience. "We do not believe in making everything nice for the flesh" is another typical comment.

Changes in Hutterite society have been limited largely to technological innovations. (See figure 41.) In the past hundred years the Hutterites have moved from ox and horse power to electricity. The blacksmith's anvil has been replaced by the electric welder. Field operations have changed from large horse teams to diesel engines. Hutterites have taken to the road, hauling their wheat and produce to market with trucks. Panel and delivery trucks are used to travel to and from other colonies and to the market centers.

These changes have not occurred without colony dialogue between those who were opposed to change and those who favored it, between

7. Cited in Bennett, *Hutterian Brethren*, p. 275.

Figure 41. *Top,* this poultry barn houses 20,000 laying hens and is tended by one young Hutterite man; *bottom,* colony machine shops are equipped not only to build modern poultry and hog barns but to adapt new farm machinery to Hutterite uses. (Photographs by Philip Garvin, 1974)

conservative and progressive elements. Typically, it is the young foremen who are the most effective innovators. They must overcome the
conservative element, which argues that the members should work
hard and not let the colony fall into luxury and laziness. When electricity came into general use, there were members who were sure that
"this great power was ignited from hell."[8] Eventually, electricity was
adopted on the grounds of its usefulness to the whole colony. The telephone was at first objected to as being too closely connected to the
world, but its value for overall colony efficiency was soon realized.
While changes in the colony are "talked through" and reasoned on
spiritual grounds, Hutterites often point out that changes in the outside
world are made on the basis of carnality and personal pleasure.

The crucial consideration in mechanization, aside from large risks
in investments, is whether the change will introduce too many elements
of personal convenience. From past experience, the leaders know the
intrinsic importance of work in maintaining a smoothly functioning
colony. Having enough work, especially meaningful, productive activity,
for all members of the colony is considered essential to success. Changes
made in the past and some now being considered revolve around the
luxury factor. The welfare of the colony must come before creature
comfort: automatic thermostats were used in hog barns before they were
used in the dwelling houses. Floor coverings first appeared in the communal kitchen before they were allowed in family apartments. Electric
floor polishers were first used in some of the wealthier colonies and are
still not permitted in others. The trend to install plumbing in family
apartments is for some Hutterites a concession to convenience, symbol-
izing spiritual decline; for others, it is justified on the basis of sanitation
and health.

On the whole, these innovations have not altered the basic social
patterns. Relationships to the outside world have not changed, although
the frequency of contacts with outsiders has increased. The authoritarian pattern has not changed, and the preacher and the council are still
in command. The younger members are still subordinate to the older,
and women are still subject to the rule of men. The introduction of sewing machines and electric irons into the family units has not greatly
altered the social relationships. By permitting all members to share an
innovation, the relative status of individuals is not changed. No person
is made richer or poorer or more powerful than another. When a colony
is prosperous, the families benefit equally, and none are excluded.

8. An observation made by a Hutterite minister, Paul S. Gross, *The Hutterite Way:
The Inside Story of the Life, Customs, Religion, and Traditions of the Hutterites* (Saskatoon, Sask.: Freeman Publishing Co., 1965).

Wealth and property, like knowledge, have never become means of social distinction. The competition that is often marked between colonies is integrative rather than disruptive to any given colony. In these several ways, material innovations are managed so as not to disrupt the social hierarchy.

Examples of innovations which would threaten the social solidarity of colony life are those improvements and practices that have been forbidden. Though heavy trucks and light panel trucks (often insulated by Hutterite mechanics for subzero temperatures and arranged with extra seats) are used for transportation, automobiles are not. Automobiles are viewed as instruments of personal convenience, scarcely usable for anything else. Worldly clothing styles and hoarding of clothing, yardgoods, and other small items of vanity are repeatedly warned against in the rules and discipline issued by the annual assemblies of preachers. Alteration of the symbols of Hutterite identity would indicate a serious erosion of discipline. A few colonies permit women to drive farm trucks and tractors in the vegetable garden, but others do not. Women never transport people on the open highway; should this occur, the social patterns would be altered. Although radio and television might benefit Hutterite foremen by bringing market and weather reports, their use would be highly destructive to the discipline of colony life.

The management of change is keenly understood by the Hutterite people. The founding colonies in the United States maintained remarkably uniform customs, epitomized in Hutterite grooming and clothing styles. As the population expanded there have been greater variations in custom but no erosion of the principle of communal living. The leaders are confident that as long as they can exercise control over change, the unity essential to communal living can be maintained. There are two formal checks for assessing the potential affect of social change on colony life; the individual colony and the annual assembly of colony preachers, which formulates the discipline for its Leut.

Individual colonies may not make major changes without the consent of the preachers, who meet annually (or oftener if required) to review any issue that threatens unity. This periodic review of disruptive colony practices, or variations within an individual colony which are considered to be in violation of tradition, perpetuates uniformity among colonies and slows down the rate of innovation. Should a colony deviate from a disciplinary rule, the preacher assembly will place the issue on its agenda. The circumstances of the violation will be discussed; the disciplinary rule may be reaffirmed by majority vote, it may be modified, or a vote may be postponed to allow time for further informal consensus.

When the young men began to wear belts instead of suspenders a few years ago, there was no problem—until belts began to be embellished, made into many styles in worldly fashion. The Schmiedeleut assembly of preachers issued a ruling against the wearing of belts. Today no man is to be seen walking about the colony without suspenders. All statements of discipline (*Gemeindeordnung*) are circulated to each colony preacher, whose duty it is to read them to the members. The colony then votes whether or not to accept the ruling.

Individual colonies may not affiliate with other communal groups, ordain a preacher or a steward, or initiate legal suits without the consent of the Leut. Each colony may manage its own economic affairs and adapt general policy to meet the specific colony needs. Decisions resulting in change depend upon the issues and context of colony life, but there is an overall pattern. Informal talk precedes any formal discussion of change. Hutterites use the power of informal, primary-group consensus. The daily, constant association between leaders and followers and between persons of all ages results in an intimate knowledge of the values and opinions held by other persons. The leaders are able to discern when a change will become inevitable. The economic factors must be weighed against kinship solidarities and loyalties, for these can impair colony unity.[9] When there is pressure for change on the part of the foreman, the council members are able to assess it informally, and after there is widespread consensus, the colony formally votes on an issue. Decisions are made on the basis of a majority vote. The acceptance of innovations by consensus before there is extensive rule-breaking and before pressures become unmanageable has the effect of maintaining members' respect for the authority system. "By bending with the wind, Hutterites have kept themselves from breaking."[10] The emphasis on group welfare and the deemphasis on individual rights minimize the friction normally associated with change. Thus, while the Hutterites give their complete loyalty to theocratic rule, the rules that govern behavior are democratically managed. The reasons for change are dictated neither by individual wants nor by expedience; they are based entirely on the welfare of the colony.

The Hutterites do not regard their way of life as a rationalized experiment in communal living or an effort to achieve a human utopia. Rather, the communal way of life is for them the practice of total Christianity. Hutterites view themselves as living according to the model described in the Bible. They attribute their success in communal living to

9. The "instrumental organization" of colony life including kinship is discussed by Bennett, in *Hutterian Brethren*, pp. 141–60, 254–65, and in "The Managed Democracy of the Hutterites," in *Communes: Creating and Managing the Collective Life*, ed. Rosabeth M. Kanter, pp. 192–205.

10. Quoted in Joseph W. Eaton, "Controlled Acculturation," which also contains a lengthy discussion of this theory (pp. 331–40).

their faith in total obedience. Faithful submission to God and commitment to one another, they say, brings about the desired attitudes that make communal living possible. The colony is for the individual Hutterite a means of salvation, an ark surrounded by vast numbers of unbelieving people whose destiny is determined by God and whom the Hutterite does not judge.

Figure 42. Resting in a park on shopping day in town. (Photograph by Kryn Taconis)

appendix one

Hutterite Historiography

Forty years after Jakob Hutter's death, Hutterite leaders began to record the events and to order the documents they considered most important. There were statements of doctrine, sermons, epistles, passionate letters, martyrs' accounts, *Ordnungen* (regulations governing the communal life), and descriptions of distinctive medical practices. This body of literature was a source of moral strength when members were confronted with problems, arguments from their enemies, or mandates from governments. They knew how to answer because they knew their faith, their history, and their identity. The most important manuscript material was copied by hand and bound into books so that copies could be circulated among the leaders.

A major step toward historical consciousness was the compilation of an official chronicle, the *Geschichts-Buch*, which came to be called the "great chronicle." During the "golden age," Kasper Braitmichel, endowed with a fine skill for handwriting, began the task of copying the "heroic beginnings" and the great happenings into a single volume. After his death in 1573 he was succeeded by seven more annalists; in 1665 work on the bulky volume (612 folio leaves) ended.

The identification with time "from the beginning of the world" and with the early Christians was of paramount importance to the chronicler. Thus, the first part of this imposing book sketches the Biblical account of the history of mankind to the year 1523, after which the authors turn to the details of their own origin, faith, suffering, and steadfastness. The impact the book conveys is that of a "suffering church," paralleling in some respects the *Martyrs' Mirror* (van Braght) of the Mennonites. The chronicle records the growth of the group in Moravia during the golden age, its great tribulations and sufferings, and its decline as a result of wars and raids by Turks, Tartars, and Hapsburg armies. The horrors of the Thirty Years' War are related as the Hutterites experienced them. The book lists a total of 2,175 martyrs and gives the deathbed instructions of leaders to their fellow believers.

Miraculously, the large book escaped the hands of its enemies. The Hutterites managed to get the book into Hungary in 1622, when the exiled Brethren were not even permitted to take tools or money away with them. Officials seized and stripped men and women, searching for money in their clothes and the soles of their shoes. When the Jesuits confiscated and burned "wagonloads" of Hutterite writings, the great book was secretly sent to a colony in Transylvania. Here it remained until 1773, when it was recovered from apostate Hutterites and taken to Russia by some of the imprisoned brethren who had managed to escape. Located at the Bon Homme Colony in South Dakota, the book is a prized possession that must always remain in the colonies.

One hundred and thirty years later, a sequel to the great chronicle was undertaken by Johannes Waldner. Waldner (1749–1824) was one of the Lutheran Carinthians who as a child had gone with his parents to Transylvania and then moved to the Ukraine where he was later ordained Vorsteher. Besides being an eyewitness to many of the most important events that befell the group in Romania and Russia, he was a capable Hutterite historian. He read all the old Hutterite books, including the great chronicle, and produced a second large volume, the *Klein-Geschichtsbuch*, or "small chronicle," as it is called. (The reference to "great" and "small" has nothing to do with the size of the books. Great indicates the esteem in which the founding period is held; small refers to the subsequent period of Hutterite history.) Waldner summarized the early part of the first chronicle and then incorporated a wealth of new historical episodes that occurred between 1665 and 1802. Not only was Waldner endowed with a fine sense of history but he was apparently a good storyteller. The only account of the Carinthians who joined the declining group of Transylvanian Hutterites is in his memoirs. Unfortunately Waldner discontinued his chronicle in 1802, although he lived until 1824.

These two chronicles constitute the major primary sources of Hutterite history. They not only comprise the documents from various periods but also the Hutterite view of themselves, the world around them, and various encounters in their history. These imposing accounts reflect the sentiments of a people who have an impregnable sense of their identity as a distinct people whose destiny is determined by God.

Although the Brethren occupied themselves with many skills and trades, they did not become printers. Their creative efforts went into handwriting, penmanship, and bookbinding. The two chronicles contain only a fraction of the prodigious literary efforts of the early Hutterites. A large body of manuscripts, including several abridged manuscripts of the chronicles themselves, have since been discovered in European libraries; most of this material was confiscated by the Jesuits in their efforts to eradicate Anabaptist heretics.

The part played by non-Hutterite scholars in the development of historical consciousness is significant. The standard interpretations of Anabaptism were usually negative, for history was written mainly by persons trained in the state churches. The publication of Joseph Beck's *Die Geschichts-Bücher der Wiedertäufer* in 1883 was a major step in the direction of objective historical research. Beck was an Austrian jurist and member of the Austrian Supreme Court who pursued historical research in his leisure time. While a judge in Bratislava, he discovered many Hutterite manuscripts in the Hungarian areas where the Brethren had lived for two centuries. He systematically gathered this material, which included sources which had not formed part of the two Hutterite chronicles, and published the most important manuscripts in a single volume. Beck died in 1887, and although he did not interpret the documents or the life of the Hutterites, his collection fell into the skillful hands of Johann Loserth (1846–1936), professor of modern European history at Graz, Austria, who was a prolific historian and interpreter. The Beck volume is today highly esteemed by the Hutterite colony leaders.

Besides his interest in the history of Austria and Bohemia, Loserth wrote extensively on Huss and Wycliffe and edited many of Wycliffe's Latin works for publication. He was ably qualified to write on nonconformists in Moravia, Lower Austria, Styria, Salzburg, Tyrol, and Switzerland. He wrote biographies of Balthasar Hubmaier, George Blaurock, Pilgrim Marpeck, and other early Anabaptist leaders. A prodigious scholar, Loserth wrote, in all, 286 separate articles. Although he did not produce any large books on the Hutterites, he thoroughly utilized the Beck materials for advancing knowledge in specialized areas. When Loserth had finished his major task, he returned the Beck collection to the Moravian state archives in Brno, Moravia, where it has been used by subsequent researchers.

Beck collected and Loserth interpreted the material pertaining to the early period, but only Loserth seems to have known that the Hutterites still survived in North America. Their research was followed by that of Rudolf Wolkan, professor of German literature at the University of Vienna, who was the first European scholar to make contact with the Hutterites in North America. As early as 1903 Wolkan had published a volume of Anabaptist hymns and had worked extensively with the Passau court records and on the origin of the *Ausbund* hymnal. His publications came to the attention of the Mennonite historian, John Horsch, in the United States, who informed Wolkan that the Hutterites were still in existence. Wolkan engaged in extensive correspondence with Elder Elias Walter of the Standoff Colony in Alberta. With the cooperation of the Hutterites, Wolkan undertook the gigantic task of publishing the great chronicle. Elias Walter meticulously copied the huge codex and sent the copy to Wolkan in Vienna, who edited the work, adding significant excerpts from other Hutterite sources and footnotes. The book appeared in gothic typeface in 1923 with the title *Geschichts-Buch der Hutterischen Brüder*, as a joint publication of a Viennese publisher, Carl Fromme, and the Standoff Colony in Alberta, Canada. Thus, for the first time, the great chronicle of the Hutterites came into the hands of a printer. The Hutterites remain deeply grateful to Wolkan for his scholarly work and for bringing the book into print.

The original copy of the old chronicle is regarded with reverence and respect but not as a relic. The Brethren have no intention of placing it in a museum, for that would mean, as one Hutterite preacher said, that "we would have given up our faith." In spite of the handling it has received, the great chronicle is well preserved, although in a few places it has begun to deteriorate from dampness and the many applications of heavy dark brown ink. The book is a monumental document of human interest, revealing many interesting sidelights from the Hutterite perspective and, for each generation of Hutterites embodying concrete vindication of their sense of identity.

Beginning with his visit to the colonies in 1930, Eberhard Arnold, founder of the Society of Brothers, collected, translated, and published Hutterite history. Rideman's *Rechenschaft* was issued in German (1938) and in English (1950). Arnold's article "The Hutterian Brothers," included in a new printing of Rideman's *Account of Our Religion* (1970), is still the best short historical account of the Hutterites. Publication of the *Klein-Geschichtsbuch*, into which Arnold incorporated "the fruits of years of research," was undertaken but never completed. Many of his writings are in German (See *Mennonite Encyclopedia*, s.v., "Arnold, Eberhard"); and much of what is in English appears in *Plough*, a journal of the Society of Brothers. The Society of Brothers (Plough Publishing House, Rifton, N.Y.) continues to play an active role in the publication of Anabaptist source material.

Also appearing on the scene of Hutterite studies was A. J. F. Zieglschmid (1903–50). Zieglschmid, who was born in Germany and came to the United States in 1922, was Professor of Germanic Linguistics at Northwestern University in Evanston, Illinois. The Hutterite materials were of great interest to him in the study of the linguistic period known as "New High German." He visited the colonies in South Dakota and studied both the great and small chronicles. Again, amiable cooperation between a university professor and the colonies resulted in major publications. The first to appear was a letter-perfect edition of the great chronicle, *Die älteste Chronik der Hutterischen Brüder* (1943), a volume of 1200 pages. Four years later (1947), the small chronicle, *Das Klein-Geschichtsbuch der Hutterischen Brüder*, appeared in a volume of 800 pages, in gothic typeface and modern German. Both volumes were edited by Zieglschmid and published by the Carl Schurz Memorial Foundation in Philadelphia, Pennsylvania. Hutterites have shown little interest in the letter-perfect edition of 1943, preferring the Wolkan (1923) edition. With the aid of Hutterite informants, Zieglschmid supplemented the Johannes Waldner chronicle with some important and other less important documents spanning the years from 1802 to 1947. Professor Zieglschmid also prepared a new, enlarged edition of the Hutterite hymnal, *Die Lieder der Hutterischen Brüder* (1914), but the work has remained unpublished (in the Mennonite Archives, Goshen, Indiana) following his untimely death in 1950.

Finally, it is to Robert Friedmann that a major advance in our knowledge of Hutterite primary sources and Hutterite life must be attributed. The large bibliography of his writings reflects the depth and scope of his contribution. Friedmann was born in 1891 in Austria and received his doctoral training in philosophy and history at the University of Vienna under Alphons Dopsch and Rudolf Wolkan. Under Wolkan he became interested in the Hutterite epistles written by their missioners and in the whole range of codices.

The most active Mennonite historian in America, John Horsch, had written to Friedmann as early as 1925. Friedmann had his first contact with Horsch's son-in-law, Harold S. Bender, in 1930, and what followed was a most productive era of scholarship. In the same year Friedmann discovered twenty-six codices of sixteenth- and seventeenth-century origin in the castle of Mittersill. He left Austria for the United States in 1935 and after a year as Honorary Fellow at the Divinity School at Yale University, he was invited to come to Goshen College where Dean Harold S. Bender arranged that he be appointed Research Fellow in Anabaptist Studies. Here he was given responsibility for the rearrangement of the Mennonite Historical Library. From 1945 until his death in 1970 he lived at Kalamazoo, Michigan, having served as professor of history and philosophy at Western Michigan University.

Robert Friedmann combined both Austrian and American scholarship. He knew thoroughly the geography, history, and theology of the various Austrian Anabaptist groups. After 1931 most of his articles were in English. In 1929 the German Society for Reformation Research commissioned him to edit a volume of Anabaptist documents for publication. Largely because of the war, the volume was delayed, but it finally appeared in 1967 as *Glaubenszeugnisse*. His penetrating study of *Mennonite Piety Through the Centuries* (1947) was written in the quiet of an English countryside while taking refuge from the Nazis.

Robert Friedmann's greatest contribution lay in his discovery and interpretation of original sources. He knew Hutterite codices, their writers, and their periods of spiritual growth and decline better than he knew contemporary Hutterite life. His articles appeared largely in German and English church history journals and in the *Mennonite Quarterly Review*. He wrote nearly two hundred articles for the *Mennonite Encyclopedia*. His most significant articles were published in a single volume, *Hutterite Studies* (1961), on the occasion of his seventieth birthday. His final important publication, after forty years of scholarship, was a catalog covering all known codices, *Die Schriften der Huterischen Täufergemeinschaften* (1965), an immensely helpful guide for subsequent scholars. The "Robert Friedmann Memorial Issue" of the *Mennonite Quarterly Review* (April 1974) contains many tributes to his life and a comprehensive list of his writings.

Robert Friedmann's writings do not tell the whole story. His colleagues, students, and friends, who have sat in on his lectures, joined in his seminars, or enjoyed delightful hours of his scholarly and engaging conversation, are grateful for the enlightenment and stimulation which they have received from him. Hutterites have become widely known in the world of historical scholarship through the efforts of Robert Friedmann.

Finally, in Austria today Anabaptist scholarship has been enriched by Professor Grete Mecenseffy of the University of Vienna, whose several publications deal with sixteenth-century primary sources, and by Dr. Adolf Mais of the Volkskunde Museum in Vienna, for his specialized studies of Hutterite folklore, ceramics, and hymnology. Centering around the person and work of Dr. Mais is the newly formed association *Arbeitsgemeinschaft für huterische Studien* ("Working Association for Hutterite Studies"), with headquarters in the restored castle at Kittsee (A 2421 Schloss Kittsee). In addition to housing ethnographic collections on eastern and southeastern European folk culture, the museum features Hutterite artifacts, especially ceramics.

This summary by no means incorporates all of the persons and publications of the movement. The interaction of Hutterite leaders with personalities outside the movement played a significant part in the formation of historical consciousness. For a comprehensive view of the literature the reader may examine the several published bibliographies and the bibliography in this book.[1]

1. Marvin P. Riley, *The Hutterian Brethren: An Annotated Bibliography with Special Reference to South Dakota Hutterite Colonies* (Brookings: South Dakota State University, 1965); John A. Hostetler, "A Bibliography of English Language Materials on the Hutterian Brethren," *M.Q.R.* 44 (January 1970): 106–13.

appendix two

Chronology of
Hutterite History

1525	Founding of the Swiss Anabaptist movement in Zürich by Conrad Grebel, George Blaurock, and others.
1526	Death penalty instituted for teaching, preaching, or listening to Anabaptist sermons, Zürich.
——	Balthasar Hubmaier (1480–1528), South German Anabaptist leader, takes refuge at Nikolsburg, Moravia.
1528	Hubmaier burned at the stake in Vienna, March 10.
——	Jakob Wiedemann and his Stäbler group of about 200 adults leave Nikolsburg, Moravia, in the springtime and en route to Austerlitz begin to practice "community of goods." Regarded by Hutterites as the occasion of their origin.
1529	George Blaurock, Swiss Anabaptist pastor in South Tyrol, executed at Klausen (Chiusa) and succeeded by Jakob Hutter.
——	Jakob Hutter, of South Tyrol, visits Moravia.
1533	Jakob Hutter takes up residence in Moravia and becomes the chief organizer of the Bruderhofs.
1536	Jakob Hutter executed by burning at Innsbruck, Austria.
——	Jakob Wiedemann executed in Vienna.
1539	Hutterites at Steinabrunn seized and after imprisonment at Falkenstein sent to Trieste as galley slaves.

c.1540   Peter Riedemann, while imprisoned in Hesse, writes the great *Rechenschaft* ("Confession of Faith") of the Hutterites.

1540-53   Time of great persecution, during which the Hutterites lived in caves and mountains.

1546   Founding of Sabatisch (Sobotište), first Bruderhof in Upper Hungary.

1554-93   The "good period" (from 1554) and the "golden period" (from 1565); ended by outbreak of war between the Hapsburg Empire and Turkey in 1593.

1558   Founding of Neumühl Bruderhof in Moravia, a center of Hutterite leadership.

——   Founding of Grosschützen (Nagy-Lévárd, or Velké Leváry) in Upper Hungary (today Slovakia in Czechoslovakia).

1561   *Ordnung* for the shoemakers. First extant Ordnung.

1576   Earliest extant Hutterite pottery trademark in Moravia (Landsfeld, *Habánské parnátky*, p. 69).

1568   First Hutterite *Schulordnung*.

1584   First Hutterite Ordnung for the potters.

1593   War between the Hapsburg Empire and Turkey, marking the end of the "golden era" for the Hutterites in Moravia.

1605   Turkish invasions and plundering.

1618-48   The Thirty Years' War, a struggle between Catholicism and Protestantism.

1621   Mandate issued on September 17 by Ferdinand II for the expulsion of all Hutterites from Moravia.

——   Hutterites, numbering 186, forcibly taken from Upper Hungary (Slovakia) to Transylvania in Romania by Prince Bethlen Gabor, resulting in the founding of the Alwinz Bruderhof.

1622   All Bruderhofs in Moravia evacuated and demolished.

1628   Ferdinand II requires Franz Cardinal von Dietrichstein to impose fines on all Moravian nobles who do not expel individual Hutterites.

1639   Andreas Ehrenpreis (1589-1662) elected leader of the Hutterian movement at Sabatisch. He collected and preserved Hutterite sermons and documents.

1665   Hutterite delegation (from Transylvania and Hungary) visits the Netherlands to secure financial aid from the Mennonites.

1690   Transylvanian Hutterites abandon communal living.

1733   A Hungarian mandate orders Hutterites to have their newborn children baptized by Catholic priests.

1740-80   Reign of Empress Maria Theresa, archenemy of Protestants and Anabaptists.

1755	Carinthian Lutheran refugees arrive in Romania and soon revitalize the declining Hutterite movement.
1757–58	First confiscation of Hutterite books in Upper Hungary by the Jesuits.
1761	Bruderhofs in Hungary (Slovakia) placed under the jurisdiction of local priests; Hutterite preachers removed from their positions.
1762	Communal living reestablished in Transylvania by the Carinthian refugees.
1767	Hutterites emigrate from Transylvania in Romania to the province of Wallachia.
1770	On August 1 Hutterites arrive at the private estate of Alexandrovich Rumiantsev in Vishenka, the province of Tchernigov, Russia.
1771–95	Seven return journeys from Russia to homesteads of Europe yield 56 more emigrants to Russia.
1782	Edict of Toleration issued by Joseph II, emperor of Austria, brings no tolerance to Hutterites. Christian Hofer interviewed by Joseph II in Vienna.
1789	First Mennonite settlement in the Ukraine, at Chortitza near Alexandrovsk, by refugees from Prussia at the invitation of Catherine the Great.
1802	The Vishenka Bruderhof moves to crown lands in nearby Radichev.
1803	Mennonites from Prussia move to the Molotschna area in Russia.
1819	Communal living abandoned in Radichev.
1824	Death of Johannes Waldner, Vorsteher (from 1794) and author of *Das Klein-Geschichtsbuch* (written between 1793 and 1802). Born in 1749 in Carinthia, Waldner journeyed from Carinthia to Transylvania, Wallachia, and Russia.
1842	Hutterites move from the Radichev area to Huttertal in the Molotschna Mennonite settlement in south Russia.
1852	Founding of Johannesruh, Hutterite village in the Molotschna area, south Russia.
1859	Communal living restored in Hutterdorf, Russia, by Michael Waldner and George Hofer.
1873	Hutterite delegates Paul Tschetter and Lorenz Tschetter investigate colonization prospects in the United States and Canada, from April 14 to June 27.
1874	The first Hutterite immigrants come from Russia to the United States. Forty families (about 250 persons) sail from Hamburg on the "Harmonia" on June 19 and arrive in New York on July 5. Among them are both Schmiedeleut and Dariusleut. On August 8 they arrive in Bon Homme County where the Schmiedeleut establish the first

Bruderhof in the United States. The Dariusleut live at Silver Lake until the following year.

1875   Wolf Creek, parent colony of the Dariusleut, founded by the 1874 immigrants. Their first preachers are George Hofer and Darius Walter.

1877   Elmspring, parent colony of the Lehrerleut, founded near Parkston, South Dakota, by Jacob Wipf, preacher. Thirteen families establish communal living after arriving in the United States.

1883   Joseph Beck's *Die Geschichts-Bucher der Wiedertäufer* appears in Vienna; the first major source book on Hutterite history to be published.

1889   South Dakota Hutterites establish a colony near Dominion City, Manitoba. The members return to South Dakota five years later.

1912   Spring Creek Colony near Lewistown, the first Hutterite colony formed in Montana.

1914   *Die Lieder der Hutterischen Bruder*, first printed hymnal of the Hutterites. Edited by Elias Walter and published at Scottdale, Pennsylvania.

1918   Hutterites from South Dakota form seventeen new colonies in Alberta and Manitoba following the deaths of two conscientious objectors, Joseph and Michael Hofer, as a result of maltreatment and starvation in the military camp at Fort Leavenworth, Kansas.

1923   Publication of *Die Geschichts-Buch der Hutterischen Brüder* (the great chronicle) by Rudolf Wolkan of Vienna in cooperation with Elias Walter of Standoff Colony, Alberta.

1930–31   Eberhard Arnold (1883–1935) of Germany, founder of the Society of Brothers, visits North American colonies. Ordained at Standoff Colony and commissioned "to proclaim the Word of God" and "gather the zealous" in Germany.

1931   *The Hutterian Brethren*, the first English history of the Hutterites, written by John Horsch and published by the Mennonite Historical Society, Goshen, Indiana.

1937   David Hofer and Michael Waldner, two Hutterite preachers from South Dakota, visit the Society of Brothers in Liechtenstein and at the European and Slovakian homesteads.

1942   The Province of Alberta enacts the Land Sales Prohibition Act prohibiting the sale of land to enemy aliens and Hutterites.

1943   A. J. F. Zieglschmid's *Die älteste Chronik der Hutterischen Brüder* is published by the Carl Schurz Memorial Foundation in Philadelphia. A letter-perfect edition of the great chronicle, it elicited more interest among philologists than Hutterites.

1947   A. J. F. Zieglschmid's *Das Klein-Geschichtsbuch der Hutterischen Brüder* (the small chronicle) is published by the Carl Schurz Memorial Foundation in Philadelphia.

1949   First colony founded in Saskatchewan, Bench Colony.

1950   Canadian Hutterite delegation visits Mexico in search of suitable locations for settlement.

——   Constitution of the Hutterian Brethren Church, a charter formed by all Canadian colonies to facilitate legal relations with the government.

1955   The Hutterites in an assembly of Schmiedeleut preachers at James Valley Bruderhof sever formal relations with the Society of Brothers on September 4.

1968   Two Hutterite preachers in North America, Paul Gross and Paul Walter, visit historic European homesteads.

1974   Formal relations restored between the Society of Brothers and the Hutterian Brethren at the Sturgeon Creek Colony, Man., on January 7, following a conference of reconciliation.

——   A century of Hutterite life in North America.

appendix three

Hutterite Place Names in Eastern Europe by Language and Country

Place Name				Location
German	Hungarian	Slavic	Romanian	Country
Alwinz, Alwintz	Alvinc		Vinţul de Jos	Transylvania
Altenmarkt		Břeclav		Moravia
Auspitz	Pusztapécs	Hustopec		Moravia
Austerlitz		Slavkov		Moravia
Bergen		Perná		Moravia
Bernstein	Borostyánkö			Hungary
Bibersburg	Vöröskö	Cerveny Kamen		Slovakia
Bodilän	Bodola			Transylvania
Bodock, Bodok	Sárospatak			Hungary
Brünn		Brno		Moravia
Budapest	Buda			Hungary
Burgenland				Austria
Dämborschitz		Dambořice		Moravia
Deutschkreutz	Sopronkeresztur			Hungary
Eisenstadt				Austria
Falkenstein				Austria
Forchenstein	Frakno (Esterhazy estate)			Austria
Göding		Hodonin		Moravia
Gran	Esztergom			Hungary
Gostolän	Kosztolány	Kostelna		Slovakia

Place Name				Location
German	Hungarian	Slavic	Romanian	Country
	Gyöngyös			Hungary
Grosschützen	Lévárd, Nagy-Lévárd	Velké Leváry		Slovakia
Hermannstadt	Szeben		Sibiu	Transylvania
Hutterdorf (Kutcheva)				Russia
Huttertal				Russia
Johannesruh				Russia
Kärnten				Austria
Karlsburg (Weissenburg)	Gyulafehérvár		Alba Iulia	Transylvania
Kirschlag				Hungary
Klagenfurt				Austria
Klausen (Chiusa)				Italy
Klausenburg	Kolozsvár		Cluj	Transylvania
Kleinsasserhof				Austria
Kräbach (near Bucharest)			Ciorogirle, Tschoregirle	Romania
Kronstadt	Brassó		Brasov	Transylvania
	Léka			Hungary
Moos				Italy
Mures (river)	Maros		Muresul	Transylvania
Neu Huttertal (Dobritcha)				Russia
Neumühl an der Thaya		Nové Mlýny		Moravia
Neusider	Nezsider			Hungary
Nikolsburg		Mikulov		Moravia
Neutra	Nyitra	Neutra		Slovakia
Odenburg	Sopron			Hungary
Ofen	Buda (Budapest)			Hungary
Olbendorf	Szentlörinc			Hungary
	Parád			Hungary
Peterwardein	Pétervárad	Petrovaradinov		Yugoslavia
Prag	Prága	Praha		Bohemia
Pressburg	Pozsony	Bratislava		Slovakia
Pribitz		Přibice		Slovakia
Protzka	Brockó	Brocké		Slovakia
Pustertal				Italy
Radichev, Radtitschewa				Russia
Radnoten	Radnóth		Iernut	Transylvania
Rossitz		Rosice		Moravia
Sabatisch, Sobotischt	Szobotist	Sobotište		Slovakia
Sárvár				Hungary
Schattmansdorf	Cseszte	Časta		Slovakia
Scheromet				Russia
Seelowitz, Gross		Židlochovice		Moravia
Siebenburgen	Erdély	Ardeal		Transylvania
St. Johann	Szent-János	Sv. Ján		Slovakia
Strassnitz		Strážnice		Moravia

Place Name				Location
German	Hungarian	Slavic	Romanian	Country
	Szombathely	Sabaria		Hungary
Temeschwar	Temesvár		Timişoara	Romania
Tövis	Tövis		Teiuş	Transylvania
Tschachtitz	Csejthe	Čechtice		Slovakia
Tura	Ó Tura	Stará Turá		Slovakia
Tyrnau	Nagyszombat	Trnava		Slovakia
Vishenka, Wischenka				Russia
Vishenau				Moravia
Wadowitz	Vagyóc			Slovakia
Wessele		Veselé (on the Vah)		Slovakia
Wessely an der March				Moravia
Wien				Austria

appendix four

The Hutterite School Discipline of 1568

Herein are recorded several necessary points which the brethren and sisters who are appointed to supervise the schools, together with their assistants, are to observe in the care and discipline of the youth.

In the first place they must constantly keep in mind that they are appointed over the children by the Lord and by His people.

Further, the school masters and school mothers, since they are the ones who are responsible for the good character of the discipline of the school, are to be peaceful and trustful in their relations one to another. There should be a willingness to assist each other with good advice and to maintain a strict and regular order in all phases of the care of the youth, for to be dutiful and peaceful is conducive to good discipline, while discord and indolence are conducive to disorder.

They shall also take proper care in directing and supervising their assistants according to the adopted discipline.

They shall take care that no disunity, strife, or boisterous speaking is heard by the children, but rather by a peaceful, cheerful, good-natured, and sober life and quiet walk they shall inspire the youth likewise to quiet and sober living and give them a good example.

Source: Harold S. Bender, ed. and trans., "A Hutterite School Discipline of 1578 [1568] and Peter Scherer's Address of 1568 to the Schoolmasters," *M.Q.R.* 5 (October 1931): 231-41.

They should avoid vain and idle words so that the children shall not have occasion to gossip.

The school masters and sisters shall admonish and ask the boys and girls in their later teens to be diligent in prayer. And it would be well if when the school masters speak with the children once or twice a week, the sisters be present if possible, and thus testify by their example and pattern to their desire to inspire the youth with ideals of piety; the sisters should not absent themselves to go to other places but should give due consideration to the honor of the Lord and the welfare of the youth. Yet the school master should not occupy the time of the children with long preaching and with much reading of many quotations because the children can understand and grasp but little.

When one or more children are guilty of something, either of unbecoming conversation or other foolishness—likewise the girls when they spin—it is ordered that not every sister should at once step in and punish but should take care in the fear of God so that the youth should not be hastily disciplined.

For this reason, in order to be better able to give account before God and man, it is believed best that the sisters should report the matter to the brethren in the school or to the school mother and should not be too severe, seeing that the Lord does not deal with us elder ones always according to our deserts, but according to grace.

The larger boys are to be punished by a school master and not by a sister, but the middle-sized boys may be punished with the rod by a school mother if the school master is absent and the boy is stubborn and will not submit to the sister's words. But if it is a larger boy, it should be noted and reported to the school master when he comes home.

Likewise the larger girls are to be disciplined by a school mother and not by a brother.

Stealing, lying, and other gross sins, whether done by boys or girls, shall not be dealt with by a sister alone, but shall be disciplined with the approval and advice of a brother.

If punishment with the rod is necessary in the case of a larger boy or girl, it shall be done in the fear of God and with discernment. In case of knavishness, lying, thieving, and unchaste conduct, severity shall be used according to desert. This shall not be done secretly or in a corner, but in the presence of all the children, so that they may learn thereby to have fear of wrongdoing.

The children shall be trained not to resist the rod, but willingly accept punishment. In this way it will be possible to always deal with them in a free manner, more than if they resist, which one shall not and cannot permit them.

A school master shall permit the boys to go out once to the lavatory mornings and evenings, and shall himself watch, but shall not refuse the children permission to go out in between times, for the natural processes cannot be controlled by law and it is harmful to obstruct nature too long. The same applies to the girls.

It should also not be difficult for a pious school mother and her assistants to counsel with a brother in the school and to inquire when one wishes to take the children out and let them go home.

Likewise a school master shall have sympathy and cooperation for the sisters and shall yield in matters which do not interfere with the honor of God and good discipline. The bread and meat (sandwiches) may and shall be handed out to the larger children by the school master, except if he does not have time or lacks the food. In that case the school mothers may do this or appoint another sister to do it.

If something special is to be given to the children, such as apples, pears, and other fruit, it shall not be done on the individual decision of anyone, but shall be done on the counsel of several at a proper time. The children's clothing shall not be had in excess; what is necessary shall be kept on hand and be kept clean. The boys' clothing shall be handed out by a brother himself.

The linen cloths shall be in the hands of a school mother and shall be given out by her, but as far as the table cloths for the children are concerned, she shall give it to the table sisters and not to the girls.

The sisters shall exercise diligence that they lift the little children out and into their beds mornings and evenings, and not leave this to the girls so that they themselves may know how the children get in and out of bed. However, the girls may help them in carrying the children to and from the beds. They shall likewise clean and wash those who are dirty.

In the morning the girls shall be called at five o'clock in winter time to spin. Then at six o'clock the boys are to be awakened and during the time that the latter are clothing, combing, and washing themselves, the smaller children are to be taken out, dressed, and washed, so that they will be quite ready for prayer and be able to sit at the table. Then the babies are to be taken out, dressed, washed, and after they have had a bit of exercise and have been walking about they may be taken to their meals, so that they are not fed at once after awakening from sleep, which is unnatural.

At evenings one should take particular care not to put the children to bed too soon after eating, which is unnatural for them, but to lead them about for a time after the meal or let them run around, small and large, in the winter time until six o'clock, and in summer time until sunset. And since it is often warm and moist in bed in summer, they shall be allowed to stay up longer at such warm times, but when it is cool they should for this reason be put to bed a little bit earlier.

During the night the nurse (*Wächterin*) shall take care that the children, both small and great, sleep well and are well covered, so that they may not become cold. Also one of the sisters should help the nurse to watch for a while when the children are going to sleep until the children are all asleep, and the children shall not be given anything to eat in bed or anything to suck except that a sick child may be given something to drink for his sickness. The children that are well shall be allowed to sleep without interruption for it is unwholesome to be feeding the children night and day. Likewise the sleeping children shall not be forced to arise during the night but shall be allowed to sleep, for if anyone has need, nature will of itself awaken them. But if a boy or a girl has some particular unclean habits, such a one may be awakened in order to be cured of such unclean habits, according to good discipline. If it happens once or twice that someone wets the bed, possibly in a dream, it shall be overlooked, with the hope of improvement, but if it occurs frequently the child shall be punished for the same.

The nurse shall likewise not at once begin to strike the child with the rod if a child begins to cry at night, but shall use other methods to quiet it.

When the innocent little children make the bed unclean they shall be diligently dried and one shall not economize with bed clothing and layettes. They shall not be left to lie because they cannot ask for help or cannot understand. The nurse shall also take good care to notice when a child cries or screams to hold it for a while over the vessel and cover it well so that it should not get cold from being without cover.

But when the little children who have begun to talk, still make a bed unclean, it may be overlooked two or three times and the children instructed with words, but if this does not help, finally they shall be punished lightly so that they shall learn to keep clean.

But the sisters shall take especial care with the little children, that they be not harsh with them but rather be sympathetic and long-suffering with them on account of their innocence and lack of understanding, just like mothers do with their own children. They shall be concerned in so training the children that they shall not be allowed to become self-willed but shall be gradually trained to love the Lord and as soon as they begin to talk they shall be taught to pray at the proper time.

Further, the brethren and sisters in the schools shall take especial care to avoid giving offence by discipline and punishment in the presence of brothers and sisters from other places who come to visit the school and observe the children. They shall be careful in this matter.

The boys and girls shall not be depended upon to take care of the little children either by day or by night, nor to take them up or lay them down, but the sisters shall be careful to be present, especially when the children get up, so that no one shall be injured.

The brethren in the schools have already been instructed by the elders that they shall not manifest wrath toward the children and shall not strike the children on the head with the fist nor with rods, nor shall they strike on the bare limb, but moderately on the proper place. It is necessary to exercise great discretion and discernment in disciplining children, for often a child can be better trained and corrected and taught by kind words when harshness would be altogether in vain, while another can be overcome by gifts. A third however cannot be disciplined without severity, and does not accept correction. Therefore the exercise of discipline of children requires the fear of God.

One should show sympathy to the little folk who have just started attending school and should not undertake all at once to break the self-will, lest injury come therefrom. For the children who are a bit larger one must also exercise very diligent care so that one can always have a good conscience.

The bed clothing shall be kept clean and shall be regularly changed, and when the little children arise in the morning a sister, or two or three girls, must always be at hand to take care on the stairways that no one falls.

When the children are brought to the school they should be carefully examined and if any one is found to have a contagious disease such as scurvy or French disease (syphilis), the same should be instantly separated from the rest in sleeping and drinking and in particular in washing. Also special brushes and combs shall be used in taking care of the hair of those having skin eruptions. Those who have such eruptions shall be put together and not kept with those who are clean. Likewise those who have head diseases. If a child suffers or receives an injury on account of carelessness of whatever sort it may be, the injury shall not be concealed, but help and counsel shall be sought as soon as possible before greater injury comes of it.

And when the school mothers examine the children for bad mouths and reach into a bad mouth with the fingers, they shall be careful that they do not at once with unwashed fingers reach into a healthy mouth and thereby contaminate it, but shall always beforehand cleanse the fingers with a clean cloth and water before they examine and cleanse mouths. They shall likewise demonstrate to the sisters with them how to heal scurvy of the mouth, and not withhold this from them that others also may be able to attend to such things if they are appointed for it.

Brushing shall not be turned over to the girls to do.

In the case of diseased heads and bad mouths the school mother shall take especial care, in particular about contagious diseases, and shall arrange for a separation in all matters, as in part already stated, as for instance in the matter of beds, washing, eating, drinking, using spoons and cups, also in the matter of examining the mouth and sitting on stools.

Once a week the clothes of the children shall be examined for lice, likewise the clothes of the children when they come to school. The new children shall have their heads and clothing examined for lice.

When boys and girls are used outside of school for help in tending the cattle or driving the horses, care shall be taken that they do not go astray since they often like to absent themselves or hide. Therefore they shall appear twice weekly on brushing day.

One should not let the shoes of the children become too hard so that they cause blisters and the parents may have occasion for complaint. Therefore care should also be taken that the clothing and everything else is regularly repaired.

The new children whose parents are still on probation shall not at once be clothed in new clothing, but shall for a time be given the old clothing until their parents have proved themselves worthy members.

The nurses (for sickness) shall diligently stay with the sick children, faithfully care for them, so that no one climbs over the bed or falls on the stairs, and it shall be earnestly impressed upon the mind of the girl in charge that they shall take good care of the children, but shall not be away from them long in case they must leave the bedside.

The food which is to be given to the children they shall not be forced to eat. Drinking shall also be attended to so that drinking is not postponed too long or refused so that the thirst does not become so great that they drink to excess, which is harmful.

And for the sick children especially one should be free to ask the cook for that which they may need; yet this should be done orderly and not each sister run to the cook on her own account, but the request should be made on advice of the school mother.

When children are sick one should not be too severe with them if they ask for this or that, but should in true faithfulness as unto God be diligent in waiting upon them, in lifting and laying down, in cleaning and washing.

And where there are two schools, the small and the large, the two shall be conducted as though they were one, and not separately. The sisters in the two schools, in whichever they may be, shall be in the proper attitude and love toward each other and shall faithfully assist one another in combing and brushing; in bathing and washing, as is necessary. That is, in everything the children of the two schools, whether sick or well, shall form a unit, and fellowship shall be exercised with open heart, without vanity or selfishness.

If the parents who are visiting a school desire to take their children home to themselves for a visit, permission may be given for a definite time by a school master or school mother but such permission shall be given with caution in the fear of God as the circumstances dictate, and those in authority shall have a definite understanding as to whither the children have been taken.

They shall also take care in supervising the larger children who serve as bread cutter, water carrier, bedroom maid, sweeper, dish washer, children's maid, sick nurse, etc., since they have often been found to be inconsiderate, mischievous, thieving and frivolous. Wherefore, those who are older shall take diligent care to supervise and watch over them so that no one shall be found guilty of permitting such conduct and have to be disciplined.

Neither brethren nor sisters shall of themselves undertake or order something without the counsel, knowledge, or will of the elders. Even though someone knows a better method, it shall not be followed without good counsel.

When the sisters go out into the field or into the garden with the children, they shall be careful, as many of them as find it possible, to stay with the children so that the children do not get into trouble. The school master shall also be along as much as possible.

The larger boys or girls should not by any means be allowed to bump or pull or hit the children.

The sisters shall take special care that the small children shall be kept clean.

The sisters shall also not go away to their rooms on their own business too much but the one shall tell the other.

They shall not carry hot water into the rooms so that no one may be injured.

They shall not bathe the children in too hot water for that is harmful.

They shall not let them sit too long on the stools lest they take cold or do themselves harm.

The wash woman shall be careful in making the fire and in heating water and shall not depend too much upon the girl who is helping her.

The night nurse (*Wächterin*) shall take good care of the light at night and shall frequently go about among the children to look at them and cover them.

The school mother shall not arrange matters for the sisters or for the girls without the counsel of the school master.

If a child will not keep quiet during the admonition it shall be taken out so that the other children may not become restless, for sometimes one child is itchy, another one thirsty, a third has some other need which one does not know. For this reason it is not possible to bring everything in order by using the rod.

During the day in school one should not attempt to settle everything with blows, but moderation should be used.

Also, no sister shall show disfavor to a child under her care or another child, nor show partiality against one that would prefer not to stay with her.

Neither brothers nor sisters shall show favoritism to particular boys or girls or send them to special places for they soon are overcome by the flattery and become proud.

Likewise the school masters shall not for any reason of their own or on account of business, without the counsel and consent of the elders, seek occasion to be absent from or leave the school. They shall not engage in work outside the school, such as planting or building or working on trifling things and thus neglect their work in the school. They must not by any means go to the markets here and there and buy according to their pleasure but rather they shall ask for the things they need at the place where these things are provided. They shall not occupy themselves with writing and reading and shall not let others take their place who often deal wrongly with the children out of favor or disfavor but they shall themselves supervise the children.

The sisters likewise shall not look after their own interests whether in sewing and mending or such work and shall not depend too much upon the girls and shall not go about too much outside the building and then when they come into the school accept a complaint from a boy or girl and then without proper consideration proceed to deal out punishment. Therefore we instruct them, faithfully to remain in the school and take care of the children since by such diligence discipline frequently becomes unnecessary and can be avoided.

No one shall unwillingly with complaint or impatience serve the needy ones of the Lord in the schools, for there would be no blessing in such work and the children would in consequence have to suffer from violence and rudeness in discipline. For where good will is lacking, there are often unkind words. Such expressions as these may then be heard: "You bad children; one must be continually occupied with you, one cannot do anything for himself," or similar improper things. By such conduct all who hear it would be grieved and the Lord, who hears all things, will take notice and He will punish it in His time. Therefore each one should willingly and gladly do his part to please the Lord.

It is therefore the appeal of us as elders to all of you who have the youth in charge, brethren and sisters, and especially you who are appointed as school masters and school mothers, that you perform your duties faithfully with all diligence as far as is possible by the grace of God, so that this and similar rules of order shall be observed by you and your assistants faithfully and harmoniously so that in these and other necessary points which would be too long to write and possibly also not necessary, a peaceful discipline may be kept in all your care and supervision of the youth, since you must give an account for the same. May you do it with joy as to the Lord in Heaven who will also be a faithful rewarder of your diligence.

In conclusion, let each one deal with the children by day and by night as if they were his own, whether in the matter of giving them to eat and drink or taking up or laying down, or leading about or carrying, or cleaning and washing, whatever is necessary, so that each one may be able to give an account before God and may have a conscience void of offense before the godly and the ungodly.

All this which has been here written and told at some length is a pattern of how counsel should be given to those who are concerned with the schools. At times more should be said and at times less, just as is necessary at each place according to the circumstances. By this each one will know how to conduct himself so that the honour of the Lord may be promoted.

The kitchen help and the waiters shall be told that they shall prepare and distribute with good will the food and drink which has been ordered for the children according to their need whether sick or well, young or old, and they shall not make many words about it.

And if it is necessary to ask for some particular food for a sick child, out of the usual order, they shall avoid using rough words. If what is asked for cannot be given, there should be a clear explanation, so that no one give occasion for complaint to another.

appendix five

Table Rules

In table prayer be serious
And fold your hands in love,
Always in reverence lifting up
Your heart to God above.

And when the prayer is ended
Turn left and right expressing
To neighbors each your wish that God
Upon this meal grant blessing.

You must never seat yourself
Ahead of all the others
Because that is the surest mark
Of most ill-mannered brothers.

Then do not upset your chair
Before you hold it fast,
And do not turn the serving dish
The way you like it best.

Source: *Gesang-Büchlein: Lieder für Schule und hauslichen Gebrauch* (Cayley, Alta.: Die Hutterischen Brüder, 1961), p. 86. Translated by Elizabeth Bender. The rules are memorized and recited daily by school children before going to the dining hall.

You must never be the first
To reach for food; no, wait
With patience till the older ones
First have filled their plates.

Do not always grasp
For only the best pieces
Or people will soon think
That with you all modesty ceases.

If a food is not prepared
The way you most would have it,
Do not speak up at once and say,
"I won't eat any of it."

You must not ask questions
About the food that's offered you,
And do not put your nose upon
The dishes passed before you.

Don't crunch things with your teeth
Or people will have fear
That wild beasts in the neighborhood
Are coming very near.

Don't dip into the salt dish
Your little bit of food,
Nor put your fingers in it,
For that is very rude.

Keep your elbows off the table
When you eat your food,
Otherwise your tablemates
Will think you very crude.

Hold your feet still while you're sitting
And keep your back up straight,
For a great amount of wiggling
Might damage cup and plate.

Handle glasses carefully
Especially when they're filled,
For if they're held up shakily
Something might be spilled.

Do not disturb your tablemates
With irritation great
By licking each crumb greedily
From your empty plate.

If you have to blow your nose
You must do it right;
Do not let it trumpet forth
And fill everyone with fright.

But turn politely to the side
To give yourself relief.
Wipe your nose with skill and speed
Using your handkerchief.

When yawning quickly raise your hand
To hide your mouth from view,
So that your neighbor need not fear
You will devour him, too.

If you get the urge to sneeze
Meet it with good grace;
Promptly hold your handkerchief
Up before your face.

When the meal comes to an end
Be thankful for the food.
Be ready with great happiness
To pray in gratitude.

For God has called each one of us
His loving child to be,
That we may in our faith persist
To serve him joyfully.

appendix six

Rites of Passage from Childhood to Adulthood

Age	Dariushof: At fifteenth birthday.
	Lehrerhof: At fourteenth birthday; girls continue to attend English school, boys English and German schools until age fifteen.
	Schmiedehof: At fifteenth birthday.
Designation of new status	The young person is now said to be *bei die Leut* ("with the people").
	The term for *boy* changes from *mandle* to *buah*.
	The term for *girl* changes from *dindla* to *die-en*.
Eating pattern	The young people eat "with the people" in the adult dining hall, the boys with the men, the youngest at the lowest ranking order of the farthest table. The girls sit with the women, the youngest at the lowest position of the farthest women's table; she waits on the men's table.
Work pattern: work no longer performed	Girls and boys no longer work as babysitters either in their home colony or for relatives in another colony.
new work	The boys work with the men, either in assigned tasks or as part of a rotating labor force. Girls work only with the women, whose major tasks are food preparation and painting and varnishing dwellings, and never do a man's work (such as helping with the cattle).

work tools	The colony gives the young adult tools he will need for his new work role. It is his responsibility to keep these tools in good working condition. Boys receive a saw, a hammer, a pitch fork, and a spade. Girls receive paint brushes, kitchen knives, a broom, a hoe, and knitting needles.
Religious observance	No longer is every aspect of religious behavior supervised by an adult. Prayers are said silently morning and evening without supervision by the German teacher, and not as part of the family group of young children. Young adults must recite memory work in weekly Sunday School, and they no longer attend German school. They must never miss Sunday service and almost never miss evening service. (A child may miss regularly if she has an assigned babysitting job.) Certain books are given to the young adult by the colony for personal use.
Social life	Visiting Hutterites will include the young adults in the hand shaking ceremony and greet them by name.
Schooling	Young adults no longer attend English school except when required by law. They no longer attend German school but attend Sunday school until baptism.
Discipline	Lehrerhof: The young person becomes subject to colony discipline in addition to (or instead of) discipline by parents and/or the German teacher.
	Dariushof: Parents take more responsibility for the young person's discipline. The German teacher is responsible in the area of religion and general moral behavior. The work foreman is responsible for work phases. A major transgression becomes a problem for the whole colony although it is usually handled through the German teacher.
Punishment	Corporal punishment is not used by the colony or colony representative. It may be used by parents but usually is not.
	Standing in Sunday School.
	For a serious offence a boy may have to stand during the evening or Sunday service. This is considered too harsh a punishment for a girl.
Furniture	A boy receives a small chest and a girl a medium-size chest in which to store personal belongings.
Clothing	Lehrerhof: Boys no longer wear a cap (Katus) but an adult-style hat. Boys and girls are given cloth for adult-style clothing.
	Dariushof: Girls get cloth for four church dresses, three black and one dark blue. They are made with large tucks to last them for the rest of their life.

Adult privileges
When cloth is passed out, young persons receive the amount, style, and quality for adults. Adult rules apply for allowance and alcoholic beverages.

Adult privileges withheld
The young adults may not attend weddings and funerals in other colonies before baptism. They must attend Sunday school and receive permission from the German teacher (instead of the preacher) to leave the colony. Misbehavior is usually handled by the German teacher rather than the preacher. Boys may not yet vote in colony affairs.

Foreman jobs are not assigned to the unbaptized.

appendix seven

Baptismal Vow

Questions asked of the applicants before the prayer:
1. Do you now acknowledge the doctrines, which have hitherto been taught to you, as being the truth and right foundation to salvation?
2. Do you also believe in and agree with the twelve articles of our Christian faith which comprise: "We believe in God the Almighty . . . ."
   [Each repeats the Apostles' Creed]
3. Do you also desire the prayer of intercession of the pious that God may forgive and remit the sins committed by you in ignorance?
4. Do you desire to consecrate, give and sacrifice yourself to the Lord God in the covenant of Christian baptism?

Here follows the prayer.
(After this prayer, while kneeling, follow these six questions:)
1. Do you now sufficiently understand the word of God and acknowledge it as the only path to life eternal?
2. Do you also truly and heartily repent of the sins which you have in ignorance committed against God and do you desire henceforth to fear God, nevermore to sin against God, and rather to suffer death than ever again to sin willfully against God?

Source: Peter Hofer, *The Hutterian Brethren and Their Beliefs* (Starbuck, Man.: The Hutterian Brethren of Manitoba, 1955), pp. 26 ff.

3. Do you also believe that your sins have been forgiven and remitted through Christ and the prayer of intercession of His people?
4. Is it also your desire to accept brotherly punishment and admonition and also to apply the same to others when it is needful?
5. Do you desire thus to consecrate, give and sacrifice yourself with soul and body and all your possessions to the Lord in heaven, and to be obedient unto Christ and his church?
6. Do you desire thus to establish a covenant with God and all his people and to be baptized upon your confessed belief?

Note: All of these questions must be answered with a "yes."

(The minister, laying on his hands and sprinkling with water, speaks the following words:)

On thy confessed belief I baptize three, in the name of the Father, the Son, and the Holy Ghost. God Almighty in heaven who has given you grace and mercy through the death of Christ and the prayer of His Saints, may clothe you with fortitude from on high and inscribe your name into the book of eternal life, to preserve thee in piety and faith until death. This is my wish to thee through Jesus Christ. Amen.

appendix eight

Engagement and Marriage Vows

The marriage vows are in two parts: the *Zusammenstellen* ("public engagement") which is held a few days before the *Zusammengeben* ("marriage"). Both services are held in the church assembly.

The Engagement Vow

Introduction:

As the brethren have talked to you individually they have understood that before God each one of you will accept the other as a gift of God in good faith. Neither a resolution nor your final approval have yet been heard.

Question to the brother:

1. Thus I ask you my brother first, do you desire to accept this sister without complaints and with good will? Say yes, so that she hears this.
Answer: Yes.

2. Do you desire to go before her in such a way that she finds in you a mirror and an example of honesty and will be led to the Lord through you, so that you may live together as Christians, one being of benefit to the other?
Answer: Yes.

Source: Michael Tschetter, *Trauungs Verhandlung für Zusammenstellen, u. Zusammengeben*, Dariushof colony document, 1913. Trans. Else Reist, 1965.

3. Marriage has its share of grief and not every day is filled with happiness, but brings suffering, too, as the women are the weaker ones. Thus I ask you, do you desire to have her for good, in health and in sickness, in love and in sorrow, never to leave her, until the Lord separates you through death? If this is not difficult for you, you may affirm it.
Answer: Yes.

Questions to the sister:

My sister, you have heard the good intentions of the brother, which will be of comfort to you.

1. Thus I ask you, will you also accept him with good will and without complaints?
Answer: Yes.

2. Since God has ordained that the husband is and should be the head of the wife, I ask you: Do you wish to obey him in all right and godly things as it is the duty of a wife, so that you can serve each other in godliness?
Answer: Yes.

3. Whether the husband can always enjoy better health than the wife is in God's hands. Will you therefore serve him also in health and sickness, in happiness and in sorrow, and never leave him? If this is not difficult for you, you may answer with yes.
Answer: Yes.

Summary:

Because of your declaration of intentions we want to publicly state before the congregation that with the counsel of your parents you want to come together. You also ask the Lord that His will be done to the glory of His name. For this the congregation will gather once more. Now you may be seated, or you can leave. Amen.

The Marriage Vow

Questions to the brother:

1. I ask you brother, first, whether you still wish to accept this sister that was introduced, in good faith as a gift of the Lord?
Answer: Yes.

2. Are you willing to be a good example for her in honesty and godliness, so that she may be brought closer to the Lord through you?
Answer: Yes.

3. Are you willing, brother, to take the introduced sister for good in love and sorrow, in health and sickness, never to leave her until death will part you?
Answer: Yes.

4. I ask you, brother, if it should happen that one or the other from the congregation should suffer shipwreck of his faith (which we would not hope for you and which God forbid) will you then be satisfied with yourself and not desire that your wife follow you from the right to the wrong and leave behind the community and the church? And would you on behalf of your woman not cause

us any trouble with the authorities; If so, you may answer with yes.
Answer: Yes.

Questions to the sister:

1. My sister, you have heard this brother in his good intentions, which will be of comfort to you. Therefore I ask you, too, do you desire to accept him in good will without complaints?
Answer: Yes.

2. Because it is ordained by God that the husband is the head of the wife, I ask you, do you desire to be obedient in all good things, as a good wife ought to be, so that one can help the other toward godliness?
Answer: Yes.

3. Whether the husband can always enjoy better health than the wife is in God's hands. Will you therefore serve him also in health and in sickness, in happiness and in sorrow, never leave him, until death will part you?
Answer: Yes.

To both: In closing, I ask you once more, brother and sister, before His church, which is a witness of this honest assembly: Will you in all that pertains to your marriage bond be faithful to each other and to your faith and never leave one another, until death will separate you? For what God has joined together, let no man put asunder. If so, both parties may answer with yes and join hands.
Answer: Yes.

Whereupon the blessing is given: We herewith bear witness that you marry each other as godfearing partners according to the order of God and the example of the forefathers and with the knowledge and counsel of the elders of the whole congregation. May the God of Abraham, Isaac and Jacob bless and keep you, may He lead you Himself together and bless you. May all godfearing husbands and wives live together peacefully and serve God all their lives. This we wish you once again from God through Jesus Christ. Amen.

appendix nine

Ordination Vow

Dear Brethren, while it has pleased God, our beloved trusting heavenly Father, to take away His servant, our beloved brother, Joseph Müller, to eternal, blessed rest, no one could help but fill his office again. We turned with heartfelt requests and supplications in our prayers to God, the Lord, that He might again supply us with a trustworthy, pious man. Now God has received our prayers and has given us one of our brothers, which pleased Him in this duty. This man has been received with great thanks and presented to the congregation according to the Christian Biblical customs of our forefathers and has been tried in this office for some time.

After he had served for a while, he proved himself so that we and all the elders were well satisfied with him. We know of no obstacle but think that if he also received the support of the congregation, he might be ordered into the service of the Word. For this reason, we will listen to his voice and determine the attitude of the congregation to see whether it also is satisfied with him.

Firstly, I am asking you, my brother, where do you stand? Do you desire to show your obedience to be given inside and outside the country, wherever needed, in good or evil times as God the Almighty does send it?

Source: This formulary was copied in 1792 by Mertl Roth from earlier editions and by custom retains the name of an early leader, Joseph Müller. Colony document. Trans. Karl Peter. The ordination takes place after a probation period of several years.

Secondly, I am asking you, do you desire to exercise punishment and admonition with the right courage and diligence so as to lead this congregation of the Lord that it might further be built and adorned in Him?

Thirdly, I am asking you, are you acquainted with the twelve articles of our most holy Christian faith, and do you acknowledge the Confession of Faith of our church as right, and do you desire to keep these, as much as possible until your death?

Fourthly, I am asking you, my brother, do you desire to keep all these points to which you have committed yourself before God and this congregation, to continue with these in good faith until death?

Now, my brother, while we have all witnessed your answers, agreement and covenant, we want to seal the work of the Lord by appealing to His name for you.

(After the prayer the brother remains in a kneeling position and the elder, standing near the table, asks further questions.)

I am asking you, my brother, whether you really mean to support those commitments into which you have entered before God and this congregation? *Answer:* Yes.

(After this, the elder, accompanied by three or four other preachers, goes near the kneeling brother and asks the following question):

Do you desire to serve God and his congregation faithfully unto death, and do you desire to be a faithful witness of the truth, particularly since we are being condemned to the fire and sword for being witnesses to the word of God? *Answer:* Yes.

The elder than says: Amen.

My brother, since we have given our confidence to you, we lay our hands on your shoulder as evidence, in the name of our Lord Christ and the power of God, that the office and the duty to serve in the word of the Lord will be trusted to you and burdened on you. You shall have the power to serve in this capacity to the redemption and improvement of mankind with us and beside us, to further the work of God with teaching, punishment, exclusion and admittance, according to the content of the Gospel and the word of God.

We wish that the grace of God may come on you, that God might draw you near to Him, overshadow you and accompany you with His grace and the gift of His holy spirit. This I wish for you from the Almighty God through Jesus Christ. Amen.

appendix ten

Agreement between a Divisional School Board and a Colony, Alberta

Memorandum of agreement made at _____, Alberta, this _____ day of
_____, 19___, between the Board of_____ Division No. ___and the Hutterite Colony located in the_____ School District No. ___ .

Subject to approval by the Minister of Education, it is hereby agreed as follows:

(1) Since the Colony has been established in a School District the pupils of
    which are now provided for by the Division and the members of the Colony
    insist that they shall have their own school apart from the schools for the
    Division, the other ratepayers of the Division should not be asked to bear
    any of the cost of the school in the Hutterite Colony.

(2) The Colony is to provide a school site of at least three acres. This is to be
    fenced to prevent the running of stock, pigs, and poultry through the school
    grounds.

(3) The Colony is to provide a school building approved by the Department
    of Education.

(4) The Colony is to provide a teacher's residence of at least three rooms with
    basement to be built at a suitable place in the school grounds.

(5) Toilets for the school and residence are to be provided by the Colony.

Note: Agreements between Divisional School Boards and the colonies are not uniform, and although this agreement has served as a model in practice, there are variations.

(6) The Colony is not to build any other buildings within one hundred and fifty feet of the school building.

(7) The Colony is to provide fuel and janitor service for the school.

(8) The teacher is to be appointed and paid by the Division.

(9) Furniture and school equipment are to be provided by the Division.

(10) The pupils of the Colony may buy their school supplies from the Division.

(11) The pupils may rent their textbooks from the Division, or the textbooks may be bought outright by the Colony.

(12) Any alternate school site or school building provided in future by the Colony shall be subject to approval by the Division and by the Department of Education.

(13) Should the enrollment of pupils in the Colony reach forty, the Colony is to provide an additional schoolroom, approved by the Department of Education, on the school site. The Division will then provide additional equipment and a second teacher.

(14) The Colony is free to use the school building for church purposes providing such use does not interfere with the use of the building for school purposes.

(15) The Minister of Education will be requested to declare the quarter section(s) occupied by the Colony buildings to be a Hamlet under Section 2(f)(ii) of The School Act.

(16) The Minister of Education will be requested to approve an additional levy upon the Hamlet as provided in Section 290 of The School Act; provided that the amount of the additional levy which the Minister will be asked to approve for   shall not exceed   Dollars.

(17) This agreement may be terminated by either party thereto giving notice to the other on or before the fifteenth day of May in any year, and, upon notice being given, the agreement shall cease and determine on the last day of the month of June of the following year.

Signed on behalf of _____   Signed on behalf of the Hutterite
_____ School Division No. ____   Colony of _____

_____   _____
Chairman   President

_____   _____
Secretary-Treasurer   Secretary

Approved this_____day of_____19__

_____
Minister of Education

appendix eleven

Holidays

Slight variations in holidays exist among the colonies. The quotations below are from the preachers of each of the three colonies and are indicated by S (Schmiedehof), D (Dariushof), and L (Lehrerhof).

January 1   *Beschneidung's Tag* ("Day of Circumcision"), comes eight days after the birth of Christ, hence the day of circumcision, which "denotes purity." (D) "On this day the child was given the name 'Jesus.' A morning and evening service is observed. The day is also honored as a thanksgiving day for God's goodness during the past year with supplication for the New Year." (S)

January 6   *Heiligen Drei Königen* ("The three wise men"), the bringing of gifts to the Christ child. "As the three wise kings were guided by the light and found Christ, so let us also be brought to the light of the Word of God." (S)

March 25   *Maria Verkündigung* ("The Annunciation") was observed nine months before Christmas in Schmiedehof until 1972. Since then it has been observed by a sermon on the Sunday nearest to March 25. Among the Dariusleut and Lehrerleut it has never been observed as a special day.

Palm Sonntag ("Palm Sunday"). If there are baptismal applicants they are baptized in the morning service. (S) The sermon stresses "humbling before the Lord. We accept Him also as the King of the New Jerusalem." (S)

Karfreitag ("Good Friday"). *Green Donnerstag*, or the night of the betrayal, requires a long sermon on Thursday evening. Good Friday is observed with a morning and evening service dealing exclusively with the suffering and crucifixion of Christ. Saturday is a "normal" work day.

Oster ("Easter") spans three holidays: Sunday, Monday, and Tuesday.
Sunday is observed with two long sermons, one in the morning and one in the afternoon, with no evening service. "We especially stress community and communion, mostly the purpose of communion." (S) Monday *Abendmahl* ("communion") is observed once each year and never on any other day of the year. The service is from nine o'clock until twelve, and there is also an evening service. Tuesday is *Auferstehungs Tag* ("Resurrection Day"). A morning and evening service is held. "We preach the resurrection texts." (D) "It's not the day Christ arose from the grave, but we observe it on this day." (S)

Christi Himmelfahrt ("Ascension Day") is observed forty days after Easter.

Pfingsten ("Pentecost") spans three holidays: Sunday, Monday and Tuesday, beginning with the ninth day after Ascension day. "For us this is an important day, for the church was formed at this time." (D) "We explain the pouring out of the Spirit, plus the development of the communal system. All but the very necessary work stops for these days." (S)

Danksagung ("Thanksgiving"), also *Hapchincka* (a Russian word meaning "celebrating the bountiful harvest"). The day is observed on a Sunday after the harvest is over. "Celebrated with a nice dinner." (S)

December 25   *Weihnachten* ("Christmas") is observed for three days, the 25th, 26th, and 27th. "These days represent the Father, Son, and Holy Ghost." (S) A morning sermon and an evening service is held on each of the three days. Should the 24th or the 28th fall on a Sunday, there are four consecutive holidays.

appendix twelve

The Liturgical Calendar

The Liturgical Calendar

Colony preachers read aloud sermons they have copied in German script from older copies, according to a yearly pattern. In colonies where there are two preachers, one is always an assistant but each takes his turn in reading the sermon. Each selects a sermon from his own collection on a theme that is seasonal. The colony keeps a record of the date and text of all sermons delivered, who delivered them, and the hymns sung. The liturgical calendar begins with the prophecy of the coming of Christ and ends with Ascension and Pentecost (the beginning of the Christian Church). (Compare also the *Lehrordnung* of Robert Friedmann in *Die Schriften der Huterischen Täufergemeinschaften*, p. 158.) Paul S. Gross gave valuable assistance in compiling this list of texts from both Testaments and from the Apocrypha.

Text	Use and Explanation
Titus 2 : 11–15	These six texts are used before Christmas but in a
Psalm 45 : 1–10	different order each year
Psalm 72 : 1–12	
Isaiah 26 : 1–10	

Source: Wie die Lehren zu Halten, Jahrlich und Feierlich. Schmiedehof colony document, 1965.

Text	Use and Explanation
Isaiah 60 : 1-6	
John 3 : 16-31	
Luke 2 : 1-20	(December 25) Christmas holiday sermons are
Isaiah 11 : 1-7	selected from these five
Micah 5 : 1-3	
Isaiah 9 : 6-7	
Isaiah 49 : 1-4	
I John 1 : 1-10	These three texts are used on Sundays following
John 1 : 6-14	Christmas
Mark 1 : 1-11	
Luke 2 : 21-32	New Year's Day, Day of Circumcision
Matthew 2 : 7-12	The Three Wise Kings from the East
Matthew 3 : 1-17	Exchanged each year as needed
Luke 3 : 1-18	
Matthew 2 : 13-23	The flight into Egypt
Luke 2 : 26-52	The twelve-year-old Jesus
Matthew 4 : 1-10	The temptation of Christ
Luke 4 : 14-28	Holy Ghost power manifest
Matthew 5 : 1-12	Advent sermons
Matthew 5 : 13-48	
Matthew 6 : 1-24	
Matthew 7 : 1-12	
Matthew 7 : 13-23	
Isaiah 58 : 1-6	
Micah 1 : 16-23	
John 3 : 1-6	
Matthew 8 : 23-27	
Sirach	
(Ecclesiasticus) 2 : 1-11	
I John 5 : 5-8	
John 3 : 7-15	Baptismal sermons
Romans 6 : 1-8	
Matthew 28 : 16-20	
Luke 1 : 26-28	(March 25) The Annunciation
John 6 : 47-48	Pre-Easter sermons
John 13 : 1-38	
Hebrews 13 : 8-16	

Text	**Use and Explanation**
Romans 12 : 1–21	
Isaiah 63 : 1–4	
I Corinthians 5 : 6–8	
Matthew 21 : 1–22	Two Palm Sunday sermons
Mark 11 : 1–10	
Luke 23 : 24–45	Good Friday
Isaiah 53 : 1–12	
Exodus 12 : 1–51	Easter Sunday, forenoon
I Corinthians 10 : 1–24	Easter Sunday, afternoon
I Corinthians 11 : 23–32	Easter Monday, communion
Matthew 28 : 1–15	Easter Tuesday, the Resurrection
John 20 : 1–18	
Luke 24 : 13–53	The walk to Emmaus
Colossians 3 : 1–8	
I Corinthians 15 : 35–44	
I Peter 4 : 1–7	
John 11 : 9–35	
Romans 14 : 7–13	
Acts I : 1–11	Ascension Day
John 14 : 15–31	
Wisdom 1 : 1–11	
Acts 2 : 1–47	Pentecost sermon in five parts
Wisdom 7 : 22–23	
Galatians 5 : 19–21	
Galatians 5 : 22–24	
Psalm 133	
I John 2 : 18–29	

appendix thirteen

Colony Menu
for One Week

	Breakfast*	Dinner	Supper*
Monday	Bacon and eggs, Bread and cheese	Hamburger and onions, potatoes, buttered carrots, cherries, plums	Fresh bread with cracker barrel cheese, baked beans, fried potatoes, hamburger, cold duck
Tuesday	Bread and cheese, celery, cooked cereal	Rice cooked in sweet milk, fried potatoes, canned chicken, sauerkraut, baked parsnips, carrots	Baked potatoes, peas, stew meat with horseradish, soup, beans, cooked eggs, bread
Wednesday	Pancakes with cheese and celery	*Schuten Krafen*† with whipped cream, stewed beef with horseradish	Creamed corn, fried potato chips, leftover chicken, sweet pickles

Source: Dariushof (April 1964)

    *Butter and honey are always on the table for breakfast and supper. Coffee or tea is served with every meal.

    †*Schuten Krafen* is made of junket, sugar, eggs, bread crumbs and onions fried in butter.

	Breakfast*	Dinner	Supper*
Thursday	Fried eggs, bread with cheese and celery	Fresh bread, jam, beef, horseradish, potatoes, buttered beets, rice pudding	French fried potatoes, ground carrots, boiled eggs, fresh bread
Friday	Cream of wheat, bread	Chicken and buckwheat grits, peaches	Fried leftover potatoes, cold chicken, carrots
Saturday	Eggs, celery, cheese, bread	French fries, pork, buttered carrots, pickles, buns	Stewed mutton and horseradish, buns, beets, cooked potatoes
Sunday	Boiled eggs, buns and strawberry jam, celery, cheese	Duck, noodle soup, buns, pears	Cold duck, cheese, boiled eggs, buns with jam and butter

appendix fourteen

Last Words of
Michael Waldner, 1823-89

On October 13, 1889, at twelve o'clock on Sunday night, the minister and *Vorsteher* (elder) of the colony at Bon Homme, Michael Waldner, fell asleep in the Lord. He was the originator and founder of this colony. He died at the age of 56 years, eight months and twenty-seven days. He served 34 years as a servant of the Word.

Before his departure he called all his children to him, admonished them sincerely in a fatherly way and bade them farewell. Among other things he said the following:

"My dear children! Fear God and keep Him constantly before your eyes and in your hearts. Be faithful and honest and let nothing improper be spoken of you, but constantly heed your father's words which I have spoken to you.

"Dear children, I have always sought to lead you to the Lord. I have given you a good example. Therefore guard yourselves against strife and disunity, which is a shattering of love. Be obedient to those who have authority over you; for disobedience is witchcraft, sin, etc."

Then he also spoke with the elders, and said, among other things, the following:

Source: Zieglschmid, *Das Klein-Geschichtsbuch*, p. 465; passage translated by Elizabeth Bender. Waldner reestablished communal life in Russia. He was the leader of the first immigrant group, which settled at Bon Homme Colony, South Dakota.

"Dear Brethren! As far as I am aware I have always desired to fear God and to serve the commune faithfully, and therefore my conscience knows itself to be free of all sin, except that I have always had to complain of my weakness like everybody else. But otherwise I have a good conscience; I have always wanted to fear God and deal faithfully and justly.

"But now, because I believe that I have probably finished my course and the Lord is calling me hence, this is my final request to you, dear Brethren.

"Let the commune be faithfully commended to your care and see that it is well cared for. And may especially the needy, the young, widows and orphans be commended to your care. And because there are so many ungodly people around us, see to it that you do not associate too much with them or grow too soft, but hold to what is right and just.

"If I have ever caused any of you sorrow or worry, I ask you to forgive it; for frequently we engaged in serious conversation, and what I said in them I always said out of zeal for God and with the best intentions.

"Dear Brethren! I ask you earnestly to guard yourselves against disunity; for you can imagine what terrible misery arises from it and how many widows and orphans are sorely afflicted as a result of it.

"See to it that you hold firmly to the old regulations of the commune and that the landmarks are not moved out of place. Persist firmly in community, which was instituted by the Holy Spirit. And resist greed and self-seeking as strongly as you possibly can.

"I can hardly talk anymore, for I am very weak; but I am confident that the Lord will not forsake His church, but will faithfully provide for it and raise up another shepherd for you that you may also be provided for. May you have a faithful concern for the doctrine and be a good example to the people; then the Lord will grant you His blessing and His strength for the task.

"Remember too, if after my departure someone should say that I had given many promises granting this or that freedom, I have not done so; I acted faithfully with counsel."

Then he folded his hand, raised himself up and said, "Lord, into Thy hands I commend my spirit."

As we all stood around the bed weeping, he said, "Dear children, don't weep on my account. My conscience is not troubling me for any part of my life. I am going to fall asleep calmly and quietly in my eternal rest."

Before his end he told this story: In a dream a man came to him, who asked how he had received all those snake and dog bites. Alas, he replied, God knows that a preacher has so much to suffer that it is beyond expression; I too have had to suffer much. Yes, one who must serve in Christ's stead is to be pitied. Not without reason they are likened to a stick that is thrown to a dog to bite upon; Yet they are the Lord's anointed and serve in Christ's stead.

And thus he fell asleep gently and rationally into the eternal rest. His last sermon was on Jeremiah 13:15, "Hear ye, and give ear; be not proud: for the Lord hath spoken."

He was a kind, modest and very sympathetic brother and was always ready to support by counsel and deed the needy ones who turned to him in their distress. He sent none away without being comforted.

He also often related that before his conversion the Lord had let him fall into a serious illness, so that he lay like a dead man and was enraptured and saw and heard unutterable things, saw heaven and hell and the damned.

He received from the Lord the command to enter the commune, which command he faithfully obeyed when the Lord gave him back his health; with God's help and support, he, together with Brother Jacob Hofer, established a commune after the pattern of the first church at Jerusalem and of our blessed forefathers, as it is written in this book.

appendix fifteen

List of Hutterite Colonies in North America

SCHMIEDELEUT COLONIES

Year Founded	Colony Name	Address	Parent Colony
1874	Bon Homme	Tabor, S.D.	From the Ukraine
1878–84	Trippe, S.D.	Extinct	Bon Homme, S.D.
1884–86	Tidioute, Pa.	Extinct	Tripp, S.D.
1886–1907	Milltown, S.D.	Extinct	Tidioute, Pa.
1900–18	Maxwell, S.D.	Extinct	Bon Homme, S.D.
1901–18	Rosedale, S.D.	Extinct	Milltown, S.D.
1906–18	Huron, S.D.	Extinct	Bon Homme, S.D.
1907–13	Buffalo, S.D.	Extinct	Milltown, S.D.
1913–18	James Valley, S.D.	Extinct	Buffalo, S.D.
1918	Bon Homme	Elie, Man.	Bon Homme, S.D.
1918	Huron	Elie, Man.	Huron, S.D.
1918	James Valley	Elie, Man.	James Valley, S.D.
1918	Maxwell	Headingly, Man.	Maxwell, S.D.
1918	Milltown	Bernard, Man.	Milltown, S.D.
1918	(Old) Rosedale	Elie, Man.	Rosedale, S.D.
1919	Iberville	Headingly, Man.	Old Rosedale, Man.
1920	Barickman	Headingly, Man.	Maxwell, Man.

Year Founded	Colony Name	Address	Parent Colony
1922	Blumengart	Plum Coulee, Man.	Milltown, Man.
1929–37	Roseisle, Man.	Extinct	Huron, Man.
1932–36	Alsask, Alta.	Extinct	Maxwell, Man.
1934–36	Teulon, Man.	Extinct	Barickman, Man.
1934	Elm River	Newton, Man.	Old Rosedale, Man.
1934	Riverside	Arden, Man.	Iberville, Man.
1934	Rockport	Alexandria, S.D.	Bon Homme, Man.
1934	Waldheim	Elie, Man.	Bon Homme, Man.
1936	New Elmspring	Ethan, S.D.	Alsask, Man.
1937	Jamesville	Utica, S.D.	Roseisle, Man.
1938	Poplar Point	Poplar Point, Man.	Huron, Man.
1938	Sturgeon Creek	Headingly, Man.	Blumengart, Man.
1942	Sunnyside	Newton, Man.	Milltown, Man.
1942	Tschetter	Olivet, S.D.	Barickman, Man.
1944	Huron	Huron, S.D.	Jamesville, S.D.
1944	New Rosedale	Portage La Prairie, Man.	Old Rosedale, Man.
1945	Rosedale	Mitchell, S.D.	Rockport, S.D.
1945	Spink	Frankford, S.D.	Bon Homme, S.D.
1946	Lakeside	Headingly, Man.	Maxwell, Man.
1946	Riverdale	Gladstone, Man.	James Valley, Man.
1947	Rock Lake	Gross Isle, Man.	Iberville, Man.
1948	Gracevale	Winfred, S.D.	Tschetter, S.D.
1949	Glendale	Frankford, S.D.	Bon Homme, Man.
1949	Maxwell	Scotland, S.D.	New Elmspring, S.D.
1949	Millerdale	Miller, S.D.	Milltown, Man.
1949	Pearl Creek	Iroquois, S.D.	Huron, Man.
1949	Platte	Academy, S.D.	Bon Homme, Man.
1949	Riverside	Huron, Man.	Rockport, S.D.
1950	Forest River	Fordville, N.D.	New Rosedale, Man.
1950	Springfield	Anola, Man.	Poplar Point, Man.
1952	Blumengart	Wecota, S.D.	Blumengart, Man.
1952	Oak Bluff	Morris, Man.	Elm River, Man.
1955	Clark	Raymond, S.D.	Jamesville, S.D.
1955	Crystal Springs	Ste. Agathe, Man.	Sturgeon Creek, Man.
1955	Greenwald	Dencross, Man.	Barickman, Man.
1956	Spring Valley	Glen Souris, Man.	James Valley, Man.
1957	Bloomfield	Westbourne, Man.	Riverside, Man.
1957	Rose Valley	Graysville, Man.	Waldheim, Man.
1958	Big Stone	Graceville, Minn.	New Elmspring, S.D.
1958	Grant	Elie, Man.	Bon Homme, Man.
1958	Hillside	Doland, S.D.	Huron, S.D.
1958	Hillside	Justice, Man.	Old Rosedale, Man.
1958	Plainview	Ipswich, S.D.	Spink, S.D.

Year Founded	Colony Name	Address	Parent Colony
1959	Bright Stone	Lac du Bonnet, Man.	Maxwell, Man.
1959	Deerboine	Alexander, Man.	Riverdale, Man.
1959	Fairholme	Portage La Prairie, Man.	New Rosedale, Man.
1960	Clearwater	Balmoral, Man.	Poplar Point, Man.
1961	Homewood	Starbuck, Man.	Lakeside, Man.
1961	Interlake	Teulon, Man.	Rock Lake, Man.
1961	Pembina	Darlingford, Man.	Blumengart, Man.
1961	Spring Creek	Forbes, N.D.	Maxwell, S.D.
1961	Whiteshell	River Hills, Man.	Iberville, Man.
1962	Cloverleaf	Howard, S.D.	Gracevale, S.D.
1963	Long Lake	Wetonka, S.D.	Pearl Creek, S.D.
1963	Thunderbird	Wecota, S.D.	Glendale, S.D.
1963	Wolf Creek	Olivet, S.D.	Tschetter, S.D.
1964	Parkview	Riding Mountain, Man.	Huron, Man.
1964	Rainbow	Isle des Chenes, Man.	Elm River, Man.
1964	Spring Hill Creek	Neepawa, Man.	Sunnyside, Man.
1964	Spring Valley	Wessington Springs, S.D.	Platte, S.D.
1964	White Rock	Rosholt, S.D.	Rosedale, S.D.
1965	Glenway	Dominion City, Man.	Milltown, Man.
1965	Ridgeland	Anola, Man.	Springfield, Man.
1967	Oak Ridge	Treherne, Man.	Barickman, Man.
1967	Poinsett	Estelline, S.D.	New Elmspring, S.D.
1968	Hidden Valley	Austin, Man.	Sturgeon Creek, Man.
1969	River Bend	Carberry, Man.	Oak Bluff, Man.
1969	Suncrest	Tourond, Man.	Crystal Springs, Man.
1970	Maple River	Fullerton, N.D.	Blumengart, S.D.
1970	Wellwood	Dunrea, Man.	Spring Valley, Man.
1970	Greenwood	Delmont, S.D.	Jamesville, S.D.
1970	Pembrook	Ipswich, S.D.	Tschetter, S.D.
1971	Deerfield	Ipswich, S.D.	Plainview, S.D.
1971	Fairview	LaMour, N.D.	Rockport, S.D.
1971	Woodland	Poplar Point, Man.	Old Rosedale, Man.
1971	Glendale Farm	Britton, S.D.	Glendale, S.D.
1972	Airport	McDonald, Man.	New Rosedale, Man.
1972	Cedar Grove	Platte, S.D.	Bon Homme, S.D.
1972	Grass River	Glenella, Man.	Grant, Man.
1972	Marble Ridge	Hodgson, Man.	Bloomfield, Man.
1972	Mayfair	Lena, Man.	Riverside, S.D.

Year Founded	Colony Name	Address	Parent Colony
1972	New Dale	Souris, Man.	Bon Homme, Man.
1972	Gracevale Farm	Bushnell, S.D.	Gracevale, S.D.
1972	Hillside Farm	Elkton, S.D.	Hillside, S.D.
1973	Pleasant Valley	Flandreau, S.D.	Big Stone, Minn.

Summary: Total number of Schmiedeleut colonies   91

Total number of extinct Schmiedeleut colonies   11

DARIUSLEUT COLONIES

Year Founded	Colony Name	Address	Parent Colony
1874–75	Silver Lake, S.D.	Extinct	From the Ukraine
1875–1930	Wolf Creek, S.D.	Extinct	Silver Lake, S.D.
1886–1918	Jamesville, S.D.	Extinct	Wolf Creek, S.D.
1890–1918	Kutter, S.D.	Extinct	Wolf Creek, S.D.
1893–1905	Dominion City, Man.	Extinct	Kutter, S.D.
1905–18	Beadle, S.D.	Extinct	Wolf Creek, S.D.
1905–18	Spink, S.D.	Extinct	Wolf Creek, S.D.
1906–18	Richards, S.D.	Extinct	Wolf Creek, S.D.
1912–20	Spring Creek, Mont.	Reestablished 1946	Wolf Creek, S.D.
1913–18	Warren Range, Mont.	Extinct	Wolf Creek, S.D.
1918–29	Raley, Alta.	Moved to W. Raley	Beadle, S.D.
1918	East Cardston	Cardston, Alta.	Warren Range, Mont.
1918	Rosebud	Redlands, Alta.	Kutter, S.D.
1918	Springvale	Rockyford, Alta.	Jamesville, S.D.
1918	Standoff	Fort MacLeod, Alta.	Spink, S.D.
1918	Wilson Siding	Lethbridge, Alta.	Richards, S.D.
1919	Stahlville	Rockyford, Alta.	Spring Creek, Mont.
1920–35	Beadle, S.D.	Extinct	Spring Creek, Mont.
1924	New York	Maybutt, Alta.	Raley, Alta.
1925	Ewelme	Fort MacLeod, Alta.	East Cardson, Alta.
1926	Felger	Lethbridge, Alta.	Beadle, S.D.
1926	New Rosebud	Beiseker, Alta	Rosebud, Alta.
1927	Pincher Creek	Pincher Creek, Alta.	Felger, Alta.
1929	West Raley	Cardston, Alta.	Raley, Alta.
1930	Granum	Granum, Alta.	Standoff, Alta.
1930	Wolf Creek	Stirling, Alta.	Wolf Creek, S.D.

Year Founded	Colony Name	Address	Parent Colony
1933	Riverside	Fort MacLeod, Alta.	Standoff, Alta.
1935	King Ranch	Lewistown, Mont.	Beadle, S.D.
1935	Lakeside	Cranford, Alta.	Wolf Creek, Alta.
1936	Cayley	Cayley, Alta.	West Raley, Alta.
1936	Sandhills	Beiseker, Alta.	Springvale, Alta.
1939	Thompson	Glenwood, Alta.	East Cardston, Alta.
1944	Fairview	Crossfield, Alta.	New Rosebud, Alta.
1945	Grass Range	Grass Range, Mont.	King Ranch, Mont.
1947	Deerfield	Danvers, Mont.	Wolf Creek, Alta.
1948	Camrose	Camrose, Alta.	Springvale, Alta.
1948	Pine Hill	Ponoka, Alta.	Lakeside, Alta.
1948	Tschetter	Irricana, Alta.	New Rosebud, Alta.
1949	Ferrybank	Ponoka, Alta.	Sandhills, Alta.
1949	Holt	Irma, Alta.	Granum, Alta.
1949	Red Willow	Stettler, Alta.	Stahlville, Alta.
1953	Leask	Leask, Sask.	Sandhills, Alta.
1953	Pibrock	Pibrock, Alta.	Wilson Siding, Alta.
1954	Scotford	Ft. Sask., Alta.	New York, Alta.
1955	Riverview	Sutherland, Sask.	Fairview, Alta.
1956	Spring Creek	Walsh, Sask.	Lakeside, Alta.
1956	Sunshine	Hussar, Alta.	Caley, Alta.
1956	Veteran	Veteran, Alta.	West Raley, Alta.
1957	O. B.	Marwayne, Alta.	Thompson, Alta.
1958	Estuary	Estuary, Sask.	Riverside, Alta.
1958	New Wolf Creek	Maple Creek, Sask.	Wolf Creek, Alta.
1959	Huxley	Huxley, Alta.	Stahlville, Alta.
1959	Turner	Turner, Mont.	Grass Range, Mont.
1960	Box Elder	Walsh, Sask.	Pinehill, Alta.
1960	Espanola	Reardan, Wash.	Pincher Creek, Alta.
1960	Mixburn	Minburn, Alta.	Holt, Alta.
1960	Ribstone	Edgarton, Alta.	Camrose, Alta.
1960	Spring Point	Brockett, Alta.	Granum, Alta.
1960	West Bench	Ravencrag, Sask.	East Cardston, Alta.
1960	Wolf Creek (North Harlem)	Harlem, Mont.	Deerfield, Mont.
1961	Cluny	Cluny, Alta.	Tschetter, Alta.
1961	Hillsvale	Ballwinton, Sask.	Springvale, Alta.
1961	Simmie	Simmie, Sask.	New York, Alta.
1961	Waterton	Waterton, Alta.	Wilson Siding, Alta.
1962	Athabaska	Athabaska, Alta.	Rosebud, Alta.
1963	Wilson Range	Stanford, Mont.	King Ranch, Mont.
1964	Bethune	Bethune, Sask.	Spring Creek, Sask.
1964	New Ferrybank	Warburg, Alta.	Ferrybank, Alta.
1964	Wildwood	Wildwood, Alta.	Red Willow, Alta.
1964	Dundurn	Dundurn, Sask.	Leask, Sask.

Year Founded	Colony Name	Address	Parent Colony
1969	Ft. Pitt	Frenchman Butte, Sask.	Ribstone, Alta.
1969	Plain Lake	Two Hills, Alta.	Scotford, Alta.
1969	Pleasant Valley	Clive, Alta.	Veteran, Alta.
1969	Smokey Lake	Smokey Lake, Alta.	New Rosebud, Alta.
1970	Vegreville	Lavoy, Alta.	Pibrock, Alta.
1971	Hodgeville	Hodgeville, Sask.	Box Elder, Alta.
1971	Morinville	Alcomdale, Alta.	Sandhills, Alta.
1971	New Raley	Turin, Alta.	West Raley, Alta.
1971	Valley View	Torrington, Alta.	Huxley, Alta.
1971	Holden	Holden, Alta.	Caley, Alta.
1972	Starland	Morin, Alta.	Lakeside, Alta.
1972	Sunshine Ranch	Hussar, Alta.	Cayley, Alta.
1972	Cameron Ranch	Turin, Alta.	Ewelme, Alta.
1973	Hughenden	Hughenden, Alta.	Athabaska, Alta.
1973	Barrens	Barrens, Alta.	Granum, Alta.
1973	Valley View	Valley View, Alta.	Thompson, Alta.
1973	**Warden**	**Warden, Wash.**	**Espanola, Wash.**

Summary: Total number of Dariusleut colonies   77
           Total number of extinct Dariusleut colonies   11

LEHRERLEUT COLONIES

Year Founded	Colony Name	Address	Parent Colony
1877–1929	Old Elmspring, S.D.	Extinct	From the Ukraine
1888–1934	Rockport, S.D.	Extinct	Old Elmspring, S.D.
1900–1918	New Elmspring, S.D.	Extinct	Old Elmspring, S.D.
1910–18	Milford, S.D.	Extinct	Old Elmspring, S.D.
1918	Milford	Raymond, Alta.	Miford, S.D.
1918	New Elmspring	Magrath, Alta.	New Elmspring, S.D.
1918	Old Elmspring	Magrath, Alta.	Old Elmspring, S.D.
1918	Rockport	Magrath, Alta.	Rockport, S.D.
1920	Big Bend	Cardston, Alta.	New Elmspring, Alta.
1924	Miami	New Dayton, Alta.	Milford, Alta.
1929	Elmspring	Warner, Alta.	Old Elmspring, S.D.
1932	Hutterville	Magrath, Alta.	Rockport, S.D.
1932	New Rockport	New Dayton, Alta.	Rockport, Alta.
1934	O. K. Colony	Raymond, Alta.	Rockport, S.D.
1935	Rock Lake	Wrentham, Alta.	Old Elmspring, Alta.

Year Founded	Colony Name	Address	Parent Colony
1935	Sunnyside	Warner, Alta.	Elmspring, Alta.
1937	Crystal Springs	Magrath, Alta.	New Elmspring, Alta.
1937	Macmillan	Cayley, Alta.	Big Bend, Alta.
1945	Milford	Augusta, Mont.	Milford, Alta.
1947	Birch Creek	Valier, Mont.	New Elmspring, Alta.
1948	Miami	Pendroy, Mont.	Miami, Alta.
1948	New Rockport	Choteau, Mont.	New Rockport, Alta.
1948	Rockport	Pendroy, Mont.	Rockport, Alta.
1949	Bench	Shaunavon, Sask.	Old Elmspring, Alta.
1949	Miller	Choteau, Mont.	O. K., Alta.
1950	Glacier	Cut Bank, Mont.	Elmspring, Alta.
1950	Hillside	Sweet Grass, Mont.	Sunnyside, Alta.
1950	Newdale	Milo, Alta.	Rock Lake, Alta.
1951	Winnifred	Medicine Hat, Alta.	Milford, Alta.
1952	Acadia	Oyen, Alta.	Crystal Springs, Alta.
1952	Cypress	Maple Creek, Sask.	Big Bend, Alta.
1952	Tompkins	Tompkins, Sask.	New Elmspring, Alta.
1953	Rosedale	Etzikom, Alta.	Hutterville, Alta.
1955	Springside	Duchess, Alta.	New Rockport, Alta.
1956	Handhills	Hanna, Alta.	Macmillan, Alta.
1959	Martindale	Martindale, Mont.	Miami, Mont.
1960	Springdale	White Sulphur, Mont.	Milford, Mont.
1961	Sage Creek	Chester, Mont.	Miller, Mont.
1962	Duncan Ranch	Harlowton, Mont.	Birch Creek, Mont.
1962	Newell	Bassano, Alta.	O. K., Alta.
1963	Glidden	Glidden, Sask.	Miami, Alta.
1963	Main Centre	Rush Lake, Sask.	Rockport, Alta.
1963	Hilldale	Havre, Mont.	Rockport, Mont.
1963	Rimrock	Sunburst, Mont.	Hillside, Mont.
1963	Waldeck	Swift Current, Sask.	Elmspring, Alta.
1964	Bow City	Brooks, Alta.	Elmspring, Alta.
1965	Castor	Castor, Alta.	Hutterville, Alta.
1965	South Bend	Alliance, Alta.	Winnifred, Alta.
1967	Haven	Fox Valley, Sask.	Acadia, Alta.
1968	Baildon	Moose Jaw, Sask.	Springside, Alta.
1968	Brant	Brant, Alta.	Rock Lake, Alta.
1968	Smiley	Smiley, Sask.	New Rockport, Mont.
1969	Casacde	Fort Shaw, Mont.	Glacier, Mont.
1969	Glendale	Cut Bank, Mont.	New Rockport, Alta.
1969	Huron	Brownlee, Sask.	Big Bend, Alta.
1970	Kyle	Kyle, Sask.	Rosedale, Alta.
1970	Roseglen	Hilda, Alta.	Crystal Springs, Alta.
1970	Rosetown	Rosetown, Sask.	Milford, Alta.
1971	Abbey	Abbey, Sask.	Tompkins, Sask.

Year Founded	Colony Name	Address	Parent Colony
1971	Clearspring	Keneston, Sask.	Bench, Sask.
1972	Parkland	Parkland, Alta.	Macmillan, Alta.
1972	Verdant Valley	Drumheller, Alta.	Handhills, Alta.
1973	Provost	Provost, Alta.	O. K., Alta.
1973	Messleigh	Messleigh, Alta.	Newdale, Alta.
1973	Grassy Lake	Grassy Lake, Alta.	New Elm Spring, Alta.

Summary: Total number of Lehrerleut colonies   61
Total number of extinct colonies   4

appendix sixteen

Branching of
Hutterite Colonies
(Dariusleut, Lehrerleut,
and Schmiedeleut) in
North America, 1874-1974

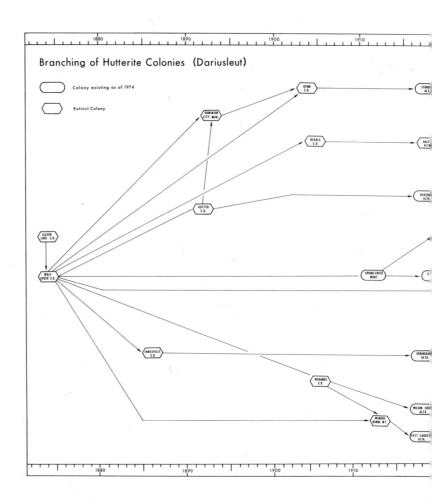

Branching of Hutterite Colonies (Dariusleut)

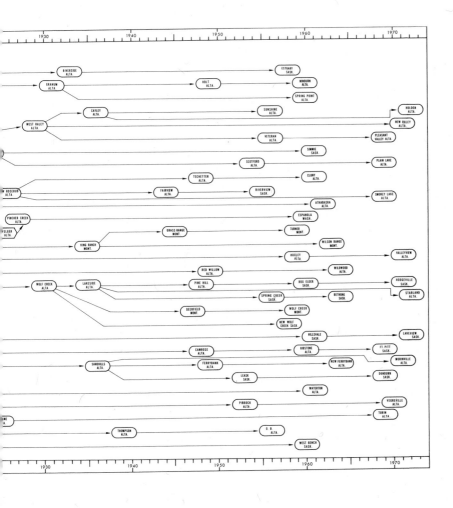

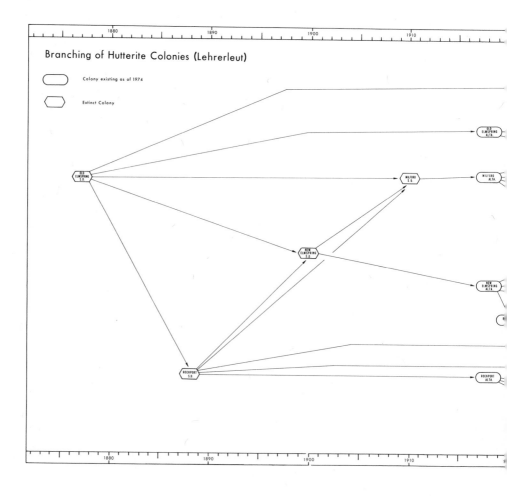

Branching of Hutterite Colonies (Lehrerleut)

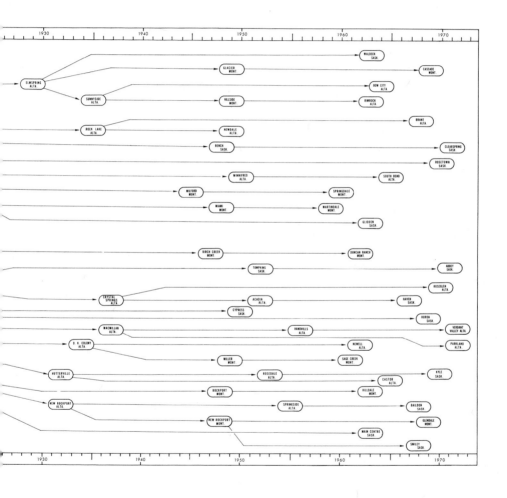

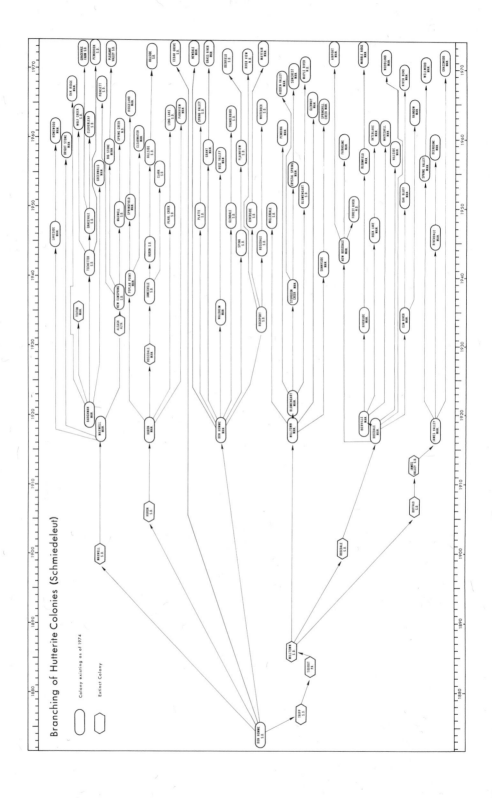

Branching of Hutterite Colonies (Schmiedeleut)

Selected Bibliography

The following short titles have been used in the citations:
M.E. (*The Mennonite Encyclopedia*)
Rideman, *Account of Our Religion*
Wolkan, *Die Geschichts-Bücher*
Zieglschmid, *Die älteste Chronik*
Zieglschmid, *Das Klein-Geschichtsbuch*

Full information about these books is given below. A short form (*M.Q.R.*) has also been used for *Mennonite Quarterly Review*.

Albert, Ethel M.
    1958   "The Classification of Values: A Method and Illustration." *American Anthropologist* 58 (1956): 221–48.
Albert, Ethel M., and Kluckhohn, Clyde
    1959   *A Selected Bibliography on Values, Ethics, and Esthetics in the Behavioral Sciences and Philosophy, 1920–1958*. Glencoe, Ill.: Free Press.
Alberta, Province of
    1947   *Report of the Legislative Committee Regarding the Land Sales Prohibition Act, 1944, as amended*. Edmonton: The Queen's Printer, 1947.
    1959   *Report of the Hutterite Investigating Committee*. Edmonton: 46 pp. and appendices. Mimeographed.

1972   *Report on Communal Property, 1972*. Edmonton: Select Committee of the Alberta Assembly. 45 pp., appendices, and map.

Allard, William A.

1970   "The Hutterites: Plain People of the West." *National Geographic*,
July 1970, pp. 98–125.

Anghel, Gh. și Ion Berciu

1968   *Cetăţi Medievale Din Sud-Vestul Transilvaniei*. Bucharest: Meridiane.

Argus, Orient, and Hardenbrook, M. B.

1903   "The Hutterische Society Home." *South Dakotan* 6 (July): 11–13.

Ariès, Philippe

1962   *Centuries of Childhood: A Social History of Family Life*. Translated
by Robert Baldick. New York: Alfred A. Knopf.

Arndt, Karl J.

1944   "The Harmonists and the Hutterites." *American-German Review*
10 (August): 24–47.

1971   *George Rapp's Successors and Material Heirs, 1847–1916*. Ruther-
ford, N.J.: Farleigh Dickinson University Press.

Arnold, Eberhard

1940   *The Hutterian Brothers; Four Centuries of Common Life and Work*.
Ashton Keynes, Wilts., England: Plough Publishing House.

1964   *Eberhard Arnold: A Testimony of Church-Community from His
Life and Writings*. Rifton, N.Y.: Plough Publishing House.

Bach, Marcus

1951   "The Hutterites." *Faith and My Friends*. Indianapolis: Bobbs-
Merrill Co.

1961   "The Hutterites." *Strange Sects and Curious Cults*. New York:
Dodd, Mead and Co.

Baden, John A.

1969   "The Management of Social Stability: A Political Ethnography of
the Hutterites of North America." Ph.D. dissertation, Indiana University.

Bainton, Roland H.

1941   "The Left Wing of the Reformation," *Journal of Religion* 21 (April):
124–34.

1952   *The Reformation of the Sixteenth Century*. Boston: Beacon Press.

Barclay, Harold

1969   "The Renewal of the Quest for Utopia." In *Canadian Confrontations*. Proceedings, Western Association of Sociology and Anthropology, December 28–30, 1969. Banff, Alta.

Barkin, David, and Bennett, J. W.

1972   "Kibbutz and Colony: Collective Economies and the Outside World."
Comparative Studies in Society and History 14 (September): 456–
83.

Beck, Josef

1883   *Die Geschichts-Bücher der Wiedertäufer*. Vienna.

Beltz, O. S.
 1943   "Historical and Doctrinal Background of German Religious Radical-
         ism, 1523-1535." Ph.D. dissertation, Northwestern University.
Bender, Elizabeth
 1963   "Grimmelshausen and the Hutterites." *Mennonite Life* 18 (Octo-
         ber): 187-89.
Bender, Harold S.
 1931   Ed. and trans. "A Hutterite School Discipline of 1578 [1568] and
         Peter Scherer's Address of 1568 to the Schoolmasters." *M.Q.R.* 5
         (October): 231-44.
 1942   "A New Edition of the Hutterian Chronicle." *M.Q.R.* 16 (October):
         269-70.
 1949   "Anabaptist Manuscripts in the Archives at Brno, Czechoslovakia."
         M.Q.R. 23 (April): 105-7.
 1950   *Conrad Grebel, c. 1498-1526: The Founder of the Swiss Brethren
         Sometimes Called Anabaptists.* Goshen, Ind.: Mennonite Historical
         Society.
 1953   "The Zwickau Prophets, Thomas Müntzer, and the Anabaptists."
         M.Q.R. 27 (January): 3-16.
Bennett, John W.
 1967   *Hutterian Brethren: The Agricultural Economy and Social Organ-
         ization of a Communal People.* Stanford, Calif.: Stanford University
         Press.
 1969   *Northern Plainsmen: Adaptive Strategy and Agrarian Life.* Chicago:
         Aldine Publishing Co.
Bennett, John W., and Tumin, Melvin
 1948   *Social Life, Structure and Function: An Introductory General Soci-
         ology.* New York: Alfred A. Knopf.
Bergsten, Thorsten
 1961   *Balthasar Hubmaier: Seine Stellung zu Reformation und Täufer-
         tum, 1521-1528.* Kassel: J. G. Oncken Verlag.
Bleibtreu, Herman
 1964   "Marriage and Residence Patterns in a Genetic Isolate." Ph.D. dis-
         sertation, Harvard University.
Boldt, Edward D.
 1966   "Conformity and Deviance: The Hutterites of Alberta." Master's
         thesis, University of Alberta, Edmonton.
 1968   "Acquiescence and Conventionality in a Communal Society."
         Ph.D. dissertation, University of Alberta, Edmonton.
Briggs, Harold
 1934   "Grasshopper Plagues and Early Dakota Agriculture, 1864-1876."
         Agricultural History 8 (April): 55-60.
Brock, Peter
 1957   *The Political and Social Doctrines of the Unity of the Czech Breth-
         ren in the Fifteenth and Early Sixteenth Centuries.* The Hague:
         Mouton and Co.
 1970   *Twentieth Century Pacifism.* New York: Van Nostrand Reinhold Co.

Canadian Mental Health Association
    1953   *The Hutterites and Saskatchewan: A Study in Inter-Group Rela-
            tions*. Regina, Sask.: By the Association.
Chalmers, Leslie E.
    1964   "A Comparison to Determine the Effect of Hutterite Culture upon
            Educational Achievement." Master's thesis, Montana State Univer-
            sity.
Clark, Bertha
    1921   "Turners of the Other Cheek." *Survey* 47: 519-24.
    1924   "The Hutterian Communities." *Journal of Political Economy* 32:
            I, 357-74; II, 468-86.
Clark, Peter Gordon
    1967   "The Brethren of Early Christianity: A Study of a World-Rejecting
            Sect." Master's thesis, McMaster University, Hamilton, Ontario.
    1974   "Dynasty Formation in the Communal Society of the Hutterites."
            Ph.D. dissertation, University of British Columbia.
Clasen, Claus-Peter
    1972   *Anabaptism: A Social History, 1525-1618*. Ithaca: Cornell Uni-
            versity Press.
    1973   "Executions of Anabaptists, 1525-1618." *M.Q.R.* 47 (April): 115-
            52.
Conkin, Paul K.
    1964   *Two Paths to Utopia: The Hutterites and the Llano Colony*. Lincoln:
            University of Nebraska Press.
Converse, Thomas A.; Buker, R. S.; and Lee, R. V.
    1973   "Hutterite Midwifery." *American Journal of Obstetrics and Gyne-
            cology* 116 (July): 719-25.
Correll, Ernst H.
    1927   "Anabaptists in Tyrol." *M.Q.R.* 1 (October): 49-60.
Correll, Ernst H., and Bender, Harold S.
    1957   "Marriage." *M.E.*
Crankshaw, Edward
    1969   *Maria Theresa*. New York: Longmans, Green and Co.
Cross, Harold E., and McKusick, Victor A.
    1970   "Amish Demography." *Social Biology* 17 (June): 83-101.
Davies, Percy G.
    1960   "Submission to the Agricultural Committee of the Legislature of the
            Province of Alberta on behalf of the Hutterite Colonies," March
            29, Mimeographed.
Dedic, Paul
    1939   "The Social Background of the Austrian Anabaptists." *M.Q.R.*
            13 (January): 5-20.
Deets, Lee Emerson
    1931   "The Origins of Conflict in the Hutterische Communities." *Publica-
            tions of the Sociological Society of America* 25: 125-35.
    1939   *The Hutterites: A Study in Social Cohesion*. Gettysburg, Pa.. By the
            author.

1945   "What Can We Learn from the Hutterites Regarding the Potentialities of Human Nature for Lasting Peace?" In *Human Nature and Enduring Peace*, pp. 341-48. Edited by Gardner Murphy. New York: Houghton Mifflin Co.

DeWind, Henry A.
1954   "Italian Hutterite Martyrs." *M.Q.R.* 28 (July): 163-85.
1955   "A Sixteenth-Century Description of Religious Sects in Austerlitz, Moravia." *M.Q.R.* 29 (January): 44-53.

Dillenberger, John, and Welch, Claude
1954   *Protestant Christianity.* New York: Charles Scribner's Sons.

Doornkaat, Koolman J. ten
1962   "The First Edition of Peter Riedemann's Rechenschaft." *M.Q.R.* 36 (April): 169-70.

Duerksen, Rosella R.
1961   "Doctrinal Implications in Sixteenth-Century Anabaptist Hymnody." *M.Q.R.* 35 (January): 38-49.

Durnbaugh, Donald F.
1974   *Every Need Supplied: Mutual Aid and Christian Community in the Free Churches (1525-1675).* Philadelphia: Temple University Press.

Eaton, Joseph W.
1952   "Controlled Acculturation." *American Sociological Review* 17 (June): 331-40.
1958   "Folk Obstetrics and Pediatrics: A Case Study of Social Anthropology and Medicine." In *Patients, Physicians, and Illness*, pp. 207-21. Edited by Jaco E. Gartley. Glencoe, Ill.: Free Press.
1963   "Folk Psychiatry." *New Society: The Social Science Weekly* (London) no. 48 (August 29): 9-11.
1964   "Adolescence in a Communal Society." *Mental Hygiene* 68: 66-78.
1964   "The Art of Aging and Dying." *Gerontologist* 4: 94-101.

Eaton, Joseph W., and Mayer, A. J.
1954   *Man's Capacity To Reproduce: The Demography of a Unique Population.* Glencoe, Ill.: Free Press. Reprinted from *Human Biology* 26 (September 1953): 206-64.

Eaton, Joseph W., and Weil, Robert J.
1953   "The Mental Health of the Hutterites." *Scientific American* 189 (December): 31-37.
1955   *Culture and Mental Disorders.* Glencoe, Ill.: Free Press.

Educational Policies Commission
1961   *The Central Purpose of American Education.* Washington, D.C.: The National Education Association.

Ehrenpreis, Andreas
1652   *Ein Sendbrief.* Scottdale, Pa.: Die Hutterischen Brüder, 1920; Wilson Colony, Lethbridge, Alta., 1953.

Eliade, Mircea
1966   *The Sacred and the Profane.* New York: Harper and Row.

Epp, D. H.
1909   *Johann Cornies.* Jekaterinoslaw and Berdiansk.

Epp, Frank
1962   *The Mennonite Exodus.* Altona, Man.: D. W. Friesen and Sons.
Erhard, Christoph
1589   *Gründliche und kurz verfasste Historia. Von Muensterischen Widertauffern.* Munich.
Falk, Robert
1931   "Hutterian Communism and Its Backgrounds." Master's thesis, University of Colorado.
Fellman, Walter
1956   *Hans Denck, Religiöse Schriften.* Gütersloh: Gerd Mohn.
Fischer, Christoph Andreas
1603   *Von der Widertauffer Verfluchten Ursprung, Gottlosen Lehre, und derselben gruendtliche widerlegung. Nach welcher gefragt wirdt Ob die Widertauffer im Landt zu leyden seind oder nicht?* Bruck an der Teya.
1607   *Vier und fünfftzig Erhebliche Ursachen Warumb die Widertäuffer nicht sein im Land zu Leyden.* Ingolstadt.
1607   *Der Hutterischen Widertauffer Taubenkobel.* Ingolstadt.
Fischer, Hans
1956   *Jakob Huter: Leben, Froemmigkeit, Briefe*, Newton, Kans.: Mennonite Publication Office.
Fletcher, E. A.
1950   "Constitution of Hutterian Brethren Church and Rules as to Community of Property." Winnipeg, Man.: [The Hutterian Brethren].
Fretz, J. Winfield
1946   Ed. *Proceedings of the Fifth Annual Conference on Mennonite Cultural Problems*, Freeman, S. Dak., August 27-28. Special issue devoted to Hutterites.
Friedmann, Robert
1927   "Die Habaner in Der Slowakei." *Wiener Zeitschrift für Volkskunde* 32: 1-11.
1931   "Concerning the True Soldier of Christ, 1534." *M.Q.R.* 5 (April): 87-99.
1943   "Adventures of an Anabaptist in Turkey, 1607-1610." *M.Q.R.* 17 (April): 73-86.
1944   Review of *Die älteste Chronik*, by A. J. F. Zieglschmid. *M.Q.R.* 18 (January): 59-63.
1945   "Reason and Obedience: An Old Letter of Peter Walpot (1571) and Its Meaning." *M.Q.R.* 19 (January): 27-40.
1946   "The Epistles of the Hutterian Brethren: A Study in Anabaptist Literature." *M.Q.R.* 20 (July): 147-77.
1946   "Christian Love in Action: The Hutterites." *Mennonite Life* 1 (January): 38-43.
1948   Review of *Das Klein-Geschichtsbuch*, by A. J. F. Zieglschmid. *M.Q.R.* 22 (July): 193-97.
1949   *Mennonite Piety Through the Centuries: Its Genius and Its Literature.* Goshen, Ind.: Mennonite Historical Society.

1950   "Comprehensive Review of Research on the Hutterites, 1880–1950." *M.Q.R.* 24 (October): 353–63.

1950   "A. J. F. Zieglschmid: An Obituary." *M.Q.R.* 24 (October): 364–65.

1952   "Of Hutterite Books." *Mennonite Life* 7 (April): 81–83.

1952   Review of *Account of Our Religion, Doctrine, and Faith*, by Peter Riedeman, translated by Kathleen Hasenberg. *M.Q.R.* 26 (April): 154–65.

1952   "Peter Riedemann on Original Sin and the Way to Redemption." *M.Q.R.* 26 (July): 210–15.

1953   "Hutterite Physicians and Barber-Surgeons." *M.Q.R.* 27 (April): 128–36.

1955   "Community of Goods." *M.E.*

1955   "Claus Felbinger's Confession of 1560." *M.Q.R.* 29 (April): 141–61; and addenda, *M.Q.R.* 30 (January): 78.

1955   "The Oldest Church Discipline of the Anabaptists." *M.Q.R.* 29 (April): 162–66.

1955   "The Anabaptists Answer Melanchthon: (II) Some Further Studies Pertaining to the Handbuechlein of 1558." *M.Q.R.* 29 (July): 223–31.

1956   "Hutterite Education." *M.E.*

1956   "Economic Aspects of Early Hutterite Life." *M.Q.R.* 30 (October): 259–66.

1956   "Huter, Jakob." *M.E.*

1956   "Hutterian Brethren." *M.E.*

1957   "The Hutterian Brethren and Community of Goods." In *The Recovery of the Anabaptist Vision*, pp. 83–92. Edited by Guy F. Hershberger, Scottdale, Pa.: Herald Press.

1957   "A Notable Hutterite Document: Concerning True Surrender and Christian Community of Goods." Translated by Kathleen Hasenberg, with an introduction by Robert Friedmann. *M.Q.R.* 31 (January): 22–62.

1958   "The Philippite Brethren: A Chapter in Anabaptist History." *M.Q.R.* 32 (July): 272–97.

1958   "Hutterian Pottery, or Haban Fayences." *Mennonite Life* 13 (October): 147–52, 182.

1959   "More About Haban Pottery." *Mennonite Life* 14 (July): 129–30.

1959   "Leonhard Schiemer and Hans Schlaffer: Two Tyrolean Anabaptist Martyr-Apostles of 1528." *M.Q.R.* 33 (January): 31–41.

1959   "The Oldest Known Hutterite Codex of 1566: A Chapter in Anabaptist Intellectual History." *M.Q.R.* 33 (April): 96–107.

1959   "The Doctrine of Original Sin as Held by the Anabaptists of the Sixteenth Century." *M.Q.R.* 33 (April): 206–14.

1959   Ed. and trans. "Hutterites Revisit European Homesteads: Excerpts from the Travel Diary of David Hofer." *M.Q.R.* 33 (October): 305–22.

1960   Intro. and trans. "Jakob Hutter's Last Epistle to the Church in Moravia, 1535." *M.Q.R.* 34 (January) 37–47.

1960   "An Epistle Concerning Communal Life: A Hutterite Manifesto of 1650 and Its Modern Paraphrase." *M.Q.R.* 34 (October): 249-74.

1961   *Hutterite Studies.* Goshen, Ind.: Mennonite Historical Society.

1961   "A Newly Discovered Source on the Transmigration of the Hutterites to Transylvania, 1621-1623." *M.Q.R.* 35 (October): 309-14.

1963   "Report on Haban Pottery." *M.Q.R.* 37 (July): 195-202.

1964   "Jakob Hutter's Epistle Concerning the Schism in Moravia in 1533." Translated by Society of Brothers with an introduction by Robert Friedmann. *M.Q.R.* 38 (October): 329-43.

1965   With the assistance of Adolf Mais. *Die Schriften der Huterischen Täufergemeinschaften.* Vienna: Herman Böhlaus.

1966   "The Re-establishment of Communal Life Among the Hutterites in Russia (1859)." *M.Q.R.* 39 (April): 147-52.

1966   "Hutterite Worship and Preaching." *M.Q.R.* 40 (January): 5-26.

1967   *Glaubenszeugnisse oberdeutscher Taufgesinnter [Österreich, pt. 2].* Quellen zur Geschichte der Täufer, vol. 12. Gütersloh: Gerd Mohn.

1968   "Newly Discovered Hutterite Manuscripts." *M.Q.R.* 42 (January): 73-74.

1970   "Peter Riedemann, Early Anabaptist Leader." *M.Q.R.* 44 (January): 5-44.

1970   "A Hutterite Census for 1969: Hutterite Growth in One Century, 1874-1969." *M.Q.R.* 44 (January): 100-105.

Gingerich, Melvin
1949   *Service for Peace.* Akron, Pa.: Mennonite Central Committee.

Gobehold, Jenser, and Lefebvre Consultants, Ltd.
1960   "Springvale Hutterian Brethren: A Report Concerning the Spending Habits of a Typical Colony of Hutterites As Compared to Those of the Individual Farmers. . . ." Calgary, Alta.: Report prepared in association with Mark and Shield, Chartered Accountants, August 24. Mimeographed.

Goodhope, Nanna
1940   "Must the Hutterites Flee Again?" *Christian Century* 57 (November 13): 1415-17.

Griffen, Dorothy
1947   "The Hutterites and Civil Liberties." *Canadian Forum* 27 (June): 125-29.

Grimmelshausen, Hans Jakob Christoph von
1668   *Der abenteuerliche Simplizissimus.* N.p.

Gross, Leonard
1968   "Newly Discovered Codices of the Hutterites." *M.Q.R.* 42 (January): 149-55.

1968   "The Golden Years of the Hutterites: Life, Mission, and Theology of the Communistic Moravian Anabaptists during the Walpot Era, 1565-1578." Ph.D. dissertation, University of Basel.

1970   "Dialogue Between a Hutterite and a Swiss Brother." *M.Q.R.* 44 (January): 45-58.

Gross, Paul S.
1954 *Hutterian Brethren: Life, and Religion.* Pincher Creek, Alta: By the author.
1955 *The Defence Against the Prozess at Worms on the Rhine in the Year 1557.* Pincher Creek, Alta.: By the author.
1959 *Who Are the Hutterites?* Pincher Creek, Alta.: By the author.
1965 *The Hutterite Way: The Inside Story of the Life, Customs, Religion, and Traditions of the Hutterites.* Saskatoon, Sask.: Freeman Publishing Co.
1970 "On the Trails of Our Anabaptist Forefathers, Summer 1968." *M.Q.R.* 44 (January): 85-99.

Gross, Paul S., and Bender, Elizabeth
1970 "A Hutterite Sermon of the Seventeenth Century." *M.Q.R.* 44 (January): 59-71.

Harada, Mary A.
1968 "Family Values and Child Care during the Reformation Era: A Comparative Study of Hutterites and Some Other German Protestants." Ph.D. dissertation, Boston University.

Harder, D. E.
1930 "The Hutterian Church." Master's thesis, Bethel College, Newton, Kansas.

Hartzog, Sandra H.
1971 "Population Genetic Studies of a Human Isolate: The Hutterites of North America." Ph.D. dissertation, University of Massachusetts.

Heimann, Franz
1952 "The Hutterite Doctrine of Church and Common Life: A Study of Riedemann's Confession of 1540." *M.Q.R.* 26 (January): 142-60.

Hiller, Harrry H.
1968-69 "The Sleeping Preachers: An Historical Study of the Role of Charisma in Amish Society." *Pennsylvania Folklife* 18 (Winter): 19-31.

Hofer, D. M.
1924 *Die Hungersnot in Russland.* Chicago: K. M. B. Publishing House.

Hofer, J. M.
1931 Ed. and trans. "The Diary of Paul Tschetter, 1873." *M.Q.R.* 5 (April): 112-27, and 5 (July): 198-220.

Hofer, Peter
1955 *The Hutterian Brethren and Their Beliefs.* Starbuck, Man.: The Hutterian Brethren of Manitoba.

Holtzman, Jerome J.
1960 "An Inquiry into the Hutterian German Dialect." Master's thesis, University of South Dakota.

Horsch, John
1931 *The Hutterian Brethren, 1528-1931: A Story of Martyrdom and Loyalty.* Goshen, Ind.: Mennonite Historical Society.
1950 *Mennonites in Europe.* Scottdale, Pa.: Mennonite Publishing House. Chapter 17, "The Hutterian Brethren," pp. 149-55.

Hostetler, John A.
    1961   "Hutterite Separatism and Public Tolerance." *Canadian Forum* 41
            (April): 11-13.
    1961   "The Communal Property Act of Alberta." *University of Toronto
            Law Journal* 14: 125-28.
    1965   *Hutterite Life.* Scottdale, Pa.: Herald Press.
    1965   *Education and Marginality in the Communal Society of the Hutter-
            ites,* Research report. University Park: Pennsylvania State Uni-
            versity.
    1968   *Amish Society,* rev. ed. Baltimore: Johns Hopkins Press.
    1970   "Total Socialization: Modern Hutterite Educational Practices."
            M.Q.R. 44 (January): 72-84.
    1970   "A Bibliography of English Language Materials on the Hutterian
            Brethren." *M.Q.R.* 44 (January): 106-13.
Hostetler, John A., and Huntington, Gertrude Enders
    1967   *The Hutterites in North America.* New York: Holt, Rinehart and
            Winston.
    1968   "Communal Socialization Patterns in Hutterite Society." *Ethnology*
            8 (October): 331-55.
Hostetler, John A., and Kleinsasser, Dennis
    1965   "A Cross-Cultural Investigation of Adolescence in Hutterite Soci-
            ety." Unpublished paper.
Hostetler, John A., and Redekop, Calvin W.
    1962   "Education and Assimilation in Three Ethnic Groups." *Alberta
            Journal of Educational Research* 7 (December): 189-203.
Howells, W. W.
    1966   "Variability in Family Lines vs. Population Variability." In *Annals
            of the New York Academy of Sciences* 134 (February 28): 624-31.
    1970   With the assistance of Hermann K. Bleibtreu. *Hutterite Age Differ-
            ences in Body Measurements.* Papers of the Peabody Museum, vol.
            57, no. 2. Cambridge, Mass.: Peabody Museum, pp. 1-123.
Hrubý, František
    1935   *Die Wiedertäufer in Mähren.* Leipzig: Verlag M. Heinsius Nach-
            folger.
Huntington, Gertrude Enders
    1965   "Freedom and the Hutterite Communal Family Pattern." In *Proceed-
            ings of the Fifteenth Conference on Mennonite Educational and Cul-
            tural Problems,* Bluffton College, Bluffton, Ohio, June 10-11,
            pp. 88-111.
Huntington, Gertrude Enders, and Hostetler, John A.
    1966   "A Note on Nursing Practices in an American Isolate with a High
            Birth Rate." *Population Studies* 19 (March): 321-24.
Hutterian Brethren of Montana
    1963   *The Hutterian Brethren of Montana.* Augusta, Mont.: The Brethren.
Jeřabek, Josef
    1966   *Žerotínové a Židlochovice.* Židlochovice, Czechoslovakia: By the
            author.

Kanter, Rosabeth M.
  1972   *Commitment and Community: Communes and Utopias in Sociological Perspective.* Cambridge: Harvard University Press.
  1973   *Communes: Creating and Managing the Collective Life.* New York: Harper and Row.

Kaplan, Bert, and Plaut, Thomas F. A.
  1956   *Personality in a Communal Society.* Lawrence, Kans.: University of Kansas Publications.

Karner, P. Lambert
  1903   *Die künstliche Höhlen aus alter Zeit.* Vienna.

Kasparek, Max Udo
  1956   "Zur Tracht der Wiedertäufer in Mähren und der Slovakei." *Südostdeutsche Heimätblatter,* 5 Jahrgang, Folge 2, pp. 91–95.
  1957   "Habanerhöfe in Südmähren." *Südmährisches Jahrbuch,* pp. 92–94.

Katona, Imre
  1963   "Sárvár und die Familie Nádasdy im XVI. Jahrhundert." *Savaria* (Szombathely): 239–55.

Kells, Edna
  1937   "Hutterite Commune." *Maclean's Magazine,* March 15, pp. 50–54.

Kirchhoff, Karl-Heinz
  1970   "Was There a Peaceful Anabaptist Congregation in Münster in 1534?" *M.Q.R.* 44 (October): 357–70.

Klassen, Peter J.
  1964   *The Economics of Anabaptism, 1525–1560.* The Hague: Mouton and Co.

Klassen, Walter
  1971   "The Nature of the Anabaptist Protest." *M.Q.R.* 45 (October): 291–311.

Klaus, Alexander
  1887   *Unsere Kolonien,* Odessa.

Klima, H.
  1942   "Das Verhalten der Wiener Regierung unter Maria Theresia gegen die siebenbürgerischen Wiedertäufer und Herrnhuter." *Südöstforschungen* (Brno, Munich, and Vienna).

Klingelsmith, Sharon L.
  1974   "A Bibliography of the Anabaptist-Mennonite Writings of Robert Friedmann." *M.Q.R.* 48 (April): 246–55.

Klusch, Horst
  1968   "Die Habaner in Siebenbürgen." *Forschungen zur Volks- und Landeskunde,* vol. 11, no. 2; 21–40; vol. 14, no. 2 (1971); 101–7. Illustrated.

Knill, William D.
  1968   "Hutterian Education: A Descriptive Study Based on the Hutterian Colonies within Warner County No. 5, Alberta, Canada." Master's thesis, University of Montana.

Knoll, Wilma I.
  1963   "The History of the Hutterites of South Dakota." Master's thesis,
          University of South Dakota.
Kraus, Frantíšek
  1937   Nové Prispevky K dejinám Habánov na Slovensku. Bratislava.
Krisztinkovich, Béla
  1958   "Nobilis amphorarius magister." ["The knighted masterpotter"].
          Müvészettörténeti értesitö (Budapest), vol. 7, no. 2/3.
  1961   "Anabaptista orvosok, gyógyszerészek a higiénia szolgálatában"
          ["Anabaptist physicians and druggists in the service of hygiene"].
          Communications ex bibliotheca historiae medicae Hungarica (Buda-
          pest), no. 20, pp. 88-117.
  1962   Haban Pottery. Budapest: Corvina Press.
  1964   "Unbekannte Messerschmied-Kunstwerke der Ungarischen Haba-
          nen." Iparmüvészeti muzeum évkönyvei (Budapest), pp. 59-82.
  1969   "Glimpses into the Early History of Anabaptists in Hungary."
          M.Q.R. 43 (April): 127-41.
Krisztinkovich, Maria H.
  1963   "Some Further Notes on the Hutterites in Transylvania." M.Q.R.
          37 (July): 203-13.
  1965   "Anabaptist Book Confiscations in Hungary during the Eighteenth
          Century." M.Q.R. 39 (April): 125-46.
  1970   "Hutterite Codices Rediscovered in Hungary." M.Q.R. 44 (January):
          114-21.
  1971   "Die verschollene Keramik der Bartmennoniten in Russland."
          Keramos (Cologne) 51 (January): 3-17.
  1971   "Wiedertaufer und Arianer im Karpatenraum," Ungarn-Jahrbuch.
          Mainz.
Krisztinkovich, Maria H., and Krisztinkovich, Béla
  1967   "Ein Habanerkrug." ["A Haban jug"]. Keramos (Cologne) 36 (Jan-
          uary): 28-34.
Kuhn, Walter
  1957   Geschichte der Deutschen Östsiedlung in der Neuzeit. Cologne:
          Böhlau.
Landgraf, Adam
  1772   Beschreibung des Habaner Strohdaches . . . . Pressburg: Printed by
          Franz Augustin in Patzkó.
Landsfeld, Heřman
  1946   "Thirty Years of Excavation." Translated from the Czech by
          Michael Mrlik and edited by Robert Friedmann. Mennonite Life
          4 (October): 167-73.
  1962   "The Discovery of Hutterite Books." Mennonite Life 12 (July):
          140-44.
  1970   Habánské památky. Strážnice: Ústav Lidhévo Umění.
Lee, C. S., and Brattrud, Audrey
  1967   "Marriage under a Monastic Code of Life: A Preliminary Report on
          the Hutterite Family in South Dakota." Journal of Marriage and the
          Family 29: 512-20.

Lee, Dorothy
   1959   *Freedom and Culture*. Englewood Cliffs, N.J.: Prentice Hall.

Lee, Richard V., and Buker, Richard S., Jr.
   1969   "Congenital Heart Disease among the Hutterite Brethren." *The New England Journal of Medicine* 280 (May 8): 1061–62.

Liebbrandt, Georg
   1932   "The Emigration of the German Mennonites from Russia to the United States and Canada 1873–1880, I." *M.Q.R.* 6 (October): 205–26; II, 7 (January, 1933): 5–14.

Lieder der Hutterischen Brüder, Die
   1914   Scottdale, Pa.: Die Hutterischen Brüder. Reprints: Winnipeg, Man., 1953; Cayley, Alta.; 1962.

Light, Charles E.
   1959   "Case Notes: Status of South Dakota Communal Corporations." *South Dakota Law Review* 4: 157–62.

Littell, Franklin H.
   1957   *Landgraf Philipp und die Toleranz*. Bad Neuheim: Christian Press.
   1958   *The Anabaptist View of the Church*. Boston: Beacon Press.
   1964   *The Origins of Sectarian Protestantism*. New York: Macmillan Co.

Loserth, Johann
   1930   "The Decline and Revival of the Hutterites." *M.Q.R.* 4 (April): 93–112.

Ludeman, W. W., and McAnelly, J. R.
   1930   "Intelligence of Colony People." *Journal of Educational Psychology* 21: 612–15.

Luthy, David
   1974   "Amish and Hutterite Relations." *Family Life* [Aylmer, Ont.], June, pp. 17–20.

Mackie, Marlene
   1971   "The Accuracy of Folk Knowledge Concerning Alberta Indians, Hutterites, and Ukrainians." Ph.D. dissertation, University of Alberta.

McKusick, Victor A., and Rimoin, David L.
   1967   "General Tom Thumb and Other Midgets." *Scientific American* 217 (July): 103–110.

Mais, Adolf
   1961   "Literarisches und Graphisches auf Habaner Keramiken." *Osterreichisches Zeitschrift für Volkskunde* (Vienna), N.S. 15, no. 64: 149–94.
   1964   "Das Hausbuch von Neumühl, 1558–1610, das älteste Grundbuch der huterischen Brüder." *Jahrbuch der Gesellschaft für die Geschichte des Protestantismus in Österreich* (Vienna), pp. 66–88.
   1964   "Der Überfall von Steinabrunn im Jahr 1539." *Jahrbuch für Landeskunde von Niederösterreich* (Vienna), Folge 36, pp. 295–310.
   1974   "The Hausbuch of Neumühl, 1558–1610, the Oldest Land Register of the Hutterian Brethren." *M.Q.R.* 48 (April): 215–36.

Manitoba, Province of
    1948   *Meeting of the Select Special Committee of the Manitoba Legisla-
            ture on Hutterite Legislation.* Winnipeg, July 23.
Mange, Arthur P.
    1963   "The Population Structure of a Human Isolate." Ph.D. dissertation,
            University of Wisconsin.
    1964   "Growth and Inbreeding of a Human Isolate." *Human Biology* 36
            (May): 104-33.
Martens, Helen
    1968   "Hutterite Songs: The Origins and Aural Transmission of Their Mel-
            odies from the Sixteenth Century." Ph.D. dissertation, Columbia
            University.
    1974   "Hutterite Melodies from the Strassburg Psalter." *M.Q.R.* 48 (April):
            201-14.
Mecenseffy, Grete
    1956   *Geschichte des Protestantismus in Österreich.* Gratz-Köln.
    1964   *Österreich,* pt. 1. Quellen zur Geschichte der Täufer, vol. 11. Güters-
            loh: Gerd Mohn.
Mendel, J. J.
    1961   *History of the People of East Freeman, Silver Lake, and West Free-
            man.* . . . Freeman, S. Dak.: By the author.
Mennonite Encyclopedia, The
    1955-59 Scottdale, Pa.: Mennonite Publishing House. 4 vols.
Meryman, Richard S.
    1958   "Hard Time Faces Fruitful Hutterites." *Life,* August 25, pp. 33 ff.
    1958   "South Dakota's Christian Martyrs." *Harpers Magazine,* December,
            pp. 72-79.
Murray, E. R.
    1914   *Fröbel as a Pioneer in Modern Psychology.* N.p.
National Film Board of Canada
    1962   *The Hutterites.* Documentary film. Black and white, 16 mm, 28
            minutes. Available from the National Film Board of Canada, 1251
            Avenue of the Americas, New York, N.Y. 10020.
Neuser, Wilhelm
    1913   Hans Hut: *Leben und Werken bis zum Nikolsburger Religionsge-
            spräch.* Berlin.
Newman, A. H.
    1926   "Balthasar Hubmaier and the Moravian Anabaptists." *Goshen Col-
            lege Review Supplement,* September.
Ong, Walter J.
    1967   *The Presence of the Word.* New Haven: Yale University Press.
    1967   *Ramus: Method and the Decay of Dialogue.* Cambridge: Harvard
            University Press.
Padover, Saul K.
    1967   *The Revolutionary Emperor: Joseph II of Austria,* rev. ed. London:
            Eyre and Spottiswoode.

Palmer, Howard
  1971   "The Hutterite Land Expansion Controversy in Alberta." *Western Canadian Journal of Anthropology* 2 (July): 18-46.
  1971   "Nativism and Ethnic Tolerance in Alberta: 1880-1920." Master's thesis, University of Alberta.
  1972   *Land of the Second Chance: A History of Ethnic Groups in Southern Alberta*. Lethbridge, Alta.: Lethbridge Herald.
Parry, John Jay
  1941   Ed. and trans. *The Art of Courtly Love by Andreas Capellanus*. New York: Columbia University Press.
Peachey, Paul
  1954   *Die Soziale Herkunft der Schweizer Täufer*. Karlsruhe: Heinrich Schneider.
Peter, Karl
  1963   "The Hutterites: Values, Status, and Organizational Systems." *Variables: The Journal of the Sociology Club* (University of Alberta, Edmonton) 2 (February): 55-59; 3 (February 1964): 7-8.
  1967   "Factors of Social Change and Social Dynamics in the Communal Settlements of Hutterites, 1527-1967." Ph.D. dissertation, University of Alberta, Edmonton.
Peters, Victor
  1965   *All Things Common: The Hutterian Way of Life*. Minneapolis: University of Minnesota Press.
Population Reference Bureau, Inc.
  1954   "The North American Hutterites: A Study in Human Multiplication." *Population Bulletin* 10 (December): 97-108.
  1968   "Pockets of High Fertility in the United States." *Population Bulletin* 24 (November): 25-55.
Pratt, William F.
  1969   "The Anabaptist Explosion: Adaptation of Pockets of Higher Fertility in the United States." *Natural History* 78 (February): 8-10.
Priestly, David T.
  1959   "A Study of Selected Factors Related to Attitudes toward the Hutterites of South Dakota." Master's thesis, South Dakota State College.
Radtke, Hans D.
  1971   *The Hutterites in Montana: An Economic Description*. Bozeman: Montana Agricultural Experiment Station.
Redekop, Calvin W.
  1969   *The Old Colony Mennonites: Dilemmas of Ethnic Minority Life*. Baltimore: Johns Hopkins Press.
Rideman, Peter
  1565   *Rechenschaft unserer Religion, Lehr und Glaubens, von den Brüdern, so man die Hutterischen nennt, ausgangen 1565*. N.p. Reprint: Ashton Keynes, Wilts., England: Plough Publishing House, 1938. English edition: *Account of Our Religion, Doctrine and Faith, Given by Peter Rideman of the Brothers Whom Men Call Hut-*

terians. Translated by Kathleen Hasenburg. London: Hodder and Stoughton; Rifton, N.Y.: Plough Publishing House, 1950. Reprint: Rifton, N.Y., 1970.

Riedemann, Peter
Spelling used by modern scholars. *See* Rideman, Peter.

Riley, Marvin P.
1956   "Communal Farmers: The Hutterite Brethren." *South Dakota Farm and Home Research* 8 (November): 5–11.
1965   *The Hutterian Brethren: An Annotated Bibliography with Special Reference to South Dakota Hutterite Colonies.* Brookings: South Dakota State University.

Riley, Marvin P., and Johnson, Darryll R.
1969   *South Dakota's Hutterite Colonies, 1874–1969.* Brookings: South Dakota State University, Agricultural Experiment Station.

Riley, Marvin P., and Priestly, David T.
1959   "Agriculture on South Dakota's Communal Farms." *South Dakota Farm and Home Research* 10 (February): 12–16.

Riley, Marvin P., and Stewart, James R.
1966   *The Hutterites: South Dakota's Communal Farmers.* Brookings: South Dakota State University.

Ryan, John
1972   "The Economic Significance of Hutterite Colonies in Manitoba." *Southern Prairies Field Excursion: Background Papers.* Montreal: Congress of the International Geographical Union.
1973   "The Agricultural Operations of Manitoba Hutterite Colonies." Ph.D. dissertation. McGill University.

Sakakibara, Gan
1962   "Study of the Hutterite Brethren: A Strophe of the Sociology of Religion." *Aoyama Keizai Ronshu* 14.
1967   *Junkyo to Bomei Hataraito no Yon-hyakaku-go-ju-Nen* ["Four Hundred and Fifty Years of Hutterite Martyrdom and Exile"]. Tokyo: By the author.
1973   "My Pilgrimage to Anabaptism." *Mennonite Life* 28 (March): 12–15.

Sanders, Douglas E.
1964   "The Hutterites: A Case Study in Minority Rights." *Canadian Bar Review* 42 (May): 225–42.

Scheer, Herfried
1962   "Sprachliche Untersuchung der Ältesten Chronik der Hutterischen Brüder." Master's thesis, University of Alberta, Edmonton.
1972   "A Lexicological Analysis of the Hutterian German Dialect." Ph.D. dissertation, McGill University.

Schilling, Arnold J.
1955   "The Music of the Hutterites of Tschetter Colony." Master's thesis, University of South Dakota.

Schluderman, Eduard, and Schluderman, Shirin
1969   "Social Role Perception of Children in Hutterite Communal Society." *Journal of Psychology* 72: 183–88.

1969   "Developmental Study of Social Role Perception among Hutterite Adolescents." *Journal of Psychology* 72: 243–46.

1969   "Scale Checking Style as a Function of Age and Sex in Indian and Hutterite Children." *Journal of Psychology* 72: 253–61.

1969   "Factoral Analysis of Semantic Structures in Hutterite Adults." *Journal of Psychology* 73: 263–73.

1971   "Maternal Child Rearing Attitudes in Hutterite Communal Society." *Journal of Psychology* 79: 169–177.

1971   "Paternal Attitudes in Hutterite Communal Society." *Journal of Psychology* 79: 41–48.

1971   "Adolescent Perception of Parent Behavior (CRPBI) in Hutterite Communal Society." *Journal of Psychology* 79: 29–39.

1973   "Developmental Aspects of Social Role Perception in Hutterite Communal Society." In *Child Development: Selected Readings.* Edited by L. Brockman, J. Whiteley, and J. Zubek. Toronto: McClelland and Stewart.

Serl, Vernon
1959   "The Hutterite Program." Final Report to the Provincial Committee on Minority Relations, Province of Saskatchewan, Regina.

1964   "Stability and Change in Hutterite Society." Ph.D. dissertation, University of Oregon.

Sheps, Mindel C.
1965   "An Analysis of Reproductive Patterns in an American Isolate." *Population Studies* 18 (July): 65–80.

Simmons, Jerry T.
1960   Ed. "Status of South Dakota Communal Organization." *South Dakota Law Review* 4: 157–63.

Smith, C. Henry
1927   *The Coming of the Russian Mennonites.* Berne, Ind.: Mennonite Book Concern.

1950   *The Story of the Mennonites.* Newton, Kans.: Mennonite Publication Office.

Sommer, Donald
1954   "Peter Rideman and Menno Simons on Economics." *M.Q.R.* 28 (July): 205–23.

Sommer, John L.
1953   "Hutterite Medicine and Physicians in Moravia in the Sixteenth Century and After." *M.Q.R.* 17 (April): 111–27.

Sorokin, P. A.
1954   "Techniques of Contemporary Free Brotherhoods: The Hutterites of the United States." In *The Ways and Power of Love.* Boston: Beacon Press.

Staebler, Edna
1952   "The Lord Will Take Care of Us." *Maclean's Magazine*, March 15, pp. 14 ff.

Stauffer, Ethelbert
1945   "The Anabaptist Theology of Martyrdom." *M.Q.R.* 19 (July): 179–214.

Stayer, James M.
1970   "Anabaptists and the Sword." *M.Q.R.* 44 (October): 371-75.
Steele, Frank C.
1941   "Canada's Hutterite Settlement." *Canadian Geographical Journal* 22: 308-14.
Steinberg, Arthur G.
1963   "Dependence of the Phenotype on Environment and Heredity." In *The Genetics of Migrant and Isolate Populations*, pp. 133-43. Edited by Elisabeth Goldschmidt. Baltimore: Williams and Wilkins Co.
1967   Steinberg, Arthur G. et al. "Genetic Studies on an Inbred Human Isolate." *Proceedings of the Third International Congress of Human Genetics*, pp. 267-89. Edited by James F. Crow and James V. Neel. Baltimore: Johns Hopkins Press.
Stella, Ado
1961-62 "Intorno al medico padovano Nicolò Buccella, anabattista del 1500." *Atti e Memorie Accademia Patavina di Scienze, Lettere ed Arti* 74.
Szövérffy, Joseph
1963   "Die Hutterischen Brüder und die Vergangenheit." *Zeitschrift für Deutsche Philologie* 82, no. 3: 338-62.
Taylor, A. J. P.
1949   *The Hapsburg Monarchy*. Baltimore: Penguin Books.
Teselle, Sallie
1971   Ed. *The Family, Communes, and Utopian Societies*. New York: Harper Torchbooks.
Thomas, Kenneth C.
1949   "A Survey of the Hutterite Groups in Montana and Canada." Master's thesis, University of Montana.
Thomas, Norman
1951   "The Hutterian Brethren." *South Dakota Historical Collections* 25: 265-99. Pierre: South Dakota Historical Society.
Thompson, Laura, and Hostetler, John A.
1970   "The Hutterian Confession of Faith: A Documentary Analysis." *Alberta Journal of Educational Research* 16 (March): 29-45.
Tietz, Christopher
1957   "Reproductive Span and Rate of Reproduction Among Hutterite Women." *Fertility and Sterility* 8: 89-97.
Troeltsch, Ernst
1931   *The Social Teachings of the Christian Churches*. Translated by Olive Wyon. New York: Macmillan.
Tschetter, Joseph W.
1931   "A Brief Biography of Paul Tschetter, 1842-1919." Translated and edited by J. M. Hofer. *M.Q.R.* 15 (April): 112-13.
Tschetter, Mrs. Joseph W.
1945   *My Life Story, 1880-1945*. Chicago: By the author.

Tschetter, Paul
  1931   "The Diary of Paul Tschetter, 1873." Translated and edited by
          J. M. Hofer. *M.Q.R.* 5 (April): 112-27; 5 (July): 198-220.
Unruh, John D.
  1969   "The Hutterites during World War I." *Mennonite Life* 24 (July):
          130-37.
  1972   *A Century of Mennonites in Dakota.* Pierre: South Dakota Historical
          Society. Reprinted from *South Dakota Historical Collections* 36
          (1972).
Valentinus, Basilius
  1717   *Currus trimphalis antimonii.* Hamburg.
Waldner, Emil J.
  1968   *Banished for Faith.* Freeman, S. Dak.: Pine Hill Press.
Waldner, Jakob
  1974   "Diary of a Conscientious Objector in World War I." *M.Q.R.* 48
          (January): 73-111.
Walpot, Peter
  1577   *Von der wahren Gelassenheit und der christlichen Gemeinschaft
          der Güter.* N.p. Translated by Kathleen Hasenberg, with an intro-
          duction by Robert Friedmann, "A Notable Hutterite Document:
          Concerning True Surrender and Christian Community of Goods."
          M.Q.R. 31 (January): 22-62.
Walter, Elias
  1908   "Wie kamen die Hutterischen Brüder nach Amerika?" *Mennon-
          itische Blatter* (November): 87-89.
Waltner, Gary J.
  1962   *The Joseph Waltner Family.* Freeman, S. Dak.: Pine Hill Printery.
Wenger, John C.
  1945   Intro. and trans. "The Schleitheim Confession of Faith." *M.Q.R.* 19
          (October): 243-53.
Williams, George H.
  1962   *The Radical Reformation.* Philadelphia: Westminster Press.
Williams, Julia
  1939   "An Analytical Tabulation of the North American Utopian Commu-
          nities by Type, Longevity, and Location." Master's thesis, University
          of South Dakota.
Wiswedel, Wilhelm
  1952   *Bilder und Führergestalten aus dem Täufertum.* Kassel: Verlag
          J. G. Oncken.
  1955   "The Anabaptists Answer Melanchthon: (I) The Handbuchlein of
          1558." *M.Q.R.* 29 (July): 212-23.
Wolkan, Rudolf
  1903   *Die Lieder der Wiedertäufer.* Berlin. Reprinted at Nieuwkoop,
          The Netherlands: B. de Graaf, 1965.
  1923   *Geschichts-Buch der Hutterischen Brüder.* Vienna: Carl Fromme;
          Macleod, Alta.: Standoff Colony.

Yoder, Don
    1968   "Trance Preaching in the United States." *Pennsylvania Folklife* 18 (Winter): 12–18.

Young, Gertrude S.
    1920   "The Mennonites in South Dakota." *South Dakota Historical Collections* 10: 470–506.

Zablocki, Benjamin
    1971   *The Joyful Community.* Baltimore: Penguin Books.

Zeman, Jarold K.
    1969   *The Anabaptists and the Czech Brethren in Moravia, 1526–1628: A Study of their Origins and Contacts.* The Hague: Mouton and Co.

Zieglschmid, A. J. F.
    1940   "An Unpublished Hausbrief of Grimmelshausen's Hungarian Anabaptists." *Germanic Review* 15 (April): 91–97. Translated by Elizabeth Bender.

    1942   "The Hutterian Chronicle." *American-German Review* (April): 18–25.

    1943   *Die älteste Chronik der Hutterischen Brüder.* Philadelphia: Carl Schurz Memorial Foundation.

    1943   "A Song of the Persecution of the Hutterites in Velke Levary." *M.Q.R.* 17 (July): 151–64.

    1947   *Das Klein-Geschichtsbuch der Hutterischen Brüder.* Philadelphia: Carl Schurz Memorial Foundation.

Zimmer, G. J.
    1912   "Huter's Religious Communism." Master's thesis, Yankton College, Yankton, South Dakota.

Index